SOVIET LAW AND SOVIET REALITY

LAW IN EASTERN EUROPE

*A series of publications
issued by the
Documentation Office for East European Law
University of Leyden*

General Editor

F.J.M. FELDBRUGGE

No. 30

1985 **MARTINUS NIJHOFF PUBLISHERS**
a member of the KLUWER ACADEMIC PUBLISHERS GROUP
DORDRECHT / BOSTON / LANCASTER

SOVIET LAW AND SOVIET REALITY

by

OLIMPIAD S. IOFFE
Professor of Law
University of Connecticut School of Law
Hartford, Connecticut

1985 **MARTINUS NIJHOFF PUBLISHERS**
a member of the KLUWER ACADEMIC PUBLISHERS GROUP
DORDRECHT / BOSTON / LANCASTER

Distributors

for the United States and Canada: Kluwer Academic Publishers, 190 Old Derby Street, Hingham, MA 02043, USA
for the UK and Ireland: Kluwer Academic Publishers, MTP Press Limited, Falcon House, Queen Square, Lancaster LA1 1RN, UK
for all other countries: Kluwer Academic Publishers Group, Distribution Center, P.O. Box 322, 3300 AH Dordrecht, The Netherlands

Library of Congress Cataloging in Publication Data

```
Ioffe, O. S. (Olimpiad Solomonovich), 1920-
  Soviet law and Soviet reality.

  (Law in Eastern Europe ; 30)
  Includes bibliographies and index.
  1. Law--Soviet Union.  I. Title.  II. Series: Law
in Eastern Europe ; no. 30.
LAW                    349.47               84-25093
ISBN 90-247-3106-2     344.7
```


ISBN 90-247-3106-2 (this volume)
ISBN 90-247-3004-X (series)

TABLE OF CONTENTS

INTRODUCTION

IDEOLOGICAL DOGMATA AND PRACTICAL TASKS OF SOVIET LAW

The supposition that Soviet law is well written, but badly applied, is widespread in the West. Such a supposition has appeared as an abstract rational deduction from two co-existing facts: Soviet law proclaims democracy, freedom, and legality, while Soviet reality proves its inseparability from dictatorship, suppression, and arbitrariness. The irreconcilable divergence between legal promises and everyday life sometimes leads to an assessment that Soviet law is a purely propagandistic phenomenon, which has nothing to do with legal regulation, and that administrative orders are the only governmental regulator of human activity in the USSR. Some authors typify the Soviet Constitution as a "form without substance."[1] Others consider the written constitution of the Soviet Union to be "a meaningless scrap of paper," behind which there is "a genuine constitution – unwritten, or rather unpublicized, yet perfectly understood and recognized by all concerned."[2] Turning to Soviet law as a single whole, the same authors admit that "any society so highly organized as the Soviet Union cannot be governed entirely on the basis of arbitrary fiat. There must be some system of regularized rules to take care of the great majority of disputes – those which are not sufficiently sensitive to be given individual political attention. Otherwise, Soviet leaders would be unable to focus their attention on the relatively small number of disputes that do have significant political implication."[3] Referring to Ernst Fraenkel who characterized Nazi Germany as a "dual state" – which in some aspects can be a "prerogative state", governed arbitrarily, and in other aspects a "normative state", where government is limited by legal norms[4] – the same authors find a similar combination in the USSR with the reservation that "the areas of jurisdiction covered by the 'prerogative state' and the 'normative state' are not fixed," but "rather they are constantly expanding and contracting as the situation demands."[5]

The latter viewpoint would already seem to be less extreme than the former one, and in this way it resembles the concepts of those scholars who are striving to find simultaneously negative and positive features in Soviet law. They criticize "the popular view of the Soviet state as a police state run by professional revolutionaries, whose actions are governed solely by the desire to extend their own power..."[6] In their opinion, this attitude "is a dangerous half-truth."[7] It is dangerous, because as a result "the inner strength of the enemy is seriously underrated", "possible avenues of reconciliation between conflicting systems are irrevocably cut off", and the West will "learn little from Soviet experience, profiting neither from its blunders nor from its successes."[8] It is a half-truth because Soviet law teaches us many very important things. According to it, "we may learn... that the balance between personal initiative and social-economic integration is one which must be struck again and again in any going legal system", that "the cohesive character of community life is an essential foundation of law...", and that "the parental character of Soviet law" contains "the great potentialities and the grave dangers inherent in the development of positive law as a guardian and teacher of the law-consciousness of persons and groups."[9] Furthermore, "the Soviets have made a genuine response to the crisis of values which threatens twentieth-century society – a response which has not merely a Marxist and a Russian but a universal significance. They have found a basis for law in a new conception of man..."[10], which considers man "as a youth to be guided and trained."[11] Therefore, "we should not allow the violence and injustice which have accompanied the birth and growth of this conception to obscure its underlying significance."[12]

The last statement is almost entirely devoid of any attention to the shortcomings of Soviet law and actually supports the view that here we simply have one of several legal systems in human history and in the contemporary world with defects and merits, which embody great services to the whole of humanity and should not be disregarded despite the dark sides of the same system. In general expression and in numerous details, this system leaves the impression of "an undoubted affinity to the Roman laws", bearing in mind its terminology and structure.[13] As for theoretical grounds, the most important of them – the "concept of the legal rule... seems no different from that of French and German jurists."[14] Nevertheless, Soviet law represents a separate, socialist legal system, which has been created under the determining influence of Marxism-Leninism and a new socio-political structure. Marxism-Leninism is important in understanding the essence and goals of law in the USSR. A Soviet law does not so much establish rules "of order by providing a principle for the solution of disputes" but rather it acts as "a means of transforming, and thus guiding society toward the communist ideal..."[15] In such a way the Soviet Union employs "social engineering through law" – to use the expression coined in a collection of articles by western scholars entitled "Soviet Law After Stalin".[16] The new socio-political structure has yielded the formation of a new terminology and the transformation of traditional vocabulary. Thus, "at the present time, fundamental differences persist between the structures, institutions, and ways of life and thought of socialist and of other countries."[17] Therefore, "the problems [of the socialist camp] are different to those in the non-socialist countries, and words themselves have a different sense. The terms 'democracy', 'election', 'parliament', 'federalism', 'trade-union', and 'collective agreement', for example, take on a very different meaning because of the existence of an all-powerful communist Party; the words 'property', 'contract', and 'arbitration' denote different realities because of the collectivization of the means of production and state planning".[18] However, later "when the present lack of understanding and suspicion are dissipated by a recognized need for participation in common tasks, these differences will one day become less marked."[19]

Some of these statements are true, if not in their entirety, then at least in part. Others seem very strange and sometimes even more than strange. The characterization of the Soviet Constitution as a form without substance is true, but only in part. When speaking, for example, about the constitutional right to work,[20] this statement cannot be disproved. In proclaiming the right to work, the constitution refers only to an economic guarantee – absence of unemployment in the USSR, which has been really reduced to almost zero by means of the low level of the average salary. Nevertheless, numerous people lose their jobs as a result of political persecution or other causes, and since neither the constitution nor the current legislation of the USSR provide legal guarantees for the right to work, no one may demand a proper job or a minimum compensation for its refusal. However, in considering the constitutional duty to work,[21] nobody would come to the conclusion that it is a form without substance. This duty rests upon strong legal foundations, including criminal punishment of "parasitic existence".[22] Thus, this duty has become so evident that there is no doubt of its existence. Side by side with negative illustrations, some positive examples of the partial reality of the Soviet Constitution can also be presented. Contemporary Soviet civil law has a provision stating that "harm suffered by a citizen while saving socialist property from a danger threatening it shall be compensated by the organization whose property the claimant saved."[23] This provision, favorable for citizens who suffer harm under the circumstances, finds sufficient application in judicial practice.[24] But actually it had appeared long before the Soviet civil codes now in force were promulgated. Already in 1940 the USSR Supreme Court applied the same rule in a particular case, referring to the constitutional duty of Soviet citizens "to safeguard and strengthen... socialist ownership,"[25] and concluding that if the performance of this duty resulted in harm for an obligor, he also had to have a right to compensation.[26] As for the general need for legal regulations, their appearance in the USSR has stemmed from the same causes as in all other countries of the world. Any state, introducing a desired order, can normally maintain it in no other way than by legal rules which are binding upon all and by compulsory measures inflicted upon violations of those rules. The Soviet state does not present an exception in this regard. And it would be very strange to look for other grounds in this case or, moreover, to find them in the economy of time for the direct solution by the Soviet leadership of especially important political disputes.

It would be even stranger – inclining almost to the opposite point of view – to commend Soviet law not for its virtues, but for the sake of purely utilitarian goals of possible "reconciliation" with another "conflicting system."[27] To say nothing about the absence of direct connections between knowledge of Soviet law and ways of reconciliation with the Soviet state, one should not forget that, according to Marxist-Leninist doctrine, law is an ideological institution, and, as Soviet leaders indefatigably repeat, the peaceful coexistence of different states does not mean peaceful coexistence in the ideological sphere. If so, then why look for political reconciliation in the laudatory distortion of Soviet law, especially when the other party sees no obstacle to political reconciliation in its humiliating distortion of western law? In addition, when one says that the Soviet experience includes, together with successes, also blunders (not governmentally organized criminality, but simple blunders), or that it teaches how important the balance is between personal initiative and social-economic integration (not a disgusting subordination, but an attractive balance),[28] one goes at least no further than Soviet legal literature. However, even Soviet scholars, accentuating the so-called nurturing role of Soviet law, have never spoken about "the parental character" of their legal system and have never called it a "teacher of the law-consciousness of persons and groups". Of course, they would agree with an opinion that Soviet law has settled the "crisis of values" threatening twentieth-century society. But to connect such a solution with "a new conception of man" as a "youth to be guided and trained" is strange, and more than strange to the citizen who does not need guiding and training so much as freedom and peace. And are there really any grounds to assume that the whole of mankind would welcome the Soviet solution of the contemporary "crisis of values" as would befit a youth who feels in need of training?

Finally, there is no doubt of the affinity of Soviet law to Roman law and to the civil law system of western continental Europe. A part of the terminology and a part of the concepts, as well as codification and some other structural components prove this affinity eloquently and persuasively. But to support the separate existence of the Soviet or, more broadly, the socialist, legal system by a semantic change of the traditional terminology – even if one points out that the terminological alteration has been predetermined by Marxist-Leninist doctrine and by new socio-political structure – means stopping at the surface of the subject of research and avoiding any attempt to penetrate into its genuine essence. However, does not the characteristic of Soviet law as a means of transforming society and thus guiding it toward the communist ideal deserve appreciation for such an attempt? Soviet history recognizes four of the most important events on the way "toward the communist ideal". The 1917 October revolution was the first of these events, but it took place before Soviet law appeared. The second event is known as the liquidation of the "Kulaks" (more or less rich Russian peasants). And Stalin himself declared frankly enough that to implement the anti-Kulak campaign successfully, it was necessary "to put laws aside" – at least for a while. So, in connection with the two above-mentioned events, Soviet law could not reveal its capacity of "social engineering" because it either did not exist or was disregarded as an obstacle to such "engineering". The third event relates to Soviet law: the 1936 Soviet Constitution declared the victory of socialism in the USSR.[29] This legal declaration, however, did not correspond to Soviet reality, as was proved by the extra-legal practices which preceded the declaration (the reprisals against the peasantry) – and which then followed it (the Stalin purges). Political and economic dictatorship, not socialism, was established at that time, and Soviet law only reflected the *fait accompli*. The fourth event is of the same nature: the 1977 Soviet Constitution proclaimed that "a developed socialist society has been built in the USSR".[30] But since the "establishment of socialism" was in itself a fiction, "a developed socialist society" could not help but be a continuation of the initial fiction. The domestic regime of barracks discipline combined with the gigantic military machine, and not "developed socialism", typify contemporary Soviet society, created independently of the law and pervertedly interpreted by it. So, in connection with the two latter events Soviet law revealed more readily its skill in concealing the actual situation by social demagogy, than its capacity for "social engineering" to prepare the triumph of the communist ideal.[31] Nevertheless, some people dream of a rapprochement of the western legal system with the Soviet system of law, hoping that this will happen when "the present lack of understanding" disappears. What does this dream actually mean? Probably nothing other than that the juridical convergence will be a part of the general convergence of the future. But the Soviet leadership rejects any type of convergence based on a modification of the Soviet system. Thus, it becomes possible solely on the grounds of a rapprochement to this system from the side of the western countries, and in such a case those who give themselves up to similar dreams should very meticulously and vigilantly check, whether they pave the road to paradise or in the opposite direction.

Soviet law, which presents a quite separate legal system, is a complicated and versatile phenomenon. Efficacious research of it supposes some indispensable prerequisites or even fundamental principles.

First of all, this research should be objective and truthful, free of any propagandistic aim and utilitarian approach. Certainly, knowledge of Soviet law can and must be used in a utilitarian way. But to reject the correct knowledge of the legal system of the USSR only because it could lead to negative practical results would be as reasonable as to repudiate the earth's gravity only because it makes it difficult for planes to take off.

Secondly, Soviet laws themselves do not assure an adequate knowledge of Soviet law. They must doubtless be known, and any scholar who deals with the USSR's legal system should study them with all appropriate seriousness. But to appreciate them without taking into consideration Soviet reality, including legal reality, would be as reliable as to judge the movement of the sun on the grounds of subjective visual perception without checking it by means of the more exact objective data.

Thirdly, Soviet law is full of numerous contradictions. Apart from internal contradictions between different parts and different norms, there are external contradictions between law as a single whole and reality in its many-sided embodiments. If the study of Soviet law has as its task real research, not a simple description, then contradictions of both kinds demand equal attention. To make an analysis of Soviet law and yet to disregard its contradictory nature would prove to be as successful as to explain electricity while ignoring its positive and negative poles.

The present book is structured in such a way as to reflect the main contradictions of Soviet law as a law of democratic centralism and centralized democracy (chapter I), of political freedom and political domination (chapter II), of economic emancipation and economic slavery (chapter III), of universal equality and universal hierarchy (chapter IV), and of proclaimed legality and legalized arbitrariness (chapter V). However, as a necessary introduction to their analysis, the ideological dogmata and practical tasks of Soviet law will be elucidated.

1. Ideological Dogmata

That which can be called ideological dogmata, forming the doctrinal basis of Soviet law, bears the official name of Marxism-Leninism. Contemporary or future historians of philosophical doctrines and political thoughts may explain its evolution, and whether more or less of what has been propounded by Marx and added to by Lenin has been preserved in Soviet ideology up to our time. But to elucidate this ideology for the sake of a theoretical analysis of Soviet law, there is no need to adduce various statements of those who are considered the founders of Marxism-Leninism. For our goals it is simultaneously necessary and sufficient to reproduce the main sociological prerequisites which have obligatory force for Soviet jurisprudence and which pertain to its impeccable and irrefutable principles independently of the concrete views developed by one Soviet scholar or another. These prerequisites are always the same whichever author one selects and whatever book one reads.[32]

The first dogma says: law is determined by the economy and cannot in its commands exceed the level of economic development, but at the same time Soviet law plays a creative role and, actively reacting to the economic basis, promotes the latter on the progressive road of building communism. This dogma, however, has never been observed in practice; rather, more exactly, it has always been disregarded cavalierly in its first part (dependence of the law on the economy) and granted exaggerated respect in its second part (the law directs the economy). In the time of the post-revolutionary devastation (1917-1920), when the country could hardly make ends meet, Bolsheviks legally declared war communism to be the shortest way to genuine communism. When, owing to the new economic policy (NEP), the country began to achieve something like an economic balance by the late 1920s, the legislation of the NEP was replaced by measures applied against private ownership in town (so-called "kooperirovanie") and in the country (the so-called collectivization), which repeatedly brought the USSR to the very brink of economic disaster. The Soviet people had not yet collected themselves after the famine of the early 1930s, when in the mid-1930s they were informed by Soviet law of the victory of socialism. The 1970s were marked by a sharp fall in productivity in all spheres of the Soviet economy, with its obsolete technology in industry and hopelessly backward agriculture, incapable of feeding the Soviet population without grain imported from the West. But in 1977 Soviet law announced all over the world that ordinary socialism had already attained the scale of developed socialism. And only when juridical disregard of economic demands results in a desperate situation, will the Soviet legislature change its mind, modifying, in order to escape wholesale disaster, extremely harmful legal rules, a procedure which has already been followed more than once in the case of legal restrictions on the private initiative or autonomous activity of economic organizations.

The second dogma declares: law is not only protected, but also created and sanctioned by the state, and since any state personifies one or another dictatorship (of the dominant class in capitalist countries or of the whole people in the USSR), so law, obligatory for everybody and everyone, cannot be binding to the state itself. In the realm of propaganda this serves to deny the very possibility of the *Rechtsstaat* (legal state) as a hypocritical fiction of bourgeois origin and, at the same time, to glorify the Soviet state where nobody but the "whole people" is free from the binding force of its own law. In practice the same dogma justifies an unrestrictedly arbitrary treatment of the law by the Soviet leadership, since the leadership represents the people, and for the whole people the binding force of legal regulations simply does not exist. As a result, the second dogma, in contrast to the first one, is actually disregarded entirely, not only in part. It is no longer a secret that the real function of law-making in the

USSR belongs to the Politbureau as the highest echelon of the Communist Party, and governmental agencies fulfill no more than a purely ceremonial role in the legislative area. From the viewpoint of ceremony, the Soviets can formally declare the whole people to be the legislature, referring either to the general election of the Supreme Soviet, if laws are concerned, or to the formation of other state agencies by the generally elected Supreme Soviet, if edicts of its Presidium or decisions of the Council of Ministers are a subject of discussion. But as soon as one turns to the actual situation, this line of argument becomes even formally futile. The Politbureau is an agency of the Communist Party, and the Communist Party is not the same as the Soviet people: the former encompasses a comparatively small part of the latter. Even if one were to ignore the fact that a party election is as fake as a general election, the Politbureau formed by the Communist Party cannot be considered an agency of the Soviet people. In the best case, it may refer to general Party opinion – whether it has been really expressed or artificially juggled. But this reference would have only quantitative, not qualitative significance. It would identify the Soviet state (as a creator of law not bound by legal rules) with the Communist Party instead of the Politbureau. However, in both cases the people remain aside. Thus, if the *Rechtsstaat* is a bourgeois fiction contradicted by the freedom of any state from its own law, then the similar freedom ascribed to the Soviet people is a socialist fiction contradicted by the real relations of forces between the people, the Communist Party and the Politbureau.

The third dogma reads: law is an expression of the will of the state as its creator, and because the state, in its turn, is an organization of political dominance implemented by the ruling class in capitalist society and by the whole people in socialist society, law virtually expresses either the separate will of the dominant class or the general "all-people's" will. The actual facts contradict this dogma. If capitalist law reflects the private owners' will, how is one to explain the numerous laws on nationalization of very important parts of private ownership in England or in France? If socialist law reflects the will of the majority in the beginning and of the entire people in the end, how is one to justify the banning of "Solidarity" with its ten million members in Poland (1981) or the compulsory collectivization of agriculture in the USSR at a time when the peasantry represented the majority of the Soviet population (1928-1932)? As a matter of course, together with its worship of the dogmatical legal importance of the general will, the Soviet leadership reduces it to nothing in actual law-making practice. Even the public issuing of laws by the USSR Supreme Soviet is not accompanied by a serious discussion with the active participation of "the people's representatives" in this "highest agency of state power".[33] Then by what miracle do the Soviet people manage to express their will in Soviet law nevertheless? But while laws adopted by the Supreme Soviet are not very numerous, the number of decisions taken by the Council of Ministers of the USSR attains astronomical proportions. In addition, they appear unexpectedly as if by a *deus ex machina*, being published in one part and unpublished in another. Can the Soviet people express its will through legal regulations, which it does not know at all or sees for the first time after their promulgation? And does not the dogma of the general will seem to be a fiction of the same character as the fiction of "the all-people's state"? In each more or less developed country the scope of legal regulations is large and their contents complicated. In this regard the Soviet Union can perhaps compete with any country of the world. Soviet legislation regulating economic activities only, encompasses more than 20,000 normative acts, and, if one takes into account ministerial regulations as well, this number will reach 100,000. Professional lawyers do not know all these acts and experience serious difficulties in explaining many of them. Under these circumstances there is no need to speak of the knowledge and understanding of the man in the street. Only a few legal rules are as simple and well-known as the commands "thou shalt not kill" and "thou shalt not steal". Most of their number is so complicated, that it is very difficult to understand them despite the great personal interest of a reader, who, for example, tries to consult the law on pensions or the law on succession. Therefore, to agree with the concept of Soviet law as an embodiment of the general will one must assume the existence of a will expressed unconsciously and without understanding. Does such an assumption have at least a remote likeness to a real truth or to any similarity of a truth?

The fourth dogma proclaims: law is protected by the state, relying upon its compulsory measures. However, while the law of capitalist countries – expressing the will of the ruling class – is observed by the other sections of the population by virtue of the fear of eventual or actual coercion, Soviet law – expressing the general will – is, as a rule, observed voluntarily and applies compulsion only in a very restricted number of cases, where an individual puts his own interests, which are wrongly understood, on a higher level than more important collective interests. In other words, the majority of people in capitalist countries would not observe the legal prohibitions of killing or stealing, were there no state coercion, while, on the contrary, the majority of people in the USSR would never kill or steal, whether state coercion existed or did not exist. And this impressive contrast does not need any sophisticated explanation. To put it bluntly, Soviet law reflects the general will not to admit such harmful behavior. But with these invaluable advantages of Soviet law in comparison with western law, many things stop being clear and simple. For example, the legislation of the USSR provides capital punishment for certain kinds of theft.[34] Western legislation does not contain similar provisions. Every Soviet city has at least one prison, and at least one labor camp exists in every Soviet province, to say nothing of territories notorious all over the world for their numerous labor camps. Western countries have nothing similar. Statistics of crimes and other violations have not been published in the USSR since the late 1920s, and only a very restricted circle of officials is granted knowledge of statistical data of this kind, despite emphatic and repeated statements by the authorities that the incidence of law-breaking, and especially of crime, is steadily decreasing. Western legal statistics are generally accessible and widely published, irrespective of the fact whether they reflect favorably or unfavorably upon the country concerned. Now and again the Soviet authorities call for an increased struggle against a certain kind of violation: hooliganism, bribery, petty stealing in enterprises, etc. Similar calls are heard very rarely in the West, although, if one were to trust Soviet concepts and the Soviet media, western countries experience a much greater vulnerability in this area. The first step taken in 1982 by the new leader of the USSR in order to improve the entire Soviet economy was aimed at the strengthening of labor discipline with the help of various means, beginning with law and ending with the police. Why was this necessary, if Soviet law had not lost its capacity to express the general will – which would be disregarded only in exceptional "pathological" cases? And how do western countries manage not to be troubled by labor discipline, if their law is generally disregarded except by the dominant class, the will of which has obtained the force of law?

The fifth dogma states: law is an institution whose purpose is to protect and strengthen a certain social order and certain social relationships on the condition that they are advantageous and convenient for the ruling class in capitalist countries and for the whole people in the USSR. However, if this were true, historical continuity would be as incompatible with Soviet law as any coincidence between the latter and Western legal regulations. Meanwhile, numerous juridical norms of the USSR repeat, in essence, or even *verbatim*, Justinian's *Corpus Iuris Civilis*.[35] An even greater number of adoptions from the *Code Napoléon* of France or from the *Bürgerliches Gesetzbuch* of Germany can be found.[36] This applies to both codifications of Soviet law: the codification of the 1920s, when, according to the official viewpoint, there was a transitional period from capitalism to socialism, and the codification of the 1960s, when, according to the same official point of view, ordinary socialism began to attain the level of developed socialism. As is well known, the social order of the USSR differs immensely from the one prevailing in Western countries, and the social order of western continental Europe is in principle of the same kind as in England or in the USA. Nevertheless, genetically the system of civil law, dominant in the western countries of continental Europe, is akin to the system of Soviet law and more distant to the English and American system of common law. Of course, peculiarities of the concrete social order cannot help influencing the content of legal regulations. On the one hand, Soviet law does not know legal institutions geared to free economic development, and, on the other hand, western law does not include juridical reprisals directed against free spiritual development. Moreover, not infrequently, legal institutions of the same title and of similar appearance prove to be diametrically opposed in their essence. General elections or freedom of speech in the USSR and in the western countries seem like manifestations of a common nomenclature, but from different planets. An analogous conclusion can be made if one compares legal regulations in the realm of other political freedoms and rights. However, side by side with the peculiarities of various countries and societies, there are general interests common to the whole of mankind, and they must be legally protected with the necessary uniformity, whether the laws in question are socialist or capitalist. Furthermore, the people of each country has its general common interest, irrespective of class, stratum or group. If this interest is not protected by law, the entire society will sooner or later collapse, notwithstanding the virtues its legal system may otherwise possess. And what seems most peculiar, the legislature itself, under the pressure of circumstances, giving in to insistent international demands or to domestic public opinion, may sometimes issue juridical norms which would be resolutely repudiated, were the legislature to take into consideration only the advantages and convenience of the dominant group. Thus, the purposes of law are broader and more versatile than just the protection of the separate social order or the demands of the ruling circles.

The sixth dogma confirms: law is an historically transient phenomenon; it appeared together with private ownership and the class division of human society; it changed its nature when the law of the exploiting society was replaced by socialist law; it plays an important role in the building of socialism and communism; it will wither away together with the state as soon as communism gains victory all over the world. It seems, however, indubitable, that no phenomenon can be preserved after the basis of its existence has been destroyed. Therefore, logical consistency demands from adherents of this thesis to select one of two alternative arguments to explain the continued existence of law in the USSR. Either hostile classes and private ownership do exist in new and peculiar forms in the Soviet Union, or the reference to the class division of human society and to the appearance of private ownership does not exhaust the essential ingredients without which law cannot come into being. In the first case, any discussion about the specificity of socialist law and its role in the building of socialism and communism becomes senseless. And in fact, the entire study shall concentrate on the peculiarities of Soviet law inasmuch as it is based upon *sui generis* private ownership and class hostility. In the second case, law has not only been serving the interests of dominant classes and protecting private ownership since its very beginning, but also something else, which Marxist-Leninist jurisprudence groundlessly describes as an exclusive function of socialist law. And if this is so, then the latter does not deserve most of the praise which Soviet jurisprudence generously heaps on to it. For better or worse, Soviet law possesses some of the inalienable virtues of law in general, modified in the Soviet's own manner, according to the level (and type) of their social development. Thus, the old is repeated in the new, and to what extent this new is better than the old will be shown by our further analysis. At any rate, this analysis shall deal with contemporary realities and, consequently, will be able to provide certain positive results, as well as verifiable conclusions. In contrast a contemplation of the future fate of law, especially in connection with the victory of communism, solemnly promised but never realized, would transport us from the ground of reality into the realm of Utopia. Visionaries who claim scientific infallibility may allow themselves to predict the fairy-tale future. Analysts who make their way to truth through doubts cannot afford to go beyond the limits of the cognizable past and the reliable present. The past as well as the present have found more than distorted reflection in the ideological dogmata of Soviet law. But ideology does not preclude distortions. Moreover, to some extent it even stimulates them. In practice it is otherwise. The practical tasks of Soviet law cannot coincide with ideological dogmata. But they do not distort reality, because they are reality itself.

2. Practical Tasks

Although the practical tasks of Soviet law pertain to reality, one should not think that Soviet legislation reflects them adequately and truthfully. The explanation for this is that the USSR legislature displays a duplicity in its activity, needing simultaneously to observe official dogmata and to pursue practical goals. As a result the legal texts that touch upon practical tasks of Soviet law combine truth, non-truth and concealed truth.

For example, according to article 1 of the Fundamental Principles of Civil Legislation of the USSR and the Union Republics,[37] "Soviet Civil Legislation shall regulate property and personal non-property relations connected therewith", and that is really so. But the same article says that this regulation has been enacted "with a view to creating the material-technical base of communism and satisfying more fully the material and spiritual requirements of citizens", and that is already a hollow declaration which has no connection with Soviet reality. Soviet civil law, regulating a section of human relationships, does indeed have its practical tasks; however, they are not expressed either explicitly or even implicitly, since in this case to remain silent seems preferable to being eloquent. A similar approach and an analogous combination can be found in any law which formulates one or another task of legal regulation in the USSR.[38] Therefore, in order to make plain the actual tasks of Soviet law, it is necessary to include in the subject of research, together with legal regulations, also legal reality, and together with legal reality, also the country's political, economic, and social structure.

The predominant component of the Soviet system is the unlimited political power of the ruling summit. It has domination over all other components, regardless of its positive or negative influence upon them. This applies to domestic relationships as well as to international affairs. The Soviet military build-up alone illustrates such a juxtaposition better than numerous other well-known facts. The tremendous expenditure of a military character long ago surpassed the strength of the Soviet economy, and has led above all to the impoverishment of the Soviet people. At the same time the Soviet Union has already managed to attain a nuclear might sufficient for the complete destruction of our world. Then why continue governmental efforts towards permanently growing strength? The answer is that as an economically backward country the USSR sees no other way of maintaining and consolidating its position as one of the two world superpowers than by continually augmenting its armaments and keeping them at the highest possible level. At this level the power of the state appears to be so strong and invincible, that the subordinate population does not counter the state's domestic arbitrariness with disobedience and other countries are in the last analysis resigned to putting up with the USSR's international conduct. Thus, the political advantage being beyond doubt, all other considerations – economic, legal or simply human – retreat into the background. And it could not be otherwise, since nothing is considered more important than unlimited political power.

The main source of this power is the economy, in its quality of the second component of the Soviet system. The economy with all its more or less significant ingredients belongs to the Soviet state which has become the economic monopolist in the USSR. As a result, each citizen and the entire citizenry depend on the state economically, and this dependence compels them to be submissive politically. Here, in the economic monopoly of the Soviet state, one can also find the explanation for Soviet style economic miracles: technological backwardness and high technical achievements, shortage of material resources and their unrestricted abundance. Owing to its economic backwardness, the USSR does not have the capacity to ensure an optimal correspondence between supply and demand. But possessing at its unfettered disposal the entire economy of one-sixth of the world, the Soviet leadership concentrates, if necessary, as many resources as are indispensable to solve those problems which the Soviet regime regards as being of paramount importance. When, for example, in the late 1970s a military pilot defected to Japan in a Soviet plane of the newest model, foreign experts were surprised by the imbalance between the advanced propulsion and the backward communications technology of the plane. However, there was nothing to be astonished about: an unequal distribution of money had resulted in inequality of technical progress. But distribution itself depends on leaders, not on subordinate executives. Such is the general rule of Soviet society. Thus, all subordinate executives are dependent on and obedient to the political leaders.

The entire complex of governing bodies, including punitive agencies (judicial system, the procuracy, the police, the KGB, etc.) is the third component of the Soviet system and, simultaneously, a subsidiary source of the unlimited political power of the Soviet leadership. The role of this complex in supporting and strengthening the Soviet regime does not provoke any doubt, since certain functions are accessible to nobody else. Inside the country the dissident movement was destroyed by the KGB, not by the economy. Outside the country new technology has been, and continues to be procured by technical espionage, not by economic activity. However, strong as they are, these agencies can be utilized only in the performance of relatively specific tasks. The general task of holding each individual and the entire population in check is beyond their capacity. Only the economy, run on a monopolistic basis by the state itself, has proved to be effective in this respect, because its pressure is limitless, while pressure from any other source cannot help being restricted to some extent. That is why the monopolistic economy is the main source of the unlimited political power of the Soviet regime, but which is additionally strongly supported by the activities of the administrative agencies.

The unlimited political power has as its subject the Soviet people which is the fourth component of the Soviet system. This component, being the largest in quantitative terms, does not occupy a qualitatively appropriate position. While political dominance acts from the top of the system, the Soviet people, as a subordinate subject, are at the bottom of it. This bottom level, however, is not homogeneous. There are different social strata. The Soviets themselves officially distinguish between workers, peasants and intelligentsia.[39] The actual social stratification of the USSR is more fragmented than the one acknowledged by the Constitution. Unskilled labor and the 'working aristocracy' are united under the general notion 'workers', well-to-do and extremely poor members of collective farms are called by one name 'peasants', to say nothing about the intelligentsia, which, in Soviet parlance, includes everybody except workers and peasants – from the new millionaires among a section of the highly paid intellectual elite, down to ordinary clerks with miserable salaries and without any hope for the future. The actual stratification of the Soviet people demands an application of different approaches toward various groups, and, on the other hand, one stratum will feel the political dominance more strongly than another. But this in principle does not change the general situation. The entire population lives under the fully unrestricted weight of political might, and the Soviet regime would cease to exist, if this relationship between the ruling power and the subordinate masses were to be destroyed or even shaken. Of course, the real circumstances are thoroughly camouflaged. In the words of the 1977 Constitution, nobody but the "Soviet people … affirm the foundations of the social system and policies of the USSR, establish the rights, freedoms, and obligations of citizens and the principles of organization and the aims of the socialist all-people's state, and proclaim them in this Constitution".[40] Meanwhile, in times of political crisis the plain or implicit recognition of the hollow ritualism of these solemn slogans slips from somebody's tongue now and again. For instance, in the post-Stalin period of the fight for personal power, Khrushchev blamed Malenkov for attempting to make advances to the people by the 1953 program for large-scale production of consumer goods. But if the supreme power were in the hands of the people, there would be no need for Malenkov's advances and Khrushchev would have had no reason to rebuke Malenkov. Nevertheless, such rebukes were made in the heat of the argument, and the unintentional truth of a few words outshone the deliberate concealment through endless loquacity. The people belong to the Soviet system, but as a subject, not as the repository of political power.

Such are the four components of the Soviet system, considered separately and in their interdependence. It is they who determine the practical tasks of the fifth component – Soviet law. Indeed, Soviet law regulates Soviet relationships, and, while on the subject of legal regulation, the normative acts of the USSR do not distort anything. The obvious distortion begins with the declaration that legal norms are enacted by the legislature and applied by a host of agencies for the sake of communist building or in order to ensure the full satisfaction of citizens' demands. The genuine tasks of legal regulation in the Soviet Union are to be found on another plane. Law is expected, first and foremost, to support and strengthen the unlimited political power of the ruling summit, which at all times should be able to solve any problem at its own discretion and to intervene in any activity of its own accord. In implementing this task, law needs to be in the closest possible connection with the Soviet economy and to protect with all its force the state's position of economic monopolist, so that even insignificant economic activity will not escape governmental subordination and control. Since law presents only a system of legal norms, and its actual realization depends upon a system of appropriate agencies, the latter shall be directed by the former through the full conformity of the practice of law-application with the politics of law-making, whether this practice corresponds with the literal meaning of the legal texts, or with their skillfully concealed sense. The successful solution of the enumerated tasks is inseparably linked with a final, but highly important function of law: unconditional subordination of the Soviet people to Soviet power, subordination in all imaginable areas – in public and private life, in economic, political and intellectual activity, in attitudes toward governmental and public agencies, and toward the Soviet state as a single unit. To a large extent the solution of this problem results from the fulfillment of the above-mentioned legal functions. But if this approach fails, then direct repressions are applied against those whose behavior is regarded as threatening.

A comparison of the practical tasks and the ideological dogmata of Soviet law reveals irreconcilable contradictions between them. It might seem as if practical tasks were entirely free of Marxist-Leninist dogmatism, and ideological dogmata were completely deprived of practical significance. But such an impression would be a serious delusion. Things are more complicated than they appear at first glance. When, for example, the Fundamentals of Civil Legislation proclaim that "in the construction of a communist society, full use is made of the goods-money relationship in accordance with the new content which it has in a planned socialist economy",[41] and "Soviet civil legislation regulates the property relations resulting from the employment of the goods-money form of economy in the construction of communism",[42] a direct reference is made to the dogma of the determination of law by the economy.[43] Such a reference provides a pretext for praising Soviet law as being scientifically justified by the adequate reflection of actual conditions and for putting the blame for all divergencies between legal regulations and human demands on these conditions, and not on the legal norms. Thus, a propagandist effect is on hand. Nevertheless, in case of necessity, Soviet practice allows the withdrawal of property from economic organizations despite the legal command to use the goods-money form. At the same time economic contracts, always supposing payment for goods supplied and services given, do not disregard this form at least within the limits of the established prices. Hence, the reference to the goods-money relationship also proves its own practical significance.

A decision of the Central Committee of the USSR Communist Party, the Presidium of the USSR Supreme Soviet and the Council of Ministers of the USSR of 2 September 1976, "On the preparation and issuing of the Collection of Laws of the USSR"[44] declares in its Preamble: "Soviet laws express the will of the people, the policies of the Communist Party and of the Soviet State." This declaration undoubtedly reflects the dogma of the creation of law by the state, and of the State not being bound by its own law. Such an interpretation can, however, be opposed by the citation of the constitutional command: "The Soviet state and all its agencies shall operate on the basis of socialist legality."[45] But the command cited, referring to the state, does not mention the other two creators of law in the USSR: the Soviet people and the Communist Party. Meanwhile, if the Soviet people play a purely decorative role in the legal formulas, the Communist Party, embodied in its summit, represents the only real power. Nevertheless, the 1977 Constitution passes it by in silence, enacting the general principle of "socialist legality", as well as concrete norms concerning the highest supervision of law-making and law application in the USSR.[46] Furthermore, if the Soviet state is a state of the entire people, and the Communist Party is "the nucleus" of the same state,[47] enumeration of all of them in one logical sequence would be unexplainable without paying attention to the hidden political objectives. And these are not too sophisticated: to disguise the real dictator (the Party top) by confusing it with decorative, ceremonial and operative holders of power (the people, the state, the state agencies). As a result this most concentrated dictatorship does not preclude the proclaiming of "socialist legality" for the sake of propaganda in the first place and also for practical purposes, but only in so far as, while keeping the decorative rulers, ceremonial bodies and operative agencies under control, subordination to law does not entail a diminution of dictatorial prerogatives.

While the decision concerning the Collection of Laws speaks of the *policies* of the Soviet state expressed in Soviet laws, the 1977 Constitution defines the USSR as "a socialist all-people's state expressing the *will*" of the whole people.[48] But because the state cannot help expressing its will other than by means of law, both legal texts taken together follow the dogma of law as an embodiment of the general will in the USSR, which is different from the will of the dominant class embodied in the law of capitalist countries. At the same time the Constitution adds the general will only to the policies of the Soviet state, not to the policies of the Communist Party. In fact, it could not act otherwise, since the Communist Party is not a party which encompasses the whole people, notwithstanding the official proclamation of the Soviet all-people's state. Nevertheless, the Communist party expresses its policies through law and does so as "the guiding and directing force of Soviet society",[49] *i.e.* as a force which subordinates to itself all other decision-making agencies and predetermines in this way all aspects of the general will. Thus, the logically inadmissible combination, on the same semantic level, of will and policies, stemming from different sources, unveils the non-coincidence of that what is with what ought to be. But to find this non-coincidence it is necessary to resort to a scrupulous analysis of legal texts. Such an analysis may be of interest to a researcher, but will hardly claim general attention. For the purpose of propaganda this is sufficient. The practical importance of such an approach should not be underrated either. If so-called all-people's discussions of certain draft laws serve to support the belief that Soviet law rests upon the general will,[50] this belief, in its turn, supports the justification of the most cruel regulations which have been or still are in force in the USSR. Not without reason did Stalin brand the victims of his purges as "enemies of the people" and introduce severe punishment for stealing of state property after having declared it "the whole people's wealth".[51] His successors dropped the label of "enemies of the people", but preserved the notion of "all-people's property"[52] and used it to justify severe repressions against anybody who attempted to appropriate some of it.[53]

A decision of 26 March 1976, of the Plenum of the USSR Supreme Court, issued with reference to the tasks of the courts defined by the 24th Congress of the Communist Party, reads that the entire future activity of Soviet courts "shall be carried out in conformity with the task, imposed by the Party, to eradicate violations of law".[54] It is to be noted that the task is not simply to cause the incidence of violations of law to be lowered, but to eradicate them altogether. An imperative demand of this kind could not be formulated, if it did not rest upon the dogma that Soviet law as the expression of the general will shall be observed, as a rule, voluntarily, and needs coercion only in a small number of cases. The same decision enumerates concrete practical means which shall be applied by the judicial system in order to ensure the actual execution of this impossible task. As a matter of fact, the means recommended (strict observance of the norms of procedure; fight against economic crimes; special attention to cases such as murder, rape, etc.)[55] have nothing to do with the goals enunciated. Nevertheless, however artificial the connection between means and ends may be, it leads to quite perceptible practical results. One can easily imagine how judges will behave, if they believe that in each criminal case they are considering they must help to eradicate crime altogether; or how they shall deal with any civil case, if they are convinced that the country needs to get rid of such cases completely and without delay. The propaganda aspect of the tasks thus defined is obvious. Would any law be more highly respected than Soviet law, if the latter is the only system to come close to transforming violations of law from everyday events into museum pieces?

"Soviet laws...", declares the decision about the Collection of Laws of the USSR, "play an important role in governing social processes in our country",[56] and the 1977

Constitution, describing these processes, typifies Soviet society as "a society whose law of life is the concern of all for the welfare of each, and the concern of each for the welfare of all."[57] Hence, it is clear that the texts cited only paraphrase the dogma of socialist law which, in contrast to capitalist law, cares about the interests of the whole people, not only of the dominant class. And if one considers this paraphrase, disregarding the reference to the contrast with other societies, it is possible to find some elements of realism in it. Apart from the general demands of the whole society, which should be taken into account by any law, Soviet law also has to settle those problems which stem from the double nature of the people in the USSR. On the one hand, the Soviet people is a subject of political domination, but, on the other hand, it is a source of fear for the ruling summit. Therefore even Stalin did not limit himself to mass repressions, but also pretended to be troubled by the people's welfare, decreasing retail prices by governmental decisions (and increasing them by the lowering of product quality) or permitting the acquisition of five-room houses by citizens (and restricting the amount of available living-space to 60 square meters).[58] The number of similar measures taken after Stalin's death has increased significantly – at times attaining a level unimaginable in the past. To say nothing about the scale of housing construction, Stalin would never have permitted the importation of consumer goods for gold or foreign currency, as practiced by his successors. With the exception of the importation of consumer goods which is considered to be humiliating for Soviet economic prestige, other actions of this kind usually become a main topic of Soviet propaganda striving to convince everybody that the Communist Party and the Soviet state have no higher task than improving the people's living standards. Similar facts are used to illustrate the contrast between Soviet law and Western law by means of an immense exaggeration of genuine practices in the form of sensational propaganda.

"The ultimate purpose of the Soviet state is the building of a classless communist society in which social communist self-administration is being developed," says the Preamble of the 1977 Constitution. Although the Constitution mentions only the state, its words doubtlessly relate to law as well, since law is a creation of the state, and both of them will share the same tasks and the same fate. So, without any difficulty one can discover in the corresponding constitutional declaration the dogma of Soviet law as a creative force which shall ensure the building of communism and then, wither away, together with its creator, the state. The propagandistic nature of this unverifiable prediction is only too obvious, but its practical advantages to the Soviet leaders should not be overlooked. Year after year legal regulations are becoming more and more widespread in the country. The number of crimes provided for in the Criminal Code has been increased. Such crimes, as, for example, the circulation of fabrications which defame the Soviet State, or the leading of a parasitic way of life,[59] were not known to the former criminal laws. The Civil Code strives not to miss any detail even when dealing with conduct which is of ethical, rather than of legal relevance. For instance, in contrast to former civil laws which did not touch upon the gratuitous use of property at all or which mentioned gifts only once in connection with the juridical forms of various acts, the Civil Code now in force devotes a separate chapter to gifts and eight articles to gratuitous use of property.[60] As for administrative regulations, the uninitiated cannot even have an approximate idea of their scale and can come across them quite unexpectedly when needing to settle a problem for the first time. Only those, for example, who have published something know the actual number of instances which must approve the publication before it is submitted to the censor. And only unusually energetic people will venture to take on the series of administrative barriers in the hope of receiving a tourist's card for foreign travel. But if Soviet law shall wither away, how is one to explain its continuous broadening? The answer is easy. Soviet law shall first ensure the victory of communism, and only then will it disappear. Thus, before withering away, it needs to exhaust all its creative potential and to encompass as many kinds of human behavior as possible. In this way the utterly propagandistic declarations serve to justify important practical activities.[61]

After all that has been said before, certain general conclusions can be made. In studying Soviet law, it is necessary to distinguish and at the same time to link its ideological dogmata and practical tasks. The practical tasks of Soviet law do not concur with its ideological dogmata. The former depend closely upon Soviet reality and reflect this reality fairly faithfully. The latter belong to the sphere of official fictions and they are preserved in immovable petrification, regardless of the changes taking place in society. But despite the tremendous gap between them, the ideological dogmata facilitate the fulfillment of the practical tasks of Soviet law, and in this way a vital connection between the two becomes visible. Of course, all this is very paradoxical and complicated. However, neither of the contradictory aspects can be abandoned and none of the complicating features can be avoided. To really understand Soviet law, it must be studied with all its contradictions and in its unembellished complexity.

18

NOTES

1. D. Barry, C. Barnet-Barry, *Contemporary Soviet Politics*, Englewood Cliffs, NJ 1978, 71.
2. T. Samuely, "Five Years After Krushchev", 12 *Survey* Summer 1969, 59-60.
3. Barry, *op.cit.*, note 1, 133.
4. E. Fraenkel, *The Dual State: A Contribution to the Theory of Dictatorship*, New York 1941.
5. Barry, *op.cit.*, note 1, 134.
6. H. Berman, *Justice in the USSR*, 2nd ed., Cambridge, MA 1978, 383.
7. *Ibid.*
8. *Ibid.*
9. *Ibid.*
10. *Ibid.*
11. *Ibid.*
12. *Ibid.*
13. R. David, J. Brierly, *Major Legal Systems in the World Today*, London 1978, 143.
14. *Ibid.*
15. *Ibid.*
16. *Soviet Law After Stalin, Part II: Social Engineering Through Law*, (D. Barry, P. Maggs, G. Ginsburgs, eds.), No.20(II), *Law in Eastern Europe*, (F.J.M. Feldbrugge, ed.), Alphen aan den Rijn, The Netherlands 1978. See, however, F.J.M. Feldbrugge, "The Study of Soviet Law", 4 *Review of Socialist Law* 1978 No.3, where in the section "Soviet Law as a Factor of Organization" one can find the following words: "Occasionally, Soviet institutions create the impression that faith in the legal machine is so great that the production of rules is the thing that matters most in Soviet law" (p.207). "Law as nothing but a reliable instrument in the hands of purposeful agents is an attractive proposition for the holders of the power monopoly in the USSR..." (p.208). "Another aspect of this way of looking at law is that it is intolerant of other views and alternative solutions." (*ibid.*).
17. David, Brierly, *op.cit.*, note 13, 144.
18. *Ibid.*
19. *Ibid.*
20. *Konstitutsiia (Osnovnoi Zakon) Soiuza Sovetskikh Sotsialisticheskikh Respublik 1977* (hereinafter cited as the 1977 Constitution), art.38.
21. *Ibid.*, art.60.
22. *Ugolovnyi Kodeks RSFSR* 1960 (hereinafter cited as Criminal Code), art.209-1.
23. *Grazhdanskii Kodeks RSFSR* 1964 (hereinafter cited as Civil Code), art.472.
24. See P.R. Stavisskii, *Vozmeshcheniie Vreda Pri Spasanii Sotsialisticheskogo Imushchestva, Zhizni i Zdorov'ia Grazhdan*, Moskva 1974.
25. *Konstitutsiia (Osnovnoy Zakon) Soiuza Sovetskikh Sotsialisticheskikh Respublik 1936* (hereinafter cited as the 1936 Constitution), art.13.
26. O.S. Ioffe, *Sovetskoe Grazhdanskoe Pravo*, Leningrad 1958, Vol.I, 60.
27. These utilitarian goals of a theoretical approach to Soviet law are no less remote from real life than is the practical justification of its study in the western countries with reference to the case if "the avenues of peace are cut off by a new World War..." (Berman, *op.cit.*, note 6, 4). It appears that in such a case "we shall surely have to know Soviet law, since if we win we shall presumably have the task of governing the Soviet survivors who have been brought up on it; on the other hand, if the Soviets should win we might possibly have to face the not so very pleasant prospect of being brought up on it ourselves." (*ibid.*) In other words, the western countries shall know Soviet law as an eventual vanquisher for better administering the people vanquished or as a people that will be vanquished for better obedience to the vanquisher.
28. An analogous euphemism sounds in the words "the violence and injustice which have accompanied the birth and growth" of the Soviet conception of law (*ibid.*, 384), as if now, when this concept has attained its maturity, no "violence" and "injustice" accompany it anymore.
29. The 1936 Constitution, art.4.

30. The 1977 Constitution, Preamble.

31. Sometimes a creative force of "social engineering" is ascribed to Soviet acts of nationalization as well as to the prohibition of private ownership. But prohibition is an act of negation, not of creation. As for nationalization, it has also been applied in some western countries and thus does not present a purely Soviet peculiarity. In addition, as a rule, Soviet legal acts of nationalization usually have followed the actual taking in possession of separate enterprises by governmental representatives. Therefore, Soviet literature considers Soviet nationalization not so much a legal act as a revolutionary measure. *E.g.* see A.V. Venediktov, *Organizatsiia Gosudarstvennoi Promishlennosti v SSSR*, Leningrad 1957, Vol.I, 3-202.

32. *E.g.* see *Marksistko-Leninskaia Obshchaia Teoriia Gosudarstva i Prava*, Moskva 1970-1973, Vols.1-4; P.E. Nedbailo, *Vvedeniie v Obshchuiu Teoriiu Gosudarstva i Prava*, Kiev 1971; A.M. Vasiliev, *Pravove Kategorii*, Moskva 1976; L.S. Iavich, *Obshchaia Teoriia Prava*, Leningrad 1976; D.A. Kerimov, *Obshchaia Teoriia Gosudarstva i Prava*, Moskva 1977; S.S. Alekseev, *Obshchaia Teoriia Prava*, Moskva 1981, Vols.I-II.

33. The 1977 Constitution, art.108.

34. Criminal Code, art.93-1.

35. O.S. Ioffe, "Soviet Law and Roman Law", 62 *Boston University Law Review* 1982 No.3, 701-730.

36. *Ibid.*

37. *Osnovy Grazhdanskogo Zakonodatel'stva Soiuza SSR i Soiuznikh Respublik 1961* (hereinafter cited the Fundamentals of Civil Legislation).

38. *E.g.* see *Osnovy Grazhdansko-Protsessual'nogo Zakonodatel'stva Soiuza SSR i Soiuznykh Respublik 1961* (hereinafter cited the Fundamentals of Civil Procedure), art.2; *Osnovy Zakonodatel'stva Soiuza SSR i Soiuznykh Respublik o Brake i Sem'e 1968* (hereinafter cited the Fundamentals of Family Legislation), art.1; *Osnovy Zemel'nogo Zakonodatel'stva Soiuza SSR i Soiznykh Respublik* (hereinafter cited the Fundamentals of Land Legislation), art.1, etc.

39. The 1977 Constitution, art.1.

40. *Ibid.*, Preamble.

41. The Fundamentals of Civil Legislation, Preamble.

42. *Ibid.*

43. See *supra*, 6.

44. *SP SSSR* 1976 No.21 item 104.

45. The 1977 Constitution, art.4.

46. *Ibid.*, art.121 (4), 164.

47. *Ibid.*, art.6.

48. *Ibid.*, art.1 (italics added).

49. *Ibid.*, art.6.

50. All-people's discussions were organized in connection with the Soviet Constitutions of 1936 and 1977, with The Fundamentals of the Housing Legislation of the USSR and the Union Republics (reprinted by *Sotsialisticheskaia Zakonnost'*, 1981 No.9, 58-71) and with several other laws. Since these discussions take the form of newspaper articles checked by the censor, meetings run by appropriate officials or letters sent to competent agencies, they do not engender any danger for the Soviet regime.

51. *SZ SSSR* 1932 No.62 item 360.

52. The 1977 Constitution, art.10.

53. Criminal Code, arts.89-93(2).

54. *Sbornik Postanovlenii Plenuma Verkhovnogo Suda SSSR, 1924-1977*, Moskva 1978, Vol.I, 50.

55. *Ibid.*

56. *Supra*, note 44.

57. The 1977 Constitution, Preamble.

58. *Ved.SSSR* 1948 No.36.

59. Criminal Code, arts.190-1, 209.

60. Civil Code, chapter XXIII and arts.342-349.

61. Soviet lawyers and the Soviet legislature itself, touching upon the functions or tasks of Soviet law, especially point out its function (task) of rearing the Soviet people in the spirit of communism. *E.g.* see *Osnovy Zakonodatel'stva o Sudoustroistve Soiuza SSR i Soiuznykh Respublik 1958* (*Ved.SSSR* 1959 No.1 item 12, art.3). At the same time, certain western authors pay serious attention to an analysis of this function. *E.g.* see Berman, *op.cit.*, note 6, 277-384. In our opinion, such a function does not exist, if not to consider legal propaganda as legal education. This is why it has not been mentioned under such a title above and will not be considered under the same title further down.

CHAPTER I

THE LAW OF DEMOCRATIC CENTRALISM AND CENTRALIZED DEMOCRACY

The Soviet approach to law as a creation of the state demands a consideration of the peculiarities of the Soviet state before turning to an analysis of the most important areas of legal regulation in Soviet law. At the same time two preliminary remarks appear to be necessary. The first one touches upon the Soviet comprehension of the state. While in Western political thought "state" refers to a country, a sovereign, or a unity of territory, population and power, Soviet political theory considers the state as nothing other than a political organization to rule all of society – an organ of the dominant class or of the entire people.[1] The discrepancy between this general doctrine of the state and the concrete concept of the Soviet all-people's state is striking. The ruler, who holds power, cannot be the same as his subject, and therefore if the state rules all of society, the entire people cannot personify the state. But that which the Soviets call "the state" – an organization of political domination – really exists in the USSR, and its structure as well as the functions of its agencies are reflected in the law of the state (according to the Soviet doctrine of the differentiation of law), *i.e.* the Soviet Constitution and numerous other legal regulations connected with it. From this point of view, the study of Soviet law begins with an initiation into the peculiarities of Soviet state law. The second remark refers to the relation between the actual structure of the Soviet state as an organization of political domination and the legal reflection of this complicated political phenomenon. In part, the Soviet state is outlined quite openly by Soviet law, and thus the latter encourages a wide dissemination of knowledge concerning the former. But occasionally, a veil is lifted by the promulgation of certain laws, and something of the hidden part is suddenly revealed. This usually happens in conditions of extreme stress, but occasionally also as the result of an oversight. The general rule, strictly observed, demands a distinction between what may be told and what must be concealed. Such a distinction, instead of being precluded by Soviet law, is silently assumed and even juridically stimulated on the grounds of two principles of the organization and functioning of the Soviet state: democratic centralism and centralized democracy. The first principle is openly declared and legally confirmed, but it plays a secondary role and mainly serves purposes of camouflage. The second principle is kept well-hidden and legally guarded, but it plays a leading role and provides the chief determinant of the Soviet government's conduct.

1. Democratic Centralism

Historically the notion of democratic centralism appeared already in Lenin's pre-revolutionary fight for the leadership of the Party.[2] It has usually been interpreted as the general electiveness of all Party agencies from the top to the bottom, and the strictest subordination of the same agencies from the bottom to the top. In theory this principle was gradually disseminated within the state structure as the new regime, established in 1917, acquired increasing political strength by means of economic transformation and repressive coercion. In law, however, democratic centralism did not find general expression before the 1977 Constitution was adopted. But its constitutional proclamation has not resulted in essential changes. Democratic centralism is one thing in Soviet law and quite another thing when being applied in Soviet reality. Thus, it must be examined from both sides with equal attention.

Democratic Centralism in Soviet Law

The Constitution now in force reads: "The Soviet state is organized and functions in accordance with the principle of democratic centralism: all organs of state power are elected from the lowest to the highest, they are accountable to the people, and the decisions of higher organs are binding for lower organs. Democratic centralism combines unified leadership with local initiative and creative activity, and with the responsibility of every state organ and official for the tasks entrusted to them."[3] However, the Constitution itself provides for two opposite deviations from the principle declared. One of them pertains to the Procuracy, which is invested with the task of supervising the observation of the law by citizens, various organizations and governmental bodies up to the rank of ministry or state committee.[4] In order to free the Procuracy from local influences and thus to ensure its independence in exercising supervision of legality, its officials are not elected. The USSR Procurator General is appointed by the USSR Supreme Soviet, and all other procurators are appointed or confirmed in their appointment by the Procurator General.[5] Further analysis will show whether this really leads to procuratorial independence from those who are to be supervised, but the independence of the entire Procuracy from the principle of democratic centralism in its democratic part is established beyond doubt. The second deviation from the same principle relates to the judicial system and goes in the opposite direction. Democratic centralism presumes subordination of the bottom to the top. In contrast, "judges ... shall be independent and subordinate only to law".[6] Since all judges of the USSR are elected,[7] their subordination only to the law means that they are also independent of the principle of democratic centralism, but, in contrast to the Procuracy, exclusively with regard to the centralized, and not the democratic part of the principle. And taking into account the specific nature of judicial activity, this is certainly reasonable and justified, although other regulations introduce in a roundabout way that which has been precluded by the constitution. Soviet judges, being elected, are not irremovable, and, as a result, they depend on agencies and officials who predetermine their re-election. Furthermore, the USSR Supreme Court, in exercising supervision over the judicial activity of other Soviet courts,[8] has the right to issue guiding explanations which concern the application of laws and are binding for all judicial agencies.[9] If such explanations did not go beyond the interpretation of law, judges would not lose their independence in the least – within the limits of their subordination to law. In reality, however, the USSR Supreme Court exercises much broader powers, now creating new legal norms under the guise of interpretation, and then issuing to all courts administrative orders which have nothing to do with the interpretation of laws. For example, article 90 of the Fundamentals of Civil Legislation deals with the liability for damages caused by organizations and citizens whose activity is connected with a source of increased danger (transport organizations, industrial enterprises, construction sites, owners of automobiles, etc.). It does not regulate cases where, for instance, an automobile or a similar "source of increased danger," belonging to one person, causes damage while being operated by another person. This problem has been settled by a decision of the Plenum of the USSR Supreme Court.[10] But what can one say of demands uttered by the same Plenum "to punish severely" people guilty "of stealing socialist property",[11] "not to admit indulgence in the fight" against hooliganism[12] or "to oblige judicial agencies to pay special attention to strengthening the fight against bribery"?[13] These are orders, not explanations. And where, for example, the law provides a penalty of from one to fifteen years of deprivation of freedom, judges ordered to "punish severely" or to "strengthen the fight" will probably not act independently within the limits of the law; they will tend to impose the maximum punishment, in an effort to avoid the accusation of not observing the Supreme Court's order and the possible consequences of such an accusation. Thus, the centralism formally abolished for judges has effectively, if not legally, been restored.

After the deviations, back now to democratic centralism. Its three principal elements are: electiveness, accountability, subordination.

Electiveness, as the first element of democratic centralism, is regulated by a special chapter of the Constitution,[14] and in greater detail by a special law.[15] Leaving aside for the time the problem of the genuineness of Soviet elections, their regularity based upon strict and unambiguous legal provisions must be recognized. In this regard democratic demands are doubtlessly observed. But the rule of general elections encompasses deputies of Soviets, from the Supreme Soviet of the USSR down to the rural Soviets, and judges of district courts – the lowest link in the Soviet judicial system.[16] Other officials and agencies are either elected by an existing body (for example, higher courts are elected by the Soviets of the corresponding level)[17], or nominated by them (for example, the USSR Council of Ministers is nominated by the USSR Supreme Soviet)[18], or simply appointed (for example, individual USSR ministers are appointed by the Presidium of the USSR Supreme Soviet).[19] This system by itself could not be blamed, if officials and agencies elected were not subordinated to agencies and officials nominated or appointed. However, when the local Soviet, a generally elected body – in enacting rules of trade for a given locality, does not have the right – without special permission, to deviate from analogous rules of the USSR Minister of Trade, an appointed official, then the democracy proclaimed loses its force in favor of centralism enforced. Meanwhile, it cannot be otherwise, because the fundamental principle of real democracy – independence of those who are elected from those who are appointed – appears to be incompatible with the very nature of the Soviet state.

Accountability, as the second element of democratic centralism, presumes direct reporting to the people, if one is to judge by the general provisions of the Soviet constitution.[20] But concrete constitutional norms related to the same problem are not always in accordance with the general rule. Only "a deputy shall be obliged to report on his work... to the electors, and also to all collectives and social organizations who nominated him as a candidate for deputy".[21] As for other officials and agencies, the constitution changes its general position. The USSR Council of Ministers, for example, is accountable to the USSR Supreme Soviet or to its Presidium, but not to the people.[22] Another solution would perhaps prove to be actually impossible under the circumstances. But why then proclaim accountability to the people, if only one case admits application of this general rule and all other cases constitute exceptions to it? On the other hand, any duty becomes a legal duty on condition that the appropriate legal regulations are in effect, and the obligor who avoids voluntary performance can be compelled by the obligee in the way provided for by law. Such regulations, however, do not exist even for reporting duties imposed upon deputies – the only officials elected by and accountable to the people. Of course, according to Art. 107 of the 1977 Constitution, a deputy may be recalled at any time by a decision of the voters. But this does not help, since the voters cannot adopt such a decision unless their meeting has been called by the appropriate governmental agency according to the established procedure. Hence, the general rule of accountability to the people stops being enforceable even in the exceptional case where it is not restricted by other concrete norms of the Soviet Constitution.

Subordination, as the third element of democratic centralism, accentuates centralism, in contrast to electiveness and accountability which emphasize democracy. Since the Soviet Union is notorious for its strong centralization, one might expect that at least in this regard democratic centralism becomes consistent to a degree unattainable by the other two elements of the principle. And subordination of elected agencies to appointed officials[23] seems to offer impressive proof of that expectation. But in reality Soviet centralization, stronger than anything known in human history, is not rectilinear in its construction and implementation. The officially proclaimed requirement of subordination suffers gross infringement to no lesser an extent than the other requirements embraced by the principle of democratic centralism. One of the most important formal infringements is the following – "The USSR Supreme Soviet shall elect the Presidium", provides Article 119 of the Soviet Constitution. Therefore, subordination of the Presidium of the USSR Supreme Soviet to the Supreme Soviet itself seems beyond any doubt. Nevertheless, the Presidium has the right, among other things, "in the interval between sessions of the Supreme Soviet with subsequent submission for confirmation at a regular session" to amend, when necessary, existing legislative acts of the USSR.[24] These amendments acquire force of law without having to wait for confirmation by the USSR Supreme Soviet. Even if in the theoretical case that confirmation would be refused (which has never happened in practice), the actual effect of the temporary application of any innovation adopted and not confirmed becomes irremovable, unless the USSR Supreme Soviet would endow its negative decision with retroactive force, and the very nature of the effect would not preclude its subsequent annulment. In this way the requirement of subordination is violated to a degree which would be inexplicable if it were not for other forces concealed underneath the restricted subordination and interested in the restrictions introduced especially for the sake of their own unlimited dominance. Formally, extraordinary prerogatives of the Presidium violate the rights of the USSR Supreme Soviet in the realm of legislation. Actually, legislation does not belong to the real activity either of the USSR Supreme Soviet or of its Presidium. Both of them fulfill purely ceremonial legislative functions, and the genuine power to legislate appertains to quite another agency which formally is not considered to be a legislative body at all. Due to such a contradiction, the real legislature needs to act through the ceremonial legislature. And this leads to numerous inconveniences, because the ceremonial legislature (the USSR Supreme Soviet) functions for only three or four days twice a year, while the real legislature (an agency not mentioned as such by the Constitution) can meet the need for legislation at any moment. To satisfy the insistent demand of the real sovereign, the ceremonial power of episodic legislation granted to the USSR Supreme Soviet has been supplemented by the ceremonial power of everyday legislation of its Presidium. Hence, by undermining subordination in the realm of ceremony, the Soviet Constitution strengthens the power of the actual rulers, which rests upon the centralized, not the democratic basis. In such a way, constitutional formulae reveal their hidden meaning, when explained by extra-constitutional considerations. However, a closer analysis of the actual situation will be attempted a little later. At this point, where the subject of study does not go beyond legal texts, another statement becomes more appropriate. Even on the basis of the Constitution alone, it is impossible to assess legal regulations of the USSR as strictly corresponding to democratic centralism. Soviet law itself proclaims and simultaneously restricts the principle formulated in the various respects and numerous directions. It is therefore no wonder, that democratic centralism will be seen to suffer even more essential transformations, when we move from the sphere of legal rules to the sphere of the application of law.

Democratic Centralism in Soviet Practice

In order to understand democratic centralism in its actual, and not only its legal dimensions, electiveness, accountability and subordination must also be considered in their practical application.

The Soviet version of electiveness, based upon the rule of "one place – one candidate", is known all over the world. But to be able to see this rule "in all its beauty" one should understand its rationale and know its ramifications. As a matter of course, there is no difficulty in finding two or three equally reliable candidates for a place, along with the one who has been recommended. If, however, real elections were held under such circumstances, the candidate deputy would depend on his electorate to at least the same degree as he would depend on the agencies who recommend him in the case of fictitious elections. It is obvious that such a state of affairs would seriously undermine the unlimited political power of the Soviet leaders.

Moreover, real elections would give voters the opportunities which they now lack: to cross out all candidates and thereby jeopardize the whole system. And, most importantly, Soviet leaders themselves would not be protected against the danger of failure, or, what seems even more probable, they would be primarily exposed to this danger. In addition, the interest of the ruling summit is not only in the election of reliable deputies, but also in such a representation of the various strata of society in the elected bodies, as would agree with the official doctrine of the social character of the Soviet state. Only persons who occupy certain positions in the Party or in the government (members of the Central Committee, ministers) are approved by name as deputies beforehand. A similar approach is taken with regard to certain national celebrities – prominent writers, actors, artists, etc. All other positions are allocated anonymously to collectives, whose duty it then is to nominate a candidate. However, the appropriate Party agency will receive detailed instructions concerning the qualifications of the person to be nominated: a worker, an engineer or a scholar, a man or a woman, a young, middle-aged or old person, a non-Party member or a Party member, and so forth. Oral instructions will even go so far as to advise against the selection of "ugly men and unattractive women". Considering all these conditions, it may sometimes be difficult to find the right candidate, and even more so to come up with two or more candidates with similar qualifications. Furthermore, within the one-candidate system, fear of failure continues to exist. This is why polling-booths are set up in such a way, that anybody attempting to use them makes himself conspicuous and, as a consequence, evokes suspicion, because one has no need to make use of the polling-booth if one votes in favor, and not against, the single candidate. Therefore, despite the alleged secrecy of voting, Soviet court practice knows numerous criminal cases of persons charged with anti-Soviet propaganda committed through writing statements on ballot papers. They would not, certainly, be in danger if "democratic elections" were not combined with police supervision in the USSR. As a result there is nothing surprising in the almost unanimous positive endorsements of candidates in Soviet elections, or in the almost total participation of the population in electoral campaigns. Anybody trying to preserve his own position will steer clear of electoral absenteeism. Otherwise, as soon as the electoral commission has reported his improper conduct to his chiefs and Party officials, he will immediately undergo repressive measures which could go as far as demotion or dismissal. Citizens who do not have valuable positions to lose will abstain from voting as often as not, and the number of such persons has been increasing through the years. But even this difficulty has not taken Soviet rulers unawares. Anybody who ever had occasion to be on an electoral commission knows that, after the time for voting has expired, the chairman of the commission, following a secret instruction, puts enough unused ballot papers in the voting box to ensure a 99% or at least 98% participation in the election. Taken together, all these stratagems transform electiveness in the Soviet Union from an important democratic institution into a badly staged farce.

The case for accountability does not look much better. Accountability, of course, can be democratic or bureaucratic. Bureaucratic accountability invariably assumes a written form, consisting of periodic reports, usually of a very detailed or even meticulous nature, being passed on from the bottom to the top: by lower-ranking officials to their immediate chiefs, as well as by subordinate to higher agencies. This type of accountability exists in the USSR and has even attained an unprecedented flowering. Democratic accountability is something else. It includes public reporting by elected representatives to those who elected them, and of agencies instituted by representative bodies to those who instituted them. For the USSR this would imply the democratic accountability of deputies of any rank, from rural soviets to the Supreme Soviet of the USSR, and of agencies such as the Presidium of the USSR Supreme Soviet, the All-Union Council of Ministers, presidia of republic supreme soviets and republic governments, local soviets and their executive committees.

The accountability of deputies to the soviets depends in practice on two factors: the level of the Soviet and the rank of the deputy. The lower the soviet, the more regular the meetings between deputies and their voters. On the other hand, the higher the rank of the deputy, the more futile is the voters' expectation of meeting him. Relatively high-ranking officials, not only members of the Politbureau but as far down as chairmen of provincial executive committees, never report to their voters. At the same time, more or less ordinary deputies, not only of local soviets but even of the Supreme Soviet of the USSR, present public reports regularly. However, deputies to soviets of any rank do not as such play a substantial role. At the sessions of the corresponding soviets they vote in favor of whatever proposal is put forward and, additionally, they participate in discussions, reading speeches prepared for them and approved beforehand in the appropriate manner. Sessions of soviets are public and are reported fully and promptly in the newspapers and other media, so that in this regard the deputy has nothing to add in his meetings with the voters. If he also happens to be a member of one of the soviet's commissions, his voters have the opportunity of hearing something about the work of the commission concerned, a subject which does not attract much attention in the press. Unfortunately, these commissions are not much more important than the individual deputies. Therefore the most significant part of the deputy's account deals with the number of visitors he has received, an analysis of the requests and complaints handled by him, a survey of his activities in helping visitors, and information concerning the results of these activities. Thus, the accountability of deputies does not contribute to popular participation in government, since the reports presented are not concerned with the exercise of real power.

The accountability of Soviet agencies exists on paper rather than in real life, judging by the absence of relevant information in the Soviet media. It is difficult to speak with absolute certainty about local executive committees. Some of them may perhaps occasionally render account to the appropriate soviets, although such a supposition seems precarious in a political system where all kinds of public activities take place only in strict conformity with standard procedure. But with regard to the highest governmental bodies, such as the Presidium of the USSR Supreme Soviet or the Council of Ministers of the USSR, the necessary data are available, sufficiently exact, and highly reliable. At each session of the USSR Supreme Soviet its Presidium reports on the edicts which have been adopted since the previous session and which require confirmation by the present session. If this is to be regarded as accountability, then it takes place without fail. No other account of the Presidium of the USSR

Supreme Soviet has ever been heard. Accounts of the Soviet Council of Ministers were known only in the earliest period of Soviet power. The USSR Supreme Soviet, which has been in existence since 1937, *i.e.* for almost half a century, does not resort to the practice at all. Only the Presidium of the USSR Supreme Soviet once included in its agenda a report on the activities of the USSR Council of Ministers. This happened in one of the last years of Brezhnev's rule, when he was simultaneously General Secretary of the Central Committee of the Communist Party and Chairman of the Presidium of the USSR Supreme Soviet. The event was so extraordinary and so significant that it deserves to be described separately.

In the evening it was announced all over the country that the next morning Soviet television would transmit, directly from the Kremlin, a meeting of the Presidium of the USSR Supreme Soviet. This promised to be interesting, since, unlike huge assemblies of thousands of people (Congresses of the Communist Party or sessions of the Supreme Soviet), smaller meetings of the highest agencies (the Presidium of the USSR Supreme Soviet or the Council of Ministers of the USSR) had never been shown before. Thus the next morning many millions of Soviet citizens were sitting by their television sets. At eleven o'clock exactly the assembly room of the Presidium appeared on the screen. Several dozen people, including certain members of the Politbureau and the fifteen chairmen of the presidia of the republican supreme soviets, were sitting at a long table. After a few seconds Brezhnev entered the room and all the members of the Presidium stood up immediately to greet him with applause. This already caught everybody's attention. One had been accustomed for a long time to such signs of servile leader worship. But people expected that small business meetings of the highest leadership circle would not waste time in similar demonstrations. Reality, however, overtook expectations. When the ceremony of the leader's entrée had come to an end, Brezhnev took the chair, opened the meeting and proposed the agenda. After his proposal had been accepted unanimously, the Presidium turned to the main item – an account by the Council of Ministers about its activities. The period of accountability was not indicated at all. The Chairman of the Council of Ministers, Tikhonov, was given the floor. Without even raising his eyes from his papers, he read a report for twenty minutes. But if the presentation was not exactly exciting, its effect was reinforced by the contents of the report itself: a downpour of verbosity, without any interesting facts or engaging ideas. Thus, the interest of the audience began to be replaced by disappointment. Immediately after Tikhonov had finished his speech, Brezhnev took the floor and read from his notes for at least twenty minutes. What he had to say was in no way more substantial than Tikhonov's account. In his speech, obviously prepared beforehand, Brezhnev, to the great astonishment of the spectators, quoted from Tikhonov's speech, which had just been pronounced minutes before. As interest was replaced by disappointment, and the latter by astonishment, amusement then took the upper hand, and finally the spectators burst out laughing, when all the participants in the meeting solemnly declined Brezhnev's invitation to ask questions or to make suggestions and without uttering a word voted in favor of the draft decision put before them. Suddenly the meeting had come to a close, the television transmission was over, the performance had ended. No sworn enemies of the Soviet regime could have done better in exposing Soviet democracy as a humiliating deception than the producers of this shoddy comedy.

If representative state agencies satisfy the people's demand for information in such an unworthy manner, what can an individual deputy expect, with his constitutional "right of enquiry" and "the right" to address enquiries and proposals to state agencies and other bodies or officials, as well as with "the right" to have these enquiries and proposals considered and answered.[25] A barber lost his only son and, after several years, he decided together with his wife to adopt a two-year old orphan, entrusted to the care of a government institution. According to Soviet law, adoption can only be effected by a decision of the executive committee of the appropriate local Soviet, if it is, in the actual circumstances checked by a special *ad hoc* commission, entirely in the interest of the child.[26] Thus, from a legal point of view, the case did not present any difficulties. Nevertheless, the requested adoption was refused without any explanation. A deputy of the USSR Supreme Soviet, who was one of the barber's customers, tried to help him, making use of his position and the rights connected with his office. All he received, however, was an explanation by the officials of the executive committee to the effect that the negative decision was made because the proposed adoptive parents were too old. Since the latter were only a little over forty, such an explanation was patently ridiculous, and this prompted the deputy to try to get to the bottom of it by all the means at his disposal. At last the unadorned truth was revealed to him unofficially, as a friendly gesture: Jews and people from other nationalities who constitute the main source of emigration from the USSR are forbidden to become adoptive parents by a secret instruction of the Ministry of Internal Affairs, in order to prevent the loss of Soviet children and unsatisfactory population growth in the country. This kind of accountability hardly needs any commentary.

Soviet style subordination is full of surprises too. If each level of the state system would be subordinate to the next higher level, with application of the rule from the bottom of the pyramid to the very top, including the highest representative body, responsible, in its turn, to the general electorate, then subordination would correspond to genuine democracy, supporting and strengthening it. As soon, however, as subordination fails to satisfy these clear and simple demands, it begins to undermine democracy and to restrict and distort the democratic character of the governing process. But precisely such a situation prevails in the USSR, where instead of a system of direct and consistent subordination, the latter is variously curtailed, circumvented, or even inverted. This statement can easily be corroborated by turning one's attention to the four bodies and agencies at the highest level of the Soviet state: the USSR Supreme Soviet, its Presidium, the USSR Council of Ministers, and the ministries of the USSR.

With regard to the relationship between individual ministries and the Council of Ministers, one may observe the ministries' direct subordination, if not to the full Council of Ministers, then to its Presidium (chairman and deputy-chairmen), or to the chairman of the Council of Ministers, or to that deputy-chairman who acts as supervisor of the ministry concerned. Nevertheless, this type of subordination does not encompass certain ministries or state committees: the Ministry of Defense, the Ministry of Foreign Affairs, and the KGB. Only at a time when the First Secretary or

General Secretary of the Communist Party was simultaneously chairman of the USSR Council of Ministers (Stalin from 1940 until his death in 1953 and Khrushchev from 1958 until his ouster in 1964), were the three agencies enumerated subordinate to one official in his double capacity. These exceptions apart, the Council of Ministers never actually controlled military, foreign and security affairs, no matter what the Soviet Constitution said about it. It is the leader of the Communist Party who runs these agencies through their chiefs, either directly, or with the help of another member of the Politbureau. So it was under Brezhnev who never occupied the position of chairman of the USSR Council of Ministers. So it had to be under Andropov, in particular if one considers the forces which helped him to attain the highest position in the country after the death of Brezhnev. So it is under Chernenko who, in contrast to Andropov, has managed – smoothly and without delay – to concentrate in his grasp the positions of General Secretary and Chairman of the Presidium of the USSR Supreme Soviet. Thus in the described cases a roundabout subordination takes the place of direct subordination. But what about the Council of Ministers itself? Is it lower or higher than the Presidium of the USSR Supreme Soviet? The question is not difficult to answer. The Council of Ministers fulfills important executive functions, while the Presidium of the Supreme Soviet deals with pure ceremony. This, however, is not a peculiarly Soviet phenomenon. In the Federal Republic of Germany the President's office is of largely ceremonial significance, and similar arrangements exist in many other western democracies. The real importance lies in the relationship between the USSR Council of Ministers and the Soviet parliament, the USSR Supreme Soviet, while the Presidium of the Supreme Soviet should only be considered within the framework of this relationship. In a genuine democracy it is the parliament which circumscribes the government's activity, defines the limits of its power, and, in the last analysis, determines its fate. In the USSR, apart from the act by which the Soviet government is formed every five years at the first session of the newly elected Supreme Soviet, there are no significant connections of subordination between one and the other. The Supreme Soviet and its Presidium do not have the right to interfere in the actual operation of the government. As for the right to demand periodic accounts from the Council of Ministers, it has already been demonstrated what this amounts to.[27] Only the government's strict observance of legal rules enacted by the USSR Supreme Soviet still appears to have been preserved. But appearances have not always corresponded to reality, as the following incident may prove. A very famous Soviet legal scholar left a will which was clearly in violation of the existing law of inheritance, a fact of which he was well aware. But rather than leaving his property to relatives who were his legal heirs and whom he considered undesirable, he chose to make an illegal will. His step proved to be quite effective. After the testator's death certain people made sure that the will was discussed by the Soviet government. And owing to the testator's very high reputation the Council of Ministers decided, in spite of the illegality of the will, to declare it valid. Consequently succession took place not in the order provided by law, but in an unlawful order confirmed *ad hoc* by the Soviet government.

With regard to the relationship between the USSR Supreme Soviet and its Presidium, the latter's subordination to the former seems certain, if one does not go beyond the constitutional provisions. Even the Presidium's right to repeal or amend laws enacted by the Supreme Soviet entails no alteration in the state of affairs, since any such decisions shall be confirmed by the Supreme Soviet itself. But what is actually practiced has more importance than legal declarations. Every session of the Supreme Soviet is prepared by its Presidium. The Presidium, following instructions from above, determines the agenda of the session of the Supreme Soviet, appoints speakers to take part in the discussions, checks their speeches beforehand (the speeches themselves being prepared by the staff of the Presidium), and, within the limits of the available time, establishes the length of every speech and other transaction which is to take place at the session. As a matter of course, the Supreme Soviet formally has the right to approve any agenda and to establish any order of its proceedings. But in the almost fifty years' history of this body there has not been a single instance of any public proposal meeting with any kind of obstacle or objection from the part of the deputies. Who then is subordinate, the Presidium to the USSR Supreme Soviet, or the USSR Supreme Soviet to its Presidium? The answer, being obvious, strikingly demonstrates that the alleged relationship of subordination of the Presidium to the USSR Supreme Soviet is inverted in its reality.

All these phenomena are inexplicable and even incomprehensible when analysed within the framework of democratic centralism. But the enigma can easily be solved by forgetting about democratic centralism and turning to centralized democracy.

2. Centralized Democracy

In contrast to democratic centralism, which is broadly described by the Soviet Constitution and other Soviet laws, centralized democracy is very seldom touched upon by legal regulations, and then not so much directly as by implication. This is why the practice of Soviet centralized democracy will demand more attention than its reflection in law.

Centralized Democracy in Soviet Law

While democratic centralism is embodied mostly in governmental agencies, centralized democracy, or, more exactly, the entire mechanism of centralization, is in the grasp of Party agencies. Therefore, Soviet law does not reflect it adequately and Stalin indeed did all he could to conceal it. The 1936 Constitution mentions the Communist Party only in the chapter on "Fundamental rights and duties of citizens", and then exclusively in connection with the citizens' right "to unite in social organizations",[28] while Communist Party organizations appear in Art.141 of the same Constitution as collective bodies which have the right to nominate candidates for election in Soviets. Art.126 states that "the most active and conscious citizens from the ranks of the working class, the working peasants, and the working intelligentsia voluntarily unite in the Communist Party of the Soviet Union, which is the vanguard of the working people in its struggle to build a communist society, and which represents the leading core of all organizations of the working people, social as well as state organizations".[29] Apart from the last words, no other hint concerning the real role of the Communist Party in the government of the Soviet Union can be found in the so-called Stalin Constitution. In the Brezhnev Constitution of 1977, which preserves its force, the matter is different. It proclaims: "the Communist Party of the Soviet Union is the leading and guiding force of Soviet society and the nucleus of its political system and of all state and social organizations. The CPSU exists for the people and serves the people. [paragraph] Armed with Marxist-Leninist doctrine, the Communist Party determines the general perspective of the development of society and the course of the domestic and foreign policy of the USSR, directs the great creative activity of the Soviet people, and imparts a planned and scientifically-sound character to their struggle for the victory of communism."[30] Although the Communist Party is not cited elsewhere in the 1977 Constitution (apart again from a mention in Art. 100, the parallel provision to Art. 141 of the 1936 Constitution, concerning the right to nominate candidates for elections to soviets), the quotation proves with all possible eloquence the real significance of the CPSU in Soviet governmental activity and social life. There is no need to discuss whether or not this utter frankness has been a tactical mistake on Brezhnev's side, but the real state of affairs has now become more manifest than at any previous moment. If, on the other hand, the CPSU occupies the supreme position within the Soviet state machinery but Soviet law, nevertheless, avoids its precise characterization, then the law of the CPSU itself – the Rules of the Communist Party of the Soviet Union, adopted in 1961 and amended several times subsequently – deserves our attention.[31] According to these Rules: "the Party Congress is the supreme agency" of the CPSU.[32] Most prominent among the duties of the congress relates to the determination of the Party line on questions of domestic and foreign policy.[33] The congress elects the Central Committee,[34] which "directs, in the intervals between congresses, the entire activity of the Party", including the selection and distribution of leading cadres, as well as the direction of central state and social organizations.[35] The Central Committee normally meets once every six months.[36] This is why it elects two other agencies: the Politbureau, "for directing the work of the Party between plenary sessions of the Central Committee", and the Secretariat, "for directing current affairs, principally the selection of cadres and the organization of verification of executive work".[37] Both agencies are headed by the General Secretary, who is also elected by the Central Committee.[38] Analogous arrangements apply at the level of republican, territorial, provincial, area, city and district party organizations,[39] with some terminological differentiation only: below the level of the Union Republic congresses are called conferences, all lower level counterparts of the Politbureau are called bureau (except in the Ukrainian Union Republic, which has its own politbureau), the counterpart to the General Secretary is named first secretary at all other levels (from Union Republic down to cities and districts). Enterprises and any other establishments with at least three party members have their own primary Party organization.[40] These organizations possess the power to oversee the activities of the administration of their respective establishments.[41] In the case of primary Party organizations created within ministries, state committees and other central or local state and economic institutions and departments, the control function does not go beyond the work of the apparatus of the agencies concerned. Partly control of the activities of ministers and chiefs of other institutions of comparable rank is not within the power of primary Party organizations, but of the central or regional Party apparatus.[42]

The content of the provisions mentioned above shows that the Rules – although as a Party document they cannot be regarded as law – provide for subordination of the state to the Party and consequently occupy a position which is higher than ordinary law, in fact acquiring the force of the supreme law. It seems fair to say the statements made in the Party Rules are generally more frank than those embodied in Soviet law. Nevertheless, the former and the latter have many features in common. Party Rules, like Soviet law, distort truth in one part and keep silent about it in another. The system of subordination at the highest level of the CPSU is described in the Rules as following: Congress – Central Committee – Politbureau – Secretariat. This description was more or less realistic at a time when the Communist Party had far fewer members and personal dictatorship or the dictatorship of a very small collective body had not reached its present intensity. Now, however, circumstances have changed. The Party congress, consisting of several thousand representatives, and the Central Committee, numbering several hundred members, have become ceremonial bodies, no less than the USSR Supreme Soviet or its Presidium.[43] Genuine power is concentrated in the Politbureau and in the Secretariat. Relations between the latter two agencies are based on the principle of subordination of the Secretariat to the Politbureau. At the same time, the Secretariat, which directs current work, has some advantages over the Politbureau, which directs the general work of the CPSU. The most powerful persons in the USSR are consequently those who hold membership of the Politbureau and the Secretariat simultaneously. The Secretariat and especially the Politbureau function in an atmosphere of the most extreme secrecy. An innovation, introduced by Andropov, in the way of information bulletins on the weekly Politbureau meetings, did not change anything in this respect. Even if the Politbureau did in effect deal with the trifles described in the weekly bulletins, its main activity is concerned with incomparably more important matters, left out or only enumerated in the information provided. As for the Central Committee, its sessions are closed. This, however, is due more to historical tradition than to practical need, because the Central Committee, as a ceremonial body, whose decisions are widely publicized, can do without secrecy.[44] Party congresses have dispensed with secrecy (with some exceptions), and their meetings have, at least in part, been broadcast and televised, to say nothing of their extensive coverage in newspapers and other media.

Such is the part of the truth reflected, albeit in a distorted manner, by the Rules and this is where the Party's written constitution comes to an end. The other part of the truth is not revealed by the Rules but reflected by the Party's unwritten constitution. It consists mainly of established customs, although it cannot help being supplemented and made more tangible in certain directions by secret instructions in written form. While the written constitution concerns the Party's structure and its elective bodies and agencies, the unwritten constitution deals with the Party's apparatus and its appointed agencies and officials. Which of these is stronger is not always easy to say. When after Stalin's death the first secretary of the Leningrad provincial Party committee tried to democratize the bureaucratic order then prevailing in Smol'nii[45] and thereby infringed the privileges of the local apparatus, he lost his position under pressure of the same apparatus, in favor of the notorious Frol Kozlov, who later on became Khrushchev's second in command and who had played the most sinister role in Stalin's purges in Leningrad in the early 1950s. Furthermore, the downfall of Khrushchev was assured not simply by certain members of the Politbureau alone, but by these members, together with the Central Committee's apparatus, displeased by the attacks against its privileges and by the continuous shake-up which had kept the Party elite in permanent danger of being ousted. But whatever power relationships between the elected and appointed sections of the Party hierarchy may exist, the latter represent the real power in the Soviet state and they should be taken into serious account.

At the all-union level the CPSU apparatus consists of departments with their chiefs and deputy-chiefs and of sectors with their chiefs, deputy-chiefs and instructors. Each department has a specific function indicated by its title (departments of propaganda, of industry, of agriculture, of transport, of relationships with communist parties in socialist states, of relationships with communist parties in capitalist states, and so on). Within the limits of the department's general functions, each sector deals with a more specific task (*e.g.* the department of culture has sectors for theaters, films, etc.). These functions become even more specific if one turns from sectors to instructors (*e.g.* the departments of science has instructors for jurisprudence, philosophy, etc.). The secretariat of the General Secretary is in fact nothing other than a department of the Central Committee, and one of the utmost importance, judging from the fact that, for instance, Chernenko, Andropov's main competitor and his successor, or Rusakov, one of the CPSU secretaries, have reached their present position through membership of Brezhnev's secretariat. At the level of the Union Republic the departmental structure is almost identical. However, since certain functions, such as foreign trade or relations with foreign communist movements, do not belong to the competence of Party agencies of the Union Republic, the number of their central departments is smaller than at the all-union level. Similarly, the departmental structure at the level of provincial CPSU committee is again simpler, and in some cases they only have separate sectors instead of departments with their own sectors. Finally, city and district Party committees, apart from certain large cities, only have instructors, and no departments or sectors, except a sector for Party records and control.

The structure described here has clearly been designed with the intention of keeping any kind of non-Party activity under the strictest control of the Party and of securing complete leadership and supervision of all Party activities for intermediate and top Party agencies. The practice of many years has not only produced a system of control and supervision, but also an original protocol governing the relationships between Party officials and officials of non-Party agencies. This protocol requires exact conformity between the levels of the Party official issuing instructions and of the non-Party official who has to carry them out. Of course, a party instructor may transmit an order on behalf of a chief of a Party department, and a chief of a Party department may transmit an instruction on behalf of a Party secretary, but a Party secretary would never turn directly to a non-Party official with whom a chief of a Party department should deal, and a chief of a Party department would never make contact with an official who falls under the sphere of a Party instructor. Such a protocol not only enhances the Party's prestige – one of the most important values from the viewpoint of the ruling bureaucracy during the entire course of Russian history – but also the efficacy of the Party governance of all sectors of Soviet society. The higher the Party official, the less available he is. Therefore, as a rule, one cannot check the correctness of instructions given by a subordinate. On the other hand, the very attempt at any check could be dangerous, because it might reveal a disagreement with a higher chief, if he turns out to have been the initiator of the instructions received. Thus, leaving aside those persons who combine non-Party functions with membership of the Politbureau (or persons with similar positions at lower levels), any word spoken on behalf of the Party, irrespective of the rank of the Party spokesman concerned, acquires imperative force and must be followed without contradiction or even discussion. The established order may lead to abuses by Party instructors or other Party functionaries. But such unavoidable losses are repaid a hundredfold by the advantages generated by the political system of severe discipline and strict subordination. Since this system proclaims democracy which in reality is replaced by centralization, it should be termed "centralized democracy". We have already seen its reflection in Soviet law and in the Party's Rules, in written and unwritten legislation. But how does it look in Soviet practice?

Centralized Democracy in Soviet Practice
The Soviet practice of centralized democracy is based upon certain fundamental principles of a general character. They can be reduced to three paramount rules: (1) those who have the formal right to adopt decisions are not empowered to actually settle problems and, vice versa, those who are empowered to actually settle problems do not have the formal right to adopt decisions; (2) those who adopt formal decisions are bound by actual decisions and, vice versa, those who take the actual decisions are bound by the requirements governing formal decisions; (3) those who take formal decisions would be doomed to inactivity without actual decisions and, vice versa, those who take actual decisions would be doomed to futility without formal decisions.[46] The principles stated apply universally. It is particularly important and highly interesting to consider their practical application in connection with problems of general regulations, operative government, and personnel selection. Of course, concrete illustration of this analysis can be taken from any level of the Soviet hierarchy, but the main attention should be directed to the highest levels.

General regulations demand general rules. These may be established by the legislature for one group of cases or by the government for another. In accordance with laws and governmental decisions, ministries, state committees and departments of equal rank (the State Bank, for example) issue legally binding orders and instructions to those who, according to law, are their addressees. As for the CPSU, its decisions adopted separately from legislative or governmental bodies are binding for Party members and agencies. They do not, however, possess a universally binding legal force, and no court considering a criminal or civil case, and no governmental body dealing with administrative or financial matters, would refer to Party instructions in their judgments or decisions. Under such circumstances, Party instructions are not enough; legal norms are necessary. But, conversely, no legal norm can be adopted without a Party directive or Party approval. All laws have to be approved by the Politbureau before the USSR Supreme Soviet may adopt them. The same procedure is to be observed in the case of more or less significant governmental decisions, and – in especially important cases – the Central Committee, through the Politbureau, adopts joint decisions together with the USSR Council of Ministers. Current governmental decisions need the approval of the Party Secretariat. A similar requirement must be satisfied in the issuing of the most important orders or instructions of ministries, state committees and other analogous departments. If the normative acts concerned are not of particular importance, the approval procedure only involves the competent department of the Central Committee.

It would be grossly mistaken, however, to assume that Party agencies only approve or disapprove, permit or forbid specific legislative initiatives. This is only the habitually used official terminology. Were it to reflect actual practice, little or nothing would be left of the "leading role" of the Communist Party in the Soviet political and social system. Of course, the suggestion to issue a specific instruction or regulation may arise from various sources, but it remains a mere idea until it has been taken over by the appropriate Party agency. Only from this moment on will and must legislative drafting begin, and its results will return to the same Party agency again and again for as long as is necessary to consider the matter solved. Once a conclusion has been reached, further discussion becomes senseless. From this moment on only the necessary formalities must be observed, whether they belong to the jurisdiction of the USSR Supreme Soviet, or to any other law-making body. To illustrate the point some examples may be useful, and the Fundamentals of Housing Legislation of the USSR and the Union Republics[47] may provide the most demonstrative ones.

The idea of such a law had appeared long before the draft of the 1977 Constitution was published in a nationwide discussion.[48] However, the absurdity of the idea must have been clear to its proponents. The Fundamentals of Civil Legislation together with the Civil Codes had already assured the necessary regulation of housing relationships, and if there were gaps or defects, these could have been removed by appropriate amendments or additions to the existing laws. As for the Fundamentals of Housing Legislation, they would make the Soviet legal system more cumbersome, necessitating the adoption of Housing Codes, and, according to their nature, both Housing Fundamentals and Codes would have to be subordinate to the Fundamentals of Civil Legislation and the Civil Codes.[49] The proponents of the Fundamentals of Housing Legislation, however, thought that by undermining civil law codification through the adoption of separate housing legislation, they would also open the way for the separation of so-called economic law from civil law, despite repeated rejection of their suggestion to regulate the property relationships of citizens by the Civil Code, and of economic and other organizations by an Economic Code.[50] This was clear to everybody, and the idea of Fundamentals of Housing Legislation was not taken seriously. It appeared, however, quite unexpectedly in Brezhnev's concluding speech on the draft of the new Soviet Constitution as a serious and important suggestion to the participants in the nationwide discussion.[51] Then the usual mechanism began to work in the predetermined direction. On 12 December of the same year the Presidium of the USSR Supreme Soviet instructed the Soviet government to start the preparation of a corresponding legislative proposal.[52] In 1980 a draft was submitted to a nationwide discussion, and in 1981 the Fundamentals of Housing Legislation were adopted by the USSR Supreme Soviet.

Along with its destructive effects on the legal system, the new law admittedly produced some positive results, in removing certain quite unbearable provisions from Soviet housing law, such as the rule which ordered the withdrawal of the so-called surplus dwelling space (*i.e.* space in excess of nine square metres per inhabitant), arising as a result of the death of a family member or from any other causes. The legislative improvements, however, were accompanied by an equal amount of the usual demagogy, such as, for example, the declaration that each Soviet citizen has a right to living space, with bland disregard of the housing crisis which still prevails in the USSR.[53] And what was even more peculiar was the resigned obedience to a demand which was in fact unacceptable: the legislature did not dare to utter one word in defense of its own legal system against the clumsy supplement thrust upon it. The Party gave the order, the legislature carried it out. And under opposite circumstances, the legislature could not have acted, because the Party had not given the order.

For instance, Fundamental Principles of various kinds of legislation, as well as the Soviet Constitution itself, contain numerous "norms with references" (in Soviet terminology), *i.e.* norms referring to other laws which have to provide the concrete regulations to make those norms operative and give them actual content. However, these laws usually did not exist at the time of promulgation of the "norms with references", and many of them have not been enacted up till now. Such is the case with the greatly important constitutional norm about actions of officials "committed in violation of law, in excess of their powers and infringing upon the rights of citizens", which "may be appealed to a court, in the procedure established by law".[54] The corresponding procedure has little chance of being introduced in the near future, and the legislature will hardly be allowed to become active in this matter, if one considers that the Institute of State and Law, which had initiated a theoretical – and not yet even practical – discussion of the topic in 1978, received orders from the Party summit to discontinue work in the aforementioned direction. Equally interesting seems the fate of the reference included in article 89 of the Fundamentals of Civil Legislation: "The respective state agencies shall bear financial liability in the instances and within the limits specially provided for by law for harm caused by the improper official actions of officials of agencies of inquiry, preliminary investigation, the procuracy, and court". The quoted provision appeared in the Fundamentals of Civil Legislation of 1961. The special law to which it referred was enacted in 1981.[55] Twenty years had passed before the Politbureau allowed the Soviet legislature to act, under the pressure of international covenants ratified by the USSR.[56] Meanwhile, the effectiveness of the new law may be regarded with some suspicion, as no case under established procedure has been mentioned in Soviet legal literature or published in the periodic reports of the Supreme Court of the USSR and the RSFSR since its enactment.

However, even the Party summit's virtual omnipotence is tempered by the objective demands of general legal regulations since without these regulations its wishes cannot be realized, and, when applying them, it is compelled to moderate its zeal. For example, the Soviet economy is not powerful enough to assure everyday repairs and other services necessary for the Soviet population. To give an idea of the real situation it is sufficient to say that for several hundred thousand private *Zhiguli* cars Leningrad has only two (large, but still two) repair shops. Naturally, people began to perform repairs privately and, from the point of view of Soviet law, illegally. Nevertheless, local and central authorities closed their eyes to such economic activity, giving precedence to the demands of reality over dogmatic orthodoxy. Still, this did not lead to the desired result, viz. satisfactory repair of personal cars, because many persons capable of performing necessary jobs abstained from taking them up for fear of the aftermaths. Consequently, the only thing to do was to legalize wholesale what had taken place incidentally and stealthily. The new Constitution now proclaims: "Individual labor activity in the sphere of trades and crafts, agriculture, serving the everyday needs of the population, as well as other forms of activity based exclusively on the individual labor of citizens and the members of their families are permitted in the USSR in accordance with the law".[57] Of course, the new rule did not immediately bring about the complete solution of the entire problem, but at least the limited efficacy of secret instructions has now been replaced by more palpable results.

In contrast to general regulations, everyday, or in Soviet parlance, "operative" governing of state agencies by Party bodies is more difficult to implement. The operative activity of the entire state consists of many millions of everyday actions performed by individual officials and collective institutions. To check all of them would be impossible and hardly necessary. A combination of direct and indirect control seems to be more than sufficient. Indirect control is assured by the subordination of operative activity to general regulations, and general regulations cannot exist without Party approval. The forms of direct control are more varied. First of all, a multitude of operative decisions demand Party sanction. For example, even within the limits of established jurisdiction,[58] no new construction plans may be embarked upon by the USSR Council of Ministers without the sanction of the Politbureau, or by ministries without the sanction of the corresponding department of the Central Committee, or by councils of ministers of a Union Republic without the sanction of the bureau (Politbureau) of the republic Central Committee. Also, there is nothing to prevent the Politbureau or other Party agencies giving operative orders to subordinate governmental institutions, economic and other organizations, and this practice is generally encountered in the USSR. Decisions on what to build in South-West Moscow or on which streets of the capital are to be closed for ordinary traffic have been taken by the Politbureau, and then the appropriate governmental agencies only performed what they had been ordered to do. Apart from this, numerous secret instructions aim to assure either control by the Party itself, or the prerequisites necessary for its realization. For instance, no film is allowed to be shown publicly until it has been approved, after personal review, by the first secretary of the provincial Party committee of the place where the film has been made, by the department of culture of the Central Committee, and sometimes by the Politbureau itself. All books and other publications, no matter where they have been produced, must be sent to the Central Committee and to the appropriate provincial committee of the CPSU, and only if no objections are made within an established period, is the publisher entitled to transfer the entire edition to the book trade. Sometimes a Party agency, through operative orders, introduces a special form of account and control. For example, in the mid-1970s the Leningrad provincial committee of the CPSU ordered Leningrad University not to admit any Jews, half-Jews, or persons who looked Jewish to the law faculty and certain other faculties. At the same time the University was ordered to inform Smol'nii (the Party headquarters) in daily written reports about the number of such persons who applied for the entrance examination and the number of them who failed their examination. At any moment and in any place the Party's agencies may order the inspection of subordinate institutions by *ad hoc* commissions or demand reports from the official heads or the party secretaries of these institutions at meetings of appropriate Party committees. Not infrequently, government officials and managers of economic associations or other establishments "coordinate" beforehand, on their own initiative, the intended execution of their plans with the appropriate Party agencies. This certainly does not exempt them from responsibility in the future, but reference to previous "coordination" may sometimes prevent the complete failure of an endeavor.

On one occasion, in the early 1960s, while Khrushchev was abroad and Brezhnev was fulfilling his functions in Moscow, the Minister of Internal Affairs of the Kazakh Republic called the latter to ask whether it would be reasonable to machine-gun students who had risen in revolt during harvesting work on virgin lands. Brezhnev sanctioned the measure. Since this became known at once in the West, Khrushchev's official trip was badly spoilt. Therefore, upon his return the Kazakh minister was committed to trial and sentenced to a long term in a labor camp, ostensibly as the only culprit in the affair. But after the fall of Khrushchev, one of Brezhnev's first actions was the release of the former Kazakh minister from the camp and his reinstatement as a minister.

When it comes to the ordinary, everyday business of government, however, where various forms of direct control operate, neither the Politbureau and its members (whose task encompasses the directing of general Party work), nor even the Secretariat and its members (whose task includes the supervision of the implementation of decisions), play the principal role. The most important part in this respect belongs to the Party apparatus. The lower the position of a link in the apparatus, the more intensive its control activity. An instructor does more than the chief of his sector, and a sector chief must be more zealous than the chief of his department. The Party apparatus of provincial committees knows its subordinates better than the same apparatus at Central Committee level. A similar correlation exists between territorial and provincial Party agencies on the one hand and city or district agencies on the other. One should also not forget that primary Party organizations have the right to control the administration of non-Party institutions and the apparatus of non-Party agencies.[59] In such a manner so-called local control acquires its own patch, which is very important, because this system allows nothing to escape Party vigilance. Moreover, each primary organization presents periodic reports to higher Party agencies, and as a result of the upward movement of papers the most complete information reaches the highest body of the CPSU. Thus operative government, although it may be more difficult to control than legislation, is so constructed that the Communist Party manages to keep everything under its dominance, even in the domain of the day-to-day business of governmental agencies and other establishments.

But the strongest weapon in the Party's arsenal, and one which assures its universal domination, is the selection of personnel or, to use the Soviet term, the *nomen-klatura*. This means briefly a list of positions which can be filled only by persons recommended or approved by the appropriate Party agencies. It encompasses Party and non-Party personnel. The appointment of each Party official, beginning with the secretary of a primary Party organization, must be confirmed by the respective Party agency, before the appointee will be able to fill his post. Beyond the Party itself, the *nomenklatura* embraces a multitude of officials of all kinds of institutions: governmental agencies, economic organizations, research institutes, universities, schools, cultural and artistic establishments, the press and other media, etc. Not only ministers and chairmen of state committees are covered by the *nomenklatura*, but also managers of enterprises, heads of libraries, chairmen of local bar associations, and chairmen of collective farms represent "nomenclature workers" (*nomenklaturnye rabotniki*). The *nomenklatura* does not distinguish between elected and appointed officials. Deputies of soviets, supreme as well as local, belong to the *nomenklatura* and must be personally approved before the start of the election campaign.

The *nomenklatura* has different levels. There are *nomenklaturas* of the Politbureau, of the CPSU Secretariat, of the Central Committee departments, of the corresponding agencies in the republics and provinces, and of city and district Party committees. For example, the Rector of Moscow University must be confirmed by the Politbureau, while the Rector of Leningrad University needs confirmation by the Secretariat. Chiefs of research institutes of Leningrad University belong to the *nomenklatura* of the bureau of the provincial Party committee, deans of faculties require the approval of the secretary of the provincial Party committee who is responsible for science, chairmen of faculty departments shall be confirmed by the science department of the same committee. Apart from this, primary Party organizations deal with appointments or elections for less important positions. The election of a new professor is preceded by the approval of the University Party committee and the nomination of the chief book-keeper as well as the election of the chairman of the local trade union likewise need the approval of the primary Party organization.[60]

Various, and sometimes quite bizarre reasons may present obstacles to recommendation or approval of *nomenklatura* officials. The Politbureau of the Ukrainian Republic once refused to confirm the appointment of a person with only one leg as the Ukrainian representative on one of the United Nations' commissions in Geneva and demanded his replacement by a similarly qualified but two-legged person. In the mid-1970s, Romanov, a Politbureau member and First Secretary of the Leningrad Provincial Committee of the CPSU, recommended his closest friend, a law professor, for the post of Rector of Leningrad University. However, Kirilenko, another Politbureau member and a secretary of the CPSU Central Committee, refused to confirm the nomination. Whether such a case revealed a personal collision between two members of the Politbureau is difficult to say. The official explanation given by

Kirilenko to the minister of higher education was that a science professor, and not a law professor should be the head of Leningrad University. But a very close connection between *nomenklatura* discussions and the struggle for influence and political power is beyond doubt and can be illustrated with numerous and impressive examples. The most recent of these may also be the most eloquent. In November 1982 the Presidium of the USSR Supreme Soviet lost its chairman with the death of Brezhnev. Subsequently, the USSR Supreme Soviet, the only body empowered to elect the Presidium's chairman, met twice, but neither session dealt with the election. As a result, something unprecedented in Soviet history occurred: the position of the official head of state of the Soviet Union remained vacant for more than seven months. The exact causes of this extraordinary development are not publicly known, but their general character is easy to guess. The Politbureau had not approved the final nomination, therefore the USSR Supreme Soviet could not proceed to the formal election. Brezhnev had combined two positions, of General Secretary of the CPSU and of Chairman of the Presidium of the USSR Supreme Soviet, and Andropov, having inherited the first position, was unable to appropriate the second one immediately, running into opposition in the Politbureau, strong enough to resist his endeavors. Only after the balance of power had shifted in favor of one of the conflicting forces, did the Politbureau at last come to the necessary decision, and in June 1983 the USSR Supreme Soviet elected Andropov Chairman of the Supreme Soviet's Presidium.

Thus, the power of the *nomenklatura* extends to all officials, from the highest to the lowest. The higher one's place in the *nomenklatura*, the greater one's political power and economic resources. This is why furtive infighting in ordinary times and almost open struggle under extraordinary circumstances are inherent to the *nomenklatura* system. However, cautiousness and vigilance are necessary in such fights, for they can end in victory as well as in defeat, and to lose one's place in the *nomenklatura* or to suffer demotion in the hierarchy means the loss or a proportional decrease of one's political power and economic opportunities. This is why discipline and obedience are no less a part of the *nomenklatura* system than are fighting and struggling. Hostility among members of the *nomenklatura* may result in personal promotion and demotion or in the appearance of new people and the disappearance of known ones, but the *nomenklatura* itself remains intact and retains its role as the personnel substratum of the Soviet system. People can be changed, the *nomenklatura* stays the same. All who belong to it are induced to be faithful and dependable, while those who stop being so are ousted by the *nomenklatura* itself. The latter may acquire democratic forms, if necessary, but in essence it manifests the most rigid centralization.

Through these various approaches, the Party's manner of personnel selection, together with general regulation and operative government, have made the Soviet political system into an organization with a double structure, a two-track Leviathan. Official rules depend on Party directives, the current activities of non-Party institutions are directed by Party instructions, public elections confirm Party appointments, and official appointments rubber-stamp Party nominations. Quite naturally the questions arise: what is this duplication for, why are the parallel functions of correlative agencies not merged, and would it not be better to economize on a governing process than to admit such a waste of time and money?

In answering these questions, one usually refers to the necessity of creating at least a semblance of democracy. This explanation is doubtlessly correct, for if the Soviet system were to divest itself of its duplicity and Party directives were to operate directly – without interference from official rules – then the Party's actual government would replace any other government activity, Party appointments would no longer be disguised by public elections, and Party nominations could dispense with official appointments. Thus, all artificial pretexts for demagogic twaddle about the sovereign people and the rulers as the servants of the people would be deprived even of the ceremonial significance which they retain in a duplicated political structure. This, of course, would be very dangerous for the entire system and its not disinterested champions. Therefore, no efforts or resources must be spared to guard against such a serious risk. From this point of view, the double nature of the Soviet system leads to reasonable expenses, not to senseless dissipation. The upkeep of a democratic facade, however, provides only a partial explanation; two other factors, less conspicuous, but equally important, should be mentioned.

The first one consists in the fact that, thanks to the duplicate organization of the Soviet system, the real culprits of evil committed by the system can often not be found; people who have suffered its harmful effects will in many cases not know to whom they should complain, and political domination will thereby remain un-accountable and unrestricted.

The Executive Committee of the Leningrad City Soviet issued an illegal decision in the area of housing legislation. The Civil Law Department of Leningrad University asked the city procurator to appeal against this illegal decision. He, however, did all he could to avoid the fulfillment of what was clearly his duty. Why? Is not the procurator independent of local government and therefore able to act freely and boldly? He is indeed, but not of the local Party agencies, and the procurator will lose his position as soon as the latter decides so. Knowing that the Provincial Party Committee had sanctioned the illegal decision of the Executive Committee, the procurator, for the sake of his own safety, was unwilling to interfere. When the Civil Law Department turned to the Provincial Party Committee, its answer was simple and curt: "Do you not know that legal rules are within the jurisdiction of the Executive Committee? The Party Committee has nothing to do with it. You appealed to the wrong quarter."

In the mid-1960s the Kirghiz Central Committee of the Communist Party, prob-ably after "coordination" with the CPSU Central Committee, instructed the Univer-sity of the Republic to admit Kirghiz girl students without an entrance examination, in order to increase the number of female Kirghiz students, although such a proce-dure was contrary to law. The Kirghiz Republic, besides being the main home of the Kirghiz population, houses many people of Korean origin, and it is difficult, if not impossible, for Russians or Ukrainians to distinguish between Kirghiz and Koreans on the basis of their appearance. On one occasion, the dean of a faculty, a Ukrainian, received in his office two girls who wanted to be enrolled as students. He assured them without delay that they would be exempt from the examination and that they could consider themselves as students of the University. Only then did the dean look through their documents and find that one of the girls was Kirghiz, while the other was Korean. He thereupon changed his decision and declared that the first girl was admitted, while the second one was only admitted to the examination. These examinations, however, were pointless, because the entire number of vacancies had been allocated beforehand according to various secret instructions. The parents of the Korean girl appealed to the republic ministry and then to the USSR Ministry of Higher Education, but in both cases received the reply that no grounds for interfering with the decisions of the University had been found. When the parents appealed to the Central Committees of the Kirghiz Republic and of the Soviet Union the stereotype answer was: enrollment as a university student is governed by existing rules and checked by the Ministry of Higher Education.

In the late 1960s twelve employees of the Leningrad Archives were fired. The reason for their dismissal was that they had admitted a well-known Soviet author, Marietta Shaginian, without special permission of the competent agencies, to certain archival documents, including some relating to Lenin and his relatives. What was even worse was that Shaginian had managed to find documents proving that Lenin's maternal grandfather, Blank, was a Jew. Soviet leaders, considering these data to be very unfavorable for the regime, persuaded Shaginian to keep them secret. The twelve employees of the Archives, however, lost their jobs on account of a "loss of vigilance". As a matter of course, Soviet labor law does not provide for dismissal on such a ground. A court therefore restored four of them to their former positions. But the eight others belonged to the *nomenklatura* and the court was not entitled to hear their cases. The head of the Archives told them frankly that he was unable to change the adopted decision, since the provincial Party committee had expelled them from the *nomenklatura*. At the same time, a high-ranking Party official who received the complainants said to them that he personally approved of the decision taken, but that the issue belonged to the jurisdiction of the Archives, and not a Party agency, so that he was unable to change anything, whatever his own attitude might be.

The conduct described would hardly have been possible without the duplicate structure of the Soviet system. Owing to this system, any unjust solution must be accepted, since the Party has ordered but not acted, and the "non-Party" has acted but not ordered.

The second factor in explaining the two-track nature of the Soviet system is even more significant. The duplicity inherent in this system ensures its almost automatic functioning, independently of the peculiarities of individual officials, and leads to self-protecting reactions against any conduct or any event which might be dangerous or unacceptable to the system.

Stalin attempted to centralize the government of the country as much as possible. He did not convoke Party congresses for thirteen years, stopped regular meetings of the Central Committee plenum, and refused to admit the collective functioning of the Politbureau during the last years of his dictatorship. Nevertheless, the USSR Supreme Soviet continued to hold regular sessions, its Presidium worked normally as a collective body, and, moreover, the USSR Council of Ministers headed by Stalin himself held its meetings and voted its decisions. This obvious discrepancy in the political behavior of one and the same dictator would be incomprehensible, if analyzed by itself, but it becomes understandable if it is viewed in the light of the demands of the system. Stalin could strengthen his personal power endlessly as long as he was acting within the realm of Party centralization, but even he would not dare to annihilate the ceremonial democracy in the realm of the government of the state. This was precluded by the very system which brought about Stalinism. The latter was not the ground for the former, but the former served as the basis for the latter.

Khrushchev strived to democratize the government of the country to as great an extent as he considered reasonable. He restored the regular work of the Party congresses, of the Central Committee plenums, and of the Politbureau – the "collective mind" of the Party. The Party also held extraordinary congresses, along with ordinary ones. Owing to "secret letters" to all Party members, which actually were known to everyone, the secrecy of the highest level of the regime lost some of its severity. Nationwide discussions of certain draft laws took place now and again. Nevertheless, real democracy did not appear, and such a thought had never entered Khrushchev's head. The system requires ceremonial democracy, being incompatible with genuine democratization. This is why Khrushchev managed to combine the denunciation of Stalin's dictatorship for the sake of democracy with the strengthening of his own personal power through centralizing measures. Thanks to this combination Khrushchev was able to hold on to power for at least ten years, despite his eccentricity and the complete unpredictability of his actions. Had he been striving towards genuine democracy, he would have been ousted long before, probably at the first steps in this direction.

Brezhnev actually aspired to nothing, or, more exactly, aspired to preserve the system as it was, without Stalin's outrages or Khrushchev's extravagance. He cancelled most of Khrushchev's innovations, but retained the most demagogic of them, primarily the concept of the all-people's state. He restored certain elements of Stalin's arbitrariness, but did not revert to Stalinism in the exact meaning of the word. He loved ostentatious ceremonies centered round his person and, by adding the post of Chairman of the Presidium of the USSR Supreme Soviet to that of General Secretary of the CPSU, introduced a reform which had never been seen before in the USSR. His personal power, however, did not increase, but simply became more imposing. Brezhnev may serve as a model of a smooth accommodation to the needs of the system, which precludes one type of behavior and requires the other. As a result, Brezhnev's rule was the most insipid in Soviet history. But this was the very reason which spared him from any trouble in the preservation of his position. He did not disturb the system, and the system supported him.[61]

Andropov's steps were too contradictory – as well as being carried out for a very short time – to serve as a ground for generalizations. At the beginning there were certain hints of economic reform. Then the question of discipline was emphasized. After this ideological restrictions came to the foreground. Finally a decision on economic experiments in the direction of economic decentralization was adopted.[62] Nevertheless, the main current seemed to be rather in the direction of Stalinism than anywhere else. As for Chernenko, only the future can tell what kind of accommodation will be preferred by him personally or by those whom he actually represents, although this future has become predictable after restoration of Party membership of Molotov, the closest accomplice of Stalin's crimes, and the erection of a monument to Kochetov, one of the most reactionary writers in Soviet history. Of course, numerous changes are possible, and domestic as well as international events may compel him to resort to them. One thing seems to be beyond doubt: nobody is considering a modification of the system, either entirely or in part. The system dominates the rulers, and the rulers correspondingly dominate the people. This state of affairs arose at the beginning of Soviet power and its nature shall remain unchanged: democratic centralism in principle and centralized democracy in reality.

NOTES

1. *E.g.* see Brezhnev's speech at the meeting of the Central Committee of the Communist Party of the USSR in May 1977 (*Pravda*, 5 June 1977).
2. V.I. Lenin, *Works*, Moscow 1970, 5th ed. in Russian, Vol.4, 190. Compare Vol.36, 151.
3. The 1977 Constitution, art.3.
4. *Ibid.*, art.164.
5. *Ibid.*, arts.165-166.
6. *Ibid.*, art.156.
7. *Ibid.*, art.152.
8. *Ibid.*, art.153.
9. "Polozheniie o Verkhovnom Sude SSSR", *Ved.SSSR* 1957 No.4 item 84, art.9(c).
10. *Sbornik Postanovlenii Plenuma Verkhovnogo Suda SSSR, 1924-1977*, Moskva 1978, Vol.II, 184-185.
11. *Ibid.*, Vol.I, 8.
12. *Ibid.*
13. *Ibid.*
14. The 1977 Constitution, Chapter 13, arts.95-102.
15. "Zakon o Vyborakh v Verkhovnii Sovet SSSR", *Ved.SSSR* 1979 No.17 item 227.
16. The 1977 Constitution, arts.89, 152.
17. *Ibid.*, art.152.
18. *Ibid.*, art.129.
19. *Ibid.*, art.122(4).
20. *Supra*, note 3.
21. The 1977 Constitution, art.107.
22. *Ibid.*, art.130.
23. *Supra*, 24.
24. The 1977 Constitution, art.122.
25. *Ibid.*, arts.105-106.
26. *Kodeks o brake i sem'e RSFSR 1969* (hereinafter cited as Family Code), arts.98-118.
27. *Supra*, 27-29.
28. The 1936 Constitution, art.126.
29. *Ibid.*
30. The 1977 Constitution, art.6.
31. An English version of the Rules of the Communist Party of the Soviet Union in *The Party Statutes of the Communist World*, (W.B. Simons and S. White, eds.), No.27 *Law in Eastern Europe*, (F.J.M. Feldbrugge, ed.), The Hague/Boston/Lancaster 1984, 415-433.
32. *Ibid.*, art.30.
33. *Ibid.*, art.32(c).
34. *Ibid.*, art.33.
35. *Ibid.*, art.34.
36. *Ibid.*, art.37.
37. *Ibid.*, art.38.
38. *Ibid.*
39. *Ibid.*, arts.41-52.
40. *Ibid.*, art.53.
41. *Ibid.*, art.60.
42. *Ibid.*
43. During about the last fifty years, the Central Committee of the CPSU has applied its power only once, when it overturned the Politbureau's decision of 1957 to dismiss Khrushchev and, instead dismissed Khrushchev's foes: Malenkov, Molotov, Kaganovich, Shepilov. But even in such an extraordinary case the Central Committee, after some discussion, simply confirmed what had been prepared by the Party oligarchy with Furtseva at the head and the military top represented by Marshal Zhukov.

44. Sometimes, however, especially when an important problem of cadres must be solved, the need to resort to secrecy appears again. Thus, for reasons which cannot be explained, the dismissal of Podgornyi, the former chairman of the Presidium of the USSR Supreme Soviet, predetermined by the Politbureau without his participation, became known to him only at a meeting of the Central Committee. That is why secrecy was necessary, and although there was a rumour about the procedure applied, nobody, except the participants in this meeting, could say with certainty how the event really happened.

45. A building, which had been the Bolshevik's staff center in 1917 and later became a residence of the highest Leningrad Party agency.

46. It is necessary to point out that the rules enumerated relate to "centralized democracy", *i.e.* to centralization concealed by democracy. In cases of unconcealed centralization or direct arbitrariness the same rules stop being applicable, and the respective Party agencies or Party leaders entirely disregard formal rights, formal procedures and formal demands. But these cases shall be discussed separately in a future chapter.

47. *Osnovy Zhilishchnogo Zakonodatel'stva Soiuza SSR i Soiuznykh Respublik*, 1981 (hereinafter cited as the Fundamentals of Housing Legislation). See *Sotsialisticheskaia Zakonnost'* 1981 No.9, 58-71.

48. "Proekt konstitutsii (osnovnogo zakona) Soiuza Sovetskikh Sotsialisticheskikh Respublik", *Izvestiia*, 4 June 1977.

49. And so it really happened. After the Fundamentals of Housing Legislation had been adopted, the corresponding articles of the Fundamentals of Civil Legislation were abolished in part (*Ved.SSSR* 1981 No.44 item 1184). Republican housing codes have already been issued, and now an analogous correlation between these and republican civil codes does not provoke any doubt.

50. For more details see O.S. Ioffe, *Razvitiie Tsivilisticheskoi Mysli v SSSR*, Part I, Leningrad 1975, 39-108.

51. L.I. Brezhnev, "O proekte konstitutsii (Osnovnogo zakona) Soiuza Sovetskikh Sotsialisticheskikh Respublik i itogakh vsenarodnogo obsuzhdeniia", *Konstitutsiia Obshchenarodnogo Gosudarstva*, Moskva 1978, 108.

52. *Ved.SSSR* 1977 No.54 item 764.

53. See note 47, art.1 which corresponds to art.44 of the 1977 Constitution.

54. The 1977 Constitution, art.58.

55. *Ved.SSSR* 1981 No.21 item 141.

56. See, for example, art.9(5) of the International Covenant on Civil and Political Rights of 1966, G.A. Res ZZO(XXI), Z1 UN GAOR, Supp. (No.16) 52, UN, Doc. A/6316 (1966).

57. The 1977 Constitution, art.17.

58. *SP SSSR* 1970 No.19 item 150; 1971 No.3 item 19.

59. *Supra*, 32-33.

60. On account of the scale of the *nomenklatura* there is no reason to consider it as a new dominant class, as a single entity (see M. Voslensky, *Nomenklatura – die herrschende Klasse der Sowjetunion*, Wien-München-Zürich-Innsbrück 1980, esp. 17-45). The new dominant class of the USSR is included into the *nomenklatura*, but the *nomenklatura* is not equal to the Soviets' new dominant class.

61. This statement touches only upon domestic politics. As for political lines in foreign affairs, including the invasions of Czechoslovakia or Afghanistan, they are beyond the given analysis.

62. *Pravda*, 26 July 1983.

CHAPTER II

THE LAW OF POLITICAL FREEDOM AND OF POLITICAL DOMINATION

Thus, the Soviet system represents democratic centralism and centralized democracy.[1] At the same time, democratic centralism, real or only proclaimed, cannot function without political freedom, actual or only imaginary. Similarly, centralized democracy, unrestricted or even mitigated, cannot operate without political domination, unlimited or even restrained. Therefore, the USSR allows political freedom and establishes political domination to the same extent as it personifies democratic centralism and centralized democracy. Each is reflected in Soviet law and embodied in Soviet life. The suggested analysis must reveal whether this reflection is veracious or inaccurate and whether this embodiment is commensurate or disproportionate. One thing, however, seems clear in advance. The very fact of the interdependence between democratic centralism and centralized democracy, on the one hand, and political freedom and political domination, on the other hand, predetermines the adequacy of their reproduction in everyday practice and legal regulation in the Soviet state.

1. Political Freedom

Real political freedom proves to be alien to the Soviet system just as genuine democracy seems incompatible with it. Nevertheless if one does not go beyond the limits of Soviet laws, only extraordinary attentiveness and extreme scrupulousness can lead to the confirmation of such a conclusion. Otherwise, it appears either as a gross mistake or as a shameless calumny. Only the comparison of legal formulae with everyday practice will put things in a proper perspective, and what may have seemed to be ignorance or malevolence becomes the irrefutable result of honest research. This again demonstrates that without an eye towards practice, the study of Soviet law is condemned to false deductions and to futile conclusions. However, Soviet legislation must not be disregarded either, not only because it expresses Soviet law formally and, as a result, can be used to cooperate with, as well as to oppose the USSR,[2] but also because the genuine content of Soviet law, though to a large degree disguised, is in some parts revealed by legal texts.

Political Freedom in Soviet Law

Soviet law settles the problem of political freedom by means of legal regulations relating to three groups of interdependent subjects: the structure of political power in the country, citizens' constitutional rights, and the development and protection of constitutional rights by civil law, criminal law and other branches of Soviet legislation.

1. The structure of political power. According to the Soviet Constitution "all power in the USSR shall belong to the people".[3] Meanwhile, as a general principle, the Constitution proclaims the indirect expression of the people's will: "The people shall exercise state power through soviets of people's deputies...".[4] Only as an exception to the rule: "the most important questions of state life shall be submitted for discussion by the whole people and also to a vote by the whole people (referendum)".[5] Such an exceptional expression of the people's will is reduced to a purely consultative function in the first case (the whole people's discussion); but it could acquire a decisive role in the second case (referendum). Therefore, since 1936, when the possibility was first introduced by Soviet law,[6] referendums have never been applied in practice. Instead of referendums, the Soviet leadership prefers to launch "whole people's discussions", when it considers these to be politically advantageous and useful from a propagandistic point of view.[7] In addition, the "whole people", although all power belongs to it, does not have a right to discussions or referendums. Referendums may be held exclusively by decisions of the USSR Supreme Soviet,[8] while decisions about discussions of the whole people may be adopted either by the USSR Supreme Soviet or by its Presidium.[9] On the other hand, discussions of the whole people which have taken place in Soviet practice on several occasions should not be equated with freedom of speech. It is enough to remember that for many people discussion of the 1977 Constitution has ended with criminal prosecutions and punitive sentences. Even comparatively innocent suggestions, if they seem suspicious or unreliable, have no chance of being published and discussed. An *ad hoc* commission comprised of more than 300 participants was created to filter citizens' suggestions during the period of the whole people's discussions of the subsequently adopted 1977 Constitution, and it was meticulously instructed on how to do its job. As a result, hundreds of thousands of opinions and remarks disagreeable to the ruling summit, did not meet any response other than judicial repression. The ficticious nature of the constitutional discussion was so well known by the Soviet citizenry that many of them sent anonymous letters of a mocking or humiliating character. One of these letters said: "The Constitution shall provide for the duty to put slightly bigger tails on the caps of vodka bottles so that horny-handed workers could open them without fail". However, "suggestions" of this kind, together with "politically unreliable" opinions were also taken into account, when the tremendous figure of those who had participated in the discussion was anounced as indisputable evidence of the high level of social activity allegedly displayed by a large proportion of the Soviet population.

The impracticability of direct rule by the people, at least in countries with large populations, has been known since Montesquieu's time,[10] and the real Soviet rulers, having proclaimed the transition of the Soviet system from the dictatorship of the proletariat to the all-people's state,[11] did not at all jeopardize their politician position. Despite the Marxist-Leninist thesis that no one ruling class gives up its power voluntarily, the Soviet proletariat did not revolt against its overthrow, nor did the Soviet people celebrate its sovereignty, after Khrushchev declared the replacement of proletarian dictatorship by the all-people's state in 1961.[12] For any Marxist in the world this must mean nothing more than the ficticious proclamation of the Soviet proletarian dictatorship, as well as of the Soviet all-people's state. Meanwhile, if a collective body does not attain the scale of the whole Soviet population and is restricted to a smaller number of participants, it acquires, according to Montesquieu,[13] the capacity of direct rule similar to the capacity of countries with small populations. But precisely in such cases Soviet law either entirely neglects collective bodies' rights or recognizes them within very modest and insignificant limits. This attitude reveals itself with peculiar clarity in the legal position of production collectives (in the terminology which preceded the 1977 Constitution) or labor collectives (in the terminology of the Constitution now in force).[14] Early in the 1920s Lenin initiated a merciless fight against *"rabochiaia oppositsiia"* (labor opposition). Adherents of the opposition thought that if political power in the country belonged to the proletariat, then administrative power at separate enterprises should belong to their production collectives, and managers of the same enterprises should be subordinated to these collectives. Lenin labeled this idea *"anarcho-syndicalism"* (anarchic syndicalism), which strived to replace one-man management based on the strongest subordination by uncontrollable collective administration based on the majority of votes. In other words, Lenin supported the unrealizable dictatorship of the whole proletariat, but he was aware and fearful of the real power of separate production collectives. As for Stalin, he alleviated such fear in a very simple way by executing all adherents of the labor opposition and simultaneously implementing severe prohibitions on any discussion about the rights and powers of separate collectives. Krushchev in his ostentatious attempts to restore democracy in the country did not go beyond *proizvodstvennye soveshchaniia* (production meetings) of collective bodies of enterprises or their representatives, which were to be called twice a year. Their functions were purely consultative and their activity was formalized to a degree that doomed them to complete degeneration even during Khrushchev's time. In contrast, Brezhnev focused in his Constitution on an alluring formula about the rights of labor collectives. Henceforth these collectives "shall participate in the discussion and decision of state and social affairs, in the planning of production and social development, in the training and placing of cadres, and in the discussion and decision of questions of the management of enterprises and institutions, the improvement of labor and domestic conditions, the use of assets earmarked for production development, and also for socio-cultural measures and material incentives".[15] However, the Constitution itself provides for only one of their rights: nomination of candidates for deputies to all soviets, both supreme and local.[16] How the deputies are actually nominated and what a humiliating role is assigned to labor collectives in this realm has already been shown.[17] In all other regards Brezhnev took no risks such as empowering labor collectives not only with "the right to discuss", but also with "the right to decide". The latter right could not become effective until a specific regulation had been established. Brezhnev himself avoided doing this. He left that task to his successor. And the successor, Yuri Andropov, carried it out by a special law on labor collectives,[18] which preserved only "the right to discuss" from the "rights to discuss and decide"[19] and which has not been changed after Andropov was replaced by Chernenko. Hence, during the whole history of Soviet law, the regulation of the organizational structure of political power has been proceeding from the principle that the larger a collective body and the less it is capable of personifying real power, the more titular power must be ascribed to it. And vice versa, the narrower a collective body and the more capable it is of governing politically, the less political power it must have even in name. Only at a certain point – to use dialectical jargon – does a transition from quantity to quality occur: those extremely narrow collective bodies or high personalities that keep a firm hand on political domination have always managed to find direct or, more frequently, roundabout ways of confirming their powerful position by law-making and still more by application of the law in the USSR.[20]

2. Citizens' constitutional rights. The Soviet Constitution classifies all citizens' rights proclaimed under it into three groups: socio-economic rights, political rights and personal rights and freedoms.[21] All of them are connected in some way with the political position of the Soviet citizenry, and therefore, despite this classification, they shall be, if not entirely analyzed, then at least exhaustively enumerated. The Constitution provides for the right to work, the right to leisure, the right to health protection, the right to material security under specially described circumstances (old age, etc.), the right to housing, the right to education, the right to use the achievements of culture, the freedom of scientific, technical and artistic creativity, the right to participate in the administration of state and social affairs, the right to submit proposals to state agencies and social organizations, freedom of speech, press, assembly, meetings, street processions and demonstrations, the right to unite in social organizations, freedom of conscience, the right of the family to be protected by the state, the right of personal inviolability, the right of inviolability of the home, the right of protection of a citizen's personal life, secrecy of correspondence, telephone conversations and telegraph communication, the right to judicial protection against infringements against a citizen's honor and dignity, life and health, personal freedom and property, and the right to appeal against the actions of officials and of state and social agencies.[22]

As indicated above,[23] some of the enumerated rights continue to exist only formally, merely in name, as for example, the right of appealing to a court against illegal actions of governmental officials, because art.58 which introduces this right refers to "the procedure established by law", and no such law has been adopted since the time the Constitution was promulgated. Therefore arbitrariness of governmental agencies preserves the same or sometimes even a broader scope under the Brezhnev Constitution, as was the case before its promulgation. A country house (*dacha*) was burned down, but the local government forbade its restoration despite Soviet land legislation which preserved the right to a plot of land if the land user began to restore the destroyed structure within two years after destruction.[24] Formerly the land user could protect his right in a judicial way. Now he can no longer do so because there is no law provided for by the Constitution establishing the necessary procedure. On the other hand, some rules, introducing constitutional rights, openly disregard the demand of equality and fairness, as for example art.52, which proclaims freedom of conscience, but includes in it the right to carry on atheistic but not religious propaganda. In conformity with it, students of Soviet universities and institutes are taught so-called scientific atheism, while the priest Gleb Iakunin has been sentenced to a long term of labor camp for religious and, consequently, anti-Soviet propaganda. However, not these but two other circumstances are the most important for a correct understanding of Soviet constitutional rights from the viewpoint of political freedom.

First, genuine political freedom assumes the possibility of choice, to agree or disagree, to say "yes" or "no". Not only Soviet practice, but Soviet law, and in the first place the Soviet Constitution precludes such a possibility. In the political realm they allow citizens no choice, legally obliging them to agree and not to disagree, to say "yes" and to avoid "no". Citizens of the USSR are guaranteed the freedom of speech, but exclusively "with a view of strengthening the socialist system".[25] They may unite in social organizations, but solely "in accordance with the aims of communist construction".[26] They are free in their scientific, technical and artistic creativity, but in this case also "in accordance with the aims of communist construction".[27] If it is impossible to accompany the formulation of corresponding rights by a similar reservation, then these rights are not mentioned at all. It would be, for example, ridiculous to say that Soviet citizens have the right to strike "in accordance with the aims of communist construction", and therefore, despite international treaties ratified by the USSR,[28] one will search in vain for this right in the Soviet Constitution. The Soviets try to explain the same fact differently, repeating now and again that because the country's economy belongs to the working masses, they have no need of the right to strike, since they cannot strike against themselves. This explanation, however, is vulnerable logically as well as practically. Logically it is vulnerable in two regards. On the one hand, if strikes are really impossible in the USSR, the Soviets could recognize the right to strike without any danger or fear. Meanwhile, they avoid doing it, and this proves without doubt that the danger positively exists. On the other hand, an official concept of Soviet leadership says that the country's economy belongs to the people in the person of the state, not to the collective bodies of separate enterprises.[29] This means that strikes at one or another enterprise are quite possible, being directed against the state, not against strikers themselves. Practically the Soviet explanation also is disproved in Soviet life. Leningrad, Togliatti, Novocherkassk and some other cities of the USSR are known all over the world as places of workers' strikes that have occured there at different times. Early in the 1980s mass strikes in Poland, another socialist country, compelled Polish leaders to recognize the right to strike and they could not find any other way of restricting its application than to introduce martial law. Instead of using such extreme measures against the legally recognized right to strike, the USSR denies its necessity for the Soviet system and leaves it out of Soviet law.

But what about the rights which cannot be omitted without political self-denunciation and which simultaneously cannot be combined with the words "in accordance with the aims of communist construction" or something to that effect? Freedom of conscience serves as a good illustration of this, and some other rights provided for by the Soviet Constitution share similar peculiarities. Bearing them in mind, the Constitution adds to the concrete reservations included in separate articles a general rule of the following content: "The use by citizens of rights and freedoms should not harm the interests of society and the state nor the rights of other citizens".[30] If nobody can be accused of disaccordance with "aims of communist construction" by exercising the right to profess any religion – since all kinds of religions are officially considered anti-communist – an accusation in harming the interests of society and the state or of other citizens' rights seems quite applicable in this case and in all other cases, where the nature of constitutional rights precludes their direct restriction. In such a way, as Marx was wont to say in characterizing capitalist law, Soviet law declares political freedom in general rules and abolishes it in numerous reservations. These reservations abolish political freedom not only in the aspect of contrasting capitalism to socialism, but also within the limits of socialism itself when a confirmed orthodoxy collides with a disapproved heresy or when a practical line adopted at a given period is contradicted by the suggestion of another practical approach. The heretical socialism of Yugoslavia was condemned ideologically; the socialism with a human face of Czechoslovakia was smashed by military invasion; the Medvedev brothers' socialism under the slogan "Back to Marx" was suppressed by punitive psychiatry and compulsory expatriation; true socialism embodied in a program of several Leningrad intellectuals was destroyed by criminal prosecution and labor camp sentences. So it is with the fight of orthodoxy against heresy. As for the fight between different practical lines, it is enough to remember that in 1957 Shepilov was declared a member of the anti-Party group because he characterized Khrushchev's administration as voluntarism, but in 1964, when Khrushchev was ousted, voluntarism appeared as the main accusation against him. Andropov considered the economic reforms under Brezhnev as insufficient half-measures,[31] and such they really were. However, up to the end of life Andropov himself had not made any significant economic steps to say nothing of his economic experiment,[32] and what is more important, during Brezhnev's life he was prudent enough either to support economic half-measures without reservation or at least to remain silent. As a matter of course, he could not have behaved otherwise, because freedom of speech within the framework of social and political harmlessness is generally binding in the USSR, although with application of different scales towards leaders and the man in the street.

Second, in proclaiming political and other basic rights of Soviet citizens, the 1977 Constitution, as well as its predecessors, does not pay adequate attention to the means of legal protection, and touches mainly upon socio-economic guarantees of constitutional rights. When, for example, article 41 states that the right to leisure "shall be ensured by the establishment for workers and employees of a work week not exceeding 41 hours, or reduced work day for a number of professions and trades and a reduced work period at night", etc., it provides for necessary legal protection, and each worker or employee, whose right of leisure has been violated, may demand its restoration in the appropriate legal way. On the contrary, article 50, speaking about freedom of speech, press, assembly, meetings, street processions and demonstrations, does not refer to legal protection and deals exclusively with socio-economic guarantees: "The realization of these political freedoms shall be ensured by granting public buildings, streets and squares, extensive dissemination of information, and the possibility of using the press, television and radio by working people and their organizations." What, however, if the granting of buildings, streets or squares has been refused, as happened with an exhibition of works by non-conformist artists near Moscow which was destroyed by bulldozers, or if disseminated information has not attained a satisfactory scale, as happened with the incident of the Korean plane when the Soviet population was not informed even about the number of passengers killed, or if press, television and radio cannot be used despite all efforts and strong insistence, as happened with open letters sent to Soviet officials by Voinovich, Vladimov, and numerous other victims of arbitrariness? Under the circumstances socio-economic guarantees do not help, and a legal way of protection cannot be used because it simply does not exist. Soviet jurisprudence has always pointed out socio-economic guarantees of constitutional rights in the USSR as an invaluable advantage of Soviet law in comparison with western law: the latter deals with formal rights, the former establishes real rights. Meanwhile, in fact, the formal right is real indeed because it admits legal protection, and the informal real right is purely formal because the legal protection becomes unachievable in this case.

As a rule, such an intentional approach used in the process of Soviet law-making remains imperceptible. First of all, the ordinary and, sometimes, professional reader, coming across the word "right" in a legal text, believes that it is a right indeed. Then, the rights deprived of legal protection are formulated by the Soviet Constitution alternately with legally protected rights, and this baffles the reader even more than the legislative way of their fixation. Compare, for example, two constitutional rules. One of them, concerning the right to material security, states that it "shall be guaranteed by social insurance... and benefits for temporary loss of capacity to work; by payment... of pensions for age, disability and loss of the breadwinner", etc.[33] The other, speaking about the right to use achievements of culture, declares that it "shall be ensured by the general accessibility of the treasures of national and world culture in state and public collections; the development and equitable siting of cultural-educational institutions on the territory of the country", etc.[34] Both rules are structured on the same model: formulation of a right and description of guarantees. The essential difference reveals itself only in case of violation. Refusal to pay due pensions protected by legal guarantees may be overcome in a legal way. Therefore, even dissidents or refuseniks[35] receive them, if the necessary conditions are satisfied. Refusal of access to the cultural treasures, since this access rests only upon socio-economic guarantees, becomes irrevocable. Therefore, even old Soviet newspapers withdrawn from general use, to say nothing of dissident's books or works published specially for the bureaucracy of different ranks, cannot be received by Soviet citizens, who do not occupy the required position or who are not admitted to *spetskhran* – special premises for the secret keeping of dangerous or suspicious cultural treasures. At last, some constitutional rights prove their meaninglessness not because nobody is legally obliged to respect them, but as a result of the legal hollowness of these obligations. Article 57 of the Soviet Constitution recognizes the citizen's right "to judicial protection against infringements of honor and dignity, life and health, personal freedom and property", and such a right really exists insofar as the appropriate branches of Soviet legislation provide for the concrete terms of its application. But the same article announces that "respect for the individual and the protection of the rights and freedoms of citizens shall be the duty of all state agencies, social organizations, and officials". It is clear that the text cited belongs rather to the category of legal slogans than of legal rules, and has hardly more sense than an appeal to be friendly or to behave decently. With the help of all these means Soviet legislature manages, if necessary, to create the semblance of rights as a convenient substitute for real rights.

3. *Citizens' ordinary rights.* While basic rights are provided for by the Constitution, which is considered as a part of state law in the USSR, ordinary rights stem from other branches of legislation, which consist of administrative law (regulations of governmental activity and of public order), civil law (regulations of property relationships and some personal non-property relationships), criminal law (definitions of crimes and regulations of punishments), law of civil procedure and law of criminal procedure (regulations of hearing of civil cases and criminal cases), labor law (regulations of labor relationships), collective farms law (regulations of internal relationships in collective farms), land law (regulations of relationships connected with land tenure), financial law (regulations of state budget relationships) and family law (regulations of marriage and family relationships).[36] The enumerated branches of law constitute numerous citizens' rights and impose upon citizens numerous duties. One part of these rights and duties, as for instance the right to have property or the duty not to steal another's property, are general for the whole human community and do not present *in abstracto* any specific peculiarity of the USSR. The other part of them, as for instance the right to be a social accuser in criminal cases[37] or the duty of contractual parties to mutual assistance in every possible way in the performance of contracts,[38] can be met only in socialist countries and, first of all, in the USSR. As for the role of all legal branches, except constitutional law or, more broadly, state law, in the realm of political freedom, they either regulate the application and protection of the constitutional rights or establish their own rights and duties having a clear or disguised political coloring.

Application of constitutional rights with a political significance is mainly regulated by administrative law. This corresponds to the task of administrative law to regulate relationships with the government and the governmental agencies and it also agrees with the particularity of the same law which more than any other branch of law consists of secret (unpublished) instructions and orders. Such a peculiarity simplifies the broadest restriction or the entire annihilation in the administrative order of those political freedoms which seem very promising at the constitutional level. The Constitution declares, for example, that "citizens of the USSR shall have the right to unite in social organizations",[39] introducing only one restriction – the accordance of these organizations "with the aims of communist construction".[40] Their actual formation requires, however, the permission of the competent agency, which may permit or refuse, referring to expediency or inexpediency and is free from any other explanation. What is expedient or inexpedient is known only to those to whom the appropriate secret instructions are available. For example, Soviet students' requests to divide the sporting society "*Nauka*" into two separate societies – one for students and another for professors – contained nothing contradictory to "the aims of communist construction", but it was refused as non-expedient, and no other explanation could be demanded. When Roy Medvedev, one of the famous dissident brothers, was nominated a candidate for deputy of the USSR Supreme Soviet by a group of his adherents, the competent powers refused to register him, because the right to nominate candidates for deputies of all the soviets belong to social organizations, and the group, which nominated him, could not be considered an organization of this kind. Since the USSR signed the 1975 Helsinki Declaration, it was impossible to prove that Helsinki groups, which monitored the observance of this agreement, contradicted the aims of communist construction; but their inexpediency did not need any elucidation and their illegality resulted from the very absence of the necessary permission. By such an approach it was not difficult to destroy them despite the right of all the Soviet citizens to unite in social organizations. Thus, administrative regulations become very helpful and particularly efficacious, when the government strives to give rights with one hand and to withdraw them with the other.

Protection of constitutional rights with political coloring rests upon administrative law or criminal law, and to some extent civil law also takes part in its application. For citizens administrative protection seems the most accessible, since in all cases, even in the absence of concrete regulations, anyone, who considers that his political rights or freedoms have been violated by lower agencies, may complain to higher agencies. For rulers the same kind of protection seems the most convenient, since it is not tied to any specific procedure and assumes, not oral and public, but written and secret examination which gives a free hand to possible arbitrariness. To refuse the registration of a new church without referring to legal grounds, as well as to disregard complaints against this refusal in secluded offices is immeasurably easier than to find legal support for obvious violations of law and to look for judicial justification of illegal decisions. Because of these peculiarities, administrative law helps not so much citizens in protecting their political rights as the government in protecting its interests against the political rights of citizens. This is why, despite the inequivocal meaning of the constitutional rule expressed by article 58,[41] judicial appeals against illegal actions of governmental officials consistently meet insurmountable resistance from the Soviet bureaucracy. In contrast to administrative law, protection of political rights and freedoms by criminal law may take place only in the cases provided for by the Criminal Code.[42] The rules of the Criminal Code – comparatively numerous – which touch upon these cases, may be divided into three groups. The first group deals with crimes, which can in fact only be committed by private citizens, and not by officials. Obviously, the legislature, in drafting such provisions, is aware of this. No other explanation for the inclusion of Article 132 of the Criminal Code about obstructing the exercise of the right to vote can be offered in the country, where citizens are compelled by all possible means to take part in general elections. The second group has been established without any serious intention of putting it in effect. Although violations of the equality of rights of nationalities belong to everyday practice in the USSR, the Soviet courts have never heard cases provided for by article 74 of the Criminal Code. similarly, article 133 of the same code about the forgery of voting documents or the incorrect counting of votes has never been used by the judicial system, despite the well-known fact that these crimes are inseparable from any general election in the USSR. The third group, disguised by the goal of protecting political rights, really has to do with their restriction or emasculation. Criminal prosecution directed against the violation of laws on the separation of church and state[43] restricts rather than protects freedom of conscience.[44] As for civil law, it touches upon political rights mainly insofar as it protects personal non-property rights. This protection, however – present copyright law and the law of inventions aside – is reduced to an insignificant number of cases. When the Fundamentals of Civil Legislation were elaborated in the late 1950s, a separate chapter was dedicated to personal non-property rights. But no other part of this draft law met with such criticism and resistance as this chapter. Under any pretext the directive agencies eliminated one article after another. After only the article about protection of honor and dignity remained in the draft law, the same agencies tried to eliminate it by reference to the fact that the whole chapter could not consist of one article. Nevertheless, it was preserved, if not as a separate chapter, then as a rule of chapter I "Basic Principles" (art.7). Later, something unprecedented happened in Soviet legislative practice: the new law, before it had time to appear, became the object of severe criticism of one of its parts – article 7. At first "Pravda", "Izvestiia" and other national newspapers raised objections: they could not work normally because citizens had received the right to sue against incorrect publications. Then the Communist Party forbade its members to use article 7 in disputes with Soviet media and governmental agencies. At last, this rule fell into disuse in judicial practice, and, having actually become a dead letter of the law, it occasionally revealed purely artificial signs of preserved life: first the USSR Supreme Court decided to interpret article 7,[45] then the Presidium of the USSR Supreme Soviet slightly changed its legal formulation.[46] Citizens, however, stopped remembering this institution, and the former enthusiasm gave way to complete indifference.

The establishment of new political rights in addition to constitutional rights can occur in the realm of administrative law and civil law, and sometimes one of them introduces a new right with possible political implications, while the other regulates its application with all the necessary details. For example, the Soviet Constitution does not formulate the right to liberty of movement and the freedom to choose one's residence. Nevertheless, the Fundamentals of Civil Legislation, leaving out the liberty of movement as a general freedom, recognize in article 9 the right to select one's place of residence. Since there are no restrictions to that right in terms of space, this provision assumes the possibility of residing either in the USSR or abroad. The problem, however, is how to apply so important a right. The necessary solution must be found not in civil law but in administrative law. The Statute on the Passport System[47] determines the choice of residence in the USSR. According to it, the passport shall contain diverse information including information about "the residence permit",[48] and that "persons, who have been refused residence registration at a population center upon their arrival shall be obliged to leave this population center within seven days".[49] The possible grounds for refusal are not enumerated by the Statute itself: they belong to the realm of secret instructions. The Statute on Entry into the USSR and on Exit from the USSR[50] determines the choice of residence abroad. According to it, Soviet citizens who are not diplomats or other officials, when going abroad on private business or because they have permanent residence there, shall receive "general citizens' passports".[51] Neither the grounds for possible refusal to issue these passports nor the way of appealing against unjustified refusals are mentioned by the Statute, although one and the other practice exist in the USSR. The Statute also does not mention cases of emigration, although it takes place in varying degrees at one moment or another. In the sphere of inter-state movement secret regulations became still more important than in the case of choice of residence within the state.

The establishment of new political duties in addition to constitutional duties[52] can be carried out by any branch of Soviet law, including criminal law. Soviet criminal codes provide for responsibility in case of failure to report crimes against the state which are known to be in preparation or to have been committed, if these crimes are treason, espionage, terrorism, sabotage, wrecking, organizational activity directed at the commission of especially dangerous crimes against the state or participation in an anti-Soviet organization, etc.[53] All the enumerated crimes have political connotations.[54] Thus, responsibility for failure to report such crimes stems from the violation of the political duty to make the required report. No Soviet law, except the criminal law, contains any hint of such a duty. Hence, this duty is provided directly by criminal law. And the majority of political cases heard by Soviet courts concern, side by side with the main accused, those who have failed to report the crimes committed or prepared. For Soviet standards, the punishment provided for the latter crime is not very severe: three years of labor camp at the worst.[55] But from the human point of view, this is sufficiently ferocious to keep people in political fear and, as a result, in political obedience. In this regard political duties differ immensely from legal duties of other kinds. They not only bind its addressees, but at the same time oppress them. The addressees become compulsorily tied to the existing regime as its subordinates and as its watchmen and spies.

Such is the situation when one considers political freedom in the light of Soviet law. Then what kind of political freedom can exist for the people of the USSR in real life?

Political Freedom in Soviet Practice

Just as political freedom in Soviet law, political freedom in Soviet practice can be studied in a threefold manner, represented by the structure of political power, the constitutional rights, and by the ordinary rights of citizens, insofar as these rights have a political content or at least a political coloring.

1. The structure of political power. Within the limits of Soviet law all power in the country belongs to the people, who, however, in principle exercise it indirectly, through soviets of people's deputies generally elected.[56] In Soviet practice this legal declaration is disproved in at least two ways. On the one hand, the soviets of people's deputies do not represent the people of the USSR, because, owing to the extraordinary specificity of the electoral system, deputies are appointed from the top and not elected from the bottom.[57] Thus, even indirectly, political power has nothing to do with the Soviet people. On the other hand, real power in the country belongs to the Communist Party summit. Formally this summit shall be elected by the members of the Communist Party, and they encompass not more than one-fourteenth of the Soviet people. Actually not even this number of Soviet citizens take part in the exercise of political power directly or indirectly, because elections to the Communist Party's agencies are no less fictitious than elections of soviets' deputies, predetermined as they are by appointments.[58] Thus, Soviet political power is separated from the Soviet people, and the very organization of the governing activity in the USSR precludes any use by citizens of their constitutional right "to participate in the administration of state and social affairs".[59]

First, a great number of political decisions are unknown to the people, and this makes their participation in governing the country simply impossible. For the whole world, the great Soviet economic expenditures aimed at supporting Cuba's daily existence has stopped being a secret for a long time; but the Soviet people can only suspect this generally known fact. The budget of the USSR does not include such an item of expenditure as economic or military help to foreign states. From this point of view, such expenditure shall be secret, since it is illegal. On the other hand, it would not be safe, considering the present economic difficulties of the country, to allow the standard of living of the people to deteriorate further for the sake of a foreign state and to proclaim this truth openly *urbi et orbi*. Therefore, in all such cases the administration of state affairs cannot but be executed without the people and unbeknownst to them.

Second, governmental decisions which are not secret can be brought to the people's notice,[60] but the people have no role to play in connection with the issuance of such decisions, even if their most important interests are involved. The freezing of payment on state loans in 1957, the repeated rises in prices of foods and other goods beginning early in the 1960s, the doubling of the price of gasoline in 1973, the annual decrees of the Soviet government concerning the participation of the urban population in the harvesting campaign with a partial loss of salary, increasing the responsibility for violations of labor discipline in 1983 – all these and numerous other governmental measures are announced to the people without any discussion, not infrequently like a shot out of the blue (such as price rises), sometimes after warning speeches by Soviet leaders (such as increased enforcement of labor discipline), and only very seldom in the form of regular acts (such as the annual organization of harvesting campaigns).

Third, everyday governmental activity is not subject even to *pro forma* control by the people and does not require token popular participation. Exceptions are made only for certain kinds of administrative activities of local governmental agencies. For example, local executive committees distribute dwelling premises among citizens with the participation of public commissions for housing.[61] As often as not, dwelling houses which have been built by order of local executive committees are checked – after their construction has been completed – not only by governmental officials, but also by the *ad hoc* public commission. One can find some other cases of a similar character. But they do not change the general situation, if one bears in mind the level of administration involved and if one takes into account the fact that they are consultative rather than decision-making bodies. It is true that Soviet citizens have the constitutional right "to submit proposals to state agencies... concerning the improvement of the latter's activity and to criticize shortcomings in work",[62] and already in 1968 the procedure for considering proposals, applications, and appeals of citizens was established. Nevertheless, up till now not one case has been heard where a citizen's proposal has led to positive governmental decisions, while cases of criminal or administrative prosecution for criticism of shortcomings in work have occurred in great number.[63]

Fourth, the Soviet authorities do not feel themselves obliged to substantially inform the people about the most important political events, to say nothing of everyday administrative activity. The denunciation of Stalin by the Twentieth Congress of the CPSU actually dealt with the crimes he committed against the Soviet state and the Soviet people in times of peace and war. However, Khrushchev's report, which referred to concrete facts and contained straightforward appraisals, was read only to Communist Party members at closed Party meetings. The rest of the Soviet population had to be content with the insipid and diffuse decision about the cult of the personality and its aftermath. The ousting of Khrushchev and the replacement of his personal power by the triumvirate of Brezhnev-Kosygin-Podgornyi in 1964 took place at closed meetings of the Politbureau and of the Communist Party's Central Committee (the so-called October Plenum). Khrushchev's resignation was publicly announced to be of his own will. Different hints about his voluntarism and other mistakes appeared in the Soviet media now and again. In all necessary and unnecessary instances the importance of the "October Plenum" was pointed out. Only one "trifle" was kept secret from everybody – non-Party as well as Party members: what really happened at the "October Plenum"? In 1982 Brezhnev died, and the position of General Secretary of the Communist Party, the actual head of the Soviet state, had to be filled first of all. This question, which represents the highest public interest, was settled in a closed meeting of the Politbureau, and its decision was rubber-stamped by a closed meeting of the Communist Party's Central Committee. The same procedure was applied after Andropov's death and Chernenko's appointment.

Fifth, the Soviet leadership has established and steadily put into practice the principle of the strongest actual separation of those who represent the ruling bureaucracy from those who belong to the ordinary people. With the exception of official receptions of citizens by governmental agencies within publicly appointed time limits, an ordinary man and a high-ranking bureaucrat will never meet. They use different department stores, different hospitals, different drugstores, different places of rest, different cinemas and libraries, different means of transportation, etc. This separation has diverse goals: to conceal the unimaginable luxury of a bureaucrat's life; to protect obedient bureaucrats, who strive to preserve their positions by hook or by crook, against the pernicious influence of disobedient people, who have no reason to value their position; to educate the ruling stratum in a special caste spirit, opposing it to the people and thus stimulating it to keep the people in check. As a result of such education, the ruling bureaucracy became accustomed – as aptly expressed by

Solzhenitsyn – to love the people and to hate the population. Contemporary Soviet folklore also has not overlooked this phenomenon. An old revolutionary song has the words: *"Vyshli my vse iz naroda, deti sem'i trudovoi"* ("We all came from the people, children of a working family"). Altered in our time, it now says: *"Vyshli my vse iz naroda. Kak nam vernut'sia v nego?"* ("We all came from the people. How can we return to them?").

Perhaps the real organization of the USSR's political power in contrast to what Soviet laws tell us about it, is more exactly reflected in the laconic words of contemporary folklore than in the broad statements of analytical research.

2. Citizen's constitutional rights. As the Soviet experience proves, it is very easy to proclaim the most democratic rights and freedoms in the Constitution: a certain combination of constitutional texts with the existing political regime reduces these rights and freedoms to nothing without serious difficulties.

The general demand to use rights and freedoms in a way, which does not harm the interests of society and the state, provides the constitutional basis for such a maneuver, and what is harmful or harmless in the USSR depends exclusively on interpretations given by the Soviet political regime. As a constitutional rule the freedom of demonstration exists in that country, but the demonstration on the anniversary of the October revolution corresponds to the interests of the state, while the demonstration of Gorbanevskaia, Litvinov, Delone and several other people under the slogan "Hands off Czechoslovakia" on Red Square in Moscow in 1968 contradicted these interests. Therefore the former rests upon the KGB's protection in contrast to the latter which was subject to KGB repression. The formally legal right to demonstrate exercised by Gorbanevskaia and her political associates provoked formally illegal actions on the part of the KGB: assault and battery of the demonstrators with shouts of: "They are all Yids (*zhidi*)! Beat them!" Nevertheless, the demonstrators were arrested and prosecuted, but the conduct of the KGB officers was irreproachable and (who knows) may be even rewarded. However, for those who take this outrageous arbitrariness seriously there is only one consolatory fact. In answer to the procurator's demand to deprive Delone of his freedom for a period of five years, the latter said: "I can stay in prison for five years in exchange for the five minutes of freedom that I have enjoyed on Red Square". Does anybody remember an expression of analogous feelings by people compelled to take part in the annual October demonstrations? Similarly to the freedom of demonstration, the Soviet Constitution recognizes the freedom of association. However, the All-Union Peace Council flourishes and prospers, but a small Moscow group of peace activists, before having the opportunity to campaign, was subjected to cruel reprisal and compulsory dissolution. Why, if the USSR is really interested in peace, does it then make a difference who supports its peaceful activity – an official society or an unofficial circle? It does indeed – for reasons which must not be lost sight of. The All-Union Peace Council as a participant of the world movement – organized and financed by the USSR itself – represents, using Bukovskii's expression, pacifism in its fight against peace by undermining Western efforts to remain in military balance with the Soviet Union and by facilitating Soviet aspirations to military superiority over Western countries. The

Moscow group, on the contrary, represents pacifism in its fight against militarism, whether it is of Western or Soviet origin. That is why one association meets official support and the other illegal repression. The same fate has befallen the freedom of meetings. Probably, no country in the world has so many meetings as does the USSR. In most cases those meetings seem interesting neither to their participants nor to their organizers. Now and again the Soviet rulers themselves initiate active campaigns against the excessive frequency of various meetings with compulsory attendance. However, after a short time everything begins anew. Unbearable boredom! But nobody may leave: the freedom of meeting! However, with the free meetings in Moscow by the Pushkin monument on Constitution Day or in Brailovskii's apartment for the sake of scientific discussion things have been different. The Pushkin Square meetings were dispersed by the police, on account of their political context: they demanded the strictest observance of citizens' rights provided by the Soviet Constitution. As for Brailovskii, he organized research discussions with Moscow scholars who, being refuseniks,[64] had lost their professional academic positions, and therefore the authorities arrested and then convicted him. Is this just? Of course it is: if you are deprived of the freedom of movement, do not dare to appeal to the freedom of meetings.

The Soviet experience also demonstrates that in the fight against the real use of nominal rights economic measures can be more dependable than political restrictions, and the freedom of the press as opposed to the freedom of religion proves this better than anything else.

Churches, synagogues and other religious establishments, in as far as their existence is admitted in a limited number, are owners of premises and equipment necessary for their religious activity. As a matter of course, they function to worship God, not the Soviet regime, and, if sometimes a service or sermon begins by blessing the Communist Party or the Bolshevik Government, this reflects a concession to political pressures or the observance of a silently established *modus vivendi*. Within the limits of voluntary goals, and not imposed tasks, they are entirely free and rely upon their own, and not upon granted, economic means. With the freedom of the press it is essentially different. Magazines and newspapers, publishing offices and printing shops, bookstores and news stalls are under state ownership, directly or indirectly.[65] Outside this legal sphere citizens can resort to *samizdat* (self-publication), restricted by the use of handwriting or typewriting and threatened by criminal or, at best, by administrative responsibility. Legally the actual implementation of this right depends on the good will of the state. Thus, economic guarantees not only do not ensure political freedoms; they transform the latter into political slavery. Reasonably speaking, the Soviet regime could do without censorship: publishers themselves will not admit any politically doubtful publication. If censorship nevertheless exists in the USSR, this is probably the result of force of habit or of exaggerated vigilance and is not primarily for the sake of checking authors but of control of publishers. Sometimes even exaggerated vigilance is not free from oversight. Thus publications like Dudintsev's book *"Ne Khlebom edinym"* ("Not by Bread Alone") appear, then their official repudiation follows, the publications are withdrawn, and the authors disappear at least spiritually, if not physically. Sometimes, "dangerous" works appear owing to a happy coincidence. Khrushchev never read books himself. Like other poorly educated people, he preferred to listen to reading aloud on the radio or by his secretary while going to bed or falling asleep. This helped to acquaint him with the manuscript of Solzhenitsyn's book "*Odin den' Ivana Denisovicha*" ("One Day in the Life of Ivan Denisovich"), which he enjoyed and his positive attitude ensured its publication. Soon after Khrushchev's ouster, the book disappeared from Soviet libraries, and the fate of the author himself is no secret to the whole world. Sometimes the powers themselves patronize the publication of books which are in practical terms necessary for them, but politically very non-prestigious for the USSR. In such cases an appropriate publication is first distributed in millions of copies, and later, when the action performed has done its bit, the authorities demonstrate, by means of mild official criticism, their non-participation in the whole affair, thus putting the lid on it. This was the case with Shevtsov who in the 1960s managed to publish two books of an openly anti-semitic character which were a match for the Hitlerite book "The Myth of the Nineteenth Century" by Rosenberg. The same method was repeated with a professional falsifier of Russian history, Pikul, whose numerous books, including "*U Poslednei Cherti*" ("At the Very Verge"), were selling like hot cakes. But there was nothing to do but to turn away from him, when his last book put in a bad light the *sanctum sanctorum* – the Russian revolution – by declaring that the Jews had created Rasputin and by hints that the latter's activity was the real cause of the revolutionary events. Relying upon means of this kind, the Soviet regime compels one section of the population to play dumb in the exercise of their constitutional rights and manages to make another section talk as the regime considers this necessary.

Lastly, the Soviet experience is almost unique in its astonishing capacity to provoke political activity, which is considered positive with the aid of approaches, which reveal themselves as negative. In the realm of political freedoms, especially those connected with oral or written activity, this result becomes attainable owing to the unwritten, unpublished but thrice repeated "no": (1) not to go too far; (2) not to generalize; (3) not to deny perspectives.

"Not to go too far" means not to go beyond a low level of Soviet bureaucracy in the criticism of Soviet shortcomings: local executive committees, officials of district Party agencies, ministers of union republics at the most but on no account higher. As far as one can remember, in the entire Soviet history, beginning with the establishment and strengthening of Stalin's dictatorship, four people who did not belong to the ruling summit, were brave enough to criticize the head of the state or the system itself: Maiakovskii, Pilniak, Mandelshtam, and Meierkhold.[66] Maiakovskii committed suicide in 1930 before Stalin's purges attained their greatest peak. Pilniak, Mandelshtam and Meierkhold were executed in Stalin's torture chambers. Turning to Soviet newspapers of our time, it is impossible to find any trace of criticism directed against comparatively high officials, such as secretaries of Party agencies in the provinces and ministers of the USSR. As scapegoats of the ostensible freedom of mass criticism officials of far less important rank appear on the pages of newspapers. For years and decades Soviet people have been educated, by means of persuasion and coercion, in the spirit of the absolute immunity of more or less high authorities, and the result proved to be so successful, that Soviet rulers could not overcome it even when they considered this necessary. At the time of the 1965 economic reform, legislation devoted to it[67] tried – for the sake of improving state planning – to impose upon economic ministries the duty to compensate all damage suffered by subordinate enterprises in consequence of wrong or unreasonable ministerial orders. There were numerous obstacles against putting this idea into effect.[68] However, the habit of absolute obedience was the most important and the most difficult to overcome. How are psychological conditions to be created which could free managers of enterprises from the fear of suing their own ministries? This was the question that demanded a solution in the first place. Different kinds of solutions were suggested by Soviet scholars, economists and jurists, but none of them appeared practicable or acceptable. Thus, all the efforts undertaken failed, and there was no other way out but to completely reject such an attractive idea. Unfortunately for its authors, after a few years there was nothing left – not only of this idea – but of the whole economic reform of 1965.

"Not to generalize" means not to go from a negative truth in particular to a negative conclusion in general. The real meaning of this demand can be elucidated by the following episode. Once, when the secretary of Leningrad's provincial Party Committee took part in a closed party meeting at Leningrad University, he was asked by one of the university professors: "Why is there prostitution in our city?" The answer sounded very eloquent: "There is no prostitution in the USSR. There are only individual prostitutes". This dialogue, akin to an anecdote, expresses the principle attitude of the Soviet regime: no society, not even Soviet society, can be immune from specific shortcomings; but a general trend of a negative character, habitual for capitalist countries, has always been foreign to the Soviet Union. For example, the very existence of drug abuse in the USSR is beyond any doubt. Otherwise it would be impossible to explain why criminal law provides for the criminal prosecution of corresponding conduct,[69] and the application of compulsory medical measures to drug addicts.[70] In addition, individual court cases of this type are well-known in large Soviet cities: Moscow, Leningrad, etc. Nevertheless, there are hardly any publications about drug abuse as such in the USSR. Even when, at a closed meeting of professors of the Law Faculty of Leningrad University in the late 1970s, a high-ranking official of the militia (the Soviet police) described the dangerous increase in the number of teenagers who used drugs, he avoided any generalization and only mentioned certain secret figures, referring to the provocative activities of Western tourists, who allegedly supplied Soviet youth with this poisonous stuff. He did not mention the mercenary activities of native pharmacists as well as of certain sections of the population in the south-east of the USSR. In order to intensify the fight against such extremely undesirable events as, for example bribery, the Soviet press will describe certain specific facts, denouncing not very highly placed officials – like the chairman of the executive committee of Sochi, who had been selling state apartments; and not making publicly known the lawlessness of high-level bureaucrats – such as the chairman of the Presidium of the Uzbek Supreme Soviet, who had been selling pardons to convicted criminals. However, when public information about individual cases seems capable of provoking or confirming political suspicions against the Soviet regime, then even such publicity becomes subject to the most severe taboo. This is why punitive psychiatry cannot be proved by reference to Soviet media, either in a general way, or even by reference to individual instances.

"Not to deny perspectives" means to appreciate any shortcoming of Soviet life as accidental (not regular!), temporary (not permanent!) and transient (not systematic!). Shortage of grain is an accidental result of climatic circumstances in the USSR, in contrast to capitalist countries where it is the result of barbarous exhaustion of natural resources. And not a single word has been said publicly about the purchases of grain from those very countries. The USSR suffers only temporary irregularities of food supply in contrast to capitalist countries where working people are doomed to permanent malnutrition. And to preempt the astonishment of those who have seen with their own eyes the daily life of working people in the West, a term of abuse "society of consumers" has been invented, as if it were possible to consume without producing. The necessity of military expenses is transient for the USSR and it will disappear together with capitalism, in contrast to capitalist countries where such expenses are systematic, being inseparable from the very nature of capitalism. As for military confrontations between socialist countries, they are explained either by the need to save socialism (as in Hungary) or by the absence of socialism during the periods of these confrontations (as in Cambodia). To understand what these rules entail in practice it will be interesting to compare the fate of two books: "One day in the life of Ivan Denisovich" by Solzhenitsyn and "That what has been suffered" (*Perezhitoe*) by D'iakov. Both books describe Stalin's labor camps. However, the former describes them truthfully without suggesting any encouraging aspect at all, while the latter confuses truth with falsehood, telling stories about the underground communist movement in the labor camps themselves and thus supporting the fantastic idea that everything will have a happy ending. As a result, the genius of Solzhenitsyn was doomed and subjected to official humiliation, and the mediocrity of D'iakov was officially declared to be an important achievement of socialist realism. Hence, the general state of constitutional rights of Soviet citizens is far from encouraging, and because of the structure of political power discussed above it cannot be otherwise with individual basic rights and freedoms.

3. Citizens' ordinary rights. The right to select a place of residence provided for by civil law, which has been presented as an ordinary, not a constitutional, right, albeit with political overtones, and established not by constitutional law, but by another branch of Soviet legislation,[71] can also be subjected to an analysis of non-constitutional rights in Soviet practice. Only one must not forget that selection of a place of residence is connected with two different spheres – movement within the state and across borders. Leaving aside a temporary change of residence, the first case can be called migration and the second case is generally known as emigration.

Migration meets general and special obstacles in Soviet practice. The general obstacle for the entire population, putting it in the grip of administrative demands, is elaborated on the model of the *circulus vitiosus:* to be registered for residence at a new place one must have a permanent job there, and to receive a permanent job at a new place of residence one must be registered there. The special obstacle deals with the rural population or, more exactly, with members of collective farms: they may not leave their rural residence without the appropriate permission issued by their collective farm. In former times, when members of collective farms did not have passports at all, illegal demands for personal permission had an undisguised practical significance. Now that the passport system has been extended to the countryside, certain peculiarities of passport numbers, known to the passport department of the MVD (the Russian acronym for the Ministry of Internal Affairs), serve as a signal to refuse an owner of such a passport registration for residence until permission from his collective farm is granted. In such a way the rural population becomes tied to agriculture, and the economic danger of mass migration to cities from villages has, to a great extent, been circumvented. To make the picture complete, it is also necessary to note the existence of special zones (military, frontier, those with certain kinds of industry, those with numerous labor camps, etc.) or so-called regime cities (Moscow, Leningrad, Kiev, etc.), where everybody, whether a town resident or villager, must satisfy numerous special demands to be registered temporarily or permanently.

This extremely rigid practice has, however, at least two limitations: official and unofficial. The official limitation relates to people who are ready to be enlisted for more or less extensive periods (three years, for example) as workers of construction or other enterprises, which have always suffered from the fluctuation in the size of the labor force. Enterprises of this kind receive a certain number of places for annual recruitment of new workers from anywhere (so-called *limit*), and these workers (so-called *limitchiki*), after the time of recruitment has expired, acquire the right of permanent residence in that place. In other words, at first you work for the time provided, and then you receive your permit of residence for an unlimited time. The unofficial limitation is due to numerous modes invented by Soviet citizens to evade this barrack like discipline. The fictitious marriage is the most common among them. It is usually effected by mutual agreement[72] and serves as an almost unconditional right of one of the would-be spouses to become a permanent resident at the place of residence of the other.[73] Later on, having exhausted all legal advantages of their marriage of convenience, the formal spouses obtain a formal divorce. Such a utilization of marriage in the USSR, determined by circumstances caused by an illegally established order, adds a comical note to a sad situation when one compares it to the solemn words of the preamble of the Family code: "Soviet legislation on marriage and on the family is called upon to actively promote the final clearing of family relations from material calculations... and to create a communist family in which the deepest personal feelings of people find their complete satisfaction".

Emigration, in contrast to migration, is considered as a politically undesirable or even hostile act. Therefore, its purely formal administration belongs to the MVD.[74] However, in reality, only the KGB has real power in this realm of governmental activity. The number of obstacles, blocking the road to emigration, are innumerable. To mention only the main ones, and not dealing with those that are secret, the following prerequisites of emigration must be pointed out. If emigration is allowed at all, the prospective emigrant must be Jewish or German, asking for permission to emigrate respectively to Israel or to Western Germany. Emigration to other countries or by members of other nationalities cannot occur at all or only as an extraordinary exception: even marriage with a foreigner does not always open the way abroad to

Soviet citizens. This practical attitude seems to be propagandistically advantageous to the Soviets, providing a pretext to say that only people alien to the USSR strive to emigrate and that the genuine Soviet nationalities do not even consider it. All other requirements play some kind of preventive function: they deter potential emigrants, by putting obstacles in their way which are insurmountable or so complicated that most of them dread the very thought of emigration. The applicant must have a formally executed written invitation from abroad. An invitation is valid, only if it has been sent by the closest relatives: children, parents, or the other spouse. In case of doubt, the applicant bears the burden of proving the necessary kinship, and it is up to the MVD to decide whether or not to believe him. Together with an invitation, an elaborate form must be accurately filled out and produced, to say nothing about documentary confirmation of numerous answers given by the applicant. The most sinister questions on the form touch upon the jobs of the applicant and his relatives, covering also the addresses and telephone numbers of staff departments. The management of the place where the applicant works receives the appropriate information immediately and, with very rare exceptions, dismisses the applicant at once. The same thing happens with the applicant's parents. All other relatives will also lose their jobs, but only if emigration is permitted and if their work is secret or comparatively important (professors at universities, research fellows, managers of enterprises, chief engineers, etc.). The applicant must receive written declarations from this relatives, that they will never emigrate, with an explanation of the grounds for such a decision (as if there is any need for this!). He is also obliged to bring his parents' written consent to his emigration; in case of their refusal emigration is not possible (as if the freedom of movement needs guardianship!).

Requests about emigration are considered secretly without any time limits. It usually takes several months and sometimes more than one year. For the applicant who has lost his job, this period is quite unbearable, because the uncertainty of his position precludes any opportunity of getting another permanent job. For the applicant's relatives the same period is equally taxing, because their future remains uncertain until the final decision is reached by the emigration authorities. The parents' fate is resolved directly after their son or daughter has sent the application. If the final decision is negative, the applicant must find a job within three months, under the threat of criminal prosecution.[75] Actually the same duty pertains to his father, if he is able to work but has been out of work as a result of dismissal from a former position. In the case of a positive decision, the parents' situation does not change while the situation of the closest relatives may further deteriorate, if they hold a more or less important job. For the applicant the way abroad is cleared. However, the latter statement needs two additional comments. On the one hand, Soviet practice knows cases when permission to emigrate once given have later been withdrawn, sometimes on the eve of departure or, still worse, just before take-off. One can imagine the situation of such a frustrated emigrant, who has already lost everything – property, apartment, etc. – and who is forced to start everything from the beginning. On the other hand, when permission remains in force, the gates abroad are still far away from the emigrant. Within a very short period of time he must fulfill numerous formalities, meeting artificial obstacles and ill treatment almost everywhere. His property must be reduced to a small volume and limited to the things allowed to be taken abroad. He needs an amount of money large enough to make official and – in principle legalized – under the table payments. Only after all these procedures are fulfilled does the emigrant, robbed and exhausted, leave his motherland for foreign soil.

Thus, while a general examination of Soviet law seems to produce a model of political freedom, this impression grows weaker after a more attentive analysis, and Soviet practice, taken broadly and in sufficient detail, destroys the original image and reveals the miserable truth.

2. Political Domination

While political freedom has brought to life numerous rules of Soviet law, political domination is poorly reflected in the same legal system. However, in providing a legal distortion of reality neither yields to the other. Therefore, in this case, the study of practice is no less important than before. At the same time, the appropriate legal texts also must not be disregarded. Strive as he might, the Soviet legislature lets out its secrets now and again. Political domination presents no exception in this regard. This is why, before turning to its application, one needs some knowledge of its regulation.

Political Domination in Soviet Law

As a matter of course, not a single Soviet law touching upon political domination connects it with a single person or with a limited ruling group. They have always talked about the broad masses of the population, although the quantitative and qualitative outlines of these masses are subject to important modifications.

The 1936 Constitution, having proclaimed soviets of working people's deputies to be the political foundation of the USSR, pointed out that they "grew" in consequence of "the victory of the dictatorship of the proletariat".[76] What does this dictatorship mean? According to Lenin, it means that "only the proletariat may dominate",[77] and proletarian domination is no other than the power that rests upon force, not upon the law.[78] It results from the words cited and the reflections presented before, to the effect that as a dictator the proletariat has unlimited power and may use it, being responsive or responsible to no one. Meanwhile, the Bolsheviks have always repeated that the October revolution replaced the domination of the minority over the majority by the domination of the majority over the minority, although at the time when the 1936 Constitution was adopted, the Soviet proletariat was inferior in number to the Soviet peasantry. How can these contradictions be reconciled? Two explanations appeared almost simultaneously. One of them actually explained nothing, since it gave unlimited power exclusively to the proletariat, with only the limitation that this power should be applied in different ways toward poor peasants, middle peasants, capitalists, etc.[79] The other attempted to combine the incompatible but its propagandistic success was so unexpectedly great, that the 1936 Constitution did not fail to take advantage of it. As if not subject to any doubt, the neighboring constitutional rules connect political dictatorship with the proletariat and full political power with the working people of the city and country.[80] But political dictatorship interpreted as unlimited domination cannot be understood otherwise than as full political power. By what kind of logic does it belong to one body under the first name and to another body under the second name? If "only the proletariat may dominate", *i.e.* if all political power is concentrated in the proletariat, is it then possible for other working people to be involved in the same power, *i.e.* to share with the proletariat its political domination? Juggling the words does not settle the problem, and the problem is not about the existence of political domination in the USSR, recognized by the Soviet Constitution, but about its personification, which the same Constitution tries to conceal from the reader by either fair or foul means. Nevertheless, one thing is sufficiently clear. Since the dictatorial proletariat humbly agrees to share all political power with other working people, and since the whole working people, endowed with full political power, submissively assents to recognize in the proletariat the political dictator, real political domination belongs neither to the proletariat nor to the working people, but to someone else.

Long before the October Revolution, when Lenin initiated the creation of the Communist Party in Tsarist Russia, he contended in his work *Chto Delat'?* ("What is to be Done?") that the proletariat was not capable of elaborating its own ideology as a necessary prerequisite to the proletarian revolution, that this ideology had to be elaborated by a comparatively small group of highly educated people – "ideologists", and that they should "introduce" their intellectual achievement "into" the proletarian masses.[81] Thus, Lenin proclaimed openly, without disguise, that ideology, proletarian in its content, belongs in its origin to those declared proletarian leaders. Meanwhile, by dividing all social phenomena into two groups – "economic basis" and "political superstructure" – Marxism-Leninism typifies the former as a material basis and the latter as an ideological ingredient of human society. Therefore, it must be clear, according to the same doctrine, that political power as an element of the "superstructure" represents ideological, not material, substance. And since the proletariat is not capable of elaborating its own ideology, it shall also be deprived of the capacity to exercise its own power. On behalf of the proletariat this power is wielded by proletarian leaders, and in the interests of the proletariat its ideology is elaborated by proletarian ideologists.

Hence, as soon as the appropriate rules of Soviet law have been collated with the corresponding postulates of Marxist doctrine, the contradiction between "proletarian dictatorship" and "full power of the working people" stops being an enigma. Proletarian dictatorship in the genuine meaning of the word is the dictatorship of proletarian leaders, and, using Lenin's expression, only they may dominate, irrespective of whether this title rests upon right or arbitrariness. All other people do not possess any power, whether it be absolute or restricted, concentrated within one class or shared by two classes. However, the proletarian leaders ascribe their dictatorship to the proletarian class maintaining that they express the interests of the proletariat better than the proletariat itself, the latter being incapable of realizing its social situation without the help of "ideologists". On the other hand, the Marxist conception accentuates the coincidence of interests of the proletariat and other working people insofar as the latter are toilers and the divergence of their interests as far as the latter are proprietors. As toilers they are considered allies of the proletariat and possessors of all power in the country together with the proletarian masses. As proprietors they have their own ways which are different from those typical to the proletariat, and therefore they cannot share the political dictatorship with the same masses. This is why, side by side with the real dictatorship in the grasp of the self-styled proletarian leaders, the nominal dictatorship can be connected with the class of proletarians and nominal power can be placed in the possession of the urban and rural working people. In such a way, declarations of the 1936 Constitution, which appear incomprehensible at a first glance, become simple and understandable as a result of a more attentive examination.

The 1977 Constitution verbally changed the former constitutional principles. As its preamble says, the October revolution "established the dictatorship of the proletariat", but now, when the proletarian dictatorship has fulfilled its tasks, "the Soviet state has become an all-people's state". Therefore, the constitutional rules do not mention the dictatorship of the proletariat, and instead of the full power of the working people of the city and country defined by the old Constitution,[82] the new Constitution speaks about the full power of the people.[83] However, nothing has been essentially changed, either in reality, or, to any extent, even in words. Having proclaimed the establishment of the all-people's state in the USSR, the same preamble does not forget to point out, that "the leading role of the Communist Party has grown", and that "the working class", i.e. the proletariat, continues to be "the leading force" of Soviet society. If the dictatorship of the proletariat means that only the proletariat may dominate, then only the entire people may dominate as soon as they have become the dictators; but if the people are ruled by the working class and by the Communist Party, then they have not become the dictators and they do not dominate. On the contrary, since ruling assumes subordination, the people shall be subordinated to the working class as a leading force of Soviet society, and the growth of the leading role of the Communist Party shall entail, as its reverse side, the growth of the subordination of the entire society, including the working class. It would also not be out of place to keep in mind that, in explaining the necessity of the Communist Party, Lenin referred to the incapability of the proletariat to create its own ideology and to realize its own interests. Proceeding from such a premise, the growth of the leading role of the Communist Party cannot be explained in any other way than by reference to the fact, that in our time the creation of ideology and the understanding of social interests have been transformed into a process even more complicated and even less available to the working people without the aid of professional ideologists and professional rulers. In its turn, this explanation leads to only one conclusion: those who have been ruling on behalf of the working class shall continue to rule with even better reason on behalf of the Soviet people. Thus, nominal sovereigns are changed by the transition from one Constitution to the other; actual rulers remain unchanged despite all the constitutional modifications.

Nevertheless, terminological replacement of "proletarian dictatorship" by "the all-people's state" must not be interpreted as a legislative enactment of a purely propagandistic character. This was predetermined by very important practical demands. The exorbitant growth of the Soviet bureaucracy deprived the proletariat of its former majority in different establishments, and notwithstanding numerous artificial measures things continue to develop in the same direction. Already for a long time enrollment in the Communist Party has been regulated by the centralized distribution of future Party membership in favor of workers and in prejudice of other strata. However, the quota allocated to workers has never been used entirely by them. They are not interested in Party membership, because an official career seems unattainable for ordinary toilers, and without this aim everything else is seen as a waste of time and money. Positions of deputies of supreme and local soviets are also allocated, but in this case other factors become insurmountable. Numerous Party and government officials shall be deputies of soviets without fail, and after this matter has been settled, the remaining number of deputies' positions are not sufficient to ensure the absolute majority of the working class. Moreover, the number of workers could not be increased even among students of Soviet universities, despite all the illegal privileges introduced for them: admittance without entrance examinations of those who have studied at special courses; preference in comparison with other applicants with equal results of the entrance examinations, etc. And there is no reason to be astonished. The salary of ordinary engineers does not attain the level of wages of skilled workers. Then why enter the university? Is it not better to improve one's working profession? All these phenomena cannot be explained, if the country is considered to be a state of proletarian dictatorship. In "the all-people's state" the situation is different. It does not matter, what kinds of Soviet strata are represented in one or another Soviet establishment. Since the Soviet state is personified by the Soviet people, this state preserves its social quality, whoever would occupy the majority in one or another Soviet establishment: workers, peasants, intellectuals or the highest, middle or lowest layers of the bureaucracy.

"The all-people's state" and the proletarian dictatorship with "all power" possessed by "the working people of the city and country", in spite of their wordy distinctions, enable the Soviet regime to suppress the individual with equal efficiency under the indisputable postulate of the supremacy of general interests over personal interests. And as long as Soviet law proclaims this supremacy, it aids suppression and, consequently, supports domination. For example, the Fundamentals of Civil Legislation, enumerating in the preamble the main tasks of Soviet civil law, relate to them "the protection of material and cultural interests of citizens and the proper combining of these interests with the interests of all of society". It is correct that the text cited does not use the word "supremacy" openly in connection with "the interests of all of society", but the euphemistic "proper combining" has the same meaning as straightforward "supremacy". At any rate, concrete regulations of civil law in the USSR prove this beyond any shadow of a doubt.

"If a citizen", states the Civil Code, "fails to take care of any property belonging to him and having an important historic, artistic or other value for the community, the state organizations whose functions include the protection of property of that kind must warn the owner to discontinue such neglect. If such owner fails to satisfy this demand, then, at the suit of the appropriate organization, the court may order the forfeiture of such property, which will pass into state ownership. The citizen will receive compensation for such forfeited property in the amount fixed by agreement, or, if there is no agreement, by the court. In cases of extreme urgency, the suit for forfeiture may be started without previous warning."[84] Neither fault nor other circumstances are taken into account: the fact that the property to be withdrawn is valuable to the community is sufficient. But what if the owner does not have the necessary material resources for the normal maintenance of his valuables? Cannot the Soviet state, instead of withdrawing them, help him financially or in another way, for the sake of community interests? Such an idea did not occur in the Soviet legislature: valuable property is to be preserved as necessary for Soviet society, or is to be handed over, against some remuneration to the individual involved, to the Soviet state, and then the interests of the entire community will be protected. Most cases of this kind relate to private collections of paintings, to valuable archives left by famous writers, scholars, etc., and possessed by their heirs, or to other similar situations. The strained housing circumstances in the USSR serve not infrequently as a pretext to sue against owners of such valuables, if they do not have room enough to ensure appropriate preservation of socially important property. However, to avoid judicial scandals the competent powers try to force the owner into a compromise: in exchange for improvement of housing conditions he will sometimes agree to give a part of his valuables to the state or to make a will in favor of the state. Thus, by hook or by crook the regime has always attained what it wished to attain.

The Soviet law on copyright proclaims that an author has the right "to publish, reproduce, and disseminate his work by all means permitted by law".[85] At the same time, "copyright in a publication, public performance, or other use of a work may be compulsorily purchased by the state from an author or his heirs in the procedure established by union republic legislation".[86] In the article cited, "supremacy" of social interests is not even hinted at. The reference to the republican procedure, which has never been established, obviates the necessity of other explanations. Application of the rule itself can take place in Soviet practice as an extraordinary exception, although this does not make its introduction into Soviet law completely senseless. It acts as a deterrent and stimulates "voluntary" agreements to avoid compulsory pressure. Moreover, if such a rule were to be formally abolished, this would not inevitably entail a fundamental change in the official attitude. Instances of this kind have occurred more than once in Soviet legislative practice. For example, before 1973, when the USSR ratified the Universal Copyright Convention, the author's heirs had had the right to royalties within the limits of 50% and for scientific works within the limits of 25% of the amount of money which would have been received by the author himself. On 1 March 1974, in conformity with the Convention, this rule was abolished as far as the Civil Codes were concerned.[87] Simultaneously, taxes imposed upon royalties due to the author's heirs were increased precisely to the level where not more than 50% or respectively 25% was left to them. In other words, the law of copyright was changed, but the real situation remained unaltered.

Incomparably more restrictive than the law of copyright is the law of invention. Generally speaking, the author of an invention may receive either a patent or a certificate. In the first case, no one may use the invention without the permission of the patentee.[88] In the second case, the right to use the invention belongs to the state, and the inventor has the right to remuneration depending on the economies or other positive effects derived as a result of introducing the invention.[89] With some exceptions provided for by special legislation, when only a certificate and not a patent is issued, the author may at his discretion demand either one or the other document.[90] Actually, however, Soviet citizens have almost never selected a patent, preferring to ask for a certificate. Such a choice is predetermined by the economic peculiarities of the USSR. In a country where the economy belongs almost exclusively to the state, the private sale of patents or the issue of licenses is a back-breaking job. Together with economic causes other inducements play an equally important role. The "supremacy" of interests of Soviet society favors the certificate, rather than the patent, which was introduced only to attract foreign inventors and to observe international legal requirements. If a Soviet citizen were to ask for a patent, he would suffer official contempt as a violator of the "proper combining" of his own interests with the interests of all of society. The aftermath of such contempt cannot be predicted beforehand. But Article 112 of the Fundamentals of Civil Legislation sounds a warning signal: "In those instances when an invention has especially important significance to the state but agreement is not reached with the patentee for an assignment of the patent or the issuance of a license, by decision of the USSR Council of Ministers the patent may be compulsorily purchased by the state or permission to use the invention may be given to the appropriate organizations, establishing remuneration for the patentee".

In the case of criminal law the matter is no better than that of civil law. In Russia, the authorities have always dreaded the free word, written or oral, spoken aloud or in a whisper, publicly or secretly, to many people or to one person. It is not for nothing that Russia belongs to those countries which have had censorship from times immemorial. Hardly any other sovereign would have behaved as did the Russian Tsar who proclaimed himself a personal censor of Pushkin's poetry. Meanwhile, this exaggerated severity resembles mere child's play in comparison with the post-revolutionary era. To say nothing of the annihilation of the multi-party system with only the preservation of the Communist Party or of the closing of publishing houses except for official establishments, oral activity has become a subject of censorship to no less a degree than printed or xeroxed works, by means of preliminary approval of public speeches or systematic control of school or university teaching and numerous other similar measures. Nevertheless, in the realm of intellectual self-expression one cannot keep everything everywhere under control. Therefore, side by side with censorship, the Soviet regime needs criminal deterrents. These are provided by article 70 of the Criminal Code which says: "Agitation or propaganda carried on for the purpose of subverting or weakening the Soviet power or of committing particular especially dangerous crimes against the state and social system, or the circulation or preparation or keeping, for the same purpose, of literature of such content, shall be punished by deprivation of freedom for a term of six months to seven years, with or without additional exile for a term of two to five years, or by exile for a term of two to five years." As has been seen, numerous actions, including even political jokes or insignificant criticism, as well as numerous cases such as possession of prohibited literature or uncensored tapes, can lead to very severe punishment, which even the Tsarist regime would not have dreamt of. How can one explain such an unexpected and extremely sharp turn from the comparatively mild and predominantly administrative measures of "bloody tsarism" to the obviously hard and exclusively criminal suppression by "the most democratic state in the world", when the question is about the expression of undesirable thoughts or the use of objectionable literature? The explanation is at hand: what was unpardonable for the Tsarist regime as a servant of the dominant minority should be just and reasonable for Soviet power, which represents the rule either of the majority or of the entire people. Unfortunately for the authors of this interpretation one thing has almost let them down.

The Criminal Code, speaking of anti-Soviet agitation and propaganda, requires intent and not simply intentional conduct, but intent specifically directed toward "the purpose of subverting or weakening Soviet power". However, when in the 1960s two writers – Siniavskii and Daniel – were accused under article 70 of the Criminal Code, they did not deny the very fact that their books (published abroad) had contained satiric criticism of negative features of Soviet reality, but rather they pointed out that criticism of shortcomings should help to overcome them and thus would not weaken, but strengthen the Soviet system. As a matter of course, these irresistible arguments had no influence upon the writers' fate: Siniavskii was sentenced to seven years of prison, and Daniel lost his freedom for five years. However, Soviet criminal legislation could not remain indifferent toward so obvious a vulnerability of some of its rules. As a result, article 70 was supplemented by article 190-1 of the Criminal Code: "The systematic circulation in an oral form of fabrications known to be false which defame the Soviet state and social system and, likewise, the preparation or circulation in written, printed or any other form of works of such content shall be punished by deprivation of freedom for a term not exceeding three years, or by correctional tasks for a term not exceeding one year, or by a fine not exceeding 100 rubles." The punishment provided for by article 190-1 is less severe than the sanction embodied in article 70, but to apply the former there is no need to prove what the latter requires: the purpose of subverting or weakening Soviet power. A loss in one direction leads to a gain in the other. As for the general question as to why such conduct should be declared a crime, can be answered without any difficulty: the importance of the all-people's interest justifies any kind of legal protection.

Thus, when Soviet law proclaims the political domination of the majority or of the entire people, this legal fiction does not remain without effect. On the contrary, it leads to very significant practical consequences. At the same time, these consequences, with all their significance, cannot replace the necessity of actual domination to be parallel to ficticious domination. One must only not forget that while ficticious domination resides mainly in the formulae of law, actual domination reveals itself first of all in real life.

Political Domination in Soviet Practice

Although Soviet law talks about the dictatorship of the people, nobody doubts that behind this proclaimed dictatorship there is an exclusive group of rulers who virtually possess and exercise unlimited political power in the country. Only the outlines of such a group differ depending on whether one uses one Western concept or another. The concept which focuses on the summit of three forces – the Party, the Army, and the KGB – seems the most interesting and, at first glance, the most realistic.[91] However, a more careful analysis from a different point of view reveals its defects. In Soviet history, the summit of the Army or the KGB has never attained a predominant position in the ruling top. In his fight for the supreme leadership, Andropov first had to leave his position as KGB chief and become one of the secretaries of the CPSU Central Committee. Only then did his appointment as General Secretary and Chairman of the Presidium of the USSR Supreme Soviet take place. Beria's attempted coup after Stalin's death failed even though as head of the KGB he appeared to have had a better opportunity for such a maneuver than anyone else. In order to become a personal dictator Beria needed a promotion to the level of the Communist Party's leader, not a demotion to the position of KGB chief. Marshal Zhukov lost his position as the head of the Soviet Army during Khrushchev's time, having been suspected of Bonapartist plans. It is difficult to say, whether these suspicions were correct. A person like Zhukov who had managed to suppress Beria's coup was probably able to execute his own coup, and if he really had had such intentions, this should prove that the summit of the Army could not control the Party's summit. To reach the very top the former should seize the latter's advantages and not the other way around. This is why there has never been a coup within the sphere of the Army or the KGB, while the Communist Party summit has known several events of this kind: the annihilation of the so-called Lenin's guard by Stalin in the 1920-1930s; the dismissal of the most devoted Stalinists by Khrushchev in 1957; the ouster of Khrushchev by a majority of the Politbureau in 1964; and the replacement of the Brezhnev-Kosygin-Podgornyi triumvirate by Brezhnev's personal leadership, prepared little by little and confirmed finally by the ouster of Podgornyi and the resignation of Kosygin. All of this means that not three forces but one force represent the supreme political power in the USSR – the summit of the Communist Party.

Political domination in the meaning of Soviet dictatorship assumes that (1) power is real, not symbolic; (2) power is all-embracing, not partial; (3) power is supreme, not subordinate; (4) power is unlimited, not in any way restricted. In these directions the political domination of the CPSU will be examined, relying mainly upon practical activities, but adducing also, when possible, the appropriate legal regulations.

Real power embraces the capacity to govern by one's own decisions, while symbolic power does not go beyond giving a legal or apparently legal form to the decisions of somebody else. In this sense all other agencies of the USSR, no matter how high they may be, fulfill symbolic functions vis-à-vis one agency of real power, the Politbureau, whether its directives affect the interests of the broadest masses of people or of separate individuals, the fate of the structure of the state or of specific officials, the perspectives of the entire economy or of its different sectors.

In the late 1920s and the early 1930s the future of the Soviet peasantry and of Soviet agriculture was tragically sealed. At present, the irrevocability of those fatal steps is an open secret. Millions of peasants were exiled, and the majority perished; private agriculture with its economic incentives gave way to collective agriculture deprived of any economic stimulus; Russia, formerly a major exporter of grain, became its main importer. But how were all these events prepared and brought about? On the eve of 1929 Moscow sent the necessary secret orders to local Party agencies. On 5 January 1930, the Communist Party's Central Committee adopted a ruling *O tempe kollektivizatsii i o merakh pomoshchi gosudarstva kolkhoznomu stroitel'stvy* (On the Speed of Collectivization and on Measures of the State to Help Collective Farm Building).[92] Only after this, in strict conformity with this Party directive and in order to confirm what had already happened, the Central Executive Committee[93] and the Council of the People's Commissars of the USSR[94] promulgated the decree of 1 February 1930 *O meropriiatiiakh po ukrepleniiu sotsialisticheskogo pereustroistva sel'skogo khoziaistva v raionakh sploshnoi kollektivizatsii i po bor'be s kulachestvom* (On Measures to Strengthen Socialist Reconstruction in Regions of Full-Scale Collectivization and to Fight Against Kulaks).[95]

So it happened with the broad masses of the Soviet population. One can predict that with separate individuals the problem would be far more simple. As the Western media have reported, in 1983 Liubimov, one of the most famous Soviet theater producers and one of the bravest theater critics of the Soviet regime, visited London upon an invitation to stage Dostoevskii's work *Crime and Punishment* (*Prestupleniie i Nakazaniie*) with English actors. There are sufficient grounds to suspect that the Soviet leaders had been wondering for a long time how to get rid of this disturbing director of the disturbing Moscow *Teatr na Taganke* (Theater on Taganka Street). The producer's courageous interview in London about the persecution of his theater could only strengthen the leadership's wish to settle their accounts with him. When the opening night of *Crime and Punishment* had taken place, a representative of the Soviet ambassador told Liubimov with an unequivocal smile: "Well, the crime was well done. Now the punishment shall have its turn." The authentic source of this undisguised threat was clear enough to everybody and to Liubimov especially judging from his subsequent behavior: a letter to Andropov, etc. Although the ambassador had no judicial power, and judicial agencies had not initiated a criminal case, this made no difference. Since the real power had taken its decision, the symbolic power simply carried it out.[96]

In 1957, with some delay, Leningrad was preparing the celebration of its 250th anniversary. As had always happened on similar occasions, portraits of Soviet leaders were exhibited on the main streets and squares of the city. Under Stalin, the order of the portraits depended on the positions of his closest collaborators at a given moment. Owing to this, the Soviet people and not infrequently Stalin's collaborators themselves found out whether their position was stable, or had improved or deteriorated. Khrushchev abolished Stalin's rule and introduced alphabetical order, but in his alphabet "kh" occupied the first place and "a" was relegated to the second place. Strange as it may seem, Brezhnev put "b" at the head of the alphabet instead of "kh", and only Andropov – as a highly educated person – returned to "a" the leading position which belonged to this letter by right. Nevertheless, for a very short time its domination was preserved. Almost all western media agree that in the realm of education Chernenko is incomparably inferior to Andropov. Was this not the reason for the priority of "Ch" over "A"? Meanwhile, in Leningrad already in the summer of 1957, something funny happened to the Russian alphabet at an exhibition of the leaders' portraits. Suddenly "kh" (Khrushchev) left the first place and moved to the last one, but a little later "kh" returned to the first place, while some other letters, "m" (Malenkov, Molotov) and "k" (Kaganovich), disappeared completely. These alphabetical manipulations were a surprise to everyone in Leningrad, except to those people who knew that in Moscow the Politbureau had had a meeting where the fight for power continued during a day and a night. Modifications of the exhibition alphabet simply reflected the varying successes of the fighting groups. However, when the fight came to its conclusion and Khrushchev emerged victorious at the Party's summit, the Presidium of the USSR Supreme Soviet formally fixed what had actually happened before its decision: Malenkov, Molotov and Kaganovich were ousted from the USSR Council of Ministers and replaced by Khrushchev's supporters.

So it happened with individual officials. One would, however, be mistaken if one thought that the entire governmental structure should be more immune than its individual representatives. Khrushchev, always obsessed with the itch to reorganize, decided not long before his ouster to divide the Party's and government's agencies in the provinces and districts into two parallel systems: industrial and agricultural. It is difficult to imagine a more extravagant restructuring of the general administration of the country than this substitution of the territorial principle by the principle of production. Nevertheless, Khrushchev thought his new reform would help overcome the hopeless backwardness of Soviet agriculture, since the entire complex of general agencies in provinces and districts would be responsible for the required effect. Therefore, he insisted upon his idea, which, as he pointed out, would stimulate one part of local agencies to concentrate on rural affairs and the other on urban matters. As it has been related after Khrushchev's dismissal, only one member of the Politbureau, the First Secretary of the Ukrainian Communist Party, Shcherbitskii, was courageous enough to retort, that this would help "neither the village nor the town".[97] As a result, Shcherbitskii lost both his positions, and the USSR Supreme Soviet rubber-stamped the Politbureau decision with corresponding amendments to the Soviet Constitution. These cumbersome innovations remained in force until Khrushchev's downfall. As soon as the new rulers took office, one of their first steps was to return to a one-track local Party and administrative system. Almost simultaneously Shcherbitskii was restored to his former positions as a Politbureau member and as First Secretary of the Ukrainian Communist Party.

Late in 1964, before the new leadership had time to settle into its position, a new fight arose between adherents of extremely centralized economic planning, headed by Brezhnev, and champions of a relatively relaxed economic management, led by Kosygin. The discussion centered on industry, and this was the first and the last time that Kosygin was the winner and Brezhnev the loser. Relying upon the majority of the Politbureau, Kosygin managed to proclaim the 1965 economic reform in the realm of industry by means of Party directives and then through appropriate legal regulations.[98] However, for Kosygin this was a Pyrrhic victory. Having received very restricted economic freedom, industrial enterprises used every opportunity to produce what was profitable to themselves rather than what was required by the center. Conflicts between the economic needs of the producers and the political needs of the rulers gradually increased, and to stop this development the 1965 economic reform was reduced almost to nothing by Party directives and administrative orders late in the 1960s and then by a new reform proclaimed under the title of improvement of industrial administration early in the 1970s.[99] This backward movement coincided with Kosygins demotion. He continued to be Chairman of the USSR Council of Ministers, but began to lose one prerogative after another, and at the time of his resignation in 1981 Kosygin officially parted with the power which had actually been lost by him long before.

This is what took place in one part of the Soviet economy. The situation does not seem essentially different if one considers the Soviet economy as a single whole. Bearing in mind the general difference between the USSR and the USA from the viewpoint of economic development, the USSR, in order to attain and in some regards to surpass the military level of the USA, needs militarization of its entire economy. All other demands must be satisfied within the limits of a hunger-ration, so that the military industry can be supplied without restrictions. This is the real situation well known not only to professional scholars and practitioners, but to everybody who is confronted with shortages in the USSR wherever he turns, except in the military realm where only those given access to secrets may be admitted. Meanwhile, every year the Soviet state budget allocates a modest amount of money for military expenditure, and thus the USSR spends less on armaments, but at the same time it is armed, at least, not worse than the USA. How can this miracle be explained? Probably, there is only one satisfactory explanation. There are two budgets in the USSR: one adopted by the symbolic power in the form of a law for the sake of general publicity, and the other confirmed by the real power in a secret order for the sake of practical application.

Distinctions between all-embracing and partial powers have a significance beyond the differences between real and symbolic powers which have been discussed before. All-embracing power encompasses the entire territory of the country and affects all kinds of governing activities, while partial power does not go beyond either certain territorial boundaries or certain governing functions.

Real power does not belong exclusively to the very summit of the CPSU. Secretaries of provincial or district party committees represent a significant force and fulfill important governing functions. At the same time, being restricted territorially, they may serve the means of political domination but not the persons. On the other hand, chiefs of the KGB or military commanders are doubtlessly very powerful officials, and without them political domination would be either impossible or at least seriously weakened. However, omnipotence and functional powers are phenomena of a different nature. One precludes the other, although each of them occupies its own quite definite place in the entire machinery of administration. It is necessary to distinguish between personification and realization of political dominance. Those who dominate politically do not always do this directly, and vice versa, those who exercise sovereign power do not always possess political omnipotence. As a rule, the coincidence of the two qualities in the same persons is simply impossible.

In cases of the highest importance and the most extreme secrecy the Politbureau rules itself and directly. No other agency but the Politbureau decides upon questions concerning new armaments for military forces, the actual volume of military expenditure, military invasion of other countries under the guise of "brotherly help" requested by their governments or politicians, etc. The majority of such decisions do not even need formal confirmation by the government or by the legislature, and only some of them, as for example those concerning military invasion, are presented *post factum* after their execution, as allegedly based on decisions of the government. If it is considered necessary to introduce a political line which would be disadvantageous to the prestige of the Soviet regime, the Politbureau may adopt generally binding secret rules which will be observed as the highest law, even though the legislature has had nothing to do with them, and only the officials immediately concerned are confidentially informed about them. In this way the Politbureau introduced a list of offices barred to any representatives of nationalities, which have their own states abroad. The nationalities concerned are not mentioned *expressis verbis*. It is clear, however, that in the case of Frenchmen or Italians, bearing in mind their insignificant number in the USSR, nobody would adopt such humiliating regulations. Two nationalities, however, which have their own states abroad, amount to millions: Germans and Jews. They are the genuine addressees of the rigid prohibition.

In cases of obligatory publicity connected with strict procedure a direct Politbureau ruling is entirely precluded. Judicial activities can serve as the most convincing illustration. During Stalin's times, execution of people according to lists signed by the members of the Politbureau, was widely practised, but this practice related to extrajudicial reprisals, not to judicial prosecution. After Stalin's death such a practice disappeared completely, although administrative punishments, like compulsory exile or expatriation, have not been rejected by contemporary rulers. As a matter of course, they intervene in judicial activities whenever they consider this useful. Without the interference of the Politbureau, Piotr Iakir or Pavel Litvinov, children or grandchildren of former high-ranking Soviet officials, would never have been committed to trial nor would Ishkov, the former Minister of the Fishing Industry, an accomplice to "stealing of state ownership on an especially large scale" – to use the terminology of the Soviet criminal codes – ever have avoided criminal responsibility. Let the Soviet psychiatrist Snezhnevskii enjoy the dishonorable glory of having invented "creeping schizophrenia" as a method of suppression of Soviet dissidents; all the same, the application of this method of punitive repression by the agencies of preliminary investigation and by the judicial system could not have occurred without the approval of the Politbureau. If judicial sentences in political cases were not predetermined from the top, in the 1960s the Soviet legal journal *Sotsialisticheskaia Zakonnost'* (Socialist Legality) could not have committed such an oversight as the publication of a sentence that was to be handed down by a court on the following day. However, exercise of the judicial function as such belongs to the jurisdiction of the courts, although they are subordinated not only to the law, but also to the general lines elaborated by the Party's summits, as well as to concrete instructions given by the Party's agencies.

In all other cases the Politbureau rules directly or indirectly according to circumstances. The removal of all monuments to Stalin early in the 1960s was ordered directly by the Politbureau; the construction of a monument on Stalin's grave near

Lenin's mausoleum late in the 1960s was prescribed by a governmental edict on the basis of a Politbureau decision. It was the Politbureau which gave the command to machine-gun the Tbilisi pro-Stalinist demonstration in the late 1950s, but it was the KGB which, following Politbureau instructions, conducted the preliminary investigation against the main instigators of these dangerous events. In order to stimulate the enthusiasm of the masses in various places of the country at different times the Politbureau annually approves lists of cities, provinces or republics which shall be rewarded with one or another decoration of the USSR; in conformity with this and on no account on its own initiative, the Presidium of the USSR Supreme Soviet issues the appropriate edicts concerning the actual awards. Hence, the practical methods of political domination vary according to transition from one to another possible procedure; its substance, however, remains as invariable as its personification.

Differences between all-embracing and partial powers, as well as between real and symbolic powers typify the subjects under discussion in other ways, along with the distinction between supreme and subordinate powers. A subordinate power can be all-embracing, such as the legislative power of the USSR Supreme Soviet formally appears to be; it can also be real to some extent, as the operative power[100] of the USSR Council of Ministers actually is. Political domination, however, remains unattainable to these agencies as a result of their subordination to other institutions. In contrast, the Politbureau is beyond any subordination, and therefore in this case all-embracing and real power acquires the character of political domination.

In the system of the Communist Party the Politbureau's position is somewhat like the position of the Presidium of the USSR Supreme Soviet in the governmental system. At the same time, edicts of the Presidium shall, as a rule, be confirmed by the Supreme Soviet, according to the direct demand of the Soviet Constitution.[101] Decisions of the Politbureau, however, are not submitted to a similar procedure. They come into force at once and without reservation. Only amendments in the Rules and the Program of the CPSU belong to the jurisdiction of the Party congress, but their preparation has always been handled by the Politbureau, and suggested drafts have never met with any objections from the congress. In addition, one must not forget that these documents, which only demand a ceremonial confirmation of Politbureau innovations, have no other but a predominantly propagandistic significance, judging, for example, from the present Party Program introduced by Khrushchev with promises of a fairy-tale life by the 1980s and doomed to replacement by Andropov as a groundless fantasy clearly disproved by harsh reality.

In the Soviet political system the Politbureau really plays the role of "the leading and guiding force" ascribed by the Soviet Constitution to the Communist Party as a single whole.[102] This conclusion can be made even on the grounds of the scant information of Soviet media concerning the weekly meetings of the Politbureau, introduced after Brezhnev's death. The head of the government or the Minister of Foreign Affairs, after having dealt with foreign leaders, renders account not to the government but to the Politbureau. The Politbureau hears reports of ministers or of provincial executive committees, addressing to them specific commands about modifications and improvements of their activities. The Politbureau first decides to experiment with less centralized methods of managing the Soviet economy, and only then does the CPSU Central Committee – in the person of the Politbureau itself – adopt together with the USSR Council of Ministers the appropriate edict in order to carry out the projected experiment at enterprises and associations of two All-Union and three republican ministries.[103] To declare a war the Politbureau needs an edict from the Presidium of the USSR Supreme Soviet.[104] In practice this formal procedure was applied in a very provocative way only in 1939, when the USSR initiated the war against Finland. In all other cases (Hungary in 1956, Czechoslovakia in 1968, Afghanistan in 1979) military actions were disguised in such a form that no edict of the Presidium of the USSR Supreme Soviet was legally necessary, and general references in official declarations to governmental decisions seemed quite sufficient. As often as not the USSR resorts to secret military actions, publicly denying any activity at all, as in the cases of the combined actions of Soviet and Cuban military forces and military instructions in Angola or Ethiopia. Then no formal governmental declaration is necessary, since the actual Politbureau decision has already been made.

In the Soviet social system the Politbureau reveals itself as "the leading core" of all other organizations, to use the terminology of the 1936 Constitution repeated in different words in the 1977 Constitution, although both speak about the CPSU and are silent about the Politbureau.[105] For example, the trade unions in the USSR are one of the adjuncts of the governing machinery. They carry out numerous functions of a governmental character: the administration of social insurance, the management of sanatoriums and resorts, participation in regulation of labor conditions, the solution of disputes between employees and employers, etc. In all these functions the trade unions are considered to be independent from governmental agencies and from management of enterprises or other establishments. There is, however, one institution to which the trade unions, as well as other non-governmental organizations – the union of writers, the union of artists, the union of cinematographers, cooperatives of any kind, and organized collectives of any character – are subordinate. This institution is the CPSU personified by the Politbureau which controls the entire system of organizations, whether they be the trade unions or anything else. As a result of Politbureau activity, such heterogenous phenomena as trade unions and the governmental bureaucracy become homogeneous ingredients of a unified political system. Thus, not subject to anyone and subordinating everybody, the Politbureau manages to maintain its all-embracing real power at the highest level of political domination.

However, to become politically dominant one needs an additional prerequisite: real and non-subordinate all-embracing power must be limitless or, in other words, dictatorial. This equals Lenin's characterization of the proletarian dictatorship as the unlimited power of the proletariat resting upon force, not upon law.[106]

Lenin, as already mentioned,[107] in speaking about proletarian dictatorship, assumed that the "ideologists" – the "rulers" – had to act on behalf of the proletariat. In a sense, Lenin's explanation was very close to the objective truth: leave out the reference to the proletariat, made for the sake of appearances, and you will have a correct idea about the actual personificiation of political dictatorship in the USSR since its inception. Unfortunately, numerous Western scholars and politicians interpret Lenin's words erroneously. Those who treat the Soviet regime with animosity deny the existence of any genuine, not hypocritical, law in the country as long as the Soviet regime rests upon force, rather than law. Others who strive to treat the same regime sympathetically consider any improvement in legal regulations as a step from dictatorship to democracy. Adherents of the first viewpoint forget that as long as only the summit of the system keeps the dictatorship in its grasp, all the subordinate agencies must follow the general commands of the dictatorial center, observing and applying its legal regulations, unless otherwise provided for by exceptional rules or by secret orders given to the bottom from the top. If any Soviet agency were empowered to act arbitrarily with disregard for the law, then not only the "ideologists" – the highest leadership – but all the institutions, including the lowest subordinates, would be dictators. Under such circumstances, centralized political domination would cease, yielding to decentralized political arbitrariness. Supporters of the second viewpoint do not take into account that when the subordinate officials or agencies are ordered to apply the law in the strictest conformity with its authentic content, this does not lead to any restrictions on the dictatorial summit, which may change an adopted attitude at any moment and in any place. If all Soviet laws were binding upon Soviet agencies and officials of any rank only on condition that special orders informed them of such a duty, then disobedience to the dictatorial center would become the general rule and observance of the dictators' demands would be transformed into an exception to the same rule. As for the practical result, it would be identical with the consequences of the first viewpoint: local arbitrariness instead of unified dictatorship. Therefore, not one of the elucidated concepts is corroborated by Soviet history.

During the civil war, Lenin ordered, in a secret instruction, the confiscation of treasures, which belonged to the church, although the Soviet laws on expropriation, nationalization, confiscation, etc. did not provide for their application to religious establishments. Thus, Lenin relied on force, not on law. However, had local officials done the same thing on their own initiative, it would have been considered as a prohibited use of force instead of an application of the law. Early in the 1930s Stalin secretly ordered that the gold, which he needed in exchange for the acquisition of western technology be extracted from Soviet citizens. To carry out his order the GPU (now KGB) arrested hundreds of thousands of people suspected of owning gold and detained them until they satisfied the compulsory demand or proved without doubt the groundlessness of the GPU suspicion. The forcible and unlawful nature of this procedure is clear, but *quod licet Jovi non licet bovi*. As the personification of proletarian dictatorship Stalin could behave in such a way. At the same time, without his command, similar GPU conduct would amount to a violation of the revolutionary legal order. In comparison with Lenin's and Stalin's orders, Andropov's approach to strengthening labor discipline, through the checking of documents of patrons in bars and of customers in department stores during working hours, looks like an insignificant prank. Nevertheless, such control has not been provided for by Soviet law and would have to be assessed as an illegal interference in citizens' privacy were it applied by ordinary officials themselves. Implementation of an order from the CPSU General Secretary is another matter. This official represents the all-people's power which has replaced proletarian dictatorship. Hence, he must always be right, whether he relies on law or on force. As these and other facts prove, unlimited political power does not preclude legal regulations just as legal regulations do not entail a denial of unlimited political power. Both are quite compatible under an utterly totalitarian system, because those who rule are not subject to regulation, and those who are do not rule. Restricting everybody by law, the dictator relies on force, and in consequence of this, everybody gives in to dictatorial force even if the matter should otherwise be settled on the basis of law.

Thus, the Soviet regime possesses all the qualities necessary and sufficient for political domination. The problem, however, is how to explain this domination, where to find its basis, what to regard as its source. Several factors, in this regard, play a more or less important role.

The structure of the Communist Party attracts the main attention. Its fundamental principles are leadership and discipline. Leadership as a structural principle means prevalence of one person's will over the will of the administered collective body and subordination of this person not to this body, but to the higher leader. Actually the First Secretary of the district Party Committee is directly subordinate to the First Secretary of the provincial Party Committee and so on right up to the position of General Secretary. In a transitional period, when the prospective leader has not been finally selected or if his position has not yet attained the necessary stability, collective administration can prevail over personal rule. At other times, members of a collective agency usually end their discussion as soon as the personal leader has expressed his opinion, and if he has acted from the very beginning, discussion normally does not take place at all. The personal peculiarities of the actual leader, of course, leave their indelible mark: Stalin differed from Lenin, and Khrushchev had no similarities with either of them. But the demand for a leader seems intrinsic to the Soviet system. This is why during the Brezhnev era the Politbureau adopted a secret ruling concerning the strengthening of the personal prestige of the General Secretary which was brought to the notice of Party members, and only then was a cornucopia of new decorations and new titles poured down on Brezhnev. It does not matter what kinds of goals have prompted the actual conduct of the various Politbureau members: personal friend-ship, self-interest, obsequiousness, or something else. Only one thing is significant. As a creation of the Soviet system, they strive to preserve this system by satisfying its vital demands and in such a way they preserve themselves as its faithful servants. In its turn, the principle of leadership entails iron discipline. Instructions of a higher Party official are unreservedly binding for his subordinate, whether the latter agrees or disagrees with the orders received. Party members are obliged to carry out the Party's decisions, whether or not they have taken part in their adoption, and whether they have voted positively or negatively at the Party meeting. Public discussions of the Party's problems by communists in the presence of non-communists belong to the most serious breaches of Party discipline. Criticism from the bottom to the top, encouraged in name,[108] meets a discouraging aftermath in deed. Even if the Party's punishment does not attain the highest possible level, expulsion from the Party, which leads to loss of all other positions, less severe Party sanctions (reproof, for example) or the simple displeasure of the Party's authority will be felt by the violator himself and not infrequently also by his children. Owing to these principles the CPSU proves its capacity to act as a united force strong enough to overcome any resistance and, moreover, to nip it in the bud.

Organizational relationships between the Communist Party and non-Party institutions are also substantial. As a matter of course, not one of the institutions mentioned can function without the Party's members as its officials, workers or other participants. It is necessary, however, to distinguish between permanently and periodically functioning institutions (for example, state enterprises or collective farms, as opposed to supreme and local Soviets or congresses of trade unions, writers, artists, composers, etc.). In the first case, as discussed,[109] the primary Party organization is endowed with all the functions of control included in its jurisdiction. In the second case, all Party members are considered to be members of a temporary Party group, and any more or less important question must be solved by this Party group before a final solution will be adopted by the institution itself. For example, the list of candidates for membership of the board of the USSR Union of Writers is to be drawn up by the Party group of the writers' congress, and only then may this list be confirmed in the established order by the congress itself. The board, in its turn, elects the First Secretary and other secretaries of the USSR Union of Writers, but this may take place only after the necessary suggestions have been approved by the Party group of the board already elected. The board and secretaries are elected by secret ballots, but lists of candidates are approved at the Party group meeting by a show of hands. Therefore, the results of elections are predetermined, because voting by a show of hands makes it dangerous to exhibit a negative attitude toward candidates nominated by the CPSU's Central Committee, and at the stage of voting by secret ballots the majority of voters avoid deviating from the prescribed scenario, knowing that otherwise they might provoke suspicion and court disaster. As often as not, the political significance of an eventual solution serves as an inducement to the Party's agencies to ensure its outcome, not simply by a majority vote but unanimously. The aspirations for a solution of this kind reveal themselves with peculiar intensity when it is desirable to deprive Soviet dissidents and applicants for emigration of their doctor's or candidate's degrees. The Party group of the Academic Council (*Uchenii Sovet*), when publicly announcing its suggestion, calls insistently upon all members of the Council to express the most severe criticism of "the apostate" by means of a unanimous vote. Sometimes such aspirations fail and at least several votes are given in favor of the persecuted victim.[110] Usually, however, the persistent activity of the Party's agencies on the one hand, and the fear of the consequences of practically useless opposition to this activity on the other hand, lead to the desired result. The party uses its preliminary meetings not only to rig the voting, but also in order to elaborate the general line of public discussions, to appoint speakers who will elucidate and protect this line, to influence the general view beforehand and in such a way as to prevent dangerous turns or undesired tendencies. All these approaches help to implement political domination steadfastly and at the same time to mask it quite skilfully with a democratic cover.

In implementing and strengthening its unlimited dominance, the Soviet leadership neither spares time nor money for political propaganda.[111] This propaganda is generally notorious as the most boring in the world. The Institute of Sociological Research of Leningrad University once undertook a survey of tens of thousands of people, representatives of different professions, educational levels and strata of the population. Anonymous forms were used in the survey, and its goal consisted of finding out the level of effectiveness of propaganda disseminated by television, radio and newspapers in the USSR. The results turned out to be deplorable. Television or radio news attracted the attention of only about a quarter of those surveyed. All other propagandistic materials did not present any interest to the overwhelming majority of the population. Nevertheless Soviet propaganda continues to be one of the strongest bulwarks of the Soviet regime. The voluntary utilization of television, radio, and newspapers[112] is supplemented by the obligatory so-called political information at each enterprise and at each establishment, and this makes propaganda all-embracing, despite the reluctance it meets among the masses. In consequence of the ideological isolation of the USSR from the rest of the world (inaccessibility of Western newspapers, jamming of Western broadcasts, etc.) official propaganda retains the position of the monopolistic informant for the whole country. Relying upon such advantages, the USSR modifies its propagandistic methods in accordance with the circumstances. The abundant arsenal of these methods includes: *omission* (for example, not one fact about the prohibited demonstrations in the USSR has been reported by the Soviet media), *half-truth* (for example, the Polish strikes of the late 1970s and early 1980s were called "work stoppages" according to Soviet sources), *distortion* (for example, the Six-day War of 1967 was depicted in the USSR as aggression by Israel against the defending Arab nations) *exaggeration* (for example, the annual statistics about economic achievements in the USSR exceed the real situation), *underestimation* (for example, the official descriptions of the economic difficulties as a temporary phenomenon despite their inseparability from the entire history of the USSR), *positive falsehood* (for example, the proclaiming of developed socialism in the USSR despite the fact that the living standards in the Soviet Union lag behind those of certain developing countries), *negative falsehood* (for example, the characterization of Western countries as countries of a decaying economy), *groundless glorification* (for example, of such charlatans of natural science as Lysenko or Lepeshinskaia), *groundless discrediting* (for example, of academician Sakharov and his wife Bonner by the false description of their private life), *modification of assessments* (for example, the transition from a negative to a positive assessment and vice versa of the French philosopher Sartre, depending on the specific political circumstances), and numerous others. However, one cannot say that by all these approaches Soviet propaganda has always hit its mark. Much propagandistic news cannot be believed by anybody, as happened, for example, with information about the direct connection between intrigues of Israeli militarists and the threat of impeachment of the then President Nixon. Sometimes such propaganda makes a fool of itself and needs additional explanations or new interpretations, as happened for example with the destruction of the Korean passenger plane in 1983, when the official Soviet version was modified several times during five or six days. However, in generally assessing Soviet propaganda, one must recognize its capacity to elaborate a certain stereotype of thinking adapted to the totalitarian system and suited to explain social events or phenomena in light of the official attitude. As a result, even those people, who were almost crushed by the Soviet invasion of Czechoslovakia, not infrequently had no doubt about the danger of a West German invasion of the same country. Moreover, one of the most difficult obstacles encountered by Soviet emigrants in their efforts to adapt to the Western system stems from a deep-rooted spiritual stereotype. Thus, poverty of content and mediocrity of form does not decrease the importance of Soviet propaganda for Soviet totalitarianism.

Alongside propaganda as a means of persuasion, suppression as a means of constraint is a basic prop of the Soviet system. In Soviet practice constraint assumes various forms. There is direct compulsion not covered by legal disguise. Its application relates to the most dangerous situations, which demand an urgent reaction: spontaneous demonstrations, unexpected meetings, collective protests, etc. In case of minor disturbances the KGB or the police cope with their suppression, as happened with dissidents' meetings in Moscow. When similar occurrences attain a threatening scale, then military forces are called to action, as happened during the protests in Novacherkassk. More often restraint combines with direct compulsion and legal procedures. Such a combination is usually directed against separate individuals or small groups in order to suppress their activity immediately and to deprive them of the appropriate capacity for a long time. In these cases the KGB or the Police apply direct compulsion and the court or the judge resort to law, as happened with participants of a sit-down strike in the reception room of the Presidium of the USSR Supreme Soviet: at first they were forced to leave the building, and then the judge sentenced several activists to fifteen days of prison for petty hooliganism. Direct compulsion must be distinguished from legal compulsion which, instead of naked violence, assumes coercion within the framework of the law. This demands a preliminary investigation, carried out by the KGB, the police or the Procuracy depending on the character of the specific cases, and a judicial hearing before general, military or special courts[113] depending on the danger of the crime and the peculiarities of the accused. If the action committed can be regarded as a crime according to Soviet law, the situation becomes very simple for the Soviet regime: it can observe legality and punish its foe, as in the case of Begun, accused of anti-Soviet propaganda and condemned to seven years of prison and to five years of exile in accordance with article 70 of the Criminal Code. When undesired political activity cannot be considered as a crime within the strict meaning of Soviet law, but the appropriate agencies or officials consider it necessary to charge the activist as a political offender, they are forced to overcome certain difficulties: to falsify the accusation with the aid of doctored evidence, to hear the case behind closed doors and only to make the court's sentence publicly known, as in the case of Shcharanskii, groundlessly accused of espionage and condemned to thirteen years of prison and five years of exile with reference to article 65 of the Criminal Code. In order not to increase the statistical number of political crimes the Soviet regime often prefers to isolate politically unreliable people by bringing false charges of non-political crimes: sponging, hooliganism, stealing, even rape. During the last few years this repressive tactic in the realm of the political struggle has been widened incessantly and numerous legally innocent people have become victims of quasi-legal judicial arbitrariness. If, in addition to the enumerated methods, punitive psychiatry – which has been already mentioned more than once – is called to mind, the pluriformity of the assortment of means of naked or concealed constraint will appear in its full extent.

The structure of the Communist Party, the organizational relationship of the Party with non-party institutions, political propaganda of a special kind and political suppression of a special character which represent the characteristics of the Soviet system, do not preclude the routine methods of ordinary government: legislative, executive, and judicial activities; legal regulations and administrative orders; formal and informal solutions of everyday problems on the basis of discretionary powers, which belong to the jurisdiction of administrative agencies and governmental officials. Taken together, all these special and routine methods serve one and the same goal: the political domination by the ruling summit. Does it, however, mean that it is precisely these methods which are the source of Soviet political domination?

As for the routine methods of ordinary government, the negative answer seems clear without any question: they are applied in every country, but not all states represent political dictatorships. The special methods, peculiar to the USSR, have been encountered in human history, if not in identical shape, then at least with an extremely similar nature. However, in the entire history of humanity no other regime has possessed political omnipotence of such magnitude as typified by the Soviet regime. Hence, these methods of government, peculiar as they are, may support the Soviet type of political dominance, but cannot have created this unprecedented phenomenon. Organized suppression, legal or illegal, seems capable of keeping a large part of the Soviet population in a state of obedience and the stupefying propaganda helps to increase the level of obedience. The structure of the Communist Party and its relationships with non-communist institutions act in the same way. However, this is not sufficient to ensure the unrestricted and invulnerable domination over the entire people. Such a result becomes understandable only if each individual in the USSR experiences a permanent and inseparable economic dependence on the political power. Thus, to find the source of political omnipotence of the Soviet leadership, the economy of the USSR and its legal regulation must be the first object of a theoretical analysis.

NOTES

1. See Chapter I.
2. In this regard it is quite remarkable that some Soviet dissidents have themselves tried to apply Soviet legal rules to protect their right to hold meetings, demonstrations, etc. (*e.g.* V. Bukovsky, *To Build a Castle*, 1978, 130-155, 187-192).
3. The 1977 Constitution, art.2.
4. *Ibid.* Being adjusted to the political domination of Soviet leadership, the indirect will of large collective bodies is preferred to their direct will in numerous other cases, *e.g.* in the case of legislative initiative, which also belongs to social organizations, but can be expressed only by their all-union agencies (the 1977 Constitution, art.113).
5. *Ibid.*, art.5.
6. The 1936 Constitution, art.49(e).
7. See *supra*, 13-14, 19.
8. The 1977 Constitution, art.109.
9. *Ibid.*, art.114.
10. Montesquieu, *Esprit des Lois*, 1877.
11. *Materialy XXII s"ezda KPSS,* Moskva 1961, 396.
12. *Ibid.*, 183.
13. Montesquieu, *op. cit.*, note 10.
14. The 1977 Constitution, art.8.
15. *Ibid.*, art.8.
16. *Ibid.*, art.100.
17. *Supra*, 25-26.
18. *Ved. SSSR* 1983 No.25 item 382.
19. The law mentioned above consists of twenty-three articles, and each of them includes several paragraphs, so that the general number of established rules is 70 or 80. However, the right not only to discuss, but also to decide belongs to labor collectives only in a few cases: to confirm the choice of people who are to be sent to study in the universities and high schools (art.13), to take part in the distribution of incentive funds (art.14) and in the improvement of socio-cultural and housing conditions of workers and officials (art.16). All other rights of labor collectives, for example, those connected with socialist competition, have either nothing to do with legal regulations or merely allow the participation of labor collectives in the discussion of law-drafts, production plans, etc., while the right of decision belongs to the legislature, managers of economic organizations, etc.
20. *Infra*, 72-93.
21. The 1977 Constitution, art.39.
22. *Ibid.*, arts.40-58.
23. *Supra*, 37-38.
24. The RSFSR Land Code (hereinafter cited the Land Code), art.89.
25. The 1977 Constitution, art.50.
26. *Ibid.*, art.51.
27. *Ibid.*, art.47.
28. See *e.g.* International Covenant on Economic, Social and Cultural Rights, adopted 19 December 1961, G.A. Res. 2200 (XXI), 21 UN GAOR, Supp. (No.16), UN Doc.A/6316 (1966).
29. The 1977 Constitution, art.10.
30. *Ibid.*, art.39.
31. *Pravda* 16 August 1983.
32. *Pravda* 26 July 1983.
33. The 1977 Constitution, art.43.
34. *Ibid.,* art.46.
35. *Otkazniki, i.e.* people whose applications to emigrate were refused.
36. The problem of legal branches is one of the most debatable in Soviet jurisprudence. Some authors consider family law as a part of civil law, but the legislature separates them. Other authors suggest

the creation of economic law on the basis of the corresponding rules of civil law and administrative law for regulations of mutual relationships of economic organizations, but the legislature rejects this suggestion. In several cases the legislature has not expressed its view at all, but Soviet jurists differ in their opinions, as is the case with financial law. At the same time, the problem of legal branches is not only theoretically significant but also practically important. If, for example, family law relates to civil law, then the general rules of the Civil Code may be applied to family relationships. Otherwise, such a possibility must be precluded. Or, if property relationships between economic organizations relate to economic law, then a number of parts of the Civil Code must be repeated in the Economic Code. Otherwise, such a necessity would not occur. For our analysis, however, it will be sufficient to use the system of legal branches which is shared and supported by the majority of legal scholars in the USSR. Only these branches have been enumerated above.

37. The RSFSR Code of Criminal Procedure (hereinafter cited as the Criminal Procedure Code), art.250.
38. Civil Code, art.168.
39. The 1977 Constitution, art.51.
40. *Ibid.*
41. *Supra*, 37.
42. Criminal Code, art.3.
43. *Ibid.*, art.142.
44. Since the illustrations referred to above do not go beyond chapter IV of the Criminal Code, entitled "Crimes against political and labor rights of citizens", other rules directed against political rights, as, for example, art.70 about anti-Soviet agitation and propaganda or art.190-1 about the circulation of fabrications that defame the Soviet state and social system, have not been included in this statement.
45. *Sbornik Postanovlenii Plenuma Verkhovnogo Suda SSSR*, 1924-1977, Moskva 1978, Vol.I, 119-122.
46. *Ved. SSSR* 1981 No.44 item 1184.
47. *SP SSSR* 1974 No.19 item 109.
48. *Ibid.*, art.4.
49. *Ibid.*, art.27.
50. *SP SSSR* 1970 No.18 item 139.
51. *Ibid.*, art.16.
52. The Soviet Constitution adds to the basic rights the basic duties of Soviet citizens: they are obliged to observe laws, to respect the rules of socialist community life, and to bear with dignity the calling of the Soviet citizen (art.59), to work in the domain of socially useful activity and to observe labor discipline (art.60), to care for and to reinforce socialist ownership (art.61), to safeguard the interests of the Soviet state and to strengthen its might and authority (art.62), to perform military service in the ranks of the USSR armed forces (art.63), to respect the national dignity of other citizens and to strengthen the friendship of nations (art.64), to respect the rights and legal interests of other persons, to be intolerant of anti-social offenses, and to promote the protection of public order (art.65), etc. (arts.66-69). Soviet official propaganda and legal theory point out with pride this peculiarity of the Soviet Constitution, which is not limited to the provision of rights but also deals with the duties. However, on second thought it becomes clear that some of the constitutional duties (to respect the national dignity of other citizens, for example) are hypocritical, some others (for instance, to safeguard the interests of the Soviet state) prove to be very dangerous, and some of them (like the duty to work in the social domain) restrict human freedom and – judging from Soviet practice of suppressing dissent – can be used for reprisals against "unreliable" people.
53. Criminal Code, art.88-1.
54. Some non-political crimes – banditry and making or passing of counterfeit money or securities – are included in the same enumeration (see, *ibid.*).
55. *Ibid.*
56. *Supra*, 52.

57. *Supra*, 25-26.
58. *Supra*, 40.
59. The 1977 Constitution, art.48.
60. The decisions mentioned above can also remain unpublished. As it is said in art.5 of the decree On the Procedure for the Publication and Entry into Force of Decrees and Regulations of the Government of the USSR (*SP SSSR* 1979 No.6 item 37), "Decrees of the Government of the USSR or in newspapers... may be published in other printed publications upon the proposal of the appropriate organizations only with the authorization of the Administrative Department of the USSR Council of Ministers".
61. RSFSR Housing Code, art.42.
62. The 1977 Constitution, art.49.
63. For example, Klebanov, a miner of Donbas, was committed to a psychiatric hospital as a result of his repeated attempts to attract the attention of some high governmental and Party agencies to the unbearable labor conditions in many mines of that area.
64. See note 35.
65. *Infra*, Chapter III.
66. After Stalin replaced Trotsky as People's Commissar for Military Affairs by Frunze in 1925, Maiakovskii wrote an epigram: *Posle Trotskogo Frunze Nam? Kakoi Sram* (To Give us Frunze after Trotsky? What a shame.) Soon Frunze died, according to official reports during an operation of the appendix, and according to broad rumor, supported by the subsequent suicide of Frunze's wife, as a result of Stalin's order. Pilniak described a similar story in his novel and, despite the absence of names, it was clear whom he meant. Still more clear was Mandelshtam's rhyme about the "Kremlin Mountaineer". In 1937 one of the most famous Soviet producers, Meierhold, publicly accused the Soviet system of the actual annihilation of genuine theater art. On the next day he was arrested and later executed.
67. *SP SSSR* 1965 No.19-20 item 152.
68. See O.S. Ioffe, P.B. Maggs, *Soviet Law in Theory and Practice*, London/Rome/New York 1983, 139-140.
69. Criminal Code, art.224.
70. *Ibid.*, art.62.
71. *Supra*, 60-61.
72. As a rule, such an agreement involves a financial interest of the corresponding partner.
73. However, in case this trick is discovered, all legal results attained will be declared null and void in consequence of invalidity of marriage according to the Family Code, arts.43-46.
74. To the department which is called by its Russian acronym *OVIR* (Department of Visas and Registration).
75. Criminal Code, art.209.
76. The 1936 Constitution, art.2.
77. V.I. Lenin, *Sochineniia* (Works), Vol.28, 5th ed., Moskva 1964, 193.
78. *Ibid.*, Vol.33, 26.
79. Lenin, *op.cit.*, note 77.
80. The 1936 Constitution, art.2-3.
81. Lenin, *op.cit.*, note 77.
82. The 1936 Constitution, art.3.
83. The 1977 Constitution, art.2.
84. Civil Code, art.142.
85. The Fundamentals of Civil Legislation, art.98.
86. *Ibid.*, art.106.
87. *Ved. RSFSR* 1974 No.10 item 286.
88. The Fundamentals of Civil Legislation, art.112.
89. *Ibid.*, art.111.
90. *Ibid.*, art.110.
91. This concept belongs to A. Avtorkhanov, *Tekhnologiia vlasti*, 2nd ed., Frankfurt am Main 1976.

92. *KPSS v rezoliutsiiakh i resheniiakh s"ezdov, konferentsii i plenumov TsK*, II, Moskva 1954, 664-667. One should not forget that when the Central Committee itself adopts one or another ruling it is called the ruling of the Plenum of the Central Committee, and when the title "The ruling of the Central Committee" is used, this means an act issued by the Politbureau.

93. An equivalent of the contemporary Presidium of the USSR Supreme Soviet.

94. An equivalent of the contemporary Council of Ministers of the USSR.

95. *SZ SSSR* 1930 No.9 item 105. "Kulak" is the official designation of a well-to-do peasant.

96. Subsequently, Liubimov lost his position in the Soviet theater and decided not to return to the USSR.

97. This is a verbatim translation of the Russian proverb *"ni k selu ni k gorodu"* used to typify impracticable or senseless suggestions, remarks, etc.

98. *SP SSSR* 1965 No.19-20 items 153-155.

99. *SP SSSR* 1973 No.7 item 31.

100. *Supra*, 38.

101. The 1977 Constitution, art.122.

102. *Ibid.*, art.6.

103. *Pravda* 26 July 1983.

104. The 1977 Constitution, art.121(17). The same rule was known in the 1936 Constitution, art.48(n).

105. Compare the 1936 Constitution, art.126 with the 1977 Constitution, art.6.

106. *Supra*, 71ff.

107. *Supra*, 73.

108. Art.3(c) of the Rules of the Communist Party.

109. *Supra*, 32-33.

110. According to his own information, such was the case of Simis, a research fellow at the All-Union Institute of Soviet Legislation in Moscow, who first was accused of being the author of an anti-Soviet book and then was compelled to emigrate. K.M. Simis, *USSR: The Corrupt Society*, New York 1982, 20.

111. As often as not this is called "educational work" or "political education" in Soviet official sources.

112. However, subscription to *Pravda* is obligatory for Party members, and other people are compelled by various methods to subscribe to at least one newspaper of their choice.

113. *Infra*, Chapter V.

CHAPTER III

THE LAW OF ECONOMIC EMANCIPATION AND OF ECONOMIC SLAVERY

Political freedom cannot exist by itself. It has numerous prerequisites, and among them economic independence seems one of the most important. However, Marxist-Leninist theory has never spoken of the economic independence of the individual after the transformation of capitalist society into socialist society. It proceeds from the assumption that capitalism is based on economic coercion – which forces the proletariat, who is deprived of any property, to work for capitalists, the owners of the means of production – while socialism ensures the economic emancipation of the proletariat, depriving capitalists of the means of production in favor of society as a whole. Therefore, from the Marxist-Leninist point of view, political freedom does not assume the economic independence of individuals, but the economic emancipation of the proletariat. As soon as such emancipation takes place, the proletariat becomes politically free together with its allies – the working people of the city and the country. The replacement of the dictatorship of the proletariat by the all-people's state signifies that the people have attained economic emancipation and, as a result, political freedom.

On the other hand, according to the same doctrine, real political freedom is out of the question while economic slavery continues to be preserved in any form: fully, as in slave-holding societies; to a limited extent, as in feudal society; or concealed, as under capitalism. At the same time, as already indicated, the USSR represents the political system of dictatorial domination, and where one dominates, another must be subordinate. This, certainly, leads not so much to political freedom as to its antipode. Thus, if Marxism-Leninism is right in affirming that economic slavery results in the non-existence of political freedom, then, reasoning *a contrario*, one must come to the conclusion that the non-existence of political freedom is an unmistakable symptom of economic slavery. This predetermines the main outlines of the subsequent analysis of Soviet law and Soviet reality. First economic emancipation and then economic slavery shall be examined in the light of legal regulations, as established by Soviet law, and in view of the actual facts, as embodied in Soviet practice.

1. Economic Emancipation

In contrast to economic slavery, which would be rejected by the Soviets with indignation even if its existence in the USSR were only hinted at, economic emancipation is assessed as being the most valuable conquest of the October revolution, solemnly proclaimed since the very beginning and persistently pointed out on any convenient occasion. However, Soviet law itself does not manage to conceal economic slavery completely, despite the fact that the latter has been created under the wordy aegis of economic emancipation, and Soviet practice, as a matter of course, is even less successful in this respect.

Economic Emancipation in Soviet Law

Among all the different kinds of legal regulations, the Soviet Constitution occupies the first and foremost place in proclaiming the economic emancipation of the working people as a consequence of the October revolution and the creation of a new society in the USSR. As mentioned in the Preamble of the 1977 Constitution, the October revolution "overthrew the power of the capitalists and landowners" and "broke the fetters of oppression"; "Soviet power has carried out the most profound socio-economic transformation, ended forever the exploitations of man by man". Similar ideas are expressed by some of the concrete rules of the Soviet Constitution. "The labor of the Soviet people, free from exploitation, shall be the source of the growth of social wealth and the well-being of the people and every Soviet person", says the Constitution in Article 14. Instead of exploitation, as under capitalism, "the ultimate aim of social production under socialism shall be the fullest satisfaction of the growing material and spiritual needs of people" – states the same legislative act in Article 15. As for the legal branches developed beyond the boundaries of constitutional law, they repeat the Constitution in this regard directly or indirectly, but only insofar as they deal with economic relationships in the USSR. For example, the Fundamentals of Labor Legislation of the USSR and the Union Republics proclaim in the Preamble that "with the triumph of socialism in the Soviet Union, the exploitation of man by man has been liquidated completely and forever".[1] The Fundamentals of Civil Legislation do not use an analogous formula directly, but their proclamations about the achievement of the full and complete victory of socialism rest upon the same assumption.[2]

This assumption, however, conflicts with other regulations. If labor is free, it does not require coercion, and, vice versa, if coercion is necessary, then labor cannot be regarded as being free. Meanwhile, Soviet law introduces compulsory methods with regard to labor activity, not only by means of the constitutional duty to work[3] and criminal responsibility for evasion of work,[4] but also through rules of a more fundamental character.

Soviet legislation confirms the fact that the means of production are objects of socialist ownership, and that only consumer goods may belong to citizens in "personal ownership".[5] But to acquire consumer goods one must work, and because the means of production are inseparable from socialist ownership, one must work at socialist enterprises or other establishments to supply oneself and one's family with the necessary goods. Marxist terminology calls this nothing other than economic coercion, and if it exists under capitalism, one may speak about economic coercion under socialism on the same grounds. The replacement of the words "economic coercion" with the words "economic stimulation" in Soviet propaganda does not change the essence of the matter. Reference to distinctions between work in favor of capitalists and work in favor of society under socialism also does not rectify the situation, even if society as a whole were the real beneficiary of individual labor efforts in the USSR. The labor of Soviet citizens is paid, not on the basis of their membership of Soviet society, but in conformity with the principle "to each according to his labor". "According" and not "equal" to labor means that the payment given does not compensate the labor invested. In complete concordance with Marxism, this is exploitation, and whether the exploiters are individual capitalists or society as a whole – the result is the same for the subjects of exploitation. Therefore, although Soviet law does not provide for the right to strike, the production process at Soviet enterprises looks like a permanently increasing "work stoppage". Several professors from Leningrad University – all customers of a car workshop – after having spent the whole day together with repair men, came to the conclusion that if you subtract periods of coming late, the increase in the length of dinner breaks, breaks for a smoke, the stopping of work before the appropriate time, etc., the actual work took no more than two hours and forty minutes, instead of eight hours. In order to compare, in this regard, work in the service sector with work in the industrial sphere, they managed to obtain the necessary information from machine-building and shipbuilding plants. The results approximately coincided. A proverb widely disseminated among Soviet working people says: "They pretend to pay us, and we pretend to work for them". In the absence of appropriate statistical data, this proverb reflects humorously to what level Soviet rulers strive to raise the degree of exploitation and to what extent working people manage to resist such an aspiration.

Soviet law deals with extra-economic, as well as economic coercion. As stated in Article 13 of the 1977 Constitution, personal ownership must not go beyond "articles of everyday use, personal consumption, convenience, and subsidiary household husbandry, a dwelling house, and labor savings". The acquisition of means of production by citizens is in principle forbidden and entails the appropriate legal sanctions for violators of the rule cited. Thus, the individual is compelled "to work for society" not only because he does not possess his own means of production, but also because he is strictly prohibited from possessing them. Individual economic production activity is accessible to the Soviet citizen solely within the limits of two constitutional rules: (1) he may receive for his use, in the procedure established by law, a land parcel for subsidiary husbandry, gardening, vegetable growing, and for individual housing construction;[6] (2) he is permitted to apply his individual labor activity in the sphere of handicrafts, agriculture, and domestic services to the populace; but the state shall regulate individual labor activity, ensuring its use in the interests of society.[7] The economic inducements that have stimulated the Soviet legislature to establish these rules are sufficiently clear. Without individual activity the socialist economy has proved to be completely incapable of ensuring even the minimum supply of agricultural produce for the Soviet population and of satisfying the demand for everyday domestic services of millions of despairing customers. The same rules, however, do not appear to be so obvious from the viewpoint of Soviet peculiarities, and therefore they deserve special attention.

The constitutional enumeration of objects accessible to personal ownership is accompanied by important restrictions in current legislation. For example, a dwelling house belongs to this enumeration, but, consulting the Civil Code, one finds out that spouses living together and their minor children may own only one dwelling house or part of one,[8] and the same family may sell no more than one house or part of a house within a period of three years.[9] There is also a general rule that "the maximum size of a dwelling or part of it belonging to a citizen by right of personal ownership may not exceed 60 square metres of dwelling space".[10] All these restrictions are not aimed at depriving Soviet citizens of the opportunity to live in large comfortable houses of their own. They have another goal, connected with the Soviet economic system and with the housing problem in the USSR. The demand for housing exceeds availability to such an extent that, by free sale and free renting, citizens could live incomparably better as sellers or landlords, than as ordinary workers or clerks. This would, of course, decrease the economic need "to work for society", and therefore the appropriate extra-economic measures are applied: the number of sales permitted is extremely restricted, the maximum size of individual dwellings usually precludes their use for renting, and in case the latter takes place the amount of rent paid must not exceed the officially established limits.[11] Violations of the mentioned rules leads to withdrawal by the state either of the income received or of the house as well. One of the most sensational judicial cases of this kind occurred in Sochi, a famous Soviet resort. The owner of a house, having rented it during the summer periods with daily payment for each bed, earned, for Soviet standards, an enormous amount of money, and, as a result, he lost both his income and his house in favor of the state.

The constitutional enumeration of aims that may serve as legal grounds for allocation of plots of land for citizens' use acquires a very peculiar coloring after a more careful study of some specific regulations. From this viewpoint, the legal regime of plots of land used for subsidiary husbandry by collective farmers seems the most interesting. Collective farmers receive their plots of land not directly from the state but through the collective farms. The collective farm is the main user, and collective farmers, receiving plots of land from their collective farm, are derivational users. As a general rule, they preserve the right to use plots of land so long as at least one of the family's members capable of working continues to work on the collective farm. Exceptions to the general rule include, among others, people called to active military service, elected to an official post, and those who became incapacitated. Beyond these exceptions, as soon as membership of the collective farm ceases to exist, the plot of land used for subsidiary husbandry must be withdrawn.[12] One should not forget that during Stalin's time, when there was no payment for labor on collective farms, subsidiary husbandry served as the only source of collective farmers' existence. They continue to play the main role in collective farmers' lives even now, when their labor is paid but in an amount much inferior to the income received from subsidiary husbandry. Hence, together with the passport system in the countryside,[13] legal regulations established for collective farmer's use of plots of land for subsidiary husbandry ensure that the collective farms are provided with the necessary labor force in extra-economic ways, since economic coercion has proved to be inefficacious in this case.

The constitutional enumeration of spheres where individual labor activity is allowed also needs some more precise definitions. As for handicrafts, they are really a sphere of individual labor separate from collective production. They may be engaged in by the observance of three demands: (1) the granting of a registered certificate for the right to exercise a specific kind of handicraft, for which one should apply to the appropriate financial agencies and for which the legally established amount of money must be paid;[14] (2) the payment of taxes, which attain such a scale in this case, that only labor unlimited in time and effort can ensure a more or less acceptable living standard; (3) the selection of handicrafts of the kind included in a special enumeration to be issued by the Council of Ministers of the USSR or of the Union Republic.[15] The most profitable kinds of private activity – despite the incapability of the state enterprises to satisfy all demands of the Soviet population (for example, transportation of passengers by motor cars) – are left out of this enumeration. Therefore, the exercise of such individual activity is characterized as engaging in a prohibited trade and entails administrative or even criminal responsibility.[16] At the same time, apart from handicrafts, all other kinds of individual labor allowed by the constitution, may be carried out only in the periods outside working time at state enterprises and other establishments. Thus, even if a citizen can earn his living exclusively by individual labor provided for by the Constitution, he is compelled in an extra-economic way "to work for society" under the threat of losing his constitutional right to individual labor activity.

Besides free labor, described above, Soviet law provides for forced labor. The latter represents one of the most important parts of the general order established for offenders whose punishment consists either in deprivation of freedom or in conditional imprisonment with mandatory imposition of labor, as well as for offenders conditionally released from places of imprisonment with mandatory imposition of labor. The appropriate rules are published as a part of the corrective labor legislation which generally deals with the execution of criminal punishment, including forced labor as an element of this execution.[17] However, the relevant regulations, which elaborate the Corrective Labor Code and supplement it with significant details, are embodied in the MVD's secret instructions. In the light of all these regulations, it is necessary to point out especially the following.

Officially "socially useful labor" pertains to "the basic means of correction and re-education of convicted persons".[18] In reality, however, two other tasks are to be resolved with the help of convicts' labor. On the one hand, all prisons and all labor camps in the USSR work on the basis of *khozraschet* (economic accountability). This implies their duty to compensate, independently of the state, all expenditures connected with the execution of a punishment such as deprivation of freedom, and the only source for meeting the demand for *khozraschet*, is the forced labor of prisoners themselves. On the other hand, the USSR has a labor shortage for work under difficult climatic conditions or for extraordinarily heavy work. To some degree the Soviet leadership tries to settle this problem by resorting to economic incentives.[19] But the first solution involves prisoners. For this reason two new institutions were included in Soviet criminal law: (1) conditional imprisonment with mandatory imposition of labor;[20] (2) conditional release from places of imprisonment with mandatory imposition of labor.[21]

To support their *khozraschet*, places of imprisonment act as economic organizations, making contracts with state enterprises or associations. These contracts, based on the principle of equivalent reimbursement, are of two kinds: sale of the manufactured produce or of the labor force. In both cases the partners deal with slave labor, and only on the surface does it appear in the shape of things or serfs. Nevertheless, the corrective labor law proclaims in general that convicted persons' work "shall be regulated on general grounds in conformity with labor legislation".[22] This general declaration, however, is refuted even by the published laws, to say nothing of secret instructions. The working day of prisoners may not exceed eight hours, but they may be compelled to work without payment for two more hours on physical or other improvements of the places of imprisonment.[23] Not two, but only one day of weekly rest is given to them.[24] A direct relationship between the work imposed and the qualifications of the prisoner is not obligatory, and those serving punishment in labor camps with a so-called special (*i.e.* the most severe) regime shall, as a rule, be employed at heavy labor.[25] For example, the writer Siniavskii was lucky to serve his sentence making boxes in a labor camp of this kind. However, another famous dissident, Galanskov, was assigned more difficult tasks and died in his place of imprisonment. The problem is even worse with regard to payment for prisoners' labor. The general proclamation also sounds benign in this regard: "Prisoners' labor shall be paid according to its quantity and quality at the norms and rates operating in the national economy."[26] The additional rules leave almost nothing over from the general rule. First of all, calculation of earnings takes into account the partial reimbursement by convicted persons of the costs of the upkeep of the corrective labor institutions.[27] What this "partial reimbursement" means in figures, the prisoner can judge only in counting the meagre amount of money that is put down to his personal account in the places of imprisonment. Sometimes his earnings amount to no more than 10% of a normal salary.[28] But even this money is not at the prisoners' free disposal. They have the right to shop only at trade enterprises on the territory of labor camps, which have an extremely restricted assortment, and with the amount of money reduced to seven rubles per month in the most favorable cases, *i.e.* in ordinary labor camps.[29] Finally, among the penalties applicable to prisoners one can find a prohibition on the purchase of food products for up to one month.[30] One must also not forget that "every convicted person shall be obliged to work",[31] and violation of this duty leads to the application of any penalty provided for by the published Code, including placement in a punishment cell (*kartser*) for up to 15 days,[32] or by secret instructions, including the cruel regime of the reduction of foodstuffs. This is why the special *khozraschet* of labor camps proves to be stronger and more efficacious than the general *khozraschet* of the Soviet economy.

To supply the economy with the necessary labor force, which cannot be ensured in the normal way, places of imprisonment sell this force by means of contracts, and the court either sentences offenders to conditional imprisonment or conditionally releases them from places of imprisonment with mandatory imposition of labor by both kinds of judicial decisions. In the case of purchase and sale the rights and duties of contractual partners are distributed in the following order. The seller receives money provided for by the contract and uses it to satisfy *khozraschet* demands, being obliged to ensure the transportation of workers and that they are looked after by armed guards during the labor process. The purchaser receives the labor force provided for by the same contract and uses it for his production needs, being obliged to observe the general rules of safety techniques and to reimburse the seller for the quantity and quality of work actually performed. In the case of conditional imprisonment or conditional release from imprisonment, accompanied by compulsory labor, convicted persons are obliged to work at the place to which they are sent by the competent agencies, with the possibility of future transfer to other places of work without their agreement. They must reside in the communal quarters especially assigned to them without having the right to leave the administrative district of their place of work during the entire term of compulsory labor and with the duty of registering at the agency of internal affairs from one to four times a month. As a reward for good behavior, they may be permitted to reside with their family in living quarters rented by them and to depart temporarily to other places for a work mission, for leave, etc.[33] Violation of labor discipline or of public order by a convicted person may entail various consequences up to a judicial decision to send him to serve his term as if he were sentenced unconditionally or were not conditionally released from a place of imprisonment.[34]

All these regulations and facts prove the real existence of slave labor in the USSR, and as far as imprisoned persons are concerned, the law itself does not seriously care whether its slave-holding spirit is sufficiently disguised or presumptuously left without any dependable camouflage. Even if the number of prisoners in the country did not exceed several hundred or even thousands, world public opinion ought to be concerned with such a situation. Unfortunately, the denunciation of Stalin's tyranny has resulted not in the annihilation of the "Gulag Archipelago", but only in the decrease of its population from dozens of millions to several million, and thus the need for economic accountability continues to victimize significant proportions of the Soviet population. The population of labor camps being what it is, compulsory labor cannot be considered an insignificant deviation from the fundamental principles. On the contrary, the quantitative indices confirm that the production activity of places of imprisonment and of convicted people presents an important ingredient of the economic system in the USSR. This system, even as a single whole, does not corroborate the official myth of economic emancipation, announced by propaganda and fixed by law. By separate analysis, what becomes clear at a first glance at special regulations, dealing with openly forced labor, demands a more thorough approach toward general regulations, dealing with allegedly emancipated work. But the final conclusion is the same, and it stems from the study of the appropriate legal phenomena. Now let us consider the problem discussed in its practical aspects.

Economic Emancipation in Soviet Practice

The economic freedom given to Soviet citizens, not by wordy declarations but by legal rules of practical importance, is extremely restricted and essentially curtailed. For the Soviet regime such an attitude seems politically necessary to ensure economic dependence of citizens on the state and to compel them on this basis to show unreserved obedience. For Soviet citizens, the same attitude seems unbearable economically, if they do not belong to the official elite with all its economic privileges and political advantages. Therefore, in studying economic emancipation as it appears not in Soviet law but in Soviet practice, one can easily notice two antagonistic tendencies: the regime strives to diminish even the economic freedom that does not go beyond the legal limits; the citizenry strives to develop even the economic freedom that transgresses the law.[35]

One of the most important elements of the private economy (individual economy in Soviet terminology) provided for by Soviet law is represented by subsidiary husbandries. Their greatest number belongs to collective farmers, but they can also be in the possession of other people, living in small cities or in villages, who are not members of collective farms (schoolteachers, doctors, workers of retail enterprises, etc.). As already mentioned,[36] Soviet rulers have mixed feelings toward this economy: they cannot do without it in consequence of the weakness of the governmental system of food supply, and they cannot tolerate it because of the economic strengthening and eventual political independence that may possibly result from this non-prohibited institution. Fear of the private economy leads to limitations on subsidiary husbandries by restricting their size, the kinds of agricultural means of production, the number of livestock, etc. These restrictions, however, are either strengthened or weakened, depending on the general economic situation in the country, as a result of decrease or increase in the needs to be served by the private economy. For example, in 1982 the RSFSR's (Russia's) Supreme Soviet confirmed the edict of its Presidium, which had increased the number of livestock allowed for personal ownership of non-members of collective farms.[37] But, if one considers the entire period from the end of World War II until present times, extreme changes of mutually opposite content in the maximum number of livestock permitted to the subsidiary husbandries took place no less than six times. Such is the frequency of variations of Soviet policy toward the individual sector of the Soviet economy, illustrated only by one example, but finding similar corroboration in all other regards.

For their part, citizens, who have subsidiary husbandries of their own, endeavor to squeeze out as much profit as is possible from them. If they use a legal route, all official attempts to diminish such profit fail as a rule. And the legal route goes through the so-called collective farm market, where citizens may sell their produce at prices agreed by sellers and purchasers. At different times, two steps have been taken, if not to eliminate, then to impoverish, the sources of the sellers' enrichment. On one occasion leaders in some provinces tried to introduce maximum prices at the collective farm markets. Immediately the markets of cities involved became empty, and there was no other way out but to reject this very radical measure. Judicial practice tried another experiment, declaring the large profit received by means of subsidiary husbandry to be unearned income and withdrawing it in favor of the state budget according to the appropriate civil law regulations.[38] The illegality of this practice is obvious. "Unearned income" in the meaning of Soviet civil law must combine two features: acquisition without one's own labor and absence of legal permission for such acquisition. Inheritance is acquired without one's own labor, but, being provided by law, it does not belong to "unearned income". A handicraft without a certificate is illegal, but, being based on one's own labor, it also does not represent "unearned income". As for sellers of the produce of subsidiary husbandries, they deal with the result of their own labor and do not violate the order established for the collective farm market. Thus, not even one of the two legal grounds needed to confiscate the "surplus" of income by application of civil law procedure is in question here. Of course, if they consider it necessary, the Soviets may disregard the existing regulation or replace it with a more convenient one. But in the case discussed, such conduct would be economically dangerous, threatening to destroy the food supply created by individuals in addition to undermining the system of governmental retail trade. Therefore, both steps have finally been rejected, and accumulation of large amounts of money by owners of subsidiary husbandries has become, though undesirable, a real fact.

This fact[39] disrupts the Soviet economy, depriving official currency of its appropriate purchasing power. Thus, unable to prevent accumulation of money by some individuals, the Soviet regime attempts to fleece the country's population by various means – not so much of a drastic nature (monetary reforms, for example) as of permanent character (mainly policies in the realm of retail trade). Since Stalin's time, the main role in this regard has belonged to vodka. During World War II the Soviet Union began to produce vodka from wood, and after the abolition of rationing in 1947 a bottle of vodka had a retail price of several rubles but the cost price of several kopeks. Stalin thought it profitable gradually to decrease its price and in such a way to increase state income. Khrushchev calculated otherwise and proved to be right. Under the slogan of the fight against alcoholism, he increased the price of vodka, but the demand increased even more. Later Khrushchev's foes developed this line, and now the state income from the sale of vodka has become one of the most important sources of state revenue. Soon after World War II the same policies were applied to cars. Strange as this may seem, in the USSR the larger the output of cars the higher their price. After Stalin's monetary reform of 1947, when, according to official explanations, the ruble became as strong as the dollar, the first Soviet compact car "Moskvich" had a retail price of 8,000 rubles, and a cost price of only several hundred rubles. Khrushchev's monetary reform of the 1960s introduced a proportion between the old and new ruble of ten to one. However, the original retail price of the new Soviet compact car "Zhiguli" was 5,500 – or in old money 55,000 rubles – although its cost price was not more than eight or nine hundred rubles. The price has increased steadily, and production of cars has been greatly developed, but the supply continues to remain lower than the demand, and as a method of squeezing money from consumers, the car trade appears more convenient than anything else. To these sources of revenue, already long in existence, Andropov managed to add his own innovation: *kommercheskie magaziny, i.e.* commercial stores with prices eightfold or even tenfold higher than in ordinary groceries. In elaborating this innovation, the new Soviet leader did not start from scratch. Similar stores had been also established by Stalin. However, there is one very specific distinction. Stalin combined such stores with rationing, and, having purchased the necessary food at low prices within the limits of rationing, citizens who had money left over could make more expensive additional purchases at the *kommercheskie magaziny*. Andropov did not establish rationing, but because ordinary stores are in principle empty, in order to buy the necessary food – except bread and certain other goods generally accessible in the majority of big cities – customers are forced to use *kommercheskie magaziny* anyway. This has led to new phenomena in the Soviet economy. It was impossible to find carpets or gold objects in so-called commission shops (shops where second-hand goods are sold on commission) while retail trade of food was carried out through ordinary stores. People who possessed such things saw no sense in selling them in exchange for money – the value of which was permanently decreasing – and people who had a lot of money managed to buy these things by payment either of high prices to the owner himself or of "under the table" money to salesmen in commission shops. But, when it is necessary to buy food sometimes at a tenfold price, the situation has essentially changed. People with a great deal of money feel this necessity themselves. Hence, their demand for valuables has noticeably decreased. Other people, in order to have money for daily purchases, need to sell their valuables with the help of commission shops, because the purchasers who previously would have bought these valuables now prefer to buy new things accessible for high prices in governmental stores. Thus the situation of the citizenry has become even more difficult. However, the withdrawal of the "surplus" of money from economic circulation in the country has attained an unprecedented volume in recent times. This would, of course, engender certain negative results too. One of them is obvious: free prices on collective farm markets would increase, as the state system of trade and supply actually works on a similar basis. In the last analysis, owners of subsidiary husbandries would compensate their losses in such a way and, as always, the broadest masses of people would be confronted with a deteriorating situation in the future.[40] Owing to these or, maybe, other circumstances, Chernenko abolished the economic innovation of his predecessor.

Besides the application of legal approaches, individual producers of vegetables and fruit, flowers and herbs do not infrequently try to overcome legal or *quasi*-legal barriers to their economic activity. The items enumerated are especially highly priced in the northern part of the country, and the profits gained compensate transport expenditures with higher returns than would the sale of the same produce in the nearest city or settlement. Sale of one's own agricultural products in remote areas is not illegal in itself. Everybody knows, however, how profitable it must be, and therefore now and again local powers use road-blocks to prevent penetration of "unbidden guests" to these areas. To give their restrictive measures an appearance of legality, they usually refer to quarantine, dangerous construction work, state of emergency, etc. In their turn, the sellers, in order to overcome such unexpected obstacles, try to find a way around this violation of the law which creates a formal pretext for confiscation of the products brought for sale. In this regard civil aviation – including transport aircraft – becomes more and more helpful. It ensures preserva- tion of the product, bringing goods to the area of sale incomparably faster than by automobile transport; further, roadblocks that can be met on a highway are not applied at airports, except in cases of real, not fabricated, quarantine, emergency, etc. Then, by means of air transport one can establish a regular supply of the product at any place and thus organize a systematic trade, as the people of the Caucasus have managed to do with the sale of flowers in Moscow and Leningrad. Finally, when it is necessary to transport a large quantity of goods at once, skillful people reveal their ability to lease a whole aircraft, although by virtue of the very strict planning of aircraft transportation in the USSR this is only possible through bribery or other criminal collusion with officials of *Aeroflot*, the only air company in the USSR. However, Soviet judicial practice does not deal with a noticeable number of cases connected with the illegal use of transport aircraft. Moreover, in the regularly established trade of produce cultivated in one area and sold in another, not only certain officials of *Aeroflot* are involved but actually something similar to private enterprise takes place. Deliverers are at the place of production, dealing with transport aircraft officials of the airport of loading; the recipients are at the place of sale, dealing with transport aircraft officials of the airport of unloading; at the place of sale apartments and other premises are rented for the sojourn of sellers and the storage of goods; prevention of discovery of this very conspicuous activity demands expenditures necessary to "cajole" those obliged to prosecute such conduct, etc. All this encompasses rather broad groups of people of different ranks, beginning with ordinary collective farmers and ending with high officials of various agencies (transport aircraft, militia, etc.). These people are bound by mutual guarantees, and only unforeseen extraordinary circumstances sometimes lead to failure. As a rule, everything is on the sly. At the same time, in analogous cases private economic activity – though permitted but simultaneously considered to be suspicious – turns into private trade, formally illegal and essentially dangerous for the Soviet system. Thus, we are confronted with the so-called underground or shadow economy in the USSR.

The shadow economy acquires various shapes and can be classified into different types. The most important of them are the following.

1. Private production as a part of socialist production. As for agriculture, this type of shadow economy is widely spread in cattle or sheep breeding regions. For example, in Kirgizia collective farms engage mostly in sheep breeding. Each collective farm has numerous flocks of many thousands of animals indistinguishable to everybody but the shepherds. The permanent succession of birth, fattening, sale and slaughter provides a unique opportunity, if one so wishes, to conceal the actual number of livestock. Therefore, having made an appropriate agreement with a shepherd, anyone can possess his own flock of sheep as a part of a collective farm flock, and all other necessary actions (slaughter, sale, etc.) may be taken in the same way as in the case of the produce of subsidiary husbandry. These tricks are so far from being a secret that even certain high officials of the Kirghiz republic sometimes say in jest: "The economy of our republic is socialist in form and feudal *bai*[41] in content".

In industry the same line of behavior is confronted with more serious difficulties. An agreement with a person such as a shepherd does not help in this case. To place a private machine tool in a shop of a state plant one must strike a bargain with the chief of the shop or maybe with the manager of the plant. This bargain has to ensure either admittance of private workers or exploitation of the private machine tool by workers of the enterprise with appropriate deals between the owner of the machine tool and those who help him on the side of the enterprise. The problem of raw materials becomes even more complicated, especially if these materials are subject to centralized planned distribution and sometimes do not correspond to the state producer's own demands. Under such circumstances the problem can be settled by illegal contacts with planning agencies or by fraudulent manoeuvres with raw materials allocated to the enterprise. The manufactured product must then be sold, and this demands the elimination of any obstacles to its removal from the factory storehouse and the finding of ways to dispose of it wholesale. If the product belongs to the category of consumer goods, and the private producer acts in complicity with the representative of retail trade, the situation becomes relatively simple. With the help of the management of the production enterprise, manufactured articles are transported without any document to the retail enterprise, whose management ensures their sale for cash, and then the entire profit will be divided in the proportion corresponding to the number of participants and the value of different efforts. If the product falls under means of production, the private producer has no other way out but to act in complicity with the representative of so-called material-technical supply and sale, which deals only with enterprises or associations and, instead of cash, receives payment to bank accounts. As a result, one additional task must be resolved: the transformation of symbolic money into real cash. There is no need to describe the various machinations applied to attain the desired goal. Soviet judicial practice, full of analogous cases, has already denounced a great number of such swindlers. Unfortunately, crime develops faster than its disclosure, and in the fight against the shadow economy the punitive agencies have always lagged behind. One concrete case may illustrate this better than the broadest abstract reasoning.

Eight people, led by a former student of the Law Faculty of Leningrad University, once made a contract under a double title: a new one, provided for by the Civil Code now in force,[42] and an old one, known to the 1922 Civil Code.[43] Its whole title was: "Contract of joint operation (society)". Having registered this contract with a notary, they sent one copy to the Leningrad militia and asked for a permit for the acquisition of their own seal. In the application addressed to the militia they called themselves only by one word of the contractual title: "society". Therefore, the permit for the seal was given because of the militia's assumption that any society must be a socialist organization, and as such it has the right to its own seal. To the seal the members of the newly-formed "society" added an account, opened not in a bank but in a savings institution, where both kinds of operations – transfer by clearing and deposit by cash – do not require strict formalities. From this moment they became free to receive money by clearing it from state enterprises and to divide the profit among themselves in cash. If the suspicion of a clerk of the savings bank had not been aroused, this "socialist society", a disguised private enterprise, could have existed and prospered till today.

2. *Private production under the mask of socialist production.* The famous Soviet authors Ilia Ilf and Evgenii Petrov described this kind of private activity in their book *Zolotoi Telenok* (The Golden Calf) early in the 1930s. Their invented enterprise *Roga i kopyta* (Horns and Hoofs) is notorious all over the country. However, literary fantasy of the 1930s is obviously backward in comparison with contemporary Soviet

practice. To prove this it is enough to tell the story of the production of ballpoint pens in the USSR. The first attempt in this direction was made, without success, by a Leningrad factory early in the 1960s. Ballpoint pens flooded the retail trade, but despite all their advantages in outward appearance one defect spoiled the whole thing: they did not write. As later discovered, a bad spring was the only cause of the defect. This spring did not push down the ink with the necessary force. Thus, ballpoint pens disappeared as quickly as they had earlier appeared. A little later ballpoint pens were reintroduced, however, not in the state retail trade, but on the black market. They were excellent, and one could buy them almost in any big city of the country. Thus, it was clear that a kind of underground industry had begun to function. Nevertheless, it was not so much the punitive agencies but the Leningrad factory – having already suffered an earlier defeat – which revealed the most vivid interest in finding the underground producer. And in this case its zeal proved to be successful. The producer was an ordinary engineer in Tbilisi, who had managed to invent the necessary spring. With this invention at his disposal he created a new enterprise, in reality his own, and a small factory of the state according to the formal registration. Its fictitious product interested no one any more than the "horns and hoofs" of Ilf and Petrov did, except for the significance of this product as an object of taxes, which were paid by the producer with extreme exactitude. As for the real product, ballpoint pens, it was in increasing demand and, being sold on the black market in numerous cities, ensured a large profit for the producer and good payment for his workers. The more they produced the higher the wages they received, and this was so stimulating that labor discipline was strengthened to an extent, which all of Andropov's disciplining detachments could only see in their sleep. Nobody was late, everybody strived to shorten the dinner break, etc. And what was the most important, the Soviet population at last received ballpoint pens that worked. Disconcerted as they were, representatives of the Leningrad factory got in touch with the producer and offered to buy his invention in an illegal way: not by means of its official registration, but in exchange of cash, which they were ready to pay. After this offer was refused, the punitive agencies intervened, and instead of an illegal bargain, a criminal case was initiated. Then three events followed consecutively: judicial conviction of the engineer, liquidation of his enterprise, and the production of ballpoint pens at first in Leningrad and later in many other cities of the USSR. Hence, the peculiarity of the case described consists in the fact that the shadow economy, in general being dangerous for the Soviet system, sometimes serves as a source of technical development for the country.

3. Socialist production for the sake of private activity. It happens sometimes that an entire enterprise or even a system of enterprises, implementing their production activity as socialist entities in accordance with planned tasks, actually function as private entities in accordance with the goal of personal gain. In 1963 the newly appointed first deputy of the Procurator of Uzbekistan, who supervised, among other subjects, preliminary investigations, found out accidentally that one insignificant criminal case had been under investigation without understandable reasons for more than two years. His curiosity led him to a very important discovery. The crime hidden by the trivial case encompassed the entire republican industry of astrakhan fur coats and involved hundreds of people from the bottom to the top of the republican hierarchy. Production of astrakhan fur coats in Uzbekistan is based on numerous production stages executed by different entities: collective farms and state enterprises. In Soviet terminology such a production system is called cooperative production (*kooperirovannoe proizvodstvo*). Each participant of the cooperative production, after finishing his part of the work, sends it to the following participant in exchange for money, and at the moment when the manufactured article has been sold to the consumer, all former payments are reimbursed with the addition of profit provided by the plan. In the case discussed, however, the usual order was significantly changed. The number of fur coats allocated for retail trade by the plan was regularly received at state stores and purchased at once by the participants of the criminal conspiracy for their own account. The circulation of those articles was endless, and it underwent a certain increase or decrease only in cases when the plan itself was changed. Beyond the planning limits, the production of fur coats could be developed as much as was allowed by the material resources on hand. The entire produce was sold on the black market at astronomical prices, and each participant of the cooperative production, as well as each trader or official involved received his share of the illegal profit. To have an idea of the real scale of this profitability, it will be enough to give only one example. The Uzbek people like *toy* – a family holiday with numerous guests and with the participation of dancers, singers, etc. Guests decide which of the dancers or singers have been the best and then the host shall award them prizes. The more expensive the prize the higher the prestige of the host. On one occasion when the host was a chairman of a collective farm which participated in the production of fur coats, he awarded the best singer with a robe made entirely of 100-ruble notes. Preliminary investigation of this case took months and years. Moscow sent seventy investigators from the USSR Procuracy to help the investigators of the Procuracy of the Uzbek Union Republic. After a large group of accomplices were convicted, they began to commit to the court comparatively small groups of accused persons. The First Secretary of the Uzbek Communist Party, an alternate member of the Politbureau Rashidov, was kept permanently informed about developments in the investigation. He also sanctioned each new arrest, while it was restricted to more or less high-ranking officials of the republic. However, the higher the preliminary investigation ascended the social ladder, the more reluctance was revealed by Rashidov in giving sanctions for new arrests, and when it came to the Chairman of the Republic *Gosplan* (the State Committee of Planning), the procedure was stopped once and for all. The First Deputy of the republican Procurator received a new office in another republic, arrests of people involved in the fur coat affair ceased, and the judicial hearing of the corresponding cases was discontinued. To understand such an ending, one must not forget that the shadow economy as a competitor of the legal economy is prosecuted in the USSR, but when this puts the Soviet political system in a bad light, the rulers consider it better to preserve the authority of the whole system rather than to denounce its shady sides without compromise.

4. Socialist production and private wholesale. Private wholesale can be combined with private production.[44] Other combinations, however, are also possible. We have already seen private production supported by socialist wholesale.[45] No less interesting is the opposite situation, where socialist production finds its continuation in private wholesale. In spite of general deficiencies as an inevitable concomitant of economic development in the USSR, certain goods, which are not in demand, or which exceed the demand of one area, may sometimes easily be sold in another area. Usually, these abnormalities result from defects of planning, if the product is allocated territorially according to the plan, or from the lack of care of producers, if they themselves must supply different regions of the country with their product. Strange as it may seem, there have been times when Vologda, without satisfying the demand of its own population, sent butter to Leningrad in such quantities that could not be consumed even by the population of that city. In respect of other goods, a similar situation could still occur at the present time. For example, department stores in Leningrad are overstocked with suits from the *Rassvet* factory and with shoes from the *Voskhod* factory. Because they are old-fashioned and poorly made, these articles are not in demand in Leningrad, where, though with difficulty, one can try to buy better things of the same kind, imported from Finland or other West European countries. In Saratov or Tambov the circumstances are different. There, western imports are inaccessible for ordinary people, and articles of local production are of such a poor quality that the products of *Rassvet* or *Voskhod* appear as genuine works of art. Nevertheless, an inhabitant of Saratov or Tambov would seek in vain in local department stores for articles spurned resolutely by Leningrad customers. It is precisely this kind of situation which promotes private trading as an adjunct of socialist production. In a case against an elderly person, accused of various economic crimes, the charge could in essence be reduced to two points: the sale of planned funds and the sale of contractual rights. If a product is distributed by planning agencies, then each purchasing organization receives a document under the title "fund" and may buy the entire quantity of goods covered by it. If distribution is not planned, any purchasing organization may contract to buy as much as the producing organization agrees to sell. The accused's activity was to find "fund" documents and contracts made in excess of Leningrad demands, and to transfer them to regions where the goods concerned would find an appropriate number of purchasers. Whenever he was successful, he received a fee from both clients consisting of a percentage of the value of the goods supplied through the transferred "fund" documents or the contracts. A certain part of the fee had to be spent for payment of services rendered by officials of planning agencies and other helpful people. The rest of the money was sufficient to make the accused a Soviet millionaire. At the judicial hearing of the case the prosecutor demanded the death penalty for the accused. In his last plea the accused expressed his astonishment at the prosecutor's demand. He did not deny his own enrichment, but he asked, who had been damaged in consequence of it. Not the Leningrad organizations, since they were able to sell unnecessary goods. Not the organizations of outlying regions, because they received the necessary goods. Not even the consumers of these regions because they had the opportunity to buy things they could not acquire otherwise. Thus, everybody gained. Then, why should the person who had satisfied all these demands be executed? Unfortunately for the accused, his arguments, persuasive in all other possible directions, were vulnerable on one point. Each participant of his wholesale enterprise may have been a winner, but one entity lost, and this entity was the Soviet system, politically incompatible with private initiatives of such a kind, and indifferent to the question of whether the latter leads to negative or positive economic results. Therefore, the court agreed with the prosecutor and the accused was executed, despite his sincere astonishment and impressive logic.

5. Socialist production and private retail trade. Socialist production is represented by enterprises of two kinds: one type manufactures the means of production, the other type produces consumer goods. This classification cannot be considered as something chemically uncontaminated, because the products of producers of consumer goods are sometimes used for the manufacturing of means of production (for instance, sacking used by plants and factories as rags in the production process), and vice versa, things manufactured as means of production are sometimes used as consumer goods (for instance, batteries of trucks used in citizens' cars). In addition, numerous enterprises belonging to the consumer goods industry have secret departments of a military character, while no less numerous enterprises belonging to the industry of the means of production have their mass consumption goods shops (*tsekhi shirpotreba*), which produce consumer goods. Bearing in mind a certain conventionality in the suggested classification, one can speak about two types of private retail trade concentrated around two kinds of socialist production.

The first type is concentrated around manufacturers of the means of production so that retail trade takes place in relationships between producer organizations and purchasing organizations. If the product is submitted for planned allocation, the producer has no right to sell it to a purchaser not indicated by the plan. However, by mutual collusion the former can manage to conceal a part of his production from the planning agencies and to sell it without the obligatory planning prerequisites to the latter. Such sales demand great resourcefulness, since they are illegal and not infrequently considered criminal. Therefore its participants try to make these sales without a written contract and by bypassing the normal order of money payments. As a rule, the representative of the purchasing organization pays cash to the representative of the producer organization, having received the necessary amount of money from the bank account beforehand, by means of one of the machinations, elaborated by Soviet economic practice for more than fifty years since the present system of bank control of financial operations was established in the USSR. Thus, retail trade of the first type, mainly concerned with machine tools and scarce spare parts, is based on a crime committed by both partners. The manager or other official of the purchasing organization commits an official crime, by illegally buying something for cash and illegally receiving cash from the bank account. In his turn, the manager or other official of the producer organization commits theft of socialist property, by illegally selling something as his own and appropriating the money received in exchange for the thing sold.[46]

The second type of private retail trade is concentrated around producers of consumer goods. Such trade takes place in relationships between workers of producer organizations and other citizens. Most often purchasers feel the need to resort to this kind of trade when there is a question of scarce goods, such as for example the replacements for automobile parts not to be found in the appropriate shops. Not infrequently, however, lower prices than those in the state network stimulate the same behavior. For example, Armenian brandy, regarded as the best brandy in the USSR, can be bought without difficulty at half price in Erevan, the capital of the Armenian Republic. Sometimes deficiencies and low prices act together as a stimulating factor. In 1980, for example, toothpaste disappeared from Soviet shops, but workers of toothpaste factories sold these articles at decreased prices, if a purchaser agreed to buy several tubes at once. In all similar cases underground retail trade is based on stealing, which is so wide-spread in production enterprises, that it has become impossible to deal with theft only by means of criminal responsibility, and Soviet legislation established administrative responsibility for so-called petty theft of social-ist property.[47] Meanwhile, there are also other sources of the underground retail trade connected, not with the production of goods, but with their realization. Workers of the state shops, having bought scarce goods for themselves, later sell them at increased prices. Sometimes, instead of goods, they sell vouchers for goods, which enable the purchaser to receive the goods at the very moment when the appropriate shop is opened. Finally, people who have nothing to do with state trade, manage to buy scarce goods at official prices and to resell them at increased prices. This conduct is also considered a crime and a very serious one at that: "speculation", *i.e.* the buying up and reselling of goods or any other articles for the purpose of making a profit.[48]

The many-sidedness of the shadow economy together with such individual eco-nomic activity as is considered normal and regular in the USSR may create the impression that the restricted limits of economic emancipation provided by Soviet law are essentially enlarged by Soviet practice. To avoid this obvious mistake, one must take into account at least four circumstances.

First, what is regular and normal individual economic activity from the viewpoint of Soviet law is in principle assessed negatively from the viewpoint of Soviet politics, and, despite the flexibility of the official attitude towards subsidiary husbandries, individual handicrafts etc. – predetermined by the extreme necessity stemming from the weakness of the Soviet economic system – Soviet citizens meet obstacles and restrictions at every step they try to make in this direction. Even within the limits established by law there is no stability which is so necessary for economic activity of any kind. Legal regulations adopted today can be changed tomorrow, and it is impossible to choose a reasonable line of behavior calculated on the more or less remote future.

Second, a shadow economy of any kind is illegal, and it can be engaged in only under the permanent risk of probable prosecution. Obviously, an activity which may be prosecuted, cannot be considered as a form of emancipation. Hence, the shadow economy relates not to the sphere of economic emancipation, but to the means of fighting economic slavery. The Soviet economy and the shadow economy are irreconcilable. Either one or the other must win. This is why economic crimes belong to the most dangerous crimes in the USSR, and the death penalty, inapplicable to them in free countries, appears to be a normal reaction of the Soviet regime against its sworn enemy.

Third, the number of people enriched by legal or illegal economic activities represents only a small part of the Soviet population. As a rule, in the northern part of the country, collective farmers can hardly manage to make ends meet by running their subsidiary husbandries. Handicrafts produce sufficient income only to very skillful workmen, and are usually only a source of supplementary income as a life-saving addition to the miserable official salary. The shadow economy, represented by the private sale of various goods stolen by workers of production enterprises, has a similar character, and private production or private wholesale cannot attain a high level owing to their unavoidable conspicuousness and extreme criminality. Thus, it is normally not the shadow economy but the official economy which determines living standards in the USSR and the entire economic structure of this country.

Fourth, to engage in individual economic activities, Soviet citizens must occupy an appropriate position in the Soviet social system. This excludes pensioners and handicapped people, and leaves workers, collective farmers, officers or officials, etc., who may possess their own subsidiary husbandries, engage in handicrafts or other private activities in the time free of their official work, or organize and run any kind of shadow economy which, being concealed as a result of its illegality, requires those who engage in it to have an official position as well. Otherwise the plot of land, the necessary prerequisite of the subsidiary husbandry, will be withdrawn, and prosecution will or may follow. Even if the latter does not involve more dangerous concealed activities, it may still lead to very unpleasant results, similar to those of malicious evasion of socially useful work. And as soon as this happens, other kinds of economic activities will cease at least until the person convicted will have finished serving his sentence.

The general conclusion to be drawn from what has been discussed above seems clear and indisputable. The Soviet interpretation of economic emancipation means neither economic freedom nor economic independence. Individuals become economically emancipated, only when they stop being economically dependent on other individuals or collective bodies. However, when one dependence is replaced by another, then economic slavery as such is preserved. The subsequent analysis will show who are the participants in this form of slavery in the USSR.

2. Economic Slavery

It would be astonishing if, along with the proclamation of the economic emancipation of the individual as a characteristic feature of the Soviet system, Soviet law openly proclaimed economic slavery as an intrinsic quality of the same system. Such a conclusion, however, logically follows from a comparative interpretation of various fragments of legal texts and undoubtedly results from a careful study of economic practice.

Economic Slavery in Soviet Law
The real nature of any historical type of human society depends – according to

Marxism-Leninism – on the dominant economic system which in its turn is determined by the dominant structure of ownership of the means of production. Soviet society is called a socialist society because, as the Constitution affirms, "socialist ownership of the means of production... shall constitute the basis of the economic system of the USSR".[49] In connection with this constitutional principle one divergence between different rules of Soviet legislation deserves to be separately accentuated. The Fundamentals of Civil Legislation provide for three forms of socialist ownership: state ownership; ownership of collective farms, other cooperative organizations, and their associations; and ownership of social organizations.[50] The same idea was reaffirmed by the draft of the Constitution now in force.[51] However, the Constitution itself has adopted a different approach. It refers to socialist ownership as "the property of trade union and other social organizations needed by them to carry out their charter tasks",[52] but, touching upon "the basis of the economic system of the USSR", it enumerates only "the form of state (all-people's) and collective farm cooperative ownership".[53] The third form of socialist ownership – ownership of social organizations – disappeared in the last enumeration, although its exposition in the Fundamentals of Civil Legislation did not undergo any change in the edict of the Presidium of the USSR Supreme Soviet, which was specifically issued to ensure the necessary conformity between Fundamentals of Civil Legislation and the new Constitution of the USSR.[54] How can one explain this obvious contradiction, which was noticed but not eliminated?

In the light of Soviet doctrine, there is no contradiction at all. When Soviet legal or theoretical sources enumerate the forms of socialist ownership, they never omit ownership of social organizations. But the problem of "the basis of the economic system" demands, in their opinion, another approach. This basis does not include the entire dominant (socialist) ownership, but only the part that does not go beyond the means of production. Trade unions and other social organizations do not engage in production. They have been created to fulfill cultural, scientific, and other purely social functions. Therefore, the means of production in principle do not belong to them. Only the Soviet state as well as collective farms and other cooperative organizations may possess the means of production, and, as a result, only their ownership embodies "the basis of the economic system" in the USSR.[55]

Legally, distinctions between the two forms of socialist ownership, which constitute the basis of the Soviet economic system, are reduced to different subjects and different objects.[56] State ownership belongs to the state and is declared to be all-people's ownership, since the Soviet state itself is typified as an all-people's state. Objects of state ownership do not undergo any restrictions. On the contrary, land, its minerals, waters, and forests are within "the exclusive ownership of the state",[57] *i.e.* nobody, except the state may own it, it cannot be sold and purchased, and the law only allows its transfer for the use of citizens and organizations in accordance with the specially established legal order.[58] At the same time, the basic means of production in industry, construction, agriculture, transport, communications, banks, the property of trade, municipal and other enterprises organized by the state, the basic city housing funds, and other property needed to carry out the tasks of the state also belong to the state,[59] although some of the enumerated objects, in contrast to the "exclusive ownership of the state", may be owned by collective farms and other cooperative organizations, provided the specifically established restrictions are observed. In the case of collective farm cooperative ownership Soviet law deals otherwise. In this case not the entire people, but the collective body of each collective farm or other cooperative is considered to be the owner. On the other hand, the number of objects, which fall under the second form of socialist ownership, is legally restricted. Collective farms and other cooperative organizations have the right to be owners only of the means of production or of other property needed by them to carry out their charter tasks.[60] It follows that, for example, a collective farm as an agricultural enterprise may possess means of agricultural and not metallurgical production, while a consumer cooperative as a trade organization may possess trade and not agricultural equipment. Such are the general distinctions between the two forms of socialist ownership outlined by the fundamental rules of Soviet law. As soon, however, as one applies the specific rules connected with the same problem, the situation essentially changes, and the generally proclaimed distinctions completely disappear.

Ownership, according to Soviet law, consists of three rights: possession, use, and disposal.[61] But in order to create ownership these rights are not sufficient. State economic associations, industrial and other enterprises, as well as other state entities possess, use, and dispose of the property allocated to them by the state. Nevertheless, Soviet law does not consider them to be owners.[62] Ownership does not only mean the unity of three rights; it also assumes application of these rights "within the limits established by law"[63] and without any other restriction. At the same time, property rights of the state entities are subordinated to different regulations. They are certainly restricted by legal limits also, but numerous other restrictions are also applied to them. In exercising their property rights, the state entities must act in conformity with (1) the purpose of their activity (for example, agricultural state enterprises shall not manufacture industrial articles), (2) planning tasks established by a higher agency (for example, an industrial state enterprise shall apply its equipment, raw materials, or money only to produce articles of the kind, quantity and quality indicated by the plan) and (3) the purpose of their property (for example, money allocated for the construction of a new shop shall not be used for the acquisition of machine-tools or raw materials for existing shops).[64] Therefore, despite possession, use, and disposal of corresponding items of property by separate state entities, the state – and not these entities – must be considered as the owner. It is not state entities but the state itself which defines the specific purposes of different activities, establishes the state planning tasks, and determines the different purposes of each property fund. Therefore, even after having distributed its property among the various entities, the state does not lose its position as an owner. This concept, supported by Soviet jurisprudence, is directly and openly confirmed by Soviet law. However, the same law proclaims that collective farm cooperative property belongs to collective farms and cooperatives, not to the state? Why? On the basis of what kind of logic? As a result of which differences between the legal positions of state entities, on the one hand, and collective farm cooperative entities, on the other hand?

"A juridical person shall possess civil legal capacity in accordance with the established purpose of its activity", states article 12 of the Fundamentals of Civil

Legislation. This general rule does not formulate an exception for collective farms and cooperatives. Thus, the first restriction established for property rights of state entities preserves its force also in the discussed case. Collective farms and other cooperative organizations, in exercising their property rights, must act in conformity with the purpose of their activity.

"The collective farm runs its economy by the plan", says article 14 of the Model Statute of the Collective Farm.[65] The plan is confirmed by a general meeting of collective farmers, but, in elaborating the draft of the plan, the collective farm must take into account various circumstances, first of all, the plan for state purchase of agricultural products.[66] The rules on the planning of economic activity of consumers cooperatives have a similar content. Hence, the second restriction established for the property rights of state entities preserves its force also in the case of collective farms and cooperative organizations. The latter, in exercising their property rights, must act in conformity with the state plans.

The collective farm creates its property funds, which "shall be used only in conformity with their purpose" (article 12 of the Model Statute of the Collective Farm). In addition, several rules of the same Statute introduce generally binding orders for all collective farms about the creation, repletion and expenditure of different funds.[67] Similar regulations are addressed to consumer cooperatives. This means that the third restriction established with regard to the property rights of state entities preserves its force also under the described circumstances. Collective farms and other cooperative organizations, in exercising their property rights, must act in conformity with the designated purpose of their property.

The only logically possible deduction from the stated arguments is that if the state entities do not own their property, then for the same reasons ownership cannot be exercised by collective farms and cooperative organizations, and vice versa: if the state is an owner of property that cannot be owned by state entities, then for the same reasons ownership of property that cannot be owned by collective farms and cooperative organizations must belong to the state.[68] In other words, the Soviet economy does not include two forms of socialist ownership of the means of production: state and collective farm/cooperative. It is based on state ownership of the means of production and nothing else.

This ownership must have its subjects. If the USSR realy had collective farm/cooperative ownership along with state ownership, then the Soviets could, at least formally, affirm that the former belonged to collective bodies of the appropriate entities: collective farms, consumer cooperatives, etc. The formal grounds for such a concept may be found in the fact that certain questions concerning collective farm property are solved by general meetings of collective farmers, and similar questions regarding the lower links of consumer cooperatives[69] are solved by general meetings of cooperatives' members. However, because collective farm/cooperative and general Soviet democracy are like two peas in the same pod, these general meetings do not so much resolve the property questions as rubber-stamp already adopted solutions, and, consequently, they do not essentially differ from production meetings of labor collectives at state enterprises.[70] On the other hand, as shown, collective farm/cooperative ownership does not exist as a separate type of ownership in the USSR. In reality, it is a part of state ownership, endowed with misleading a name on account of considerations of a political, economic, and even a demagogic character.[71] Therefore, collective farms headed by their boards and their chairmen, in deciding questions of property, do not become owners to the same extent as state enterprises, despite property decisions adopted by their managers personally or with the approval of their labor collectives.

The question of state ownership requires another approach. This form of ownership does not merely exist in the USSR; it occupies the dominant position and encompasses the Soviet economy completely. Then, who is its subject, to whom does it really belong? The most simple and natural answer is: the state. Unfortunately, under the circumstances, such an answer obscures and complicates, rather than explains the matter. To be clear, the reference to the state requires one very important addition in order to be able to define who personifies the Soviet state. The USSR Constitution is not sufficiently precise in this regard. Its formula "the all-people's state"[72] allows for two interpretations, and each of them can be textually supported by the Constitution itself.

The first interpretation of "the all-people's state" proclaims that the Soviet state is none other than the Soviet people themselves. This interpretation stems from the constitutional phrase that "all power in the USSR belongs to the people".[73] The constitutional provision that "state ownership is the common property of the whole Soviet people"[74] leads to the same conclusion.

The second interpretation of "the all-people's state" announces that the Soviet state is the governing body of the Soviet people. This interpretation stems from the constitutional provision that "the people exercise state power through soviets of people's deputies, which constitute the political foundation of the USSR".[75] The constitutional passage about the Soviet state as "the principal instrument... for the construction of socialism and communism",[76] leads to the same conclusion.

Since our analysis does not deal with the general notion of the Soviet state *in abstracto*, and is aimed only at revealing the personification of state ownership in the USSR, in the following argument both interpretations of "the all-people's state" shall be checked exclusively within the limits of the topic discussed.

If "the all-people's state" means the Soviet people themselves, then they must be the only subject of state ownership as the trinity of possession, use, and disposal exercised directly or indirectly within the limits of the law and without any other restriction. But that direct possession, use, and disposal of the entire economy of the country seems inaccessible to the whole people. Not even a single object can be in their direct possession, use, and disposal. Thus, the whole people, if they were owners, would be very peculiar kinds of owners, unique and remarkable in their being incapable – in contrast to all other owners of the world and throughout history – of exercising their ownership directly in any imaginable case. As for indirect exercise, the Soviet Constitution – having established the appropriate rule about political power – dropped its analogous regulations with regard to state ownership. "The people exercise state power through soviets of people's deputies", says article 2 of the Soviet Constitution. Well, but who acts as an intermediary in the people's exercise of possession, use and disposal of state property? One would look in vain for the necessary indications in the Constitution or any other law, and so there is nothing left but to examine all the possible practical variants.

Does this role belong to citizens as members of the Soviet people? In numerous cases they use different objects of state ownership, however, not representing the owner but relying upon other legal titles, such as tenants of state apartments, users of state land, etc. At the very moment when a citizen begins to treat any object of state ownership as his own, he commits a crime and must be punished. Unlike strikes which have been declared unimaginable as a protest of Soviet citizens against themselves,[77] stealing of state property has not been denied as a senseless appropriation of one's own property. Thus, the problem of indirect exercise of the people's ownership cannot be settled by citizens' activity.

Then, maybe, state enterprises and economic associations can exercise this necessary function? As has been shown,[78] separate parts of state property are allocated to them, and they have certain rights toward such parts. However, allocation to economic organizations does not encompass state ownership completely. Money from the budget, state reserves and certain other objects are not distributed temporarily or permanently. At the same time, state property allocated to a specific entity consists of different funds and engenders different rights. For example, an enterprise uses but cannot sell its equipment, and, the other way around, the product can be sold but not used by the same enterprise. As a rule, economic organizations have never combined the three rights of possession, use and disposal with regard to specific parts of their property. But even if such a combination took place, the enumerated rights of state entities would never attain the level of full ownership.[79] Hence, state enterprises and economic associations can ensure the indirect exercise of the people's ownership, but not with regard to all objects and the entire spectrum of state ownership.

Finally, would it not be reasonable to suppose that the Soviet people, incapable of exercising their ownership directly, do so indirectly, owing to the various activities not only of economic organizations, but of all state agencies? Each of them has its own task and a restricted number of rights and duties. One regulates and another orders, one plans and another fulfills plans, one produces and another sells, one distributes and another consumes. However, if one would collect all these kinds of activity together with all corresponding rights and duties, the multivarious forms necessary for exercising state ownership would be described without gaps and omissions. In all probability, such a solution would be correct, but it means that the Soviet people exercise state ownership through the Soviet state, because the state and all its bodies and agencies are the same thing. Therefore, the only solution, which seems acceptable, disproves the first interpretation and leads us to the second interpretation of "the all-people's state". If this notion is to have any sense at all, it must be understood in the meaning of, not the people themselves, but the governing body of the Soviet people. Then it becomes clear that because the Soviet people and the Soviet state are not one and the same, state ownership in the USSR cannot be "the common ownerhip of the whole Soviet people".[80] It has been, and continues to be, the ownership of the Soviet state.

In the political realm, the fact that the Soviet state and the Soviet people are not one and the same has compelled the Soviet regime to proclaim the superiority of the people over the state in the USSR. It is only in such a way that the concept of "the all-people's state" becomes, if not truthful, then at least understandable. Soviet law itself, however, discredits this concept, introducing as a general rule the indirect exercise of political power by the people and admitting the people's direct political activity solely in the form of referendums, based exclusively on decisions of those who formally are not the bearers of the highest authority, but only the subordinate intermediaries in its execution. Soviet reality is far removed from the concept of the all-people's state. Instead of political power subordinated to the people, the USSR practices subordination of the people to political power. Its subordination is as unrestricted as political power is unlimited. Political freedom in words and political domination in reality: such is the Soviet system, if one considers it as a governing structure with all the peculiarities of its ingredients and methods.[81]

In the economic realm, the fact that the Soviet state and the Soviet people are not one and the same has compelled the Soviet regime to proclaim the double nature of the dominant ownership in the USSR as belonging simultaneously to the Soviet state and to the Soviet people. Only in such a way does the concept of "all-people's ownership" become explainable if not logically, then at least pragmatically. Soviet law itself, however, disregards this concept, passing over in silence all the ways in which the people might exercise their rights of ownership and enumerating only the property rights of different state agencies.[82] Soviet reality has no concern with the same concept at all.[83] Instead of the economic omnipotence of the people, the USSR practices the permanent strengthening of the people's economic dependence on the state. Their dependence is as strong as the state is economically powerful. Economic emancipation in words and economic slavery in reality: such is the Soviet system, if one considers it from the viewpoint of economic activities in all their varieties.

Thus, the Soviet regime belongs to the category of monopolistic regimes, but it is a monopolistic regime *sui generis*, combining in one entity two monopolies: political and economic. As the only personification of unlimited political power it is monopolistic politically, and as the only owner of the means of production it is monopolistic economically. Both monopolies are interdependent, and their mutual interdependence receives a certain reflection in Soviet law.

The political monopoly has helped to introduce the economic monopoly with its subsequent confirmation by law. Property owned by capitalists and landowners was at first actually expropriated by the new political power, and only then was this factual event legalized by the well-known Soviet decrees. Collective farms were created and the individual peasant economy was liquidated through political compulsion, and only after this did collective farm law appear as a separate branch of the Soviet legal system. Collective farms gradually lost their original, more or less significant, property independence, and only when the desired result was attained, were they in one part transformed into state agricultural entities and in another part subordinated to legal regulations, which were not essentially different from those applicable to state enterprises. Centralized planning of economic activities was applied with growing intensity, but only when it became actually all-embracing, did the law proclaim that "the economic life in the USSR shall be determined and directed by the state national economic plan",[84] or, using contemporary legislation, "the direction of the economy shall be carried out on the basis of state plans for economic and social development".[85] From time immemorial, Soviet leaders have been accustomed to doing whatever they consider necessary or reasonable with the budget, paying little attention to the funds allotted for different purposes by budget laws. However, only after Stalin's constitutional reform – and up to the present time – have they used the form of a budget law so skillfully elaborated that nobody is able to check reliably whether actual state expenditure on various needs corresponds to the budget provisions or not.

The economic monopoly is the main source of the political monopoly which is concentrated in the same grasp in fact and legally supported by the appropriate regulations. Under the existing economic monopoly, Soviet citizens cannot earn their living without establishing labor relationships with the State. The overwhelming majority of citizens must take part in such relationships in order not to starve to death, being deprived of their own economy and having the state as their only possible employer. The insignificant minority of citizens who operate legally, as owners of subsidiary husbandries, or illegally, as participants of underground economic activities, must at the same time be workers of the state in order to preserve the necessary prerequisites for legal status (a plot of land, for example) or the indispensable disguise for an illegal existence (an official position of a clerk, for example). Due to these causes, all citizens are afraid of losing their job, and political disloyalty has always resulted in dismissal, even where it did not entail more dangerous consequences. There are certain legal rules which directly provide such a sanction. For example, labor contracts can be terminated in cases of the "commission by a worker performing educational functions of immoral misconduct incompatible with the continuation of such work".[86] And there is nothing easier than to declare political disloyalty immoral misconduct. When a specific job demands KGB clearance (*dopusk*) in consequence of its secrecy or importance, the cancellation of such clearance, which does not demand any explanation, is equal to dismissal. Relying upon an artificial interpretation, one can prove that political disloyalty leads to "unsuitability of the manual or office worker for the position occupied by him",[87] which also serves as a legal ground for terminating a labor contract. There are numerous other approaches ensuring the unhindered dismissal of "politically unreliable" people. While criminal punishment or direct suppression are capable of insulating the existing regime against the most extreme danger, the universal political obedience of the many millions of USSR citizens is due to their economic dependence on the strongly organized political force. This is why the unlimited political power of the Soviet regime can apply different measures and use various means, but the economic monopoly and only the economic monopoly serves as its basis and its foremost bulwark.

The joining of economic and political monopolies in the same grasp exhaustively explains all those Soviet "miracles" which sometimes so delight certain foreign observers. According to them, "communism as embodied in the Soviet system, offers its followers economic security, military power and sensational technological progress, all in return for one thing: absolute subservience to ... the party leadership".[88] Even if such an exchange between the party leadership and the Soviet citizenry really took place, it would be impossible, nevertheless, to understand such admiration from an American who receives more of all these goods including welfare payments that are higher than the average salary in the USSR, and who at the same time preserves his political freedom without returning "absolute subservience". His admiration, however, must be factually corrected not for the sake of polemic, but of truth. As for the military power of the USSR, there is no doubt of this, but as it is not under the threat of foreign attack or invasion, why does the Soviet citizenry need such power, created at the people's own expense and to their huge economic detriment? As for economic security, it does not go, in the span of a month, beyond the average salary of 180 rubles (about 155 dollars). Would Americans accept similar economic security in replacement of their economic insecurity? "Sensational technological progress" also needs to be elucidated. If the observer in question means military achievements in the broadest sense, including space exploration, he is certainly right, although in this case his information stems from the media, not from visiting of military plants, which are closed to Soviet citizens, and not only to foreigners. If he is talking about the Soviet economy as a single whole, he should check his impression by visiting any department store, open to foreigners as well as to Soviet citizens. Only then will it be discovered that the "sensational technology" of the USSR has not yet attained the American level of the 1920s or 1930s.

However, there are genuine, not invented, miracles in the USSR, and it is necessary to explain them. The Soviet Union is far from being the richest country in the world. Nevertheless, the Soviets can make investments, if necessary, which would be too much for incomparably richer countries, for example, military expenditure. Where does this capacity originate? It is rooted in the combination of the economic monopoly with the political one. As the economic monopolist, the Soviet state has at its disposal all of the country's material and financial resources. By their even distribution some demands (for example, the people's demands for goods) would be better satisfied and some other demands (for example, the state military demands) would not be so well satisfied. But as the political monopolist, the Soviet state may distribute material and financial resources unevenly, directing them as much as possible towards one goal (military, for instance) and reducing them to a *minimum minimorum* in connection with another goal (consumption, for instance). On the other hand, the Soviet Union is one of the most populated countries in the world. Despite this – as proved by, for example, growing food difficulties in recent years – the Soviets manage to permanently keep the whole people under control and obedient, whatever the concrete historical situation. What is the source of this capacity? The answer must be the same: the combination of the economic monopoly with the political one. As the political monopolist, the Soviet state has at its disposal all legal and illegal means of prosecution and suppression. Through their broad application, certain kinds of disobedience (for example, dissent) are overcome and certain other kinds of disobedience (for example, discontent) are left without any political reaction. But as the economic monopolist, the Soviet state may suppress even uncontrollable disobedience, keeping everybody under the threat of economic sanctions for political unreliability.

Political monopoly is not a new phenomenon in human history, but in the past it has never been combined with an economic monopoly. Economic monopoly also is not an invention of our time, but in the past it has never been supported by a political monopoly. The Soviet regime is the first historical model that unites both. This leads to unlimited political obedience as well as to firm economic slavery. The latter has already been shown in its legal aspect. Now let it reveal its practical manifestations.

Economic Slavery in Soviet Practice

The Soviet state, combining political and economic monopolies, is simultaneously a political and an economic organization. As a political organization it functions and acts through agencies of political power: leading and subordinate, legislative and executive, judicial and suppressive, guarding and attacking. As an economic organization it functions and acts through agencies of economic activity: separate enterprises and economic associations of industry, agriculture, construction, transportation, trade, banks, insurance, etc. The Soviet state supports its political power by strengthening its economic potential and consolidates its economic forces by exercising political domination. Special agencies of political power, such as, for example, *Gosplan* (the state planning committee), authoritatively direct economic activity, while economic activity, in its turn, supplies the entire political structure with the necessary financial and material resources.

The result of economic activity is embodied in the product produced, whether it be goods (machines, raw materials, etc.) or services (transportation, restoration, etc.). However, because the Soviet economy is based on exchange of money, no matter who its participants are – whether they be citizens or enterprises – the economic result, achieved in the form of the product, returns to the state in the form of income.[89]

Income received may be divided into two parts: one represents cost price, the other embodies profit.

Since the state is the owner of the Soviet economy, cost price represents a peculiar issue in the USSR. It includes the usual components: expenditure for the means of production and for wages or salaries in the sphere of production. Along with this, all maintenance costs of state machinery, not compensated by income taxes of citizens, are, in the appropriate proportion, distributed among economic entities as an obligatory addition to the cost price of their product. On the other hand, certain services, and among them several very important ones, are provided to the Soviet citizenry free of charge (education, medical aid, etc.) or below cost price (rental for state apartments, payment for urban transport services, etc.). The state cannot, of course, work miracles and create sources for its largesse from nothing. Increments to cost price together with citizens' income taxes also provide governmental generosity with the necessary resources as well. To ensure that citizens – within the limits of their meagre incomes – receive at least the unconditionally indispensable means of human subsistence, the Soviets have fixed quite low prices for bread and certain similar consumer goods, but the unavoidable loss on this account is compensated by artificial gains in other areas, originating from increments to cost price or increases in the retail price. Therefore, when, in describing the economic situation of the people,

Soviet propaganda speaks of additions to salaries and wages in the form of goods supplied to citizens by the state without charge or for a modest charge, it simply distorts the real situation. Nothing is received by citizens without complete compensation. They pay for everything either directly, when the retail price corresponds to cost price increased with a fair profit, or indirectly, through income taxes and payment of excessively high retail prices. An analysis of the ostensibly or inadequately remunerated services supplied by the Soviet state confirms the old maxim: *ex nihilo nihil fit*.

Profit, extracted from the Soviet economy, also has its peculiarities due to the monopolistic state ownership of the means of production. When production is based on private ownership, it becomes clear that one person works, receiving a salary, while another person owns, receiving profit. Hence, the recipients of salary and profit are not the same. With production based on state ownership, when in addition the latter is proclaimed to be "all-people's ownership", the situation changes radically, at least in appearance. As an individual the worker receives his salary, but as a component of the people, and through the people in their capacity of collective owner, the worker receives profit. Hence, the recipients of salary and profit are one and the same. They are the same person, however, with different qualities under different circumstances. Different qualities allow them to be employers as well as employees. But, being the same person, they can neither exploit nor become an object of exploitation. The salary is a result of the citizen's work for himself as a member of society, and profit is a result of the citizen's work for society whose member he is.

To get out of this sophisticated labyrinth of Marxist phraseology one needs to clarify who is the real owner of the Soviet economy in accordance with the same Marxist doctrine. As Marxism affirms, those who appropriate profit, generated by the use of the means of production, are the owners of these means. In the USSR the state appropriates profit, and, consequently, it is an owner. But what is meant by the state under such circumstances; who personally stands behind it as a genuine beneficiary? After being received, profit falls into two parts from the point of view of its destination. One part is to be applied for expanded production: construction of new plants and factories, enlargement of existing plants and factories, etc. Within the limits of this part the Soviets may pretend with a certain semblance of truthfulness that profit serves the interests of the whole society, and that therefore state property belongs to the whole people. However, their efforts prove to be in vain as soon as the second part of profit, used for the owner's personal needs, becomes the main object of analysis. The labor of Soviet citizens, whether mere workers or high officials, is paid by salary and wages. Let us ignore the fact that the Bolsheviks' slogan "the salaries of governmental officials must not exceed the wages of an average worker" has nothing to do with Soviet reality, and let us suppose that even despite the proportion of ten to one between the former and the latter, the socialist principle "to each according to his labor" remains inviolate. These considerations do not affect the correctness of our analysis, because wages and salaries are compensated not by profit, but by the equivalent of cost prices and by the payment of income taxes. It seems more important that governmental officials in the broad meaning of the word (including the Party bureaucracy and the technocratic rulers) receive part of the profit – which remains after production demands have been satisfied – on top of their salaries as a general form of payment for labor. This process, not provided for by law, but actually occurring with great regularity, reveals itself in the following features.

First, distribution of profit assumes such forms as allocation of all kinds of goods either gratis or at a discount. Such goods include foodstuffs and manufactured articles, apartments and country houses, transportation, domestic and cultural services, special treatment and convenient holiday arrangements, etc. To conceal this shameful system the Soviets have created so-called closed establishments (shops, hospitals, sanatoriums, etc.).[90] Nevertheless, the system itself has stopped being a secret for a long time, and sometimes high Party officials are forced to explain its existence publicly. They, however, do not feel embarrassed when faced with such a necessity. For example, early in the 1960s, when L. Il'ichev in his capacity of a secretary of the CPSU Central Committee was asked for an appropriate explanation by participants of meetings of chairmen of departments of Leningrad University and Institutes, he, without batting an eyelid, referred to Lenin as an enemy of *uravnilovka* (wage-levelling), as if legally established payment of labor has anything in common with illegally introduced bonuses for officials.

Second, the proportions of the distribution depend directly on the level that one or another official position occupies on the scale of ranks intrinsic to Soviet bureaucracy. The higher the position in question the larger the part of distributed profit. The desired effect is achieved by taking into account the different quantities and qualities of allotted goods, the various proportions between goods given gratis and at discount, the several levels of discount, etc. To conceal these gradations the Soviets have created closed establishments of different ranks, and each of them is accessible only to the corresponding stratum of governmental officials. For example, the Leningrad Committee of the CPSU has its country houses situated in the Komarovo settlement. All these houses are surrounded by a high fence. At the same time, inside the large area there are internal fences that separate country houses of officials of one rank from those given to officials of another rank. A similar order is applied in all other cases, and this leads to such mutual separation inside the ruling elite that, according to one high-standing lady, the circle of her acquaintances changed completely each time her husband was promoted from one hierarchical rank to another.

Third, participation in the distribution of profit is derived from participation in the exercise of political power. As long as an individual belongs to the politically ruling stratum he preserves the economic advantages stemming from his appropriate share of distributed profit and, the other way around, the same individual loses all his economic privileges at the very moment when he is expelled from the politically ruling stratum. To conceal the predetermined relationship of strict dependence, the Soviets created the institution of *trudoustroistva* (job arrangement) for politically ruling officials. If anyone of them loses his position, all possible measures are taken to give him another position, albeit at the lowest level, but within the framework of political rule. This ensures him a certain residue of economic advantages and stimulates his support for the very important collective secret involved. However, in the most extreme cases it may become necessary to deprive an individual of all participation in political rule, and, as a result, he loses all the economic advantages connected with such participation. Then everything possible is done to isolate him completely from the stratum whose representative he has been until then. To further these goals all means are acceptable, including violations of law or disregard of individual rights. When Adzhubei, Khruschchev's son-in-law, was ousted together with his father-in-law, he became an ordinary journalist. Soon after his ouster he was evicted from an apartment in the governmental apartment building, in contradiction to Soviet law, which does not provide for such sanctions under those circumstances, but in conformity with the needs of the ruling elite interested in being divested of those people who stopped belonging to it.

Thus, each shareholder of political power takes part in the distribution of economic profit destined for personal consumption, and as a single entity the same profit belongs to the comparatively restricted collective body acting under the name of the Soviet state. Since the state, personified by its real beneficiaries, appropriates economic profit destined for personal consumption, their interests, and not the interests of the whole people, are also satisfied by the economic profit destined for production. Hence, the politically ruling stratum is the genuine owner of the USSR economy, and as soon as this truth has been learned, all mysterious secrets of the Soviet system come to light.

The state, on the one side, and the people, on the other: these are the principal components of the Soviet system. The state is the politically ruling and economically dominant collective body; the people, politically ruled and economically dominated, makes up the balance. Using official Soviet terminology and calling the USSR a socialist country, the following juxtaposition of socialism, capitalism, and feudalism can be articulated. Socialism combines political and economic power in the same body. In this regard it differs from capitalism, where ownership of the economy and the exercise of power are separated, and rather resembles feudalism, where the owners of the land are simultaneously the political rulers. However, under feudalism political power stems from land ownership, while under socialism economic might results from political puissance. The Soviet system is based upon the primacy of politics over the economy, and only in light of its political structure, which is labelled as the Soviet state, can one understand its economic essence, which is labelled as socialist ownership.

The Soviet state is a *sui generis* political organization united as a single whole and differentiated as a complicated social mechanism.

Its unity is based upon the common interest of the dominant political body to strengthen political power in the country, to make it unassailable, invulnerable and virtually unlimited. Everything is subordinated to this aspiration, including a peculiar relationship between legal and administrative ways of managing the Soviet economy. Laws, adopted by the Supreme Soviet of the USSR, although they are normative acts of the highest order, only play a very modest role as an instrument of economic regulation because otherwise they would restrict the necessary freedom of the administrative agencies. In contrast to this, governmental edicts concerning the economy are adopted by the hundreds and thousands: they ensure complete freedom for any kind of centralized commands. For example, the Fundamentals of Civil Legislation include only twelve articles concerning the contract of delivery,[91] while two statutes concerning delivery issued by the USSR Council of Ministers in 1981[92] together consist of 205 articles. Furthermore, to assemble all the governmental edicts on any particular economic topic, one would need to publish a legislative collection in many volumes. A similar situation exists in construction, transportation and other spheres of economic activity. The political needs of economic centralization have also led to the established system of economic planning. The Soviet constitution speaks in a very general way about the all-embracing importance of the plan for the Soviet economy,[93] but a law specifically devoted to economic planning does not exist in the USSR. A modest number of rules concerning different kinds of applicable plans are scattered over separate governmental decrees.[94] In essence, however, everything depends on established practice which has been developing, with certain deviations, in accordance with the general tendency of increasing centralization. Deviations usually have a forced character. To save the economy – brought to the brink of disaster by excessive centralization – strict planning from the top has been somewhat relaxed, together with a broadening of the independence of lower economic entities, the introduction of a certain amount of freedom in their own planning and an increase in the role of their own contracts, etc. Centralization, however, remains the general tendency and is not only proclaimed with enthusiasm by Soviet rulers but supported quite willingly by economic managers. The replacement early in the 1920s of centralized war communism with the decentralized new economic policy (NEP) was given a hostile reception, while the transition from the decentralized NEP to an extremely centralized economic policy in the late 1920s and early 1930s took place without noticeable resistence; similarily the 1965 reform with its economic liberalization threw economic managers into confusion, while the rejection of this liberalization, ensured by the 1973-1974 reform, was met by them with unconcealed relief.[95] The primacy of political tasks as opposed to all other practical problems demands an assessment of specific circumstances from the point of view of the very summit of Soviet society – and not from the perspective of lower positions and secondary interests. If, for example, the organization of the 1980 Olympic Games in Moscow had depended upon economic considerations and the opinions of those directly involved, these Games would have never taken place, because it was obvious from the beginning that they would lead to nothing but unjustified expenses and unpredictable troubles. However, the Soviet leaders – despite their vows about the separation of sport from politics – considered the Olympics as a trump-card in the political game and insisted upon Moscow as the venue with utter disregard for the negative economic and other consequences.

Side by side with its unity, the political organization called the Soviet state, has its inner differentiation. One part of this organization implements unrestricted political domination, another engages in exercise of daily (in Soviet terminology, operative) activities, and a third deals with purely ceremonial functions.[96] Its members staff high-ranking and subordinate agencies, directive and executive bodies, important and not very significant levels. There are rulers and executives; executives who at the same time rule, and rulers who at the same time execute; rank-and-file officials who nevertheless may issue orders, and officials of high, higher or the highest rank who do little or nothing else but issue orders. And this very complicated table of ranks is far from being neutral in practice. It plays a very important role in the economic competence of each agency as well as of every official. The higher a position the broader its economic competence, whether this is provided for by law or not. The First Secretary of the Central Committee of the Kazakhstan Communist Party, as well as the First Secretary of the Leningrad Party Committee have no economic rights at all, if one is to judge from the texts of Soviet laws. Nevertheless, they managed to build the Palace of Sport in Alma-Ata and a Leningrad copy of the Moscow Palace of Congresses without budget financing, but with money supplied according to their orders by industrial enterprises and other economic entities of Kazakhstan and Leningrad. They are, however, subordinate, though very high-ranking, officials, whose orders may not go beyond their territory and may be countermanded by higher agencies. At the very top of the Soviet system – unlimited politically – there are no economic restrictions, and the Politbureau disposes of state property entirely at its own discretion. This relates equally to either part of economic profits, whether destined for production or for personal use. Moreover, where the interests of the highest summit are concerned, any orders may be given, and any whim satisfied. When Ekaterina Furtseva lost her position in the Politbureau and became only the USSR Minister of Culture, she constructed a luxurious country house for her daughter at the expense of the ministry. Legally she committed a crime, but actually there were no grounds to blame Furtseva, who had simply become accustomed to the rules of conduct appropriate for Politbureau members and could not immediately free herself of a deep-rooted habit. Furtseva's situation was understood by her former colleagues in the Politbureau, and, as a result, she retained her ministerial office, losing only her status of a deputy to the USSR Supreme Soviet by way of punishment. The economic privileges of the politically ruling caste are guarded to an extent that completely precludes any sacrifice connected with them. At one time during the mid-1960s, in the summer, there was a very difficult situation in the cancer hospitals of Leningrad. Because most parts of the hospitals were closed for repairs, only 60 patients could receive in-house treatment in July and August. At the same time, *Sverdlovka*, a closed hospital for the Leningrad bureaucracy, usually had several buildings empty during the summer. Nevertheless, the request of Leningrad oncologists to allow the temporary use of one of those buildings was refused pitilessly by the first secretary of the Leningrad Party Committee. Even for such an official it would have been dangerous to admit ordinary people to a closed establishment and to place the caste interests of the Leningrad elite under a rather improbable threat.

In accordance with the demands of the Soviet state as a political organization the Soviets exercise the management of socialist ownership as an economic phenomenon.

The method of management most appropriate to the demands of unrestricted political power, would appear to be the centralized distribution of the product, as well as the centralized supply of the production mechanism from the top without exchange of money and any initiative from the bottom. On the model of this method Lenin introduced war communism immediately after his seizure of power. But the system did not work, because it deprived producers of all possible economic incentives. Another method, better adjusted to the demands of economic development, consisted of the decentralized sale by the producers of their product, as well as the decentralized supply of the production mechanism on the basis of money exchange at the initiative from the bottom and without interference from the top. On the basis of this model, or a near replica of it, Lenin introduced the NEP as soon as war communism revealed its destructive forces. But the new system, although it worked economically, became dangerous politically, because it deprived the ruling summit of the economic monopoly as the main source of Soviet political power. The "golden mean" – which had been found by Stalin shortly after Lenin's death – was chosen and was preserved with certain contradictory modifications by all subsequent leaders of the USSR. This "golden mean" is based upon two methods: plan and *khozraschet* (economic accountability).

The plan represents the centralizing trend: it expresses the views of the top concerning the prospects and directions of economic development. Centralized planning can be imperative (mandatory) or indicative (advisory). The Soviet regime prefers imperative (mandatory) planning. It is true, that, in addressing collective farms as formally independent owners, the Soviets like to use the word "recommend", instead of the word "oblige". This is, however, nothing more than a *modus dicendi*. Not a single collective farm has ever understood such recommendations to be other than commands. To some extent and in some economic sectors the imperativeness of economic plans was relaxed a little in comparison with the former rigidity. For example, in the realm of supply the purchaser has the right, while observing certain conditions, to refuse execution of a planned contract completely or in part.[97] Nevertheless, in principle, Soviet plans preserve their mainly mandatory character. On the other hand, centralized planning can include detailed and general indices. The Soviet regime prefers detailed planning. The attempted transition from detailed to general planning, provided for by the 1965 reform, failed because in consequence of it the ruling summit began to lose control over the Soviet economy. Therefore, detailed planning was restored first by administrative order and ultimately by virtue of the 1973-1974 reform. Moreover, even the economic experiment, proclaimed by Andropov in 1983 and supported by Chernenko after his ultimate promotion, did not liberate from detailed planning those ministries and their economic entities that were outlined as the object of the experiment.[98] Thus, the plan as the first method of the "golden mean" is imperative and detailed.

The second method, *khozraschet*, represents the decentralizing trend: it ensures initiatives from the bottom in economic processes. The entire reservoir of the means of production is distributed among state enterprises and other economic entities, which become economically and legally independent from the moment of their creation. As economically independent units, they possess, use, and dispose of the corresponding items of state ownership, make a profit and compensate expenses, settle accounts with the state budget in conformity with established quotas and utilize the remainder of their funds to satisfy the demands of expanded production. As legally independent units, they are in the position of juridical subjects, *i.e.* they may acquire property rights and duties in their own name, and be plaintiffs or defendants in court and other agencies which hear and solve property disputes.[99] As administrative orders are the means of planning, so economic contracts are the means of *khozraschet.* Based upon *khozraschet*, economic entities conclude contracts such as those of delivery, capital construction, carriage of freight, bank account, bank credit, etc. Economic contracts are secured by mutual liability within the limits of actual losses and liquidated damages. Liability does not, however, preclude specific performance. The contractual partner ought to perform the contract itself, despite reimbursement of losses and payment of penalties.[100] Thus, *khozraschet* as the second method of the "golden mean" provides for legal security and economic freedom.

There is no need to point out that both methods basically countervail one another, as diametrically opposed economic approaches, while the Soviet leadership insists upon "the correct combination" of plan and *khozraschet*. This, as one would think, must unavoidably lead to insurmountable difficulties. The Soviet regime, however, has managed to avoid these in a very simple way: it subordinates *khozraschet* to the plan just as generally any decentralization is turned into rigid centralization in the USSR. As a result, almost nothing of the economic and legal independence, connected with *khozraschet*, remains, under the pressure of centralized commands which are inseparable from planning. Basic assets of economic entities may be transferred to other economic entities by administrative order at any moment according to direct statutory provisions.[101] As for circulating assets, legal regulations provide for their withdrawal by a superior agency only in the case of a surplus as compared to the standard set, and solely in conformity with the annual report.[102] But this restriction is virtually paralyzed because of the ability of a superior agency to change the plan and to withdraw the surplus of circulating assets resulting from such a change at any moment. Moreover, even economic incentive funds – which, according to the legal rules, cannot be withdrawn at all, and of which the balance, unused during one year, shall be left at the disposal of economic entities in the next year[103] – are nevertheless redistributed in practice, if the USSR Council of Ministers considers it necessary to use them for road building or another important goal. So much for economic independence, and it is no wonder that legal independence has suffered the same fate. Economic entities act as juridical subjects only in relationships with equal partners. In connection with superior agencies they are considered, not so much possessors of definite rights, but strictly subordinated obligors. Freedom of contract, albeit restricted in matters of price and several other terms, exists only for unplanned contracts, which play an insignificant role anyway and even so have sometimes to be engaged in compulsorily.[104] Planned contracts depend on planning tasks, either completely (*e.g.* capital construction), or in their most important conditions (*e.g.* delivery). Losses reimbursed and penalties paid must be transferred by their recipients to the state budget at the end of the economic year, and this so jeopardizes the willingness to demand them, that in order to preserve the effectiveness of such remedies, special legal rules have been created which proclaim the right to exact penalties from a violator to be the duty of the creditor toward the state.[105]

That is what the Soviet system looks like from the aspect of one of its principal components – the Soviet state taken as a politically unlimited power and an economically omnipotent entity. The second component, the Soviet people, does not change the general conclusions about the nature of this system already made on the grounds of the previous analysis. On the contrary, it confirms and strengthens the same conclusions.

Marx holds that to become an object of exploitation the legally free worker must at the same time be divested of ownership embodied in the means of production. Both prerequisites described by the founder of theoretical communism are on hand in the society of "developed socialism" engaged in the "construction of communism".[106]

The worker is legally free in the USSR. Numerous Soviet laws proclaim and confirm his freedom. It is true that workers suffer some noticeable restrictions. The facts of compulsory labor have been already stated above.[107] It seems necessary to add to the facts enumerated that, on the one hand, "young manual workers who have graduated from professional-technical and technical schools, and young specialists who have graduated from higher and secondary special educational institutions shall be assured work in accordance with the skills and qualifications acquired".[108] On the other hand, these young manual workers and young specialists are obliged to work according to obligatory appointments for two or three years in the first case and for three years in the second case.[109] Beyond directly provided cases the formal freedom of the Soviet workers is not in doubt.

It also seems beyond doubt that the Soviet worker is free from the ownership of means of production. Therefore simple economic necessity compels him to sell his labor permanently and on terms imposed by the purchaser. In the situations already discussed,[110] when Soviet citizens operate legally in subsidiary husbandries or illegally in underground enterprises, the compulsion to work in the monopolistic economy remains just as strong. However, under such circumstances, not so much economic as extra-economic coercion plays a compulsory role. People work as a result not of economic necessity, but of the legal threat of economic sanctions such as the withdrawal of their plot of land or the confiscation of their enterprise together with more serious criminal punishment. Nevertheless, coercion "to work for society" whether – generally – by economic, or – exceptionally – by extra-economic means, has become all-embracing in the Soviet Union.

Hence, even according to Marxist-Leninist doctrine, both conditions necessary for exploitation exist in the USSR. Attempts to conceal the obvious truth with references to "all-people's ownership" do not stand the test. When it comes to the crunch, not the people but the state reveals itself as the owner of the whole Soviet economy. It means that the two principal components of the Soviet system – the state and the people – are correlated: (1) in the realm of politics as the ruler and the ruled; (2) in the realm of economics as the exploiter and the exploited.

Marx further holds that there are varying degrees of exploitation, which are determined by the proportion between the "necessary" product assigned to the worker as payment for his labor and the "additional" product appropriated as economic profit by his master. In all the mathematical illustrations contained in Marx's principal work *Das Kapital* he never went beyond 100% exploitation, and one can assume that this probably reflected his abstract ideas about the normal level of economic cruelty of capitalism in his time.

Since exploitation also exists under socialism, estimates as to its extent are possible. The difficulty one meets in this respect is connected with the unreliability and inaccessibility of statistics in the USSR. Nevertheless, with the aid of certain published data – and despite their inexactitude and lack of authenticity – at least an approximate figure is attainable. Let us suppose that the average salary of 180 rubles applies to all working people, including peasants, although collective farmers' labor is lower paid than industrial labor. With a population of about 270 million, the working population cannot be more than 60% and, consequently, numbers approximately 162 million. Thus, the total payment for labor does not exceed 29 billion rubles a month and 348 billion rubles a year. At the same time, the law on the budget of 1984, issued by the USSR Supreme Soviet in December 1983,[111] provides for a net annual revenue in the amount of 366 billion. This shows the degree of exploitation – only within the limits of the state budget and without the profit retained by economic entities – is 105%. The latter is far from being insignificant, especially for a country that has "ended forever the exploitation of man by man".[112]

Marx holds, finally, that salaries ought to be equal to the expenses necessary for the replenishment of the labor force, including the worker himself and his family. The cruelty of capitalism, in his opinion, is that it leads to the establishing of salaries lower than the labor force is worth, and, as a result, the capitalists increase their profit, while the workers send their wives and children to work.

The Soviets explain the same phenomenon in their regime in another way. They appeal to women's social need to work as the most active and most respectable form of human activity under socialism. They also employ child labor, not, however, in the form of hiring, which is legally forbidden,[113] but by recruiting children under the age of sixteen or sometimes fifteen for "socially useful" work during summer vacations. As the Soviet media inform, "the experience of 1981 demonstrated the broadening of the engaging of schoolboys and schoolgirls from the fourth to the sixth grades and even from the first to the third grades in socially useful labor during the last summer vacations".[114] B. Pastukhov, the former secretary of the Komsomol's Central Committee, told the Komsomol congress in the same year that "only last summer they [schoolboys and schoolgirls of Ivanovo province] produced products worth 14 million rubles and ensured the opportunity for two thousand textile workers to have a holiday during the summer".[115] And this becomes even more profitable because, in contrast to hiring, childrens' "socially useful" work is unpaid or is rewarded with a very modest amount of money. Therefore the "Principal directions" of the reform of Soviet general education and professional schools, approved by the Plenum of the CPSU Central Committee on 10 April 1984 and the USSR Supreme Soviet on 12 April 1984 and published by *Izvestiia* on 14 April 1984, provide for a more extensive use of schoolboys' and schoolgirls' labor than before.

However, the real causes of female and juvenile labor under socialism do not differ from those described by Marx in *Das Kapital*. 180 rubles is only the nominally average salary in the USSR. About 18 rubles are deduced for income taxes. By the most modest calculations, a typical Soviet family of two parents and one child spends not less than 32 rubles a month for rental, municipal services, urban transport and personal demands. Thus, the net average salary equals about 130 rubles. This money is sufficent to buy one suit of sub-standard quality, or one dress of more or less standard quality, or one overcoat of sub-standard quality, or three pairs of shoes of normal quality. Suppose that each of the parents buys one suit or dress, one overcoat and one pair of shoes every three years, which requires about 600 rubles for this period or about 200 rubles a year. Without risk of exaggeration one can also assume that clothing for the child and all other clothes for the parents increase this amount to 260 rubles or two months' net salary. The remainder is 1300 rubles a year or about 109 rubles a month. If for the sake of simplicity we assume that the parents have ten rubles a month for small out-of-pocket expenses (such as for movies, theaters, newspapers, books, magazines, etc.), 99 rubles will allow the typical Soviet family to spend 3 rubles and 30 kopecks (about 2 dollars and 55 cents) a day for food. With such resources one can only live at a subsistance level. This is why usually all adult members of a family work in the USSR, and many of them strive to increase their earnings by additional work of a different kind.

In such a way the extent of exploitation and the living standard of the working masses in the Soviet Union can be elucidated realistically even by applying figures which are the most favorable for the Soviet system. However, this very deplorable situation, as it emerges from statistical calculations, conflicts with the usual impressions, as expressed by certain detached observers. According to one of them, he is ready "to present evidence of substantial improvement of the Soviet economy in each decade since World War II, showing that the USSR population has never before been better fed, better clothed and better housed; and that consumer goods such as automobiles, television sets and a host of other items have never before been so abundant".[116] Then, what is more reliable: the mere listing of figures or an emotional description of feelings,

To some extent the daring readiness of our observer is at least premature, if not groundless. Beginning with 1947, when rationing was abolished, the food supply actually improved, and with some interruptions this process developed positively until the early 1960s. Then the development was reversed. To say nothing of the increase in prices, in most Soviet cities, including such industrial centers as Sverdlovsk or Cheliabinsk, even the necessities of life, such as milk and butter, vegetables and eggs, became scarce, while meat, sausage, and cheese stopped being an object of free sale altogether and were subject to disguised distribution among citizens on the principle of actual rationing. Moscow and Leningrad, formerly sources of food supply used by many hundreds of thousands of visitors, have lost most of their past advantages, and if meat or cheese can be bought by lucky people early in the morning, with sausages and fish the situation is almost the same as in Sverdlovsk or Cheliabinsk. Of course, the increasing scarcity has not yet attained the level of World War II, but any Soviet citizen of the appropriate age knows with absolute certainty that in this regard not only post-war progress, but even pre-war achievements were better than contemporary accomplishments.

In another area the same observer is right, but only in part. Automobiles and television sets for personal use were not produced at all in the USSR up to the recent post-war period, and their production, having been initiated, was gradually increased. Therefore, there is no cause for wonder that these objects "have never before been so abundant", although the word "abundant" seems hardly applicable to automobiles that can be bought after three to five years of waiting in the registered line. Housing construction was greatly increased under Khrushchev and, after his denunciation of Stalin, this was his second great service toward the Soviet people, despite all the shortcomings of his personality. Now, however, the situation has changed immensely. Instead of the government, first of all housing cooperatives construct apartment buildings, which demand significant outlays from citizens as members of cooperatives. The amount of housing construction has sharply decreased, and since one needs to wait in turn for allotment of a state apartment from eight to ten years and for admittance to a housing cooperative from three to five years, the time has not yet come to be delighted by the scale to which "the USSR's population has been... housed". It is true that the new Housing Code provides not for nine but for twelve square meters as the maximum size of dwelling space permissible for each member of the family in state apartment buildings.[117] But to be registered as a family that needs new housing, the limit is no more than five square meters for each family member, and, in any event, one may receive no more than seven square meters per person.[118] As for clothing, it has certainly improved, especially if one compares the direct post-war period with the contemporary situation. One must not, however, confuse Moscow and Leningrad, which are supplied by numerous imported articles, with other areas, which have to rely upon domestic production. But even in Moscow and Leningrad acquisition of more or less fashionable clothing demands such efforts that only young people or people who have appropriate acquaintances are capable of finding it. All other people must be content with clothes that, bearing in mind the differences in general economic development now and almost forty years ago, are of the same kind and quality as their predecessors of the post-war period.

It is also no wonder that with an average salary of 180 rubles a month Soviet citizens buy television sets for 250 rubles or automobiles with prices from 3,000 up to 10,000 rubles and more. Leaving aside those individual owners who could acquire even more expensive objects, one should not forget two very important economic factors: as a rule, all adult members of the family work and the durability of expensive objects is comparatively long. Automobiles, furniture, television sets are acquired by Soviet citizens usually only once. On the other hand, money for such purchases has been accumulated by the entire family for months, years or even for the better part of their lives. If a western observer disregards all accompanying factors and appreciates only the result, a Soviet citizen who wears an overcoat, who drives his car and does not go on foot, who watches his television and not his neighbor's, is either an inexplicable miracle or undeniable proof of Soviet achievements. From the viewpoint of Soviet people, these are neither miracles nor achievements. Expensive objects are the result of joint work and demand lasting thrift, and the lasting thrift of a permanently working family only aggravates its economic difficulties.

At the same time, to assess the economic situation in any country exclusively by the number of things in citizens' possession compared with the coinciding index of forty or fifty years earlier cannot be correct in principle. In order to understand the vulnerability of this approach some analogous illustrations are appropriate and instructive. Russian pre-revolutionary agriculture depended upon the wooden plough as the principal means of production, while contemporary agriculture of the USSR is equipped with new types of machinery. Does this mean that "never before" has the agriculture of the country been as highly developed as now? Then why, instead of being the main exporter of grain in the world, has Russia become its main importer? Timber as an object of foreign trade was the second main export after grain in pre-revolutionary Russia, and this did not entail any deficiency in the home market, despite the very backward technology which was applied in the timber industry at that time. However, with all the technological improvements that the timber industry has undergone during the Soviet period, citizens need to receive special planning permission in order to buy wooden materials for construction of houses, having waited their turn for years and after satisfying all the necessary prerequisites provided by law. Such things have really "never before" taken place. The practical application of atomic energy belongs to the inventions of recent time, and, being used in the USSR, it has ensured a new industrial progress in the country. Nevertheless, its influence upon the citizens' standard of living was negative, not positive, because it resulted in the production of nuclear weaponry which drew away material resources from consumers' needs to an extent, which has been known "never before".

The correct idea of the standard of living assumes the assessment of the satisfaction of the individual from the viewpoint of the level attained by economic development and by personal demands. If one judges the level of economic development in the USSR on the basis of its military industry it becomes clear that the satisfaction of the individual is beyond criticism. The country that has managed to create the most terrible weapons in the world and to compete in this regard with the most powerful country in the world, has proved its inability to produce its own jeans, as has been discussed in the Soviet media by various people, beginning with consumers and ending with ministers. In the Soviet Union, demand for consumer goods has always exceeded supply not because of the prosperity of Soviet people, but because they have never been supplied in sufficient quantity and quality with the daily necessary goods, to say nothing about articles of convenience or comfort. On the other hand, if one judges the level of personal demands of Soviet citizens, taking into account their cultural development in the present time, one cannot have any doubt about the enormous divergence between this level and the degree to which it is satisfied. The country which boasts about universal literacy and the greatest number of people with a higher education, has such a restricted choice in bookstores, such insufficient quantities of clubs and cinemas, such an insignificant number of cafes and reading halls, that almost any foreign literary work, no matter how mediocre, is greedily devoured, and almost any more or less roomy porch of a big house is used as a place of entertainment by youth, but, unfortunately, not only for entertainment and not only by youth. In the Soviet Union demand has always been considered firstly in connection with objects of daily consumption. If there is not enough bread for the population's supply, this is politically dangerous for the Soviet leaders, who respond with alarm in order to remove such a serious threat, without sparing anything, including gold and foreign currency so necessary for other purposes. However, when hospitals are overcrowded or the number of children exceeds the number of schools, this is certainly undesirable, but seems quite endurable as it would hardly lead to political trouble and, consequently, does not represent a direct political danger.

Without bread even the slave cannot live and work. As for the other goods, they seem desirable but are not vital under the system of economic slavery supported by political domination.

The poor living standard of the Soviet people is revealed with particular force when compared with the living standard of the Soviet bureaucracy. The appropriate comparison, however, relates to an analysis of the Soviet system not only from the aspect of economic emancipation reduced to actual slavery but also from the viewpoint of legal equality transformed into actual inequality.

NOTES

1. Hereinafter cited as the Fundamentals of Labor Legislation.
2. Preamble of the Fundamentals of Civil Legislation.
3. The 1977 Constitution, art.60.
4. The Criminal Code, art.209(1).
5. The 1977 Constitution, arts.10, 13; the Fundamentals of Civil Legislation, arts.20, 25.
6. The 1977 Constitution, art.13.
7. *Ibid.*, art.17.
8. The Civil Code, art.106.
9. *Ibid.*, art.238.
10. *Ibid.*, art.106. Only when a citizen has a large family or the right to an additional dwelling space (for example, as a scholar or as a high official), may the executive committee of the local Soviet permit him to acquire a larger house or part thereof.
11. The Housing Code, art.134.
12. The Land Code, arts.60-62.
13. *Supra*, 68-69.
14. *Grazhdanksoe Zakonodatel'stvo*, (A. Kabalkin, ed.), Moskva 1976, 41-44.
15. *E.g.* see *SP RSFSR* 1965 No.18 item 110, taking into account its numerous modifications in later periods.
16. The Criminal Code, art.162.
17. Arts.37-42, 78-1, 78-6 of the Corrective Labor Code of the RSFSR (hereinafter cited – the Corrective Labor Code).
18. *Ibid.*, art.7.
19. For example, the work day in uranium mines is one hour long with extraordinarily high wages and an excellent supply of food.
20. *Ved. RSFSR* 1977 No.12 item 255; 1980 No.20 item 535.
21. *Ved. RSFSR* 1977 No.12 item 255.
22. The Corrective Labor Code, art.38.
23. *Ibid.*, arts.38 and 41.
24. *Ibid.*, art.38.
25. *Ibid.*, art.37.
26. *Ibid.*, art.39.
27. *Ibid.*, art.39.
28. *Ibid.*
29. *Ibid.*, art.62. As a reward for good behavior they may be allowed to spend and additional four rubles per month (*ibid.*).
30. *Ibid.*, art.53.
31. *Ibid.*, art.37.
32. *Ibid.*, art.53.
33. *Ibid.*, art.78(2).
34. *Ibid.*, art.78(3).
35. In assessing these two tendencies, one must not forget that while the Soviet regime acts as an organized force, the Soviet citizenry acts as an unorganized mass. In addition, the greater part of the Soviet population has either submitted to its economic situation or is deprived of any opportunity to engage in prohibited kinds of economic activity. Thus, despite the indisputable existence of countervailing tendencies in the Soviet economy, they are of such unequal a strength that the suppressed activity by itself has no chance of overcoming the dominant system.
36. *Supra*, 100.
37. *Ved. RSFSR* 1982 No.49 item 1830. Similar decisions were adopted by all the union republics. They deal only with non-members of collective farms, because the Model Statute of the Collective Farm and statutes of separate collective farms formally have to resolve the same problem toward collective farmers. As a matter of fact, in accordance with the Party directive this problem has

already been settled for collective farmers in the same way as toward non-members of collective farms.

38. The Fundamentals of Civil Legislation, art.25.
39. It is connected not only with family husbandries. *Infra*, 110-116.
40. It is very remarkable that the USSR State Committee of Prices introduced, together with the establishment of *kommercheskiie magazini*, rules providing for the compensation of damage, caused by stealing or loss of meat, milk and related products, on the basis of retail prices with a coefficient of 3 in some cases and 2.5 in others (*Biulleten' Verkhovnogo Suda SSSR* 1983 No.4, 46). The same Committee also decreased prices of some unmarketable goods (*Izvestiia* 1 December 1983).
41. *Bai* means a rich landlord in Central Asia.
42. The Civil Code, Chapter XXXVIII.
43. The 1922 Civil Code, Law of Obligations, Chapter X(1).
44. *Supra*, 109-110.
45. *Supra*, 107-108.
46. This type of private retail trade is also used for the sake of acquiring machine tools or other means of production, with the purpose of applying them in the realm of private production activity.
47. *Ved. RSFSR* 1982 No.49 item 1823.
48. The Criminal Code, art.154. So-called petty speculation is known to Soviet law as well as petty stealing of socialist ownership. Both regulations are predetermined by similar causes. Speculation is considered as petty if the amount involved does not exceed 30 rubles, *Ved. RSFSR* 1983 No.31 item 1126.
49. The 1977 Constitution, art.10.
50. The Fundamentals of Civil Legislation, art.20.
51. The draft of the Constitution, art.9.
52. The 1977 Constitution, art.10.
53. *Ibid.*
54. *Ved. SSSR* 1981 No.44 item 1184.
55. This thesis also is not exact if assessed in the light of Marxist-Leninist orthodoxy, because some cooperatives, as for example housing or garage cooperatives, do not possess means of production, while the Soviet Constitution speaks generally about cooperative ownership. To say nothing about collective farms, among other cooperative organizations only the consumer cooperatives may have means of production as a part of their property.
56. The 1977 Constitution, arts.11-12; the Fundamentals of Civil Legislation, arts.21, 23.
57. The 1977 Constitution, art.11.
58. For example, the Land Code in arts.12-19 deals with the procedure for the granting of land for use.
59. The 1977 Constitution, art.11.
60. *Ibid.*, art.12.
61. The Fundamentals of Civil Legislation, art.19.
62. Under Soviet legislation their property rights are not called ownership but rather "operative management" (art.26(1) of the Fundamentals of Civil Legislation).
63. Note 61.
64. The Fundamentals of Civil Legislation, art.26(1).
65. *SP SSSR* 1969 No.26 item 150.
66. *Ibid.*, art.14.
67. *Ibid.*, arts.36-38, 40-41.
68. This deduction does not touch upon property of housing, garage and other similar cooperatives that are more analogous to individual than to so-called socialist ownership.
69. The rural consumer societies, created in each village of the USSR, are such a link. In the higher links of consumer cooperatives – district, provincial, republican, and USSR associations – representative bodies (conferences, congresses) rather than general meetings exercise a similar jurisdiction. In contrast to consumer cooperatives, collective farms are not united in an All-Union system, whereas they represent not one of the levels but the only possible link of agricultural cooperatives.

70. *Supra*, 52-54.
71. See, for further explanations, O.S. Ioffe, P.B. Maggs, *Soviet Law in Theory and Practice*, London/Rome/New York 1983, 159-161.
72. The 1977 Constitution, art.1.
73. *Ibid.*, art.2.
74. *Ibid.*, art.11.
75. *Ibid.*, art.2.
76. *Ibid.*, Preamble.
77. *Supra*, 55.
78. *Supra*, 115-116.
79. *Supra*, 116.
80. The 1977 Constitution, art.11.
81. See Chapter II.
82. *E.g.* see the 1977 Constitution, art.131 (about the right of the USSR Council of Ministers to ensure the direction of the national economy and to work out state plans for economic development) or art.146 (about the right of local soviets to direct economic construction on their territory and to confirm local plans and budgets).
83. See *infra*, 123-136.
84. The 1936 Constitution, art.11.
85. The 1977 Constitution, art.16.
86. The Labor Code, art.254(3).
87. *Ibid.*, art.33(2).
88. *Newsweek*, 9 May 1983, 8.
89. More exactly, at first the purchaser pays money to the seller, and only periodically – as installments to the budget or at the end of the economic year as a "surplus" of money funds – does the seller transfer his income to the state, retaining a certain part of this income for incentive funds in the amount provided for by the law. Statutory regulations also predetermine to what extent the sale of a product shall compensate its production. But all these rules belong to bookkeeping techniques. Substantively, everything is at the state's disposal, exercised either in the form of general regulations (as in the case of incentive funds) or by way of accumulation and distribution of money resources (as in the case of installments to the budget and financing by the budget). This is why the ultimate conclusion, disengaged from passing details and concentrated around the final result, deals with the state itself and not with the separate economic entities. As for details, see *e.g. Polozheniie o sotsialisticheskom gosudarstvennom proizvodstvennom predpriiatii* (*SP SSSR* 1965 No.19-20 item 155), arts.11-22, 71-80; *Polozheniie o proizvodstvennom ob"edinenii (Kombinate)* (*SP SSSR* 1974 No.8 item 38), arts.38-53, 123-136.
90. Those who are interested in details should read M. Voslensky, *Nomenklatura – die herrschende Klasse der Sowjetunion*, Wien-München-Zürich-Innsbrück 1980.
91. Arts.39-50.
92. *Khoziaistvo i Pravo* 1981 No.4, 73-96; No.5, 75-96.
93. The 1977 Constitution, art.16.
94. *E.g.* see *SP SSSR* 1965 No.19-20 item 155; 1974 No.8 item 38.
95. In more detail see O.S. Ioffe, "Law and Economy in the USSR", *Harvard Law Review* 1982 No.7, 1617-1624.
96. See Chapter II.
97. Note 92.
98. *Pravda*, 26 July 1983.
99. The Fundamentals of Civil Legislation, art.11.
100. The Civil Code, arts.191, 221.
101. *Polozheniie o proizvodstvennom ob"edinenii* (note 90), art.43.
102. *Ibid.*, art.42.
103. *Ibid.*, art.51.

104. See the Civil Code, art.166: "Disagreements between such state, cooperative, etc. organizations arising in the course of concluding a contract not based on a planned task binding on both parties may be resolved by the appropriate court or *arbitrazh*, if this is specifically provided by law."
105. See *e.g.* note 92.
106. The 1977 Constitution, Preamble.
107. *Supra*, 101-103.
108. The Labor Code, art.182.
109. The appropriate legal rules are stated by *Kommentarii k zakonodatel'stvu o trude*, Moskva 1975, 581-583.
110. *Supra*, 103-113.
111. *Izvestiia*, 30 December 1983.
112. The 1977 Constitution, Preamble.
113. Fundamentals of Labor Legislation, art.74.
114. This citation is borrowed from an excellent article "Shkola v tochke izloma", written by D. Shtruman and published in *Vremia i my* 1983 No.70, 167.
115. *Ibid.*, 168.
116. *Newsweek*, 9 May 1983.
117. The Housing Code, art.38.
118. These rules, unpublished, are in force in Leningrad. Every other big city or province has its own, in principle similar, rules.

CHAPTER IV

THE LAW OF UNIVERSAL EQUALITY AND OF UNIVERSAL HIERARCHY

A society with economic emancipation and political freedom assumes the equality of its members. Because the USSR pretends to be such a society, it necessarily proclaims the universal equality of its citizenry, free of economic slavery and political domination. Slavery and domination, however, despite all wordy declarations, are the cornerstones of the Soviet system, and they inevitably entail a universal hierarchy, which markedly distinguishes between subordinate and commanding positions. As a matter of course, equality and hierarchy do not simply contradict one another; they are mutually exclusive. It is also clear that in their polar opposition one pole, universal equality, appears as the only one existing in law, while the other pole, universal hierarchy, reigns as the only one significant in practice. The fiction of this equality and the reality of this hierarchy are most noticeable in practice, although certain traces of them can also be observed in Soviet law.

1. Universal Equality

With regard to equality, one usually has in mind individuals in their mutual relationships and especially in their relationships with the state as a single whole and with governmental agencies as representatives of the state. Equality, however, can also be applied in respect of collective bodies, or of states, as members of a federal state, or of the international community of states. As for the USSR, the notion of equality may be used in one way or another, depending on the specific circumstances. This relates to Soviet law as well as to Soviet practice.

Universal Equality in Soviet Law

The USSR is a federal state.[1] As a state, it proclaims the equality of citizens; as a federal state it proclaims the equality of its members: fifteen union republics. Each type of equality has certain peculiarities.

Union republics are formed on the basis of nationality. Therefore, they are called the Russian, Ukrainian, Belorussian Republic, etc. Accordingly, the Constitution itself points out that the USSR is an "association of equal Soviet Socialist Republics".[2] Meanwhile, there are numerous other nationalities in the Soviet Union, who have not been granted union republic status and who cannot be considered members of the "federal national state".[3] In order to universalize equality at a higher level than that of nationalities, which form the basis of union republics, the Preamble to the Constitution accentuates the "legal and actual equality of all nationalities" present in the USSR. However, actual equality is impossible in practice. The levels of economic development in Russia and, for example, Kirgizia are beyond all comparison, and during the entire history of the Soviet regime the budget maintenance of the latter has always, even relatively, fallen far short of that allocated to the former, although any serious aspiration to actual equality would have required just the opposite. With regard to legal equality, the situation is even worse, because, being realizable in practice, it conflicts with the evolution of Soviet legislation and its present state.

First of all, only fifteen nationalities are granted union republic status, and this gives them "the right of free secession from the USSR".[4] Of course, the right of secession is nothing more than an empty phrase, and all attempts to realize it have been mercilessly suppressed in Soviet history. But other nationalities do not have, even formally, a similar right, and therefore they are legally unequal to those who possess union republic status. Sometimes there are no obvious arguments which can justify their inequality. For example, in the Kazakh Union Republic, Kazakhs compose a minority of the entire republican population. Nevertheless, they occupy the position of the "leading" nationality on the republican level. Sometimes certain arguments seem convincing, although they do not remove all possible doubts. For example, alongside with Union republics, the Soviets have invented several other forms of national state autonomy: the autonomous republic as a part of a Union republic,[5] the autonomous province as a part of a Union republic or a territory,[6] and the autonomous national area as a part of a territory or province.[7] Various kinds of autonomy follow one another in an order of diminishing political power, and this is officially explained as a result of diminishing numerical importance of the nationalities concerned. The official explanation refers, in addition, to the fact that only Union republics border on foreign countries, and that this is why only they may have the right of secession from the USSR. If these explanations were absolutely reasonable, they still would not disprove the legal inequality of various nationalities, despite the opposite principle confirmed by the Soviet Constitution. Unfortunately, even their reasonableness is subject to criticism. Numerous nationalities of the USSR are not provided with any form of autonomy, although many of them live as a compact majority in a given area. Moreover, where autonomy of any kind, except the Union republic variety, exists, it totally lacks the right of self-determination. The Abkhazian Autonomous Republic is a part of the Georgian Union Republic. Hostility between these two nationalities and the dominant position of the Georgians induced the Abkhazians, in the person of their most active representatives, to appeal to the Soviet leadership with a request to transfer the Abkhazian Autonomous Republic from the Georgian Union Republic to the Russian Union Republic. If the right of self-determination was respected, such a modest request would have been satisfied without obstacles and delay. The Soviet leadership, however, refused it immediately, because the Constitution does not grant the autonomous republics with such a right, and the International Covenants ratified by the USSR speak about the self-determination of an entire people, not of its representatives.[8] To discourage other nationalities from engaging in similar attempts, and to avoid repetition of the Abkhazian demand, the request was rejected peremptorily, and the most dangerous Abkhazian representatives were committed for trial, accused of anti-Soviet propaganda, and convicted to long terms of deprivation of freedom. Such was the legal result of the legal equality of Soviet nationalities in the case discussed.

No more consolation may be derived from a historical comparison of various Soviet laws which retraces the evolution of the Soviet legal system in this very important sphere of extremely fragile human relationships. To be brief, one may omit current legislation and concentrate only on the 1936 and 1977 Constitutions. In the case of Union Republics, the former provides for sixteen while the latter deals with only fifteen of them.[9] This happened because the Karelo-Finnish Union Republic was transformed into the Karelian Autonomous Republic,[10] and the transformation itself has its own political peculiarities. Before the 1939-1940 Soviet-Finnish war a Karelian Autonomous Republic existed in the USSR. Stalin, to support his claims to a part of Finnish territory, at first created a Finnish government in exile with a Soviet communist, Otto Kuusinen, at its head. After an attempt to found a separate Finnish socialist state had failed, Stalin proclaimed the creation of a new Soviet union republic – the Karelo-Finnish Republic – a combination of the former Karelian Autonomous Republic and new territory seized from Finland by the USSR as a result of the 1939-1940 war. The newly formed Union Republic, with a population of little more than one hundred thousand, was smaller than many autonomous republics, and it contained no Finns, except for Kuusinen and several other officials. Thus, it was clear from the very beginning that this phenomenal creation was due to political goals rather than to the national equality of eight or ten Finns with the other many-millioned nationalities of the country. Although the obvious political goals instantly proved unattainable, Stalin's death was necessary to recognize his failure, and only then did the Karelo-Finnish Union Republic return to its initial status as the Karelian Autonomous Republic. However, if anyone's pride was wounded by the described result of the Karelian national state formation, one must not forget the tragic fate of several other state entities in the USSR. In 1936 the Constitution knew such autonomous republics as the German Republic, within the limits of the Russian Union Republic,[11] and the republic of the Crimean Tatars, within the limits of the same Union Republic.[12] During World War II Stalin liquidated the first autonomous republic under the pretext that, being populated by Germans, it might support Nazi Germany, not the USSR. The second autonomous republic was also liquidated on the grounds that the entire people of Crimean Tatars were in collaboration with the German Army. Both peoples – Germans and Crimean Tatars – were exiled to the eastern part of the country with such a drastic change in life-style that their very survival was threatened. Stalin applied the same approach to certain other peoples of the USSR, for example to Chechens and to their autonomous republic as a part of the Russian Union Republic. Under Khrushchev, all these peoples were rehabilitated, but with one essential difference. The Checheno-Ingush Autonomous Republic appeared again,[13] and Chechens, exiled in the past, were allowed to return to their native places. The German Autonomous Republic, on the contrary, and the Autonomous Republic of the Crimean Tatars fell into oblivion, while secret regulations of the KGB and the MVD introduced passport conditions and other insurmountable obstacles to the return of any representatives of the peoples concerned to their destroyed homelands. Such was the real result of the restored equality of the Soviet nationalities in the case described.

Dealing with nationalities, Soviet law speaks about legal and actual equality. As for citizens, a similar method becomes inapplicable. Actual equality of citizens would mean in the first place their economic equality. However, the principles of socialism confirmed by the Constitution read: "From each according to his ability, to each according to his labor."[14] Even if the Soviet system precluded exploitation – which in reality does exist in the USSR[15] – inequality of citizens would stem just the same from the fundamental principle of socialism. "To each according to his labor" assumes equal payment for equal labor, but "from each according to his ability" assumes unequal abilities of various people. Hence, equal payment for equal labor leads to unequal earnings of people with different abilities and, as a result, to the economic inequality of Soviet citizens. This inequality becomes more palpable owing to the difference in demands, even in the case of equal payment, if one is single and another is married, or if one has a small family and another has a large family, etc. Marxist doctrine itself recognizes this kind of inequality under socialism, postponing full economic equality until the complete victory of communism, when, instead of the socialist principle "From each according to his ability, to each according to his labor", the communist principle will triumph with its alluring slogan "From each according to his ability, to each according to his needs". In as far as the promised paradise has not yet appeared, actual equality of the USSR citizenry cannot be declared. Thus, only legal equality may be proclaimed: "Citizens of the USSR are equal before the law."[16] Their legal equality, as it is said in the same article of the Constitution, exists "irrespective of origin, social and property status, racial and national affiliation, sex, education, language, attitude toward religion, type and nature of occupation, place of residence, and other circumstances".[17] Two circumstances enumerated in the article cited – sex and racial or national affiliation – are repeated in a broader way by other articles of the Constitution: "Women and men have equal rights in the USSR";[18] "Soviet citizens of different races and nationalities have equal rights".[19] Both articles refer to actual and legal guarantees of their effectiveness. Besides this, the general rule of article 34 points out that "the equality of citizens of the USSR is ensured in all areas of economic, political, social and cultural life".

The actual situation of citizen's equality in the Soviet Union will be considered later.[20] For now Soviet laws themselves will attract all our attention, and in this regard the enumeration of areas where the equality of citizens is ensured, according to article 34 of the Constitution, seems especially important. If the constitutional principle "From each according to his ability, to each according to his labor" precludes actual equality in the economic area, what other meaning, apart from a purely formal one, can the proclamation of legal equality in the same area have? Moreover, is not this proclamation reduced to a mere formality also in regard of political, social, and cultural activities, when their realization demands individual expenses under different economic conditions? Finally, does not real participation in political, social and cultural life depend on different abilities as well as economic activity, and is not actual inequality something which all enumerated areas have in common? If so, then the only thing the Soviet Constitution may affirm without contradicting itself is universal equality in the sense of equal legal opportunities and equal legal demands. However, even within this restricted framework, general constitutional declarations conflict with specific legal regulations. Legal education in the USSR can serve as one of the best illustrations. On the one hand, it encompasses all kinds of activities. As any educational process, legal education by itself means participation in cultural life. In its turn, entry into the legal profession clears the way to various political, social and even economic activities, bearing in mind, for instance, the office of jurisconsult in Soviet enterprises and other economic entities. On the other hand, perhaps no other sphere of education is subordinated to such legal rules of direct inequality, as is the case in legal education. For the most part, these rules have not been published, but their existence and application are an open secret.

In the mid-1960s the USSR Council of Ministers sanctioned a list of offices which may be occupied only by people with a legal education. This fact, taken separately, does not present anything abnormal. Numerous professions assume professional education, and just as one cannot be a doctor without a medical education, one cannot be a lawyer without a legal education. Adoption of the list mentioned would not violate legal equality, if legal education were equally accessible to any Soviet citizen. The case is, however, somewhat different. In the USSR there are three legal institutes[21] and numerous legal faculties of state universities. To be admitted to a legal institute one must be 21 years old[22] and have a recommendation from a CPSU provincial committee. Students of legal institutes are better provided for, with allowances and various conveniences (hostels, etc.), than students of law faculties. As people checked beforehand by the CPSU agencies, those who graduate from legal institutes also receive higher appointments than their colleagues from law faculties. As for the latter, all student vacancies for a given year are divided by each university into two unequal parts. One part consists of 80% of the vacancies which are assigned to 21 year olds who have served for not less than two years as manual or office worker. The other part is reduced to 20% of the vacancies and is available to 18 year olds who have not worked after finishing their secondary education. This differentiation, unequal in itself, entails another, more striking inequality. In the first case, vacancies and applications are usually in a proportion of one to three, and quite mediocre results in the entrance examinations prove to be sufficient for admission to the university. In the second case, the proportion is often as high as one to twenty-five, and therefore even a highly successful score in the entrance examination does not ensure the desired result. In light of the data stated, the list of offices that demand a legal education acquires unexpected significance. Inequality in admittance to legal education engenders inequality in numerous areas of economic, political, social, and cultural life.

Not only legal education but Soviet higher education as a whole, with its secret instructions and other governmental regulations, completely undermines constitutional references to numerous circumstances that must not affect the legal equality of Soviet citizens. There are closed educational institutions, such as the Higher Diplomatic School, which is not subject to any demand of equality. The CPSU Central Committee, in the person of the appropriate secretary, has exclusive powers to decide who shall be sent to study at this establishment. The decision may be adopted only after meticulous verification of all data concerning a potential candidate, whether they relate to his origin or social status, national or racial affiliation, sex or any other peculiarity. However, such a process is only necessary in a few cases, because the vast majority of vacancies at the Higher Diplomatic School are distributed among children of the ruling elite whose social or other characteristics are known beforehand. At the same time, in this exceptional case, one privilege is not extended, not even to the highest elite: women are absolutely not admitted to diplomatic education. Alongside with closed, there also are half-closed educational institutions, such as the Institute of Foreign Trade, where applicants' political reliability is checked by the KGB, and origin, social status and nationality must meet Soviet standards, to say nothing of the religious beliefs of applicants, which precludes admittance to any Soviet higher educational institution, not only to higher foreign trade education. Besides closed and half-closed there are, finally, partially closed educational institutions, such as the University and the *Fiztekh* (physical-technical) Institute in Moscow, certain departments of the University and the Electric-Technical Institute in Leningrad, physical and mathematical departments of the University of Novosibirsk, etc., hermetically sealed against Jews, Germans, and several other unreliable nationalities. In addition, equality applied at the beginning is sometimes replaced by inequality at the end. This happens, when as a result of entrance examinations several people attain achievements necessary to be admitted to one and the same vacancy. Under such circumstances, other data acquire a decisive significance. Representatives of unreliable nationalities must lose out to representatives of other nationalities. Children of workers have advantages over children of peasants, while the latter are more favored than children of office workers. Women are considered inferior to men, except in those national areas where women continue to avoid higher education and need to be stimulated to change their minds under the influence of special privileges.[23] Inhabitants of the city, where the University or the Institute is situated, defeat their competitors from other cities or villages. A Party member is more agreeable than a Komsomol member who, in his turn, has superiority over non-Party members. These criteria do not stem from local arbitrariness. They are applied in a unified way all over the country. Some of them, as for example, being domiciled in the same city, are not concealed in cases of conflict, and complaints made to higher agencies are always declined, if the grounds for the adopted decision answer at least one of the criteria described. Thus, without reading secret instructions, one can have no doubt as to the existence of corresponding general rules, adopted by appropriate Soviet agencies and therefore being law, despite their unconstitutionality, until they are abolished or replaced in the established order by the competent governmental body.

The example of higher education has been taken because of its comprehensive illustrativeness. But it does not represent anything extraordinary. Each type of human activity, submitted to legal regulation in the USSR, can serve as a source of similar contradictions between the equality proclaimed by the Constitution and the inequality introduced by subordinate normative acts.

Article 54 of the 1977 Constitution formulates a rule of general importance and of special significance for criminal law and criminal procedure. According to this rule "citizens of the USSR shall be guaranteed inviolability of the person. No one may be subjected to arrest other than on the basis of a judicial decision or with the sanction of a procurator". The necessary details concerning the grounds for and procedure of arrest at the stage of the preliminary investigation or inquiry and at the stage of the execution of the judgment are provided for by the Code of Criminal Procedure[24] and the Corrective Labor Code.[25] The first stage, as described by the published rules, demands the sanction of a procurator, given either beforehand or not later than 72 hours after confinement under guard.[26] However, if an accused or a suspect is a Party member, he may be arrested only if the procurator's sanction has been preceded by the sanction of the appropriate Party agencies, beginning with the district committee and ending with the Politbureau, depending on the position of the person to be arrested. This rule, unpublished but binding, introduces an obvious inequality between Party members and non-Party members. At the lower levels of the Soviet bureaucracy it stimulates criminal relationships between party bosses and criminal offenders, when the latter serve as a material source of economic gain. A secretary of a Party district committee, who has received his share of the criminally attained gains as "a gift" or as a direct bribe, would apply all his authority to refuse a request for the Party's sanction to arrest a Party member. At the higher and especially at the highest levels of the same bureaucracy, considerations of prestige lead to identical results. In the early 1960s all of Leningrad was excited by the notorious Romanov case. Romanov, using his position as the chief of the trade department of the Leningrad executive committee, had systematically engaged, together with numerous accomplices, in theft of state property, not simply on a large, but on a colossal scale. The criminality of his behavior was so evident and conspicuous that, despite all his connections in "high spheres", it was impossible to refuse the Leningrad procurator's request for the Party to sanction Romanov's arrest. Thus, he was arrested, and the preliminary investigation began to operate at full speed, involving new accomplices and discovering new incidents each week and each day. At last, evidence from the investigation engendered suspicion against two persons of very high rank: Nikolai Smirnov, the chairman of the Leningrad executive committee, and Frol Kozlov, the former first secretary of the Leningrad CPSU committee, and at the time of investigation, a secretary of the CPSU Central Committee, and a member of the Politbureau, in fact the second in rank after Khrushchev. This caused a sharp turn in the whole situation. People, who had already been arrested, were committed to trial and sentenced to various terms of deprivation of freedom. However, all materials connected with Smirnov and Kozlov were withdrawn from the investigatory documents, and the investigator who dealt with the case was removed and then fired. Despite various rumours in Moscow and Leningrad, it is difficult to say with any certainty to what extent the careers of both leaders were affected by the case discussed. Only two things are certain. Shortly after this affair, Smirnov perished in an automobile accident, and Kozlov, after suffering a stroke, lost all his positions and then died.

In civil law one of the most important areas of legal regulation relates to so-called housing law. This law introduces the maximum norm of dwelling space that can be rented by citizens in state apartment buildings. As mentioned above, in the Russian Union Republic this size is 12 square meters *per capita.*[27] Dwelling space that exceeds the established norm becomes a surplus subject to a special regime. However, certain categories of citizens have the right to supplementary living space in the form of a separate room or of 10 square meters. Article 39 of the Housing Code, articulating this rule, refers for the necessary details to USSR legislation, partly published. Those who know the appropriate legislation can easily prove its tendency towards inequality. The right mentioned is granted to ordinary people, if they suffer certain chronic diseases in grave forms or if they need supplementary living space for their work as writers, scholars, etc.[28] But they do not receive and cannot demand supplementary living space. Only if a surplus of such space occurs as a result of a decrease in the size of the family, does the right to retain this space, not as a surplus, but as a supplement, arise. In contrast to ordinary people who acquire the right concerned only under special conditions, "responsible executives" (*otvetstvennye rabotniki*) – as representatives of the bureaucracy are called in the USSR – acquire a similar right exclusively on the basis of their official position. The general norm of supplementary living space – one room or 10 square meters – is not applicable to them. Everything depends on the level of the office occupied. The higher this level, the larger and more comfortable the apartment. Executives receive such apartments together with their offices, and elevation of official rank entails improvement in housing conditions.

In administrative law rules concerning public order occupy a prominent position, and among them traffic rules form a significant part. The latter are elaborated, formally adopted, and actually enforced by the MVD department known as GAI (acronym for the Russian words "State Automobile Inspection"). Owing to their very nature, traffic rules demand complete uniformity and universal force. Otherwise it would be impossible to ensure the safety of traffic. At the same time, some of these rules, not published but well-known to any GAI officer, have an exceptional character. According to them, automobiles with certain signs and numbers, which reveal that they belong to representatives of the Soviet middle and high-ranking bureaucracy, cannot be stopped and given a ticket, whatever violations their drivers may have committed. They may park anywhere, whether or not parking is prohibited. Speed limits and traffic signals are not obligatory for them. Moreover, in Leningrad, for example, one of the main city thoroughfares *Moskovskii Prospekt* – always busy with various means of transport – is burdened with additional difficulties of a purely artificial character. The extreme left part of the road, in both directions, has been separated from the rest of the road by a solid line, and may not be used by anyone, except automobiles of the local bureaucracy. In Moscow, even more radical steps have been taken: whole squares, passages and streets are closed for ordinary cars and reserved exclusively for official transport.

In labor law, the general principle "to each according to his labor" – which has only the appearance of equality, but in reality preserves inequality even by Soviet understanding[29] – is further transformed in the latter direction. According to two rules of labor law (with certain exceptions): (1) "payment for labor by manual workers shall be effected on the basis of wage scale rates (salary scales) approved by the central authorities";[30] and (2) "payment for labor by office workers shall be effected on the basis of schedules of official salary scales, which have been approved by the central authorities".[31] The problem, however, is that the central authorities also introduce different scales for establishments of the same kind. There are, for example, three categories of research institutes, and, although there is no distinction in the nature and quality of work, official salary scales and wage scale rates for manual workers, affirmed in the centralized manner, differ, from one to another, being highest for institutes of the first category, and lowest for institutes of the third category. As a result, up to the late 1960s, two legal research institutes of otherwise equal status – the Institute of State and Law and the All-Union Institute of Soviet Legislation – were subject to different pay scales for equal work, because the former belonged to the first category and the latter to the second. This striking injustice was removed after the All-Union Institute of Soviet Legislation acquired, at last, first category status, on the condition that staff reductions would compensate the additional expense resulting from the increase in salaries and wages of the remaining employees. Similar consequences are attached to distinctions between enterprises, associations, and other establishments as entities of local, republican and all-union significance. Not infrequently, they execute identical functions with equal efficiency. The only distinction consists in different payment for equal work owing to different official rank. The situation becomes absurd and intolerable, when two establishments of different rank merge to create a united establishment. Each of them brings its own wage scale rates and schedules of official salaries, and until the appropriate central authority puts things in order, manual and office workers in the same positions at the same establishment receive unequal payment for equal work. The Soviet Constitution talks about ministries and state committees, governing bodies of Union and Autonomous republics, local agencies of power and administration, as if there were complete equality among them at each hierarchical level. However, along with the publicly enunciated constitutional enumeration there are unpublished groupings within the framework of this enumeration. For example, the Ministry of Defense and the Ministry of Justice or the Leningrad and Voronezh executive committees are agencies of different rank with all ensuing consequences, especially with regard to salaries and wages which are based – in contrast to the constitutional requirement – on the principle of unequal payment for equal work.

In collective farm law the situation is even worse. As a general rule, all collective farm work shall be performed by the personal labor of collective farmers,[32] and in this case labor is paid in accordance, not only with its quantity and quality, but also with the level of income of the collective farm's economy.[33] An exception to the general rule admits the hiring of specialists and other workers from outside in instances where the necessary specialists are not available at the collective farm or where agricultural and other work cannot be performed by the collective farmers themselves within the period required.[34] Specialists and other workers hired by collective farms are paid according to their labor contracts, independent of the results of the collective farm's economic activity, because these relationships belong to the realm of labor law, not to collective farm law. Therefore it is possible that two or more people, executing the same specialist job (agronomists, veterinarians, etc.) or ordinary agricultural work (during harvesting or sowing campaigns), will receive different payment, if some of them are collective farmers and others are hired by the collective farm. Such arrangements would be unjustifiable and even unconstitutional, were state ownership openly declared to be what it really is[35] – the united "basis of the economic system of the USSR", to use an expression from the Soviet Constitution. The Constitution distinguishes, however, between two forms of this "basic" ownership allegedly inherent to the Soviet system: state and collective farm/cooperative. It also considers the former as the property of the entire people and the latter as the property of separate collective farms or other types of cooperative entities. Due to this attitude, different systems of payment for equal work acquire reasonable justification. State ownership belongs to the entire people, and those who work at state enterprises or other state establishments ought to be paid in the order and on the scale established in a centralized way. Collective farm ownership belongs, in its different parts, to separate collective farms, and those who are members of these farms ought to be paid within the limits of collective farms' economic resources. In this particular case the state may only recommend and not command. State commands continue to apply to the hiring of specialists and workers, since labor relationships are regulated by the state. Collective farm relationships are regulated by the collective farms themselves, and differences of payment for labor due to this cause cannot be imputed to the state. Analogous reasoning justifies numerous other differences between collective farmers and other manual or office workers. Along with differences in payments for equal work there are differences in pensions, working and rest time, labor discipline, etc. In principle, all these differences allow the state to economize on the labor of collective farmers in comparison with the labor of hired workers. Here, and also in some other factors,[36] one can find the real cause of legally groundless differences between state ownership and collective farm ownership, insistently preserved by the Soviet Constitution and current legislation.

All the illustrations given prove that Soviet law, although it declares universal equality as a general principle, does not follow its own declarations. In numerous cases specific regulations leave almost nothing of the appropriate general rules. Thus even formal equality, which does not go beyond legal texts, has been disregarded in the USSR, and this is especially ominous, if one remembers that, according to Marxist doctrine, formal equality has no meaning unless it is supported by actual equality, equality in real practice.

Universal Equality in Soviet Practice

Providing for universal equality of Soviet citizens, article 34 of the USSR Constitution mentions ten circumstances which should not affect the proclaimed principle. The words "and other circumstances", which end the text of this article, indicate that the enumeration is not exhaustive. Hence, the equality of citizens shall be observed in the Soviet Union irrespective of any circumstances, whether or not expressed by law.[37] However, in order to form a correct idea of universal equality as it reveals itself in Soviet practice, an analysis of all the circumstances included in the legal enumeration is required.

1. Origin. In using this word, the Constitution, certainly means social origin, *i.e.* the belonging of parents of individual citizens or of citizens themselves to a specific social stratum in the past. During the first two decades of the Soviet regime, certain social origins entailed far-reaching discrimination according to direct provisions of Soviet law. Former landowners and capitalists, representatives of the tsarist bureaucracy and members of the priesthood, petty traders in the city and well-to-do peasants in the countryside were deprived of political rights, Soviet higher education and governmental office – all of which were closed to them and to their children, etc. The 1936 Constitution formally put an end to these restrictions, having provided for citizen's rights without any reference to citizens' origins.[38] As for the 1977 Constitution, it is indisputably superior to its predecessor in the comprehensiveness and legal technique of equality provisions, without, however, being essentially different.[39] This sharp turn for the better, introduced by Soviet legislation, has not been fruitless in practice. On the contrary, new opportunities, tightly closed in the past, have now been opened for *ci-devants* (*byvshie liudi*). Moreover, the more Soviet leaders prided themselves in the past of the country, the stronger aristocratic origins were favored. In 1937, when the first elections for the USSR Supreme Soviet took place, Molotov boasted in his speech at a session of this Soviet that one of its deputies was the writer Alexei Tolstoy, a count in pre-revolutionary Russia. After World War II, the situation changed to such an extent that people, instead of concealing their aristocratic origins, began to speak openly about their genealogy, and impostors, referring to the sound of their names, also proclaimed themselves noble. However, at the time of Stalin's purges, when the GPU (the present KGB) received daily "planned" tasks of arrests of "enemies of the people" in each city and in each village, these tasks were executed mainly by *ci-devants*, first of all by members of the pre-revolutionary nobility. An aristocratic or other unreliable past provokes distrust also in present times in cases of high appointments, official promotions, admittance to a secret job or missions abroad. In all such cases meticulously elaborated questionnaires are required, and a point concerning social origin is one of the inevitable items. In addition, the USSR already has its own history and its own past which gives new meaning to the notion of "origin". "Have you or your close relatives been in military captivity?" "Have you or your close relatives been taken to court or investigated?" No questionnaire omits these questions, and no unfavorable answer remains without effect on the fate of an applicant. Although legally social origin must not entail either positive or negative results, the appropriate authentic or artificial data are used, if necessary, to attain one of these opposite goals. When Khrushchev was leader, he did not miss any opportunity of reminding people of his origins as a poor peasant and an ordinary miner. After his ouster, rumors were spread all over the USSR that his parents had been rich peasants and that he himself had never been down a coal pit, and, judging from the insistence and the scale of the rumors disseminated, the central Party apparatus had to be the main source of these rumors. In order to compromise Alexander Solzhenitsyn, the Soviet media, and especially the writers' newspaper *Literaturnaia Gazeta*, published articles with assertions that Solzhenitsyn's father had been a landowner deprived of former advantages by the October revolution, and that therefore the son tried to take vengeance on Soviet power by means of slanderous literary works. In all such cases the constitutional principles of universal equality, independent of social origin, were not considered a serious obstacle to soiling somebody's reputation.

2. Social status. According to the Constitution, there are only three social strata in the USSR: the workers, the peasants and the intelligentsia.[40] This enumeration, however, contradicts reality, and seems all-embracing only as a result of the distortion of the very term "intelligentsia". According to its constitutional interpretation, everyone who is not a worker or a peasant, belongs to the intelligentsia, whether one is an intellectual, a bureaucrat or an office clerk. Nevertheless, even with such an arbitrary application of the notion discussed, two circumstances ought to be taken into account. On the one hand, to belong to one of the three social strata recognized by the Soviet Constitution is not meaningless for the actual equality of Soviet citizens. The practical importance of the constitutional stratifications in the realm of higher education has already been discussed above.[41] Similar illustrations can be found in numerous other spheres of public activity. If one leaves aside the privileged elite, which is *hors concours*, then the rule is that workers are superior in comparison with peasants, and that both of them are superior in comparison with the intelligentsia. This rule makes itself felt when deputies to Soviets or people's assessors of courts are elected, when representative agencies of purely ceremonial character[42] are created, when delegations of different kinds are formed, and so on and so forth. On the other hand, even under the broadest interpretation of the word "intelligentsia" in the Soviet Constitution, many strata of Soviet society are not included in the constitutional *nomenklatura*. This relates not only to those whose existence is officially denied, as, for example, the ruling bureaucracy, but also to separate groups of the population, which are mentioned in certain official documents, including normative acts of current legislation, as, for example, the priesthood or craftsmen working by themselves. Meanwhile, when we are dealing with the real stratification, whether reflected in Soviet law or omitted by it, actual inequality replaces legal equality in practice. Thus, craftsmen working by themselves are inferior to the social strata enumerated by the Soviet Constitution, not only in real fact, but also from the viewpoint of legal opportunities granted to them.[43] As for the priesthood, it occupies virtually the lowest place in the Soviet social structure, as well as in the Soviet legal system.[44] Here is one sufficiently convincing illustration. A priest's daughter made three unsuccessful attempts to be admitted as a student to Leningrad University. Each time she indicated in the questionnaire the real profession of her father, and each time she failed the entrance examination, despite her great abilities and excellent preparation. In attempting the fourth time, she answered the same question falsely: instead of "a priest", her father became "a worker". The situation immediately changed, and the brilliant results of her entrance examination helped her to be enrolled on the list of students. A little later, however, one of the University clerks identified her, and she was immediately expelled. All her complaints with reference to a violation of the constitutional principle of legal equality were rejected with indignation. As the official explanations stated: three times running she had not been admitted to the University as a result of her failure in the entrance examinations, and on the fourth time, she lost her position because of dishonest behavior. One way or another, Soviet higher education is closed to people of this particular social stratum: such is the simple truth.

3. Property status. Separately analysed, property status does not really affect the general principle of legal equality in the USSR. As a matter of course, economic prerequisites, which make various goods accessible, depend on the scale of property which is in the possession of different citizens. But this has nothing to do with legal equality and relates to economic inequality, confirmed, not denied, by the constitutional rule: "From each according to his ability, to each according to his labor."[45] To understand the legal significance of property status in Soviet society, one must not forget that under socialism economic might, instead of being a cause, has become an effect of political power. Therefore property status influences legal capacity in the USSR not directly, by means of its own force, but indirectly, by means of its political connotation. For example, in addition to free hospitals, certain Soviet cities have hospitals that require payment. If the former are full or if they do not have sufficiently skilled doctors, the latter remain the only alternative for the ordinary citizen, and in the absence of the necessary means even this ultimate remedy is beyond reach. With the Soviet bureaucracy the case is somewhat different. They have their closed hospitals which are always ready to render the necessary services, relying upon their own staff or upon specially invited professionals, and the lack of means is of no importance for the patient in question. Hence, in this case, the legal inequality of one person in comparison with another can be strengthened or neutralized by economic inequality, depending on its manifestation in the same or in the opposite direction. Since, however, as a rule, those who hold political power also have greater economic might, economic inequality more often strengthens legal inequality than neutralizes it. At the same time, legal inequality due to political differentiations cannot be neutralized exclusively by an opposing economic inequality in numerous important situations. New medicines imported from foreign countries are not distributed among ordinary hospitals and drugstores in the USSR. As long as their production has not been planned for by Soviet enterprises, only closed hospitals and closed drugstores may receive them through the channels of centralized supply. Hence, in this case, economic advantages do not compensate legal disadvantages. The desired medicines can be procured either *po blatu* (using "pull"), *i.e.* relying upon other people's privileges, or by bribery, *i.e.* by taking criminal steps. Thus, even money that should be equal according to its very nature is unequal under the Soviet system. One person is forced to buy what another person receives gratis, and another may buy what the first cannot acquire with money. Political inequality leads to monetary inequality and in such a way supports legal inequality by economic means.

4. Racial and national affiliation. Since national discrimination in the USSR has become universally acknowledged, no one takes seriously the constitutional declaration on this point, and there is no need to disprove national equality by illustrating the situation of Jews, Germans, or other nationalities oppressed almost without disguise. Probably, it is more important to focus on circumstances that until now have undeservedly remained in the background. The promising slogan of national equality was twice qualified with the restriction of *primus inter pares*: the first time with regard to the Russian union republic in the rulers' speeches at the time of the promulgation of the 1936 Constitution, and the second with regard to the Russian people in Stalin's toast on the occasion of victory in the second World War. These additions were not a play of words. They closely resembled Orwell's *Animal Farm* with its general rule about universal equality and its exceptional rule about those who are "more equal". Communist Party and governmental agencies of all national republics are headed by representatives of local nationalities, but the second position always goes to Russians, and the actual power of the latter is based on principles similar to those known for a long time as applicable to political commissars. No decision vetoed by these commissars may be adopted unless the appropriate central agency in Moscow abolishes their veto. Each national republic has the right to its own language in all legislative, governmental and judicial affairs, but the Russian language preserves equality, and not only equality. Legal regulations must be published in Russian along with the national language. At least one newspaper, but usually more than one, must be in Russian. Local radio stations and television centers must interrupt national programs at assigned times in order to relay Moscow transmissions in Russian. In all national schools the Russian language must be studied separately, while in Russian schools in the same localities the national language can be either obligatory or optional. Such rules, unofficial in the past, have now become binding. The CPSU Central Committee's draft of the reform of Soviet schools of general education, published by *Pravda* on 4 January 1984, and the USSR Supreme Soviet's law on the same reform, published by *Izvestiia* on 14 April 1984, order the application of "additional measures to improve the conditions for studying – along with the native language – also the Russian language, voluntarily accepted by the Soviet people as the means of international communication". There is no need to point out how negatively this affects national culture in general, and national languages in particular. The Baltic republics, whose nationalities have never been reconciled to joining the USSR, continue to resist cultural russification, and the majority of the local population either refuses to speak Russian or pretends not to know it. In light of the directive cited, their attitude will be overcome in the very near future. In the Ukraine the concealed resistance is to a great extent combined with a conformist attitude. The Belorussian language has actually stopped being used, and, except in remote villages, it has become a dead or dying language. In the Soviet Asian republics (Uzbekistan, Kazakhstan, etc.) national languages survive, but the local elite and national urban population strive to give their children a Russian education for the sake of their future careers. The same tendency prevails in the Soviet Caucasian republics (Georgia, Armenia, Azerbaidzhan). Meanwhile, a new situation has developed in relation to the dominant and subordinate nationalities which has given rise to alarm among the Soviet rulers and hope among some of the oppressed peoples. Following the Soviet invasion of Afghanistan, western scholars and politicians began to study, more attentively, the demographic shifts among the population concentrated mainly in the Asian republics and considered to be Moslem by western observers. Although figures published by the western media do not always coincide with each other, the majority of reviewers affirm that every fifth Soviet citizen is a Moslem. In connection with events in Afghanistan they pay attention almost exclusively to personnel changes in the Soviet military forces that have already taken place and will continue more strongly in the future, judging from these demographic data. As for the Soviet leaders, they have been aware of this problem for a long time and not only with a view towards military personnel. They have taken into account the eventual overall influence of this trend of demographic development upon the political, economic and cultural situation in the USSR. Before the invasion of Afghanistan, at an all-union seminar of chairmen of civil law departments of Soviet law schools in 1975, a lecturer from the CPSU Central Committee devoted a part of his lecture to the problem of demographic trends, having stressed the pressing need of raising the birth-rate in the European area of the country in order to maintain a reasonable economic and cultural balance in the Soviet Union. Everyone understood what was really meant. The problem is how to replace the "one-child-system" by the "many-children-system" in Russian families in the first place and thus avoid a future Asian majority in the country. The modest incentives for child-bearing, which existed at that time, were not sufficiently effective in this regard, and certain additional measures introduced later on (an increase in state aid, certain housing privileges, etc.) were not enough to achieve the desired goal. The problem retains its acuteness, and future developments seem unlikely to counteract existing national inequality, which has arisen during the last four or five decades.

5. *Sex*. Formally there is not only equality of sexes in the USSR but even a privileged position for women provided by various kinds of legal regulations, first and formost by labor law and family law. Labor law establishes special rules for work by women, enumerating types of jobs from which women are excluded, limiting night work for women, etc.[46] Family law pays special attention to the protection and encouragement of motherhood, to the wife's right to material support during pregnancy and for one year after the birth of a child,[47] etc. However, beyond these privileges, determined by the biological specificity of the female sex and fixed directly by law, the inequality of women in comparison with men is striking. Discrimination in admittance to higher education has already been mentioned.[48] Its secret justification by Soviet rulers consists of the reference to the fact that higher education is free of charge in the USSR and that in cases connected with women this can lead only to a waste of money after their marriage and the birth of their children. In addition, generally speaking, the higher the step on the social ladder, the less accessible it is for a woman. Soviet people have already grown accustomed to the usual picture of road building carried out mostly by women and supervised mainly by men. The low salaries of ordinary teachers or ordinary doctors have resulted in a preponderance of women in such professions. Higher salaries for university professors or scientists in medical and other research institutes have resulted in a preponderance of men in such establishments. The USSR Supreme Soviet and other purely ceremonial agencies of Soviet power include a sufficient number of women, although they are outnumbered by men. Operative agencies with the same degree of power,[49] beginning with local executive committees, function with noticeably fewer women, and their participation gradually decreases at each higher level of the system, so that there is not a single woman in the Council of Ministers of the USSR. As for the Politbureau – the highest body of the Soviet system and the real bearer of political power in the country – Ekaterina Furtseva was its only woman member during a short period of time under

Khrushchev. However, she lost her position in the first and only case when, in 1961, in conformity with a rule introduced by Khrushchev, one-fifth of the Politbureau members had to be replaced. Of course, the comparatively restricted representation of women in the highest bodies of political power continues to be a common feature of modern states. However, in the USSR, where everything is predetermined from the top to the bottom, this is the result not of a free competition, but of a deliberate policy.

6. Education. In the present world legal equality independent of education is practically impossible and virtually inadmissible. It is not only the professions of medicine or law which demand special education,[50] but numerous other kinds of professional occupations are unattainable without proper preparation. This relates also to activities connected with economic management or governmental administration. Lenin's assertion that each cook must be taught to govern the state[51] was shelved long ago and has never been applied in practice. There are no obstacles to electing a cook as a deputy to the USSR Supreme Soviet – bearing in mind the extreme simplicity of the deputy's functions: to be present at each session, to vote always positively and to read speeches written beforehand by other people – if such an honorable duty has been imposed upon him. To perform these functions is easier than to work as a cook, which nowadays also requires professional training. Meanwhile, the real execution of governing functions assumes – together with a certain general level of culture – professional understanding of numerous problems, which is gained by practical experience and, more often than in the past, by special education. This is why, at each nomination of candidates to official positions, the Soviet leadership takes these indispensable prerequisites into account and, if necessary, makes them publicly known through speeches at sessions of the USSR Supreme Soviet, through information in newspapers and other media, etc. No one can hold such a practice against the Soviet regime. But this regime deserves a serious rebuke for its combination of fictitious equality irrespective of education with real inequality in the realm of admittance to higher and professional education.[52]

7. Language. The problem of languages has already been touched upon in connection with the problem of nationalities.[53] It is necessary to add that certain nationalities are in principle deprived of their own language, and that the corresponding secret restrictions are supported by organized coercion, including criminal punishment. As is known, Jews have two languages: Yiddish and Hebrew. Before the notorious campaign against so-called cosmopolitans (1949-1953), Soviet Jews had their national theaters, newspapers, literature, and schools in Yiddish, not only in the Jewish autonomous province of Birobidzhan (in the Far East of the USSR), but also in Moscow and some other cities. The campaign resulted in the liquidation of all these establishments and installations, except for one official newspaper in Yiddish preserved in Birobidzhan. After Stalin's death, one newspaper and one magazine were restored in Moscow, and from time to time Jewish singers or Jewish plays began to appear on the Soviet stage, but Jewish culture expressed in Yiddish could never attain its former level and actually ceased to exist. In the case of Hebrew the situation is even worse, because it is the official language of Israel, which is considered an enemy of the USSR, and because Soviet Jews who want to emigrate to Israel study this language to prepare for their new life. Therefore, instruction in Hebrew is tacitly forbidden, and Soviet judicial practice has already had a certain amount of experience with criminal prosecutions of the numerous attempts to violate this prohibition. The formal equality of different languages, proclaimed by the Constitution, is usually observed in judicial activity, owing to the concrete guarantees provided by the rules of judicial procedure.[54] However, if the court of a national republic hears a case in Russian, this is not considered a violation of judicial procedure. Aside from events which have taken place in a courtroom, it is very difficult and sometimes even impossible to receive a copy of an official document in a language other than Russian or that of the national republic. In Leningrad, one notary lost his position after having attested English translations of certain documents of several people who were preparing to emigrate, and the Leningrad CPSU committee secretly instructed all notarial offices to refuse similar applications as allegedly belonging to the exclusive jurisdiction of the corresponding Moscow agencies. In this case, the unequal treatment of languages stemmed from secret instructions and local initiatives. In other regions, for example in Estonia or Lithuania, nothing like that has ever occurred. However, there are certain legal regulations which introduce the unequal treatment of languages as a general rule without any secrecy. For example, to be awarded the academic degrees of candidate or doctor one must produce and defend a thesis (dissertation) in the established order. According to this order, a thesis written in any language other than Russian, must be accompanied by a Russian translation, and a synopsis of the thesis, which shall be disseminated long before the public discussion and must be written only in Russian and in no other language. This rule and other similar regulations, which are in open violation of the equality of languages, become serious obstacles to a balanced development of national cultures and ensure the dominant position of the Russian culture.

8. *Attitude toward religion.* Discrimination against religious groups in the USSR is no less notorious than national discrimination, and therefore no special efforts are needed to disprove the constitutional equality, irrespective of one's attitude toward religion. Only in order to enlarge the volume of illustrations does it seem appropriate to adduce some examples, which immediately come to mind. For instance, a legal scholar lost his position as chairman of the civil law department in a Ukrainian University not because he himself was a religious person, but because, having yielded to pressure of his closest relatives, he buried his mother with observance of Christian customs. In a case that occurred at Leningrad University, freedom of religion was violated after a violation of the right to privacy. First a student's diary was secretly removed from his suitcase in the student hostel, and then, when the entries in the diary revealed his religiousness, the student was expelled from the university. As a matter of fact, not only higher education with all its future opportunities, but any comparatively respectable career is closed for people who, being religious, have not managed to conceal their beliefs. And another point which is usually disregarded, is even more peculiar. Along with general discrimination against religious people, the

Soviet regime treats different kinds of religion differently. Russian Orthodoxy represents the most widely followed persuasion in the country, while the number of Catholics is incomparably smaller. In addition, Catholicism, headed by the Pope, gives rise to greater political fear among Soviet rulers than does Orthodoxy, which is not united on a world scale. As a result, despite the general oppression of any religion, Catholicism suffers more restrictions than Orthodoxy. Similar distinctions reveal themselves in Soviet attitudes toward Islam and Judaism or even toward the same religion in different regions of the country, depending on the concentration of its adherents in one area and their small number in another. The most cruel methods of oppression are applied toward religious communities labelled as sects in the official terminology: Baptists, Adventists, Pentecostals (*Piatidesiatniki*), etc. The Soviets consider any type of sectarianism as being very dangerous and therefore undesirable. Sectarianism leads to secrecy, and religious fanaticism promotes adamant resistance against official demands to reveal secrets. This is why, if one assumes that a religious sect might engage in anti-Soviet activity, one must take into account the almost insurmountable difficulties of the process of its denunciation. Thus, it is easier to forbid religious sects completely than to be regularly informed about their activities. As a result of this, while the Orthodox Church meets obstacles in receiving the necessary governmental permission for opening new establishments, for performing certain services, etc. and while these obstacles become stronger and even malicious with respect to the Catholic Church, religious sects have been completely deprived of similar opportunities, as they are considered to be illegal entities whose very existence is at the best a misdemeanor and usually a crime. Hence, it must be clear enough that such a political system – which actually denies the equality of various religions – cannot separate different attitudes toward religions from the legal equality of citizens. Both equalities, being fictitious, serve as legal masks for real inequalities.

9. Type and nature of occupation. "Any labor is honorable" according to a Marxist slogan. Nevertheless, during the 1980 USA election campaign, Soviet propaganda, directed against Ronald Reagan, spoke with indignation about the possibility of making a former actor the head of a superpower. In the USSR actors are respected people, who are awarded state decorations and honorary titles in great number, and often elected as deputies of various Soviets. However, it is simply impossible to imagine the appointment of an actor as a minister or other higher official of the Soviet Union. From this viewpoint, Soviet indignation about Reagan's eventual presidency was quite sincere, and not purely propagandistic. The same attitude can be met with in some cases of internal significance. For example, up until the early 1960s, the salaries of judges were so low that one of them, in order to support his family, decided to earn additional income by working in the evenings as a porter at one of Leningrad's railroad stations. After this was discovered, he lost his judicial position because according to the official decision his conduct disgraced the judge's office. One could understand his removal, if it were explained by the incompatibility of an official legal profession with another, unofficial, occupation. But if one considers employment, which is legally permissable, as being shameful for those who fulfill official functions, then legal equality – irrespective of type and nature of occupation – is not treated seriously. Such equality was also openly disregarded when Leningrad University refused to recognize two years of work as a manicurist as the length of service generally necessary to be admitted as a student in Soviet law schools.[55] One must not lose sight of two other circumstances. There are certain kinds of occupations that the Soviet regime needs to permit even though they contradict its real interests, as for example the occupation of clergyman. In these cases direct discrimination acts in its true colors. There are various kinds of occupations with different levels of importance to the Soviet system, as is the case with labor of industrial workers in comparison with labor of trade workers. Soviet rulers strive to have representatives of all kinds of occupations in central and local soviets; however, in proportions that correspond to their importance and with the exception of undesirable professions. Both facts prove reliably what legal equality irrespective of occupation actually means.

10. Place of residence. A country that has an internal passport system cannot boast of legal equality irrespective of residence. This equality becomes impossible simply because citizens who visit a given area are not equal to citizens who live there. The former need a temporary registration for residence, which may sometimes be refused, while the latter have permanent registration in their place of residence, which may sometimes be annulled.[56] The proclaimed equality also conflicts with the double passport system, which functions secretly together with the official one. The urban population is covered by a comparatively liberal regime which in principle allows a change in the place of residence at one's own will. The rural population, in so far as it is represented by collective farmers, is subjected to an extremely restricted order that completely precludes a change of residence without the permission of the collective farm.[57] The equality discussed ultimately resembles a legal mirage, if one takes into account the special (*rezhimnye*) cities and territories generally closed to other sections of the population and only temporarily accessible to specific individuals with personal permits.[58] It would be, however, a mistake to think that the place of residence affects legal equality exclusively within the limits of the freedom of movement. Numerous other prerequisites of everyday life depend to a considerably greater extent on this place. Strange as it may seem to the uninitiated, the entire territory of the USSR is divided into different zones from the viewpoint of supply. Moscow, as the capital, occupies the most favorable position, and all other zones are ranked as first, second or third category with a corresponding deterioration of supply from the higher category to the lower. As a result, in Leningrad one can find more food than in any other city of the Leningrad province. However, if one tries to visit Luban, a city that is about 70 kilometers away from Leningrad, one will find the general situation with regard to foodstuffs essentially no better than it was for Russian peasants in the same place nearly two centuries ago – according to "Journey from Petersburg to Moscow" (*Puteshestvie iz Peterburga v Moskvu*) by Radishchev, a Russian writer of the eighteenth and early nineteenth centuries. Moreover, even Leningrad itself is supplied differently in the center and in the suburbs, in Nevsky Prospekt and in the outskirts. Of course, inhabitants of other places are not forbidden to visit Leningrad with a view to purchasing food, and those living in the outskirts can go shopping in

Nevsky Prospekt. However, to say nothing about the waste of time, only a small part of the population can afford such travel, even infrequently and at additional cost. Thus, economic inequality, which results from the very essence of socialism and which is strengthened by the political structure of the Soviet system, relies upon various other circumstances, and among them the place of residence plays no insignificant role. This place is also important for educational goals and cultural development. Throughout the provinces, the educational and cultural levels are inferior to those of the capitals and other centers. In this regard the Soviet Union is not to blame. However, the rulers who have established centralized planning of economic and social development, disregard their own duty, proclaiming legal equality irrespective of place of residence, on the one hand, and on the other hand, not letting the provinces have their fair share of resources so as to preserve the economic and cultural advantages of capitals and central cities. As for higher education, inhabitants of the provinces manage sometimes to overcome provincial disadvantages, by entering universities or institutes in Moscow, Leningrad or Kiev, although they meet numerous obstacles along the way.[59] With general education the case is essentially different. Children and teenagers must and can study only in their place of residence. Meanwhile, for numerous reasons and, due first of all, to the incomparably lower level of financing of provincial schools, their students prove to be worse prepared for higher education than students from capital and central cities. Therefore, cultural and educational inequality created during childhood continues, as a rule, to be preserved and intensified into adulthood. Thus, as in other cases in which legal equality is not affected under Soviet law – but is inevitably affected in actual fact – one's place of residence has the same effect – sometimes supported by law but more often reinforced by practice. However, in contrast to universal equality which is proclaimed in law and curtailed in practice, universal hierarchy prospers in practice without adequate reflection in law.

2. Universal Hierarchy

Soviet law does not entirely disregard the hierarchical character of the Soviet system, although it speaks only about a fictitious hierarchy and passes over in silence the real hierarchy. To reveal the latter, Soviet practice is more enlightening than Soviet law. At the same time, one must recognize the hierarchy acknowledged by Soviet law in order to discover the legal distortion of real phenomena. In addition, words of truth are sometimes blurted out by Soviet law, either through negligence or because it cannot be avoided. They also command our attention.

Universal Hierarchy in Soviet Law

The Soviet system, as described by legal texts and, especially by constitutional provisions, is similar to a pyramid with a broad foundation and a truncated top. At the base of this pyramid there are the people, since the USSR has been typified as an all-people's state.[60] The people consist of workers, peasants and intelligentsia;[61]

however, the latter two are subordinated to the former, because – as the Preamble of the Constitution says – the working class continues to be "the leading force" of Soviet society. Hence, the working class towers above the foundation and occupies a higher position than the peasantry and intelligentsia. But its position is not supreme, in so far as the CPSU "shall be the guiding and directing force of Soviet society"[62] in all its ingredients, including the working class. At this point, constitutional descriptions stop moving upwards and return to the lower levels of the Soviet hierarchy: trade unions, the All-Union Leninist Communist Youth League (Komsomol in Russian terminology), other social organizations, and labor collectives of enterprises and institutions.[63] Their relationships with the CPSU are sufficiently clear, being based on the principle of subordination, since the CPSU is the "nucleus" of all social organizations.[64] There is also no doubt that trade unions, the Komsomol and other social organizations, which "take part in the administration of state and social affairs",[65] are higher than labor collectives of enterprises and institutions, which "participate in the discussion and deciding of state and social affairs".[66] Because of the absence of any indication concerning the "leading role" of the enumerated entities, they cannot formally claim to be higher than the people or the working class. However, this claim may be substantiated logically if one remembers that the people as a whole or the working class as their leading force are incapable of expressing their will directly and must do so indirectly: through soviets and other state organizations or through trade unions, the Komsomol, and other social organizations. Owing to the fact that the logical conclusions do not tally with the formal provisions, a certain ambiguousness remains in the case discussed, if the analysis does not go beyond Soviet law. Nevertheless, the Soviet pyramid, considered from the bottom to the top within the framework of constitutional regulations, can be outlined as consisting of the people, the working class and the CPSU with subordinate social and state bodies and entities. But what about the very top of this pyramid? Does it exist or is everything crowned by the CPSU as such – with millions of members and thousands of agencies? Soviet law remains silent in this respect, and the Party Rules mention various agencies of the CPSU, as if they were not governing but subordinated to those who created them. At the same time, without doubt, the Party as a single whole does not rule and cannot do so. Therefore, the legal description of the Soviet hierarchy seems incomplete, leaving an impression of a pyramid provided with a foundation and deprived of a top. However, as has been shown,[67] the top of this pyramid exists, and, although concealed legally, it acts in fact with unlimited political power based upon an economic monopoly. Thus, the Soviet political system appears in all its fullness – and not in a disappointing truncation – as a political hierarchy with a ruling summit and a dominant peak.

At the same time, the existence of a hierarchical structure is not peculiar to the Soviet system. Any political system must be hierarchical, whether it is democratic or totalitarian, and whether its totalitarianism is open or disguised. The real peculiarities of the Soviet political hierarchy are revealed in the combination of the most extreme totalitarianism with the most demagogic democratism. The combination includes universal equality in verbal declarations and all-embracing hierarchy in daily life. What this means from the viewpoint of the organizational, political and economic structure of the USSR as a whole, we have already seen in analysing correlations between democratic centralism and centralized democracy, political freedom and political domination, economic emancipation and economic slavery.[68] In terms of daily life, embellished by equality and impregnated by hierarchy, elucidation of the same feature will follow now. As soon as one passes from universal equality to universal hierarchy, Soviet law loses its habitual eloquence and becomes extremely laconic, if not completely dumb, at least in its published part. Nevertheless, this must not discourage us from investigating the matter. Nothing sought, nothing gained.

For example, the Statute on the Manner of Assignment and Payment of Pensions[69] provides that, in general, old-age pensions shall be no less than 45 rubles and no more than 120 rubles.[70] Other kinds of pensions – for disability and for the loss of the breadwinner – also have their minimum and maximum limits. However, these rules, as well as the Statute on Pensions, are applicable only to manual and office workers and not to collective farmers, whose pension allowance is less favorable both in size and on grounds of eligibility. Moreover, even manual and office workers, who are not collective farmers but live permanently in rural areas and are engaged in agriculture – being hired by collective or state farms – are less favored in this regard to their urban colleagues. They may receive only 85% of the pension granted under the same conditions to people who do not live in villages or who do not work in agriculture.[71] No other kind of pension differentiations, except certain privileges for especially heavy labor, injuries suffered in the defense of the USSR, etc., are known to the Statute of Pensions. However, in reading certain other Soviet laws, one can come across additional differentiations. For instance, the Housing Code speaks of personal pensioners (*personal'nye pensionery*), providing them with certain housing privileges. What does this mean and how can one distinguish between personal and ordinary pensioners? Everyone is aware of such an institution, and the Soviet leadership itself does not keep its existence a secret. For example, when Khrushchev died, official information issued on behalf of the CPSU Central Committee and the Soviet government called him "a personal pensioner". Similar communications often appear in national and local newspapers on the occasion of the death of former officials of different ranks. However, the Statute on Personal Pensions, affirmed by the edict No.1128 of the USSR Council of Ministers of 19 December 1977, has not been widely published, and instructions supplementing this edict, being more important than the edict itself, are altogether beyond publicity. It is, however, known that personal pensions may be assigned exclusively to people who have worked for a long time as officials of the Party or governmental bureaucracy. It was only in 1983 that the same privilege was also extended to participants of World War II. The very complicated procedure for assignment of personal pensions serves as a filter to prevent penetration into such privileged ranks of those who do not belong to "minions of fortune" or whose former positions are not sufficiently important, or of politically failed bureaucrats (with a possible exception to the latter rule, when the persons in question are the highest leaders ousted from the Politbureau, the Secretariat of the CPSU Central Committee, etc.). The personal pension is a greater privilege than any other. Apart from higher monetary awards, it entails certain additional payments (for example, annual allowances for treatment), certain special rights (for example, the right to be admitted to governmental sanatoriums), certain significant advantages (for example, one or several complimentary railroad trips a year), certain important privileges (for example, to have a permanent job without suspension of pension payments), etc. All these circumstances leave no doubt that personal pensioners occupy an incomparably higher rank than ordinary pensioners, who represent three successively ascending groups: collective farmers, manual or office workers living in rural areas and engaged in agriculture, and other manual or office workers. However, personal pensioners do not represent a homogeneous entity either. There are personal pensions of local, republican and all-union importance, and accordingly the corresponding persons are called (similar to enterprises, roads or property) pensioners of local, republican or all-union significance. Although such a nomenclature would seem humiliating to normal people, it has been introduced all the same and publicly applied as an honorable table of ranks, and not only honorable, but quite important from a financial point of view. While local and republican pensions have their own, though different, limits, the exact amount of all-union pensions depends exclusively on decisions of the highest agencies adopted in various cases. To receive a country house (*dacha*) or a car for life, it is not enough to be a local or even a republican pensioner. Such benefits are granted only to pensioners of all-union significance.[72] The same distinctions make themselves felt in the right to treatment in the Kremlin or another governmental hospital, to rest at sanatoriums of the USSR or republican governments, of the CPSU or republican central committees, etc. The hierarchy established for Soviet bureaucrats stays with them for life, and if changes occur, they are caused by a shift either within the framework of official ranks, or by the transition from active to pensioned status. However, be that as it may, within the limits of the pension hierarchy alone we have already counted six different degrees: three ordinary and three personal. And to make the picture complete, two other kinds of pensions should be mentioned.

One of them, encompassing Soviet scholars, was established in 1949.[73] Its main peculiarity consists of monetary awards. The maximum pension of a scholar is not 120, but 160 rubles. In addition, after retiring, scholars preserve some of their privileges, for example, the right to supplementary living space, etc.[74] The second kind of special pensions concern officers and generals of military forces and other services equated to them (the MVD, the KGB). It is not easy to explain the motives, which induced the authorities to keep the legal regulation of military pensions as even more secret than that concerning personal pensions. Nevertheless, certain things are not a mystery. Relying upon personal information, received directly from a pensioner or indirectly from his surroundings, everyone knows that a colonel's pension is 300 rubles; and marshalls, even if they stop serving, continue to receive their salary, since they are never considered as being pensioners.[75] In comparison with personal pensioners, military pensioners may be more or less privileged, depending on the level of the particular official. For example, the pension allowance of a colonel is higher than that of a pensioner of local significance and lower than that of an all-union pensioner. However, generally speaking, personal pensions are the highest and military pensions follow behind them. Thus, in the realm of pension allowances alone, the Soviet hierarchy consists of no less than eight levels: the six already mentioned before, scholars, and military officials.

An analogous situation exists in the realm of housing, taking into account state apartment buildings and leaving aside citizens' houses. In this respect, the entire Soviet population can be divided into two parts. The first part is formed by people provided with sufficient living space according to Soviet standards. It includes different levels of housing: without limits for certain representatives of the Soviet bureaucracy; within the limits of the established norm (12 square meters *per capita* in the RSFSR) plus supplementary living space (10 square meters or a separate room in the RSFSR) for citizens whose type of occupation or official position entails the right to supplementary living space; to the limits of the established norm for any citizen who has managed to receive such living space at the very beginning or whose housing conditions have been improved in consequence of a decrease of the size of his family; within the limits, though less than the established norm, but more than is necessary for acquisition of the right to improvement of housing conditions (more than 5 square meters *per capita* in Leningrad).[76] The second part is formed by people who do not have living space at all or whose housing falls short of minimum standards (below 5 square meters *per capita* in Leningrad). In this case there is also a more complex differentiation. As a general rule, citizens, registered by local executive committees as being in need of living space, shall be granted housing in order of priority, depending on the time when registration took place.[77] As an exception to the general rule, certain people have the right to receive housing immediately after being registered and independent of the time of registration.[78] Along with certain disabled persons and large families, those decorated with certain high governmental awards have such an exceptional right. It is, however, worth noting that the legal text devoted to the problem discussed ends with the words: "Legislation of the USSR and RSFSR may grant the preferential right to receive housing also to other categories of citizens."[79] As a result, housing demands of Soviet officials can be satisfied, owing to non-published rules, before similar demands of ordinary people. But this order has one disadvantage: it assumes registration by local executive committees before housing may be granted. Therefore, as a special exception to the exception itself, the Housing Code provides for extraordinary allocation of living space, which need not be preceded by any registration.[80] An "exceptional exception" seems quite just when applied in cases of natural calamities which have destroyed living quarters. But the legal enumeration concerned ends again with a reference to other cases provided for by all-union or republican legislation,[81] thus introducing for the Soviet bureaucracy even more favorable opportunities than those connected with the first exception. One noteworthy feature of both regulations, concerning pension allowances and allocation of housing, consists of the fact that not only are they based upon the hierarchical idea, but it is put into practice on an all-embracing scale, encompassing the population from the top to the bottom. This creates an illusion of everyone being able to participate in common affairs, although in different roles, with abstractly equal potential. In such a way the legalized hierarchy preserves an appearance of legal equality.

Soviet legislation, containing few direct indications of hierarchical privileges, does not miss any opportunity to introduce them in a disguised way by the expedient legislative technique of "rule-exception", so highly appreciated and so often applied in the USSR. As a general rule, holding down more than one office is forbidden in the realm of higher education, but, as an exception to the general rule, it is permitted to "prominent scholars", who may simultaneously work in the Soviet economy, and to "leading specialists", who may simultaneously work at universities and institutes.[82] In practice, however, "prominent scholars", busy with teaching and research, seldom use this opportunity and do not often receive the appropriate offers. On the other hand, "leading specialists", or more exactly, high-rank bureaucrats, willingly exploit such an easy way of additional enrichment, and the administrations of institutions of higher education are glad to offer them lucrative sinecures as a reward for eventual support or actual assistance. What their activity really boils down to has been eloquently demonstrated by a former USSR Minister of Justice who, at the same time, was a professor at the Law Faculty of Moscow University. When he was dismissed as a Minister, the Law Faculty found out that only two classes had been given by him during the whole academic year, despite the enviable punctuality of his paycheck. The unlucky ex-Minister did not deny this finding and returned the unearned salary without uttering a word. Along with the occasional plurality of offices, Soviet law admits, also as an exception, the so-called personal salary (*personal'nyi oklad*), with only one difference between the two: the first has been published, the second is not subject to publication. The legal meaning of this very peculiar institution consists in the right of appropriate governmental agencies to replace the standard salary established for a particular office (for example, 120 rubles a month) by an extraordinary salary (for example, 250 rubles a month), granted exclusively to an individual official. So long as the latter continues to occupy his office, he will receive the increased payments under the title of personal salary. These payments may be preserved by an order of the competent body in case he is removed to another office. As soon, however, as a new official replaces him, the payment will be reduced from the increased level to the ordinary standard (in our example, from 250 to 120 rubles a month). The institution of the personal salary is applied in various instances, but mainly to the advantage of officials, who have failed in comparatively high positions and must be provided with good rewards of another kind or who prefer a not very conspicuous cushy job to retiring on pension owing to age or health, which would hinder the execution of more important administrative functions. Thus, all more or less significant establishments have their special departments (*spetsotdeli*) dealing with secret objects and documents, supervising personnel and being in permanent contact with the KGB. Usually their chiefs have been KGB officials and receive a personal salary in these new positions. Along with these, numerous managers of secondary schools, local theaters and clubs, libraries and cinemas are appointed with personal salaries as a reward for their bureaucratic past. A similar approach is applied to many chiefs of staff departments, "honorary" consultants at various establishments, etc. In a word, governmental charity in favor of former bureaucrats, failed or weakened, is the principal goal of this inglorious but lucrative institution.

In studying Soviet law from the point of view of universal hierarchy, it is very important to be equally attentive toward legal stability and legal change.

As noticed more than once, the housing question has been, and continues to be, one of the most difficult problems in Soviet society. That is why Soviet housing legislation employs such notions as a norm and a surplus of living space.[83] In the past, the surplus of living space could be withdrawn if it consisted of at least one separate room, and in other cases, when withdrawal was impossible, the tenant was obliged to pay three times as much as the statutory rent established for living space within the limits of the norm.[84] The first rule represented no danger to Soviet bureaucrats, because if they retained their apartments which exceeded the norm, after they lost their official positions, no one would withdraw the surplus rooms and thus transform a separate apartment into a communal (*kommunal'nyi*) one in a governmental apartment building. Hence, this rule was abolished in the Housing Code, not for the sake of the bureaucrats, but in order to liberate housing legislation of provisions which made daily life unbearable for a large part of the urban population. As for the second rule, it was doomed to another fate during the preparatory work connected with the drafting of the new housing legislation. Since the housing shortage is far from being overcome, there have been suggestions to increase the rent for surplus dwelling space from three to twelve times in comparison with statutory rent, in order to induce the tenants concerned to avoid accumulating living space and not to insist upon its retention in excess of the established norm. However, the suggestion described contained an obvious threat to Soviet bureaucrats. The apartment itself might sometimes be retained after one had been ousted from the ruling hierarchy, but the privilege concerning the amount of the rent would unquestionably be withdrawn. Foreseeing even the slightest possibility of this kind, high-ranking bureaucrats blocked the suggested innovation, supporting the stability of the corresponding regulation first of all for their own sake and only secondarily for the sake of ordinary people. Similar factors help to explain certain other cases of legal stability that would otherwise be simply incomprehensible. Thus, despite numerous discussions and insistent demands to decrease the comparatively high salaries of university professors and other scholars, Soviet legislation has shown great steadfastness in this case, due, however, to the interests not so much of present, as of future beneficiaries, when a bureaucrat would lose his office and receive a plain sinecure in the field of higher education or scientific research.

The following illustrations relate to bureaucratic interests, not in preserving, but in amending the law in force. Thus, on 3 December 1982, the Presidium of the RSFSR Supreme Soviet, following corresponding all-union decisions, adopted an edict[85] which may be called – with good reason – a reform of Soviet criminal law. In changing no less than one-third of the criminal legislation, this reform seems to be unprecedented in itself. In addition, it has one very important peculiarity. Article 141 of the Criminal Code consists of two paragraphs. The first paragraph deals with "issuance under one's own name of another's scientific, literary, musical, or artistic work, or any other appropriation of the authorship of such a work, or the illegal reproduction or distribution of such a work, or the compelling of someone to be a co-author". The measure of punishment provided for originally was deprivation of freedom for a term not exceeding one year or a fine not exceeding 500 rubles. At present, this measure is not deprivation of freedom of up to one year, but correctional tasks of up to two years, or a fine within the limits, not of 500, but of 300 rubles. Thus, the measure of punishment has obviously been decreased. The same thing has happened with the second paragraph which prohibits "the public disclosure of an invention before it is registered without the inventor's consent, the appropriation of the authorship of an invention, the compelling of someone to be a co-inventor, or the appropriation of the authorship of a rationalization proposal". Instead of deprivation of freedom for a term not exceeding one year, or of correctional tasks for the same term, or of a fine not exceeding 500 rubles, the new measure of punishment excludes deprivation of freedom and provides for either correctional tasks of up to two years or a fine of up to 300 rubles. This mitigation of punishments seems especially astonishing in view of the aggravated repression of all other crimes affected by the reform. Yet there is no reason to be astonished. During the last couple of decades the crimes mentioned in article 141 have developed into something like professional crimes of the Soviet bureaucracy. Not infrequently managers of enterprises, design offices or research institutes compel subordinate workers to insert managers' names among the genuine authors of inventions, rationalization proposals, scientific books or descriptions of research performed. In order to prepare a dependable way of retreat in case of a sudden ouster from the ruling bureaucracy, many of its representatives defend their theses in good time and thus acquire academic degrees, which will make them eligible as departmental heads or professors at universities or institutes in the future. However, the real authors of these theses are not those mentioned on the title page, but their subordinates, who sometimes let "the author" down, by using other people's works without the necessary references or by exposing the truth as a result of a conflict or other circumstances. Brezhnev, as far as it is known, has been the first Soviet leader to introduce a new kind of plagiarism, having published under his own name three novels evidently written by professional writers. In such a way writers reappeared among the Soviet rulers – although they were not unlike Lunacharskii, Lenin's minister of education, who, for better or worse wrote his own plays – in the shape of persons who, without sufficiently mastering the Russian language, proved to be ingenious enough to create Russian literature. Obviously, these rulers cannot help being complacent toward plagiarism, no matter how intolerant they are of other offenses. Therefore, despite the absence of frank arguments, penalties for plagiarism are mitigated, reflecting an aspect of the system of universal hierarchy in Soviet law.

Universal Hierarchy in Soviet Practice

To explain the universal hierarchy in Soviet practice simply as a conglomerate of concrete facts would mean telling a long story without a beginning and without an end. All of Soviet life – political, economic, cultural and even private – is subject to hierarchical subordination. Let anyone try to express a pro-Soviet political slogan, not confirmed by the Politbureau, on the event of the October anniversary or the May Day holiday, and his career will be destroyed. Let the management of an enterprise try to introduce new economic methods, quite efficacious but not yet approved by the highest summit, and the whole affair will surely end in a complete crash. Let an author try to write a book dealing with theoretical problems of any kind, whether sociological or technical, without referring to Soviet ideology or omitting reference to the country's contemporary leader, and the book will never be published. Let people criticise in private conversations what has been approved by the ruling summit or let them privately support what has been officially rejected, and, if this somehow becomes publicly known, the consequences will be unpleasant at least, if not tragic. However, along with a tremendous collection of hierarchical commands and prohibitions, there is a system of unwritten rules, elaborated by Soviet practice over many years and strictly observed by Soviet people of different levels, owing to habit, instruction or trained intuition. These rules, systematically stated, help more than anything else in understanding the essence and character of the Soviet hierarchy.

1. Suum cuique. With good reason *suum cuique* may be considered as the most basic and all-embracing rule of any hierarchy, and especially of the one that exists in the USSR. We have already seen[86] that the hierarchical level, attained by an individual official, predetermines his political power, economic capacity and all other social opportunities. But these data are not exhaustive. The rule now discussed has even ritual significance. The Soviet system is based upon numerous rituals, and not one of them disregards the demands formulated. Any newspaper or magazine is free to publish pictures of members of the Politbureau; however, in connection with official state holidays they may do so only on condition that all members appear in the established order. Pictures of single Politbureau members may be published only in connection with an event concerning such a person, for instance an award made on the occasion of a birthday. In all other cases a picture may be officially published only by permission of the CPSU Central or Regional Committee, depending on the level of the media where the eventual publication shall take place. Deaths of ordinary people are either not mentioned in the media at all, or an appropriate communication may be published by relatives and friends in the same way as any paid advertisement. As for the Soviet hierarchy, leaving aside the highest rulers, who occupy a peculiar position even in this regard, three types of official reactions to deaths of its representatives may be encountered: obituaries with pictures, obituaries without pictures, and short advertisements. The funeral itself may relate to the first, the second or the third category. And the necessary choice is not made arbitrarily. It depends on the position of the deceased and on the decision of the appropriate agency. Meanwhile, these and similar rituals belong to the external trappings of the Soviet hierarchy, and although they may by themselves appear repulsive, they are harmless in practice. The situation is, however, essentially different when the practical activity of the USSR's ruling mechanism cannot take place without observing the same rituals, which seem only decorative in non-practical realms.

In the mid-1970s, when a very important draft law was being elaborated, a divergence of opinion, expressed by the working commission, compelled the Politbureau to create an *ad hoc* commission to discuss this divergence and to present an objective finding. Two members of the *ad hoc* commission supported opposite points of view. One of them was Fedoseev, a member of the CPSU Central Committee and

Vice-President of the USSR Academy of Sciences, and the other Terebilov, a member of the CPSU Auditing Committee and the USSR Minister of Justice. Therefore, the final finding depended on which one of them would command a majority in the *ad hoc* commission. Bearing in mind the importance of the forthcoming discussion, Terebilov invited several prominent legal scholars, who shared the same theoretical attitude, to accompany him to the meeting of the commission in order to ensure, if necessary, the possibility of a professional opinion. The most remarkable part of the story was that the Minister did not fail to impress upon the scholars their duty to advise only him and to avoid any direct discussion with Fedoseev. This peculiar instruction was explained by pointing out that discussions could be permitted between Terebilov and Fedoseev as persons of equal Party rank, but that there would be a violation of hierarchical etiquette, if one of the consultants was ranged against Fedoseev, disregarding his incomparably higher Party position. And Terebilov was doubtlessly right: *suum cuique*, to render to everyone his own.

2. Sic volo, sic jubeo. These rules determine the attitude of commanding parts toward subordinate links of the Soviet hierarchy – the relationships between those who give orders and those who are obliged to execute them. When an order has been given in the form *sic volo*, the subordinate must do his best to achieve the desirable result. If he fails, this may, but need not affect his career, depending on what has caused the failure: incompetence of the executor or objective circumstances. When an order has been given in the form *sic jubeo*, the subordinate must carry it out, whether this order is just or unjust, humane or cruel, legal or illegal. If he abstains from doing so, his career will be doomed, and sometimes not only the official career, but also the whole life of a disobedient official will be ruined. In Soviet practice, however, disobedience of *sic volo* orders is almost completely impossible as well as disobedience of *sic jubeo* orders.

When the draft of the 1977 Constitution was published for an all-people's discussion, Romanov, a Politbureau member who was at that time the first secretary of the Leningrad CPSU Committee, invited three professors of the Law Faculty of Leningrad University to help him in connection with a very delicate, although in practice insignificant question. In the 1936 Constitution the union republics were enumerated according to the size of their population. As a result, the Kazakh Republic occupied the fifth place in the Constitution, following the Uzbek Republic, and, according to the explanation Romanov gave to the three professors of law, "comrade Kunaev, the first secretary of the Kazakh Central Committee, felt hurt" by this situation. Therefore it would be expedient to find a reason for its modification. No one could understand why Kunaev took this formality to heart. As for the problem revealed by Romanov, it was to be surmised – since Kunaev was not only a Politbureau member, but also a close friend of Brezhnev – that Romanov had a serious interest in playing up to him, thereby strengthening his position within the Brezhnev-dominated leadership. Nevertheless, the very problem was of a nature that precluded a categorial command. *Sic volo*, "thus I will" was the only possible approach under the circumstances. The poor professors tried to settle the problem in the direction indicated by means of various logical speculations, but either Romanov did not make use of their recommendations at all or their arguments did not command sufficient persuasiveness; at any rate, nothing was changed, and the Kazakh Union Republic preserved the same place in the new Constitution as it had in the previous one.

One of Romanov's predecessors in the office of first secretary of the Leningrad CPSU Committee, Spiridonov, was obsessed by the idea of evicting from state apartments those Leningrad inhabitants who had their own country house (*dacha*) in the Leningrad region. Late in the 1950s, when he expressed this *sic volo*, no legal rule in force at that time could justify such a judicial decision. On the contrary, its illegality was indicated by certain regulations. For example, in order to receive a plot of land for the building of a *dacha* in the Leningrad region before the prohibition introduced in 1961,[87] one had to be registered in Leningrad as a permanent resident, and to possess an apartment in a state-owned building as a permanent tenant. Hence, it is clear that the legislature could not, on the one hand, demand possession of state living space for acquisition of a *dacha*, and, on the other hand, withdraw it as soon as a *dacha* was acquired. Nevertheless, certain legal scholars and legal practitioners attempted to fulfill the task imposed from on high by a contrived interpretation of the law in force. Since allocation of dwelling premises assumed the need for living space, they argued that after a *dacha* had been built this need had disappeared, and its owner had to lose the right of a tenant. The fact that the demands satisfied by apartments and *dachas* were not the same was disregarded by such an artificial interpretation, because otherwise the ruler's wish could not have been met as required under the hierarchical system. In a very restricted, hardly recognizable shape the same idea was later adopted by Soviet law. As the Fundamentals of Civil Legislation state, eviction from state apartments may take place "in instances when a lessee possesses by right of personal ownership a dwelling house in the same population center, which is suitable for permanent residence, and it is possible for him to occupy it".[88] Meanwhile, in this formulation, the rule cited could not acquire any practical importance, but its very existence compromised Soviet housing legislation. Therefore, it has been omitted in the elaboration and promulgation of the Housing Code now in force. Thus, not only Spiridonov himself, but even his shameful monument of legislative activity sank into oblivion.

In contrast to *sic volo*, which expresses only the wishes of ruling circles, *sic jubeo* implies a higher level of imperativeness, expressing the rulers' commands. In this regard, Leningrad practice proves to be no less varied than in the aspect discussed above.

In the late 1970s, the same Romanov ordered, through his ideological assistant Khodirev, a secretary of the Leningrad CPSU Committee, that all persons who had applied to OVIR to emigrate be deprived of their academic degrees and titles. According to Soviet regulations, only one agency has the right to adopt such a decision – VAK (Russian acronym for Supreme Certification Commission), which functions as a department of the USSR Council of Ministers. However, individual universities and institutes may send the appropriate proposals to VAK, and, having brought his order to the notice of the Leningrad establishments concerned, Romanov could not mean anything else than the adoption of such proposals by decision of the academic councils of the institutions where "a culprit" worked. If there is no other pretext, as, for example anti-Soviet activity or other crimes committed, VAK never confirms similar proposals, not because it is more liberal than the Leningrad rulers, but because otherwise the genuine attitude of the USSR toward the right to emigration would be exposed. This practice is an open secret, but just the same all Leningrad establishments of higher education and of scientific research obeyed the command received, without missing even one case. Nothing could be done – *sic jubeo*: orders are orders.

One of Romanov's predecessors in the office of first secretary of the Leningrad CPSU Committee, Tolstikov, was obsessed by the idea of preserving a post-war privilege for Leningrad, despite the emergence of a new situation and the issuance of new legal rules. As discussed above, the surplus of living space consisting of a separate room had to be withdrawn according to a general procedure established by legislation then in force.[89] However, the tenant had the right to find a new neighbor by himself, and the local executive committee was obliged to accept the person thus chosen as being entitled to the vacant dwelling space. In such a way the law strived to alleviate the original tenant's hardship caused by the withdrawal of a part of his apartment. In Leningrad, which was very heavily destroyed during the war, the latter rule was abolished by the Soviet government, and in all cases surplus rooms withdrawn from tenants were allotted only by the local executive committee and exclusively to people officially registered as being in need of living space. When the Fundamentals of Civil Legislation were adopted in 1961, they did not reaffirm this Leningrad privilege and proclaimed as a general rule for the entire country the tenant's right to choose his neighbor.[90] Nevertheless, Tolstikov ordered the Leningrad executive committee to promulgate a local regulation, which recognized the above-mentioned right of choice, but only within the limits of people registered with the housing agency. The illegality of this regulation was obvious from the very beginning, and it retained its effect for no more than several months, when its abrogation became inevitable. Thus, there were no reasonable grounds to issue a regulation which ran counter to a newly adopted law. Unfortunately, all reasons lose their significance when a hierarchical order appears on the scene. Is a command unreasonable? Well, it could be, but it is a command just the same. Therefore, there is no arguing; one must only be obedient and execute it: *sic jubeo*.

3. *Non est corrigendum, non est disputandum.* While *sic volo, sic jubeo* belongs to the rulers' prerogatives, *non est corrigendum, non est disputandum* determines the subordinates' behavior. In Stalin's time this not infrequently led to humiliating extremes. In 1938, for example, all Soviet newspapers published Stalin's letter *Otvet Tovarishchu Ivanovu*, ("Answer to Comrade Ivanov"), which touched upon the problem of the fate of the state in connection with the construction of communism. To the great astonishment of most readers the word "restoration" was written not in its contemporary spelling (*vosstanovlenie*) but in the old-fashioned way (*vozstanovlenie*). However, no one dared to correct this archaism. Stalin was beyond correction. The word *spodruchnyi* means "handy", but in Stalin's vocabulary it meant "assistant" (*podruchnyi*). His writing and speeches were published verbatim, even where certain alterations would have ensured grammatical correctness. *Imperator*

Romanus super grammaticam est.

Similar anecdotes disappeared together with Stalin, but the general directive of *non est corrigendum, non est disputandum* has preserved its effect as a necessary prerequisite for the regular functioning of the hierarchical machinery.

Late in the 1950s, Khrushchev's deputy in the USSR Council of Ministers, Kosygin, headed an *ad hoc* commission of the Politbureau and the Government which supervised the elaboration of the draft of the Fundamentals of Civil Legislation. When the draft was almost ready, with only a few problems still unresolved, Kosygin invited the entire working commission to the Kremlin for a direct and informal conversation. The affair, however, took another turn. After entering the office once all were already assembled there, Kosygin began to look through the draft law, as if it were the first time he had seen it. His attention was attracted by an article which dealt with the contract of carriage of passengers. Like other people without a legal education, Kosygin could think of a contract only in terms of a complicated document signed by both contractual partners, and he was very astonished by the idea of contracts with passengers who simply purchased tickets, but did not make a contract according to Kosygin's understanding. Bearing in mind his profession as a textile engineer, no one was surprised by his self-confident remark about the sheer nonsense of combining the legal notion of a contract with passengers' tickets. Therefore, and because of a well-known understanding not to correct the rulers and not to argue with them, everyone kept silent with the exception of one woman professor whose venerable age and strong principles precluded her playing mum under such circumstances. Her clear voice sounded: "Yes, there is a contract, and it is not nonsense." "You will even say that purchase of bread in the shop is also a contract", parried Kosygin. "Yes, I will", continued the same voice with increasing insistence. At this, Kosygin got up and left the office. The informal discussion was over, but its participants felt perplexed. What were they to do with all similar contracts? Failure to use this notion would imply legal ignorance, but its use would demonstrate open disregard for authoritative displeasure. The only person who preserved complete calmness was Kosygin's legal assistant. He also did his best to calm the other participants of the failed meeting, expressing the strong hope that Kosygin would never remember his criticism, and that the word "a contract" might be preserved in all appropriate cases. But what if Kosygin would remember? This question was in the air, and no one, including the optimistic assistant, could give a reassuring answer. But Kosygin perhaps really did forget or pretended to have done so, since in all cases which elicited his sincere astonishment the word "a contract" was not left out of the Fundamentals of Civil Legislation.

Another incident took place at a comparatively lower level but with a different result. In the mid-1970s a post-graduate student from the German Federal Republic came to Leningrad University to study Soviet law and economy for one year. As is common in such cases, the newly arrived student, together with his consulting professor, worked out a plan for the whole year, which was later sanctioned by the university's foreign department. Among other commitments, the plan provided for a one-week visit to the Novosibirsk department of the USSR Academy of Sciences to meet a famous scholar who was engaged in research on mathematical methods of economic management. When the time came, the trip took place, but owing to a mistake by the university's foreign department, the document given to the western research fellow indicated, instead of the Economic Laboratory of the Novosibirsk Department of the USSR Academy of Sciences, the Legal Faculty of Novosibirsk University. Unfortunately, there is no such faculty at this university. Therefore, when "a vigilant" official from the University of Novosibirsk found an obvious incongruity in the document of a foreigner, and not simply a foreigner but a citizen of Western Germany, he decided that there was something wrong and ordered the astonished visitor to go back to where he came from. The student, having returned to Leningrad, informed his ambassador about what had happened; the ambassador complained to the USSR Ministry of Foreign Affairs, which in its turn got in touch with the USSR Ministry of Higher Education; then the mistake came to light, the culprits were punished, and the conflict was settled.

Such is the real content of this story. But some months later at a professors' meeting of Leningrad University Zinaida Kruglova, one of the secretaries of the Leningrad CPSU Committee, described it in essentially different terms. In her version, the West German intelligence service sent a spy to the USSR in order to meet a German secret service man in Novosibirsk. The KGB knew of this plan from the very beginning and took all necessary measures to ensure its failure. However, according to Kruglova's own words, a happy-go-lucky professor of law ruined all the KGB's efforts by giving the West German spy a document for an official trip to the Novosibirsk Faculty of Law – which really did not exist – and, owing to an astonishing lack of vigilance, an undesirable meeting took place. Leningrad University officials involved in this case knew that her statement had nothing in common with reality. Moreover, the entire audience understood the evident defects of the report, as it was unimaginable that the KGB – informed about the future meeting of two West German spies – could not prevent it because of a document which justified the trip of one of them to Novosibirsk. However, as a matter of course, no one, including the unlucky professor, tried to refute Kruglova's information by speeches or even by questions. *Non est corrigendum, non est disputandum* against a Party official of such rank. Meanwhile, despite its incorrectness, the statement put the professor's career in serious danger, and he managed to speak with Kruglova personally in order to clear the matter. To his surprise, Kruglova not only heard him out quietly, but, after he had ended, replied that she knew the truth and had no objections against the explanations presented. Then what was the problem? According to her, the problem was the necessity to educate the university's professors in the spirit of vigilance, and, in the absence of other examples, she considered it reasonable to use the incident mentioned, having modified it in such a way as to make it fit the appropriate educational purpose. She also added that her statement would not result in any sanctions against her interlocutor, and the only thing the latter had to sacrifice to the Party's demand was his reputation, which certainly would be quickly restored, since no punishment was in store for him. For the victim of this official calumny there was no other remedy. To demand the public refutation of a Party secretary's speech would mean the undermining of the very foundations of the Soviet system. For the author of the same calumny, her subtle understanding of foreign affairs, revealed probably not only in the case mentioned, had its positive effects. Soon afterwards she was appointed chairman of the Union of Soviet Societies of Friendship with Foreign Countries, and in this office she continues to be until today.

4. Per ordinem and extra ordinem. This set of rules opens a whole series of diametrically opposed principles, connected with the same conduct, but addressed to rulers in one case and to subordinates in the other.

Per ordinem refers to subordinates. In dealing with ruling agencies or officials, they must strictly observe the existing order and not transgress it from the viewpoint either of procedure or of instances. For example, late in the 1970s a famous woman professor lost her office in the Herzen Pedagogical Institute of Leningrad because of her son's emigration to Israel. She was not only disappointed but indignant with this decision and, referred not to the illegality of reprisals against emigrants' parents, but to certain peculiarities of the case. In her opinion, as a soldier of the Soviet Army during World War II, injured several times in battle and decorated, she deserved to be immune from such extreme measures. On the other hand, after the divorce from her husband twenty years previously, she was unable to educate and supervise her son, who lived separately from his mother with his father. Moreover, when, according to the emigration procedure established in the USSR, the son asked her written consent, she refused his demand and addressed a request as a Party member to the Institute Party Committee to help her in this complicated situation. However, instead of help, she was expelled from the Party and from the Institute on the grounds that as a person who proved to be incapable of educating her own son, she could not be trusted with the education of other people's children. Her immediate reaction to this hypocritical cruelty was a complaint in the form of a telegram sent directly to the CPSU Central Committee. As provided for by the Party Rules, "a Party member has the right to . . . address questions, applications, and proposals to any Party instance up to and including the Central Committee of the CPSU".[91] Thus, by sending a telegram directly to the Central Committee and by-passing all other links of the Party bureaucracy (committees of district and province), the complainant did not violate so-called Party discipline. One can also understand the complainant's impatience, since, in addressing all instances in consecutive order, she would have to spend months or even years without a job and without a salary. Nevertheless, the Central Committee returned the complaint to the complainant because she had disregarded the normal sequence, and each lower instance which heard her case afterwards broadened the main accusation with an additional rebuke concerning a gross violation of established procedure. Only when the case at last came to the Central Committee, was the punishment somewhat mitigated: a strict reprimand instead of expulsion from the CPSU, and a pension combined with occasional teaching assignments, instead of the complete deprivation of professional employment. But it was already too late. The *per ordinem* procedure so exhausted its victim that any thought of pedagogical or research work resembled a fantastic dream rather than even a remote reality.

Extra ordinem refers to the rulers. In dealing with subordinate agencies or officials, to say nothing of individual citizens, rulers are not bound by any order either of procedure or of instances, with exceptions only for judicial activity, though even in this case they do not stop at disregarding the established order, when its violation can be justified by the "highest interests". Artificial transformations of open judicial hearings into closed ones, groundless refusals to call witnesses suggested by defense counsel in political cases, the formal independence of judges combined with actual predetermination of their decisions in cases of "governmental necessity" have been depicted so extensively in numerous publications of Russian emigrants and Western scholars, journalists, politicians and even ordinary tourists that it is hardly necessary to adduce similar data again. It will be far more interesting to examine more closely, not the exceptional, but the routine application of the *extra ordinem* principle, when Party and governmental activities are dealing with subordinate agencies or persons and remain totally unchecked.

In 1963 the Faculty of Law of Leningrad University organized a conference about contemporary problems of criminal law. Numerous theorists and practitioners from many cities and different establishments were present. The head of the Criminal Law Department was the main speaker at the conference. Soon after the conference's completion a group of participants, headed by a deputy chairman of the USSR Supreme Court, sent a letter to the CPSU Central Committee, accusing the conference in general and the main speaker in particular, of "gross political mistakes". The speaker had affirmed that jurisprudence would help the legislature only if it was brave enough to say "no" when necessary, and this – according to the signatories of the letter – meant a call for disagreement between jurisprudence and the legislature in the USSR. As the letter stated, the same scholar put in bad light a new Soviet law providing for criminal punishment for feeding livestock with bread bought at state shops, since he defended the point of view that a scarcity of fodder had to be overcome by enhanced supply, not by criminal punishment. The authors of the report were especially indignant at the fact that an American lawyer used the platform of the conference to criticize Soviet criminal theory under Stalin, and that this was not met with an adequate rebuttal from the side of the Soviet scholars. In following the established order, the CPSU Central Committee should have sent the letter mentioned to the university Party committee for investigation and the elaboration of a finding. Thus it would have been *per ordinem*. But the question concerned "gross political mistakes" with the participation of an American and under the influence of his "hostile propaganda". Under such circumstances it would be pointless to waste time in the observation of established procedure. The state of emergency demanded *extra ordinem* actions. A Central Committee *ad hoc* commission was created, numbering about 30 members. It arrived in Leningrad and meticulously studied all aspects of the actual situation at the University's Faculty of Law, which suddenly became politically unreliable and demanded urgent political sanitation. As a matter of course, attention was paid primarily to the unfortunate conference itself and to its main speaker first and foremost. Then the *ad hoc* commission presented its findings to the CPSU Central Committee, and none less than the Secretariat itself – the most important body after the Politbureau – heard the case together with numerous other problems of all-union significance. The main speaker at the conference was called to this meeting, but he did not have the opportunity to provide the necessary explanations, due to incessant interruptions by Brezhnev, who was acting as a chairman because of Khrushchev's absence. After a short discussion the case was resolved. The chairman of the criminal law department of Leningrad University lost his office and his position as editor-in-chief of the legal journal *Pravovedenie*, and for almost the rest of his life he was unable to publish his works or regularly engage in research and pedagogical functions. The Faculty of Law of Leningrad University remained under political suspicion for several years, and was deprived of the rights to convoke conferences with participation of representatives of other cities or establishments. Direct contacts of Leningrad professors of law with foreign scholars, which had already attained considerable success, were reduced to the previous low levels. And among all these circumstances, the most sinister was the fact that the initial resolution was simultaneously the final one in consequence of the replacement of *per ordinem* by *extra ordinem*. This precluded any change for the better, because no one could ask the Secretariat to abrogate its own decision, and at the same time no one would modify his attitude toward the accused while the Secretariat decision remained in force. These peculiarities of the *extra ordinem* procedure reveal its advantages in comparison with its *per ordinem* counterpart, in cases where reprisals are required to be as severe as possible. Therefore the former is preferred to the latter whenever it is considered necessary to deliver a strong blow from the top to the bottom.

5. Imperium rationis and *ratio imperii*. When the lower links of the Soviet bureaucracy or individual Soviet citizens consider it necessary to introduce certain innovations, they may act only by force of reason (*imperium rationis*), presenting their arguments to the higher instances and doing this with the utmost circumspection in order to avoid any accusation of superfluous activity or – what is incomparably worse – of political immaturity. Preparations and executions of various economic reforms in the USSR illustrate the practicability of such an approach better than anything else.

The only economic innovation carried out by Khrushchev and preserved after his ouster pertained to the MTS's (Russian acronym for Machine and Tractor Stations). They existed as state enterprises, fulfilling all kinds of mechanical jobs for collective farms and receiving in exchange collective farms' grain and other produce. As a result, collective farms were deprived of most of their produce by obligatory deliveries to the state on the one hand, and by payment in kind to the MTS on the other. To liberate collective farms at least from the latter burden, Khrushchev ensured, in the late 1950s, that the CPSU Central Committee passed a decision concerning the liquidation of the MTS's and the selling of agricultural machinery to the collective farms. Some months before the issuance of this decision, an economist sent an article with the same suggestion to the leading economic journal of the USSR *Voprosi Ekonomiki*, and just a month before the problem was officially resolved he received a negative review from the journal with such political accusations as could have ended his professional career. He was saved only because of the short period of time separating the journal's negative stance and the positive decision of the CPSU. Meanwhile, when the final decision was published, the author again addressed the journal with an insistent demand to have his groundlessly rejected article published. However, he also failed this time, although owing to other circumstances. For now the editors of the journal referred not to the political defects of the article but to its obvious obsoleteness on account of the official decision already adopted. And, despite contradictions, this answer was quite logical, according to Soviet standards: no other authorship may exist where the leader has established his authorship.

In contrast to Khrushchev with his uncoordinated tinkering, Kosygin managed to proclaim a general economic reform of Soviet industry in 1965, despite Brezhnev's resistance at a time when his struggle for personal supremacy was just beginning – instead of the established triumvirate (together with Kosygin and Podgornyi). On the other hand, while Khrushchev kept the projected liquidation of the MTS's secret until the last moment, the 1965 reform was preceded by a broad theoretical discussion. Maximum economic freedom for Soviet enterprises was defended by a famous Kharkov economist, E.G. Liberman.[92] The reform itself did not, certainly, go as far as he had suggested, but his position could not be faulted, since it remained within the limits of the discussion stimulated, if not officially, then at least semi-officially. However, after public promulgation and partial execution of the economic reform another capable economist, the Moscow scholar G. Lisichkin, published a book in support of even greater economic freedom than that advocated by Liberman.[93] But this was a thoughtless action, because an attempt to strengthen that what had officially been settled – once the initiative did not come from the leadership itself – could only be assessed as revisionism or, at best, as frivolity. Thus it happened with Lisichkin whose book was given a hostile reception by official doctrine and whose name actually disappeared from economic literature.

Like Kosygin, Andropov also began his rule with some ideas about possible changes in economic management. It is true that his ideas seemed extremely vague, because it is only after an economic experiment, encompassing two all-union and three republican ministries and timed to begin on 1 January 1984, has revealed palpable results, that the concrete direction of economic reorganization will be determined. In addition, except for a short meeting with so-called Party veterans during which Andropov outlined his projected experiment,[94] no public discussion took place and no suggestions were published. The western media disseminated a manuscript allegedly compiled by a group of Soviet economists and destined for the Politbureau, but nevertheless quite mysteriously transmitted to western journalists. However, in the USSR this manuscript has never been published, and its very existence has never been confirmed. There are serious grounds to throw doubt on the authenticity of the document mentioned, whose content contradicts the Soviet understanding of *imperium rationis* and thus makes it improbable that it has been drawn up officially at research establishments at the demand or for the use of the ruling summit. Judging from extracts that have appeared in certain Western newspapers, the document declares the entire economic system of the USSR to be completely defective, and demands a radically new approach. One may admit the validity of this conception and recognize its rationality, but it certainly stems either from western sources or has been created in dissident circles and on no account can it be the result of official research. The Soviet hierarchy is based upon the Soviet system, where unlimited political power originates from established might.[95] To suppose under these circumstances that suggestions from the bottom to the top may be directed against the basis of the Soviet hierarchy and therefore against the hierarchy itself would mean nothing less than to assume that the Soviet regime recognized the right of lower strata to deal with the ruling group not only according to the principle of *imperium rationis* but also of *ratio imperii*. As a matter of course, there is no need to refute this assumption, because its groundlessness is quite obvious.

Ratio imperii as a method of hierarchical activity may only be applied in a downward direction and its peculiarity consists precisely in the power to give orders, which are to be carried out, whether accompanied by any grounds or not, and whether the grounds given are reasonable or irrational. In this regard, the notorious case of Rokotov and Faibishenko, heard by a Soviet court in the early 1960s, is especially illustrative.

Both persons had committed a crime which could be considered as "speculation in currency . . . as a form of business" – to use the language of Soviet criminal law.[96] The preliminary investigation had not yet been completed, when the Soviet media trumpeted the materials all over the country, and the main *dramatis personae* were described as hardened criminals who deserved the worst fate. Everyone was therefore sure that they would be sentenced to death. However, this did not and could not happen, because the criminal law then in force did not provide for capital punishment for the crime committed. Nevertheless, nobody except lawyers, knew of such "legal niceties", and it was no wonder that the sentences to long terms of deprivation of freedom provoked universal astonishment. Strange as it may seem, even the head of the Soviet state, Khrushchev, was astonished and indignant. By coincidence, a meeting of the CPSU Central Committee took place a few days after the passing of this sentence and Khrushchev publicly expressed his indignation, directly addressing Roman Rudenko, the late Procurator General of the USSR. Rudenko's reference to the law in force – which precluded capital punishment – did not impress Khrushchev who retorted with a question, ironical in form but quite clear in meaning: "Are not we those who make Soviet laws?" If the rule of *ratio imperii* were not behind this question and if Rudenko had acted as a genuine legal consultant, and not as a disciplined *apparatchik* (bureaucrat), he would have explained that, even if adopted, a law providing for capital punishment could not be applied to Rokotov and Faibishenko owing to its non-retroactivity, and that if, nonetheless, the new law did include a direct provision or *ad hoc* decision concerning retroactivity, this would have compromised Soviet legislation from the viewpoint of the elementary principles of genuine legality. Such an explanation, however, was not put forward, as Rudenko knew quite well, what kind of commands were implied in Khrushchev's question and in which way his dictatorial will had to be put into effect. Therefore, the necessary legislative steps were taken immediately, the law concerning capital punishment for currency speculation was passed,[97] and a secret edict of the Presidium of the USSR Supreme Soviet made this law retroactive in respect of Rokotov and Faibishenko, whose case was reconsidered on the demand of the Procuracy and who were subsequently executed in accordance with a new sentence.

The case is well known to western readers, and it has been recalled here, on the one hand, because of its obvious straightforwardness, and, on the other hand, in order to present its occurrence without any distortions. Beyond these considerations, one cannot complain of a noticeable lack of similar illustrations. Commands are not to be discussed; they must be carried out. And the higher the level that issues the order, the more inadmissible is any discussion. This is the general principle of governing activity in the USSR, whether it touches upon economic or political problems, military or cultural commitments, internal or foreign affairs. It has therefore become typical of the Soviet system that, in contrast to *imperium rationis*, which is just as rare as an initiative from the bottom, *ratio imperii* belongs to the routine methods inherent to the prevailing system of administration from the top.

6. Ratio decidendi and *nuda decisio*. When a lower link of the Soviet hierarchy decides upon any problem, it must explain the step taken either directly in the adopted text or at the first demand of higher agencies. Without a *ratio decidendi*, expressed or implied, not one decision of this level can be valid, and, if the *ratio* is vulnerable, the *decisio* is under threat of abrogation.

However, if one leaves aside court decisions, where any other approach would be simply unimaginable, this principle, which is quite reasonable, has a very restricted application in its proper meaning. In issuing regulations at their own initiative, lower governmental agencies usually refer to the appropriate reasons for them. During periods of summer drought, the local executive committees of Moscow and Leningrad adopt rules that forbid driving and parking in forests, directly pointing out their purpose of fire-prevention. By introducing an order that allowed the selling of alcoholic beverages no earlier than at 11 in the morning and no later than at 8 in the evening, the Leningrad executive committee openly directed its measures against alcoholism. The Moscow executive committee did not keep its goals a secret either, when in order to prevent abuses, it introduced special rules for selling cars with the obligatory participation of GAI.[98] The problem, however, is that most general regulations adopted at lower levels do not go beyond solutions promoted by the top. Then these solutions themselves serve as *ratio decidendi* for public activities of subordinate agencies, even if the higher commands are not supported by proper explanations and have the form of pure imperatives. Thus, numerous edicts of Presidiums of Union republic Supreme Soviets begin with the words "in conformity with such-and-such an edict of the Presidium of the USSR Supreme Soviet"; similarly numerous regulations of local governmental agencies are preceded by the formula "in conformity with such-and-such an edict of the Council of Ministers of the USSR" or of the corresponding Union republic. These words and these formulae not only replace *ratio decidendi*; they disprove at the same time the constitutional declarations about the sovereignty of the Union republics[99] and about the independence of local administration within the limits of its jurisdiction.[100] Bodies and entities, which cannot function otherwise than "in conformity" with what has been solved without them and "in correspondence" with what has been imposed upon them, can neither be sovereign nor independent. As simple executors of a higher will they act automatically, without arguing and without explaining, not so much with *ratio*, as *sine ratione*. Why may individual housing not exceed 60 square meters in the RSFSR and 100 square meters in Estonia? Why have the local executive committees of all cities opened to foreigners established identical rules concerning the duty of foreigners to pay more for hotel rooms than Soviet citizens? Why are some hotels in these cities closed to foreigners, while others are closed to citizens? Is there any reason for such regulations? Of course there is. They originate, however, not from the reflections of those who have adopted them, but of those who have ordered them to be adopted.

And the latter are not obliged to explain, since they have the actual right to decide. It is true that beginning with Khrushchev Soviet legislation has followed the practice of attaching preambles to normative acts, which technically are similar to *rationes decidendi*. One must not, however, forget that preambles usually accompany only the most important enactments: constitutions, fundamentals of separate legislative branches, the most important republican codes, etc. In addition, they fulfill exclusively propagandistic functions, proclaiming political slogans instead of giving substantive explanations. As soon as it is understood that this is the task of preambles, it becomes clear that the principle of *ratio decidendi* is alien to Soviet government activity. At the hierarchical peak, decision without argument, *nuda decisio*, plays the main role in the governing of the country. To prove this assertion let us resort to one example only, not very impressive at first sight but extremely demonstrative after a more careful investigation.

An edict of the USSR Council of Ministers, issued on 30 December 1961,[101] begins with the following: "To forbid the granting of plots of land to citizens for the individual building of country houses [*dacha*] in all localities." This prohibition was not explained in any way either by the edict or by an additional act. One could only guess at its hidden causes, although two things were clear from the very beginning. Neither agricultural demands nor the eventual construction of sanatoriums played an important part in the matter. Agricultural land has never been used for *dacha* building, and the construction of sanatoriums does not occur "in all localities" but only within the limits of well-known resort areas. To understand the real causes of such a rigid and quite unexpected legal innovation, one episode is especially symptomatic. Not long before the promulgation of the edict a group of about forty writers addressed, to the competent Leningrad agencies a common application for the granting to them of plots of land for the building of *dachas* in the village of Komarovo. In the end their request was satisfied, but initially they met with serious obstacles, which compelled them to ask for a meeting with the first secretary of the provincial CPSU Committee. To the writers' astonishment the secretary, instead of supporting them, tried to persuade them of the groundlessness of their demand. His main argument was that, having been provided for with good apartments in the city, writers could use them to adequately develop their creative activity without the benefit of country houses, which were objects of luxury, and not instruments of labor. When one of the writers, probably the bravest among them, exclaimed in the heat of the argument, that the secretary himself had a *dacha* at his disposal, the latter gave a very peculiar answer: his *dacha* belonged to the state and would be withdrawn immediately in case of his dismissal, while country houses built by writers themselves would be in their ownership, whatever change took place in their positions. This definitive objection betrays one of the most basic features of the Soviet hierarchy.

Essentially, economic advantages shall correspond to hierarchical levels. Meanwhile, in the case discussed the law encouraged those who did not belong to the political hierarchy to be economically equal or even superior to those who represented its various links. Such legal regulations contradicted the prevailing political system, and they were doomed to be abrogated sooner or later.

The enumeration and illustration of principles, which eloquently express the universal hierarchy existing in the USSR as a real counterbalance to a fictitious equality, could be prolonged. However, additional analytical efforts are not required to substantiate the appropriate general conclusions. It should be clear enough that unlimited political power, which rests upon monopolistic economic might, entails a hierarchical structure of the corresponding society as its natural consequence and logical completion. Legal regulations are aimed at disguising this fact, but they lack the necessary consistency, because irrepressible reality breaks through the legislative camouflage now and again. In turn, daily practice does its best to keep the hierarchy inviolate – despite the inadequacy of legal regulations – but these aspirations are sometimes seriously thwarted by the impossibility of disregarding completely a certain part of the adopted rules. Therefore, the hierarchical approach, victorious as a general rule, must occasionally retreat, and legal equality, which is mostly pure propaganda, exceptionally succeeds in becoming effective. At the same time, it would be a gross mistake to confuse ephemeral cases with stable factors. The Leningrad writers won. This was very impressive, but only as a deviation from the norm. The individual building of country houses has now been forbidden. This is also very impressive, but now as a norm, and not as a deviation.[102]

However, if the Soviet system heaps one contradiction upon another, combining the uncombinable – democratic centralism and centralized democracy, political freedom and political domination, economic emancipation and economic slavery, universal equality and universal hierarchy, does it not mean that so-called socialist legality also pertains to the contradictory phenomena of the Soviet system? The closing chapter shall try to answer this question.

NOTES

1. The 1977 Constitution, art.70.
2. *Ibid.*
3. *Ibid.*
4. The 1977 Constitution, art.72.
5. The 1977 Constitution, art.82.
6. The 1977 Constitution, art.86.
7. The 1977 Constitution, art.88.
8. Art.1 of Part I of the International Covenant on Civil and Political Rights, adopted December 19, 1966, 21 U.N. GAOR, Supp.(No.16)52, U.N. Doc. A/6316 (1966); Art.1 of Part I of the International Covenant on Economic, Social and Cultural Rights, adopted December 19, 1966, 21 U.N. GAOR, Supp.(No.16)49, U.N. doc. A/6316 (1966).
9. The 1936 Constitution, art.13; the 1977 Constitution, art.71.
10. The 1977 Constitution, art.85.
11. The 1936 Constitution, art.22.
12. *Ibid.*
13. The 1977 Constitution, art.85.
14. The 1977 Constitution, art.14.
15. *Supra*, 130-133.
16. The 1977 Constitution, art.34.
17. *Ibid.*
18. The 1977 Constitution, art.35.
19. The 1977 Constitution, art.36.
20. *Infra*, 150-160.
21. There is also a fourth legal institute – the All-Union Institute for Extra-Mural Legal Studies, but it is of no particular interest in the present analysis.
22. As a general rule, one must be 18 years old in order to become a student in a Soviet university or institute.
23. *Supra*, 42.
24. Arts.89-90, 95-98.
25. Arts.12-13.
26. Note 25.
27. *Supra*, 134.
28. It is not sufficent, however, to be a writer or a scholar in order to acquire the appropriate right. The latter belongs only to writers who are members of the Union of Soviet Writers, or only to scholars who have academic degrees of "doctor" or "candidate".
29. *Supra*, Chapter III.
30. The Labor Code, art.80.
31. The Labor Code, art.81.
32. Model Collective Farm Charter, art.24.
33. Model Collective Farm Charter, art.27.
34. Model Collective Farm Charter, art.24.
35. *Supra*, 119.
36. Note 71 to Chapter III.
37. As a matter of course, inequality conditioned by minority or insanity is known to Soviet law (*e.g.* see the Civil Code, arts.13-15) as well as to any law in the world. Since, however, another solution would be impossible due to natural rather than social causes, this would not contradict the principle of equality if it were observed in all other matters.
38. The 1936 Constitution, arts.118-128.
39. The 1977 Constitution, arts.33-36, 39-58.
40. The 1977 Constitution, art.1.
41. *Supra*, 145-146.

42. *Supra*, 23-24, 25-26.
43. *Supra*, 100-101.
44. This does not, however, relate to the ruling summit of the Orthodox Church and some other churches, owing to their unofficial bargain with the Soviet ruling summit. See, *e.g.* Mark Popovskii, *Zhizn' i zhitiie Voino-Iasenetskogo, archiepiskopa i khirurga*, Paris 1979.
45. *Supra*, 144.
46. The Labor Code, arts.160-162.
47. The Family Code, arts.5, 25.
48. *Supra*, 145-146.
49. *Supra*, 38.
50. *Supra*, 145.
51. These words of Lenin, so popular in the beginning, went out of fashion some time after his death.
52. *Supra*, 145-146.
53. *Supra*, 154.
54. According to art.17 of the Code of Criminal Procedure, "persons who do not have command of the language in which the judicial proceedings are conducted shall be secured the right to make statements, give testimony, speak in court, and submit petitions in their own language, as well as to make use of the services of an interpreter in accordance with the procedure established by the present Code". An analogous rule is provided for in the Code of Civil Procedure, art.8.
55. *Supra*, 145.
56. Art.22 of the 1974 Statute on the Passport System in the USSR. It deserves to be pointed out that the Statute cited is more lenient in its demand of temporary registration than were its predecessors.
57. *Supra*, 68-69.
58. *Ibid.*
59. *Supra*, 145-146.
60. The 1977 Constitution, art.1.
61. *Ibid.*
62. The 1977 Constitution, art.6.
63. The 1977 Constitution, arts.7-8.
64. The 1977 Constitution, art.6.
65. The 1977 Constitution, art.7.
66. The 1977 Constitution, art.8.
67. *Supra*, Chapter III.
68. Chapters I, II, III.
69. *Polozhenie o poriadke naznacheniia i vyplaty pensii, SP SSSR* 1972 No.17 item 8 with subsequent amendments (hereinafter cited: the Statute on Pensions).
70. *Ibid.*, art.19.
71. *Ibid.*, art.102.
72. See, *e.g.*, art.108(9) of the Housing Code.
73. *Sotsial'noe obespechenie v SSSR*, Moskva 1979, pp.273–278.
74. *Supra*, 147-148.
75. The same monetary regime has been introduced for officials with the title of ambassador. Therefore, when a high official loses his position and is sent abroad as an ambassador, this often means a demotion in office, compensated, however, with stable pecuniary maintenance. For example, the former first secretary of the Kazakhstan Communist Party, Penteleimon Ponomarenko, was Brezhnev's chief at the time when the development of virgin lands in Kazakhstan was initiated. Later he lost his office in favor of Brezhnev, but was appointed Soviet ambassador to The Netherlands. However, to some extent his position became stronger, and as an official – equal in rank to marshal as far as pensions were concerned – he preserved his former salary after a scandal with a Soviet defector in The Netherlands compelled him to retire on a pension.
76. See references to laws *supra*, notes to 138, 142, 145, 154, 169.
77. The Housing Code, art.33.
78. The Housing Code, art.36.
79. *Ibid.*

180

80. The Housing Code, art.37.
81. *Ibid.*
82. *SP SSSR* 1972 No.14 item 73.
83. *Supra,* 134, 137, 140, 147-148, 162.
84. The Civil Code (before the 1983 amendments) arts.303, 316; *SZ SSSR* 1926 No.44 item 312; *SU RSFSR* 1928 No.53 item 402.
85. *Ved. RSFSR* 1982 No.49 item 1821.
86. *Supra,* 39-41.
87. *SP SSSR* 1961 No.1 item 2.
88. The Fundamentals of Civil Legislation, art.61.
89. *Supra,* 166.
90. The Fundamentals of Civil Legislation, art.59.
91. Rules of the CPSU, art.3(e).
92. See, e.g., E. Liberman, *Economic Methods and the Effectiveness of Production*, White Plains, NY 1971, which is a translation of an earlier work in Russian.
93. G. Lisichkin, *Plan i rynok*, Moskva 1966.
94. *Izvestiia*, 16 August 1983.
95. *Supra*, Chapters II, III.
96. The Criminal Code, art.88.
97. The second paragraph of art.88 of the RSFSR Criminal Code allowing capital punishment as a possible penalty for currency speculation was added on 25 July 1962 (*Ved. RSFSR* 1962 No.29 item 449).
98. *Supra,* 148.
99. The 1977 Constitution, art.76.
100. The 1977 Constitution, art.146.
101. *SP SSSR* 1961 No.1 item 2.
102. Those who know this Soviet practice not only from books but also from experience, from the inside and not from the outside, are utterly astonished at certain western discussions about how significant Soviet decisions are made. The incident with the South-Korean airliner in September 1983 is a comparatively recent and extraordinarily striking example of this kind. Most participants of oral discussions, witnessed by the author of this book, referring to reasonable practice as they understood it, had no doubt that the decision to shoot down the plane had been made by local commanders. They did not change their mind even after, in contrast to the Soviet practice of keeping such things secret, Marshal Ogarkov declared that the fateful decision was taken by a local commander of the air force. Why Ogarkov deviated from usual practice in this exceptional case is more or less clear. To shoot down the plane without the highest order after its flight in Soviet airspace for more than two hours would be simply impossible in the USSR, considering the extremely hierarchical order which prevails in that country. By his declarations, Ogarkov tried to provoke at least some hesitation in quite natural assumptions. However, he hardly knew that there was no actual need for his far-fetched explanation, because even before the notorious press conference in Moscow took place, numerous people in the West were sure it could not have been otherwise.

CHAPTER V

THE LAW OF PROCLAIMED LEGALITY AND LEGALIZED ARBITRARINESS

Among the verbal symbols of Soviet totalitarianism, legality occupies one of the most honorable places. It has always accompanied the Soviet state, beginning with the October coup d'état down to our time. The only thing that has changed is the terminological designation. After the seizure of power and during the atrocities of the *Cheka* and the *GPU* (predecessors of the KGB), the words "revolutionary legality" were used. Following the promulgation of the 1936 Constitution they were replaced by the words "socialist legality", and this designation has survived from the times of Stalin's purges into the present. The difference in terminology reflects to some extent a conceptual evolution. "Revolutionary legality" refers not so much to law as to the so-called revolutionary legal conscience, *i.e.* instead of legality, it openly proclaims undisguised arbitrariness.[1] "Socialist legality" refers to nothing other than to Soviet law itself, *i.e.* independently of the specific content of legal rules, it assumes their observance to be the main demand of legality.[2] Until recently the problem of the legality of laws themselves had not been touched upon at all since Soviet laws are considered legal as such and must be beyond dispute from this point of view. The discussion concerning the notion of law, resumed late in the 1970s,[3] stimulated scholars to pay increased attention to the question of the legality of laws, and some of them attempted to overcome a purely formalistic approach to this problem. However, their arguments were concerned only with an abstract definition of law and did not specifically consider Soviet law by itself.

Meanwhile, in analysing Soviet law from the point of view of legality, one is not bound by the Soviet doctrine concerning this principle. To understand the genuine meaning of the latter one has to study legal rules and legal reality in their congruency and discrepancy, their conformity and contradictions, their correspondence to official jurisprudence or lack of it. Therefore, legality, as it is reflected in Soviet law, seems no less interesting than legality, as it is applied in Soviet practice. At the same time, both law and practice require elucidation in order to understand the proclaimed legality and legalized arbitrariness.

1. Proclaimed Legality

Hardly any other notion is repeated by Soviet laws with such persistence as the notion of legality. This practice would be pointless and banal, if the fixation on legality could not be counterbalanced by the intentionally disguised actual arbitrariness. Although strict legality is widely proclaimed in legal texts, striking arbitrariness is a routine phenomenon in legal practice.

Proclaimed Legality in Soviet Law

The Soviet Constitution, in typifying "the basic orientation of the development of the political system", especially stresses "the strengthening of the legal basis of state and social life".[4] It also proclaims that "the Soviet state and all its agencies shall operate on the basis of socialist legality and ensure the protection of the legal order, and the rights and freedoms of citizens".[5] The same constitutional rule provides for a general duty of "state and social organizations and officials . . . to observe the USSR Constitution and Soviet laws".[6] Another article of the Soviet Constitution addresses a similar command to the Soviet citizenry, adding to the observance of legal rules the duty "to respect the rules of socialist community life".[7] In following the Constitution, numerous current laws also appeal to the principle of legality. This is particularly true with regard to legislation, regulating civil or criminal legal procedure. "Civil procedure shall further the strengthening of socialist legality, the prevention of violations of law, and the education of citizens in a spirit of undeviating execution of Soviet laws and respect for the rules of socialist community life."[8] "Criminal procedure shall further the strengthening of socialist legality and the legal order, the prevention and eradication of crimes, the protection of the interests of society, the rights and freedoms of citizens, and the education of citizens in a spirit of undeviating observance of the USSR Constitution and the law and of respect for the rules of socialist community life."[9] Within the limits of its operation, substantive law also underscores the importance of socialist legality. "Soviet civil legislation is an important means for the further strengthening of legality in the domain of property relations and the protection of the rights of socialist organizations and citizens", states the preamble to the Fundamentals of Civil Legislation. In enumerating the tasks of criminal law, the Fundamentals of Criminal Legislation, in article 1, point out separately the protection of "the entire socialist legal order against criminal infringements". Laws dealing with supervision by the Procuracy or with the organization of the courts quite naturally pay great attention to socialist legality. "The purpose of the supreme supervision over the strict execution of the laws is the strengthening of socialist legality", reads the Statute on Procuracy Supervision in the USSR in article 2.[10] "The activity of the court in the administration of justice shall be directed towards a comprehensive strengthening of socialist legality and the legal order", provide the Fundamentals of Legislation on Court Organization of the USSR and of the Union and Autonomous Republics in article 3.[11]

After Stalin's death, numerous steps were taken which are known as measures to strengthen socialist legality. One of these measures was the abrogation of legal rules and the liquidation of state institutions that contradicted the principle of legality by the very fact of their existence. For example, among the legal rules abrogated in such a way were those that established a summary procedure in criminal cases of a political character, and among the state institutions liquidated in the same process was the *Osoboe Soveshchanie*, an extra-judicial agency that had the right to hear political cases secretly, without a strictly prescribed procedure or the participation of the accused, and to apply any penalty including capital punishment. However, in some instances the reforms were reduced only to a modification of titles, accompanied by not very consistent substantive changes. For example, corrective labor camps were renamed corrective labor colonies in 1957. At the beginning, renaming entailed mitigation of the former inhumane regime, but little by little, especially when the campaign against dissidents reached its apogee, many methods of formerly condemned brutality were restored, despite the earlier rejection of the discredited title. Another measure directed at strengthening legality was actually a renovation of Soviet laws, mainly in the form of their new codification, beginning in the late 1950s. The movement differed in three ways from the codification of the 1920s. First, it was more centralized, since in all cases where the enactment of codes belonged to the jurisdiction of the union republics, the USSR first adopted Fundamentals regulating the branch of law concerned, and thus republican codification depended not only in essence but even in formal terms on the legal rules of all-union nature. Second, it was more complete than its predecessor owing to the elaboration of certain codes which were unknown beforehand, such as, for example, the Water Code, the Code of Mineral Resources, or the Forestry Code. Third, it was used to eliminate obsolete institutions (for example, various kinds of private societies provided for by the Civil Code, but later eradicated from the Soviet economy), to fill gaps in previous legislation by introducing new institutions (for example, the system of administrative violations established by the Fundamentals of Legislation of the USSR and the union republics on administrative violations),[12] and to clean up the entire body of current legislation by amending normative acts that were impractical, inefficient, or defective, etc.

In addition, codification has been supplemented by two other kinds of systematization. In the mid-1970s the Ministry of Justice of the USSR completed the issuance of the *SDZ* (Russian acronym for "Collection of legislation in force"), making up 51 volumes. The *SDZ* encompasses the bulk of Soviet legislation, whether expressed in laws or in subordinate normative acts (decrees of the USSR Council of Ministers, for example). However, since this is not a codification, but an ordinary systematization – carried out not by the legislature but by the Ministry of Justice – all normative acts, included in the *SDZ*, have been reproduced verbatim with amendments adopted beforehand by the competent agencies at the suggestion of the Ministry of Justice. The latter has also used this opportunity to present its suggestions about the abrogation of numerous obsolete or awkward legal regulations. In this respect the preparation of the *SDZ* played, in general, a positive role in the improvement of Soviet legislation. It also helped in the search and discovery of appropriate rules owing to a certain logic of the system applied. Nevertheless, since it was not a work of codification, the *SDZ* could not avoid repetition, a certain lack of coordination between different normative acts, and a certain cumbersomeness or even clumsiness which hampered its practical applicability. One should also not forget that, although the *SDZ* had been prepared by the Ministry of Justice in conformity with government instructions, approved by the Politbureau, it did not possess the force of an official legal collection, and in all practical cases the appropriate agencies and officials must refer to the law or other normative act itself, and not to the appropriate volume, chapter and page of *SDZ*. On 2 September 1976, the CPSU Central Committee, the Presidium of the USSR Supreme Soviet, and the Council of Ministers of the USSR proclaimed the need to prepare and promulgate a Collection of Laws of the USSR (*Svod Zakonov SSSR*).[13] Its publication has already begun,[14] and, as the decision about the adoption of a Collection of Laws and the individual volumes published since 1980 show, this legal collection differs essentially from the *SDZ*. The official significance given to the Collection of Laws is a very important advantage – but unfortunately the only one – which the Collection possesses in relation to the *SDZ*. As the Introduction to the first volume provides, "the Collection of Laws of the USSR is an official publication of the Presidium of the USSR Supreme Soviet and the Council of Ministers of the USSR".[15] This means that direct references to the Collection are permissible in all appropriate cases of the practical application of Soviet law, although there can hardly be any doubt that because of a deeply-rooted practice of many decades governmental and judicial agencies will continue to quote the individual laws, in spite of the promulgation of the Collection, even if the former are included in the latter. In all other respects the Collection has the same short-comings as the *SDZ*, and some additional ones as well. The Collection, like the *SDZ*, being an exercise in systematization, rather than in codification, does not present a united law, consisting of interdependent parts and logically coordinated ingredients. It is true that in this case, even more than in case of the *SDZ*, the USSR Ministry of Justice – which was again responsible for all preparatory work[16] – has made use of the opportunity to remove many defects from Soviet legislation by means of official suggestions addressed to the competent agencies. Moreover, the edict about the Collection of Laws considered it necessary – in order to ensure the issuance of this legal collection – to enact codification and other consolidated normative acts as well as normative acts indispensable for the removal of gaps in legislation.[17] But all these wishes and recommendations cannot be carried out consistently, when a legal collection is not envisaged as a unified piece of codification. Therefore, cumbersome-ness and clumsiness can be found in those volumes of the Collection that have already appeared. At the same time, another factor seems even more important. The *SDZ* is a collection of the entire legislation in force. With the Collection the situation is different. It will include only laws, the most important joint decrees of the CPSU Central Committee and the USSR Council of Ministers, as well as decrees of the USSR Government, if these are of a general character.[18] Hence, the Collection of Laws will not satisfy practical demands even within the limits of normative acts, which are of the highest rank in formal terms, to say nothing of substatutory (*podzakonnye*) instructions, without which nothing can function in the USSR. The eventual publication of republican Collections of Law, foreseen for the remote future,[19] does not save the situation, because they too will have the same short-comings on the republican level as their prototype on the All-Union level. In the decree on the further improvement of economic legislation, adopted by the CPSU Central Committee and the Council of Ministers of the USSR on 25 June 1975,[20] the USSR ministries were obliged to ensure the reform of their own normative acts and the completion of the issuing of collections or enumerations of these acts not later than in 1976.[21] But the decree touches only upon economic legislation, which concerns primarily the activity of economic ministries, and even these ministries have not yet carried out the task imposed. Thus, the knowledge of the law in force as an elementary condition of genuine legality is not, in principle, ensured in the USSR, despite the new codification, the issuing of the *SDZ*, the promulgation of several volumes of the USSR Collection of Laws, the prospect of similar Collections in the union republics, and special measures connected with the improvement and systematization of economic legislation. Moreover, there are various other circumstances related to legislative practice and sometimes to legal principles, that obviously contradict this most important demand of the principle of legality.

First of all, any legality assumes the publication of legal regulations. The secrecy of these regulations in the Soviet Union, sometimes even on the level of decrees of the USSR Council of Ministers, to say nothing of ministerial instructions and orders, has already been pointed out,[22] and is known all over the world. But the most peculiar thing is that the *SDZ* itself is kept a secret. It was published under the title "For official use" (*Dlia sluzhebnogo pol'zovaniia*). This title only serves as a sign of secrecy, which can have different degrees of practical application. No book or booklet, bearing such a sign, is officially for sale. The price is simply not indicated, in contrast to the general rule in force in the USSR. Nevertheless, some such publications are on the shelves of Soviet establishments and may freely be used by any officials. Moreover, to receive them in personal possession is, although illegal, not difficult in numerous cases. As for the *SDZ*, it was subject to a very severe order, which itself was kept a secret until an unexpected event revealed the truth. The Law Faculty of Leningrad University, having some spare money earned through research ordered by certain Soviet institutions, decided to buy the complete *SDZ* through the channel of closed selling operated by the USSR Ministry of Justice. The appropriate amount of money was transferred, but not one of the 51 volumes of the *SDZ* appeared in the library, despite the written notice of the Ministry that all of them had been sent to Leningrad University. Only after a long search was the complete *SDZ* at last found in *spetskhran*[23] of the University library, where solely those people who had personal access were permitted to use secret literature. It is also important to remember that, beginning with World War II and up to 1958, decrees of the USSR Council of Ministers were not published at all, and only a part of them appeared in the *SDZ*, while another part, having preserved legal force, did not leave "the kingdom of secrecy". After 1958, the same regime continued to be practised toward those decrees of the all-union government which were classed as secret and therefore exempted from publication. This means that from the viewpoint of public knowledge Soviet legislation consists of three divisions: (1) secret legislation known only to a very restricted circle of bureaucrats, directly concerned in that area of activity, which has engendered such peculiar ways of legal regulation; (2) legislation for official use available to a comparatively broader circle of people, but not to the man in the street and sometimes not to all participants in the administrative process; (3) legislation brought to universal notice either by Soviet media or exclusively by special publications of the Presidium of the USSR Supreme Soviet, of the Council of Ministers of the USSR, etc. Meanwhile, socialist legality, according to Soviet doctrine and the

Soviet Constitution,[24] presupposes the strictest observance of Soviet law by state agencies and social organizations, all officials and all citizens, whether this law is publicly known, half-secret or completely concealed. How can one reconcile one thing with another? And, if they are irreconcilable, then Soviet law does not go beyond a purely verbal legality which, being proclaimed officially, does not possess a clearly outlined content and a firm and dependable foundation.

The main approach to the notion of legality in the USSR is also unacceptable. This approach rests upon the observance of law as a demand addressed with the same force to governing agencies and to subordinate citizens. Meanwhile, in the realm discussed, the latter and the former play essentially different roles. Citizens may break specific laws, but they cannot violate legality. If there are larcenies, murders or other crimes committed by individual citizens, but all necessary measures to expose the criminals are taken and while all intentional accusations of innocent persons are prosecuted, legality rises to the occasion, despite the violations of numerous laws. Governing agencies, on the contrary, may violate legality not only in breaking specific laws but also by means of their formal observance. When a procurator refuses to initiate a criminal case because the person to be charged belongs to the CPSU, whose corresponding agencies do not sanction prosecution, the procurator breaks the law of criminal procedure, which does not provide for the Party's approval to be imposed upon practice in an extra-legal way.[25] Simultaneously, however, legality suffers a gross violation too, since the state disregards its own orders established in the legal sphere of criminal procedure. Another situation occurs in the case when a chief of a labor camp concludes a contract with a state enterprise about the "delivery" of a labor force of prisoners at a certain time and for a certain payment.[26] Because the regulations mentioned above permit such a contract, an actual agreement of this kind does not break Soviet law, but the regulations themselves contradict the legal order of the country, which boasts the absence of any exploitation – not only that of universally forbidden slave labor. In his turn, the chief of the labor camp, having engaged in a contract – known in Ancient Rome as *locatio conductio operarum* and disingenuously called *kontragentskii dogovor* (contractor's contract) in Soviet corrective labor legislation, as if any other contract exists without contractors as its participants – cannot defend himself before a court by referring to the legal permissibility of his actions. First of all, permission is not an order, and therefore, one may make use of it, or not. Then, even an order does not free the executor from responsibility, if this order is illegal itself. At last, the duty of management of a labor camp involves the observation of *khozraschet*,[27] but it is up to its chief whether the task of *khozraschet* is to be carried out by selling the prisoners' labor or by the exploitation of the enterprises of the labor camp itself. Thus, he has a choice and may not refer to orders, even if the latter precluded responsibility. But the problem at hand is not so much about official crimes, as about violations of legality. In actual fact this problem is not difficult, and the Soviets themselves would hardly support the opposite point of view. If prisoners' slave labor did not violate legality only because it was provided for by Soviet law, then, in the discussion about the use of slave labor in the construction of the gas pipeline from the USSR to Western European countries, the Soviet Union would not waste so much energy and effort to disprove similar assertions. The same fact also illustrates an integral defect of such an understanding of legality, which assumes complete equality of its demands, irrespective of its addressees, and a complete vulnerability of its functioning, irrespective of the acting officials. In contrast to law consisting of legal commands, legality means nothing other than the establishing and supporting of the legal order. The legal commands are addressed to everybody and can be violated by everyone – by private citizens, state and other officials, state and other agencies or organizations, or by the state as a single whole. The legal order shall serve the general welfare, but only the state as a single whole, directly or through the competent agencies, may establish and support it, and, as a result, only the state, its agencies or its officials can violate legality. While law deals with relationships between citizens, between citizens and various agencies and organizations, between these organizations and agencies as well as between any of them and the state, legality reflects the status of relationships exclusively between citizens, acting separately or as collective bodies, and the state, functioning directly, through its agencies or through its officials. When these relationships are based upon the legal order – firmly established and strictly supported by the state – then legality exists in all its fullness. On the contrary, when the state abstains from establishing the legal order or establishes it without sufficient fullness, as well as when the state allows violations of the legal order, if not always then at least in principle, or if not as a general rule then at least as exceptions to the general rule, legality either does not exist at all or at best is combined with arbitrariness. If this is so, then two circumstances must be considered separately.

The first relates to the slogan of the "further strengthening of socialist legality", proclaimed by Soviet law and supported by Soviet doctrine. It must be clear without saying that legality needs strengthening if it conflicts with arbitrariness. Hence, the slogan, attractive at first sight, sounds more like a self-denunciation, when it is tested. The Soviets apparently admit the existence of arbitrariness in the country, since they have tirelessly repeated an insistent appeal to strengthen legality during their entire history, beginning with the NEP and up to the present period. This deduction, to be sure, could be disproved by the fact that strengthening of legality to no inconsiderable degree means the toughening of the fight against crime and other violations of law, committed by hostile or irresponsible people, in spite of the strictest observance of the legal order by the Soviet state. As long as legality is regarded simply as the non-violation of law, such an argument seems quite convincing. Moreover, relying upon the same interpretation, Soviet propaganda retained the opportunity for praising socialist legality and proclaiming its uninterrupted progress during Stalin's purges. Only when Stalin was denounced, did Khrushchev connect the task of strengthening legality with violations of law, committed not by subordinates but by the leadership. However, even in this unprecedented case only one individual and his closest assistants, such as Beria or Abakumov, were to blame. As for the Soviet state, it was declared not the principal tool, but the main victim of Stalin's arbitrariness. Nevertheless, the Soviets cannot succeed in being sufficiently consistent in their adherence to a notion of legality which distorts its own original meaning and undermines its essential characteristics. Perhaps without noticing it, they sometimes raise the question of legality in its genuine content, acknowledging, if not *expressis verbis*, then implicitly, the urgent necessity to remove arbitrariness from the legal order and thus to strengthen the order of legality. The 1975 decree of the CPSU Central Committee and the USSR Council of Ministers[28] provided for various measures of further improvement of economic legislation, pointing out that the previous state of the same legislation "hampers its application, does not correspond to the task of the future strengthening of socialist legality and, in the final analysis, affects negatively the raising of efficiency of social production".[29] It does not matter, whether the discussed realm of human activity really belongs to the weakest spheres of Soviet legality or not. What is most significant is the unequivocal acknowledgement that negligence has been admitted, not by citizens, but by the state in ensuring the legality of economic activity in the USSR, because no one other than the state should establish – yet has not introduced – the appropriate legal order in this decisive sphere of the country's well-being. Similar arguments can be found in the 1976 decree of the CPSU Central Committee, the Presidium of the USSR Supreme Soviet and the Council of Ministers of the USSR about the Collection of Laws of the USSR.[30] As the decree states, "fulfillment of this task will help the further strengthening of legality, of public discipline and of the legal order".[31] The task outlined may be imposed and must be fulfilled not by citizens, but by the state. However, because the Collection of Laws of the USSR is not restricted to specific spheres of the country's life and encompasses it in all possible aspects, absence of the required legality due to a lack of the work mentioned, wherever it is felt and whoever becomes its victim, must be imputed to the state as a defect of the existing legal order and not as a result of violations of existing law. This approach to the notion of legality, being the only correct and entirely dependable one, proves with absolute certainty the erroneousness of the slogan about the further strengthening of socialist legality as it is often expressed in Soviet law. Either socialist legality is all-embracing, in which case it cannot be strengthened; or it leaves room for arbitrariness, in which case it must not be strengthened but extended to those spheres deprived of an appropriate legal order.

The second circumstance stems from the assessment of law as a self-sufficient value. Generally speaking, this attitude is foreign to Marxism, including law as part of the "superstructure" of society, allegedly determined by the dominant "economic structure".[32] As soon, however, as the question of legality arises, the strictest observance of any legal rule becomes *conditio sine qua non* and is indisputable proof of its firmness and dependability. In Ancient Rome a similar demand was expressed simply as an unalterable imperative. Roman jurisprudence did not deny that laws could be unjust and that sometimes *summum ius est summa iniuria*. Nevertheless, they had to be observed: *dura lex, sed lex*. In the USSR other arguments affect the matter. Because it is Soviet, any law shall always be *summum ius* and can never lead to *summa iniuria*. By its very nature Soviet legislation does not know any *dura lex*. Only *iusta lex* is compatible with this legislation, which must therefore be observed not only because it is *lex*, but also because it is *iusta*. If Soviet legislation is amended, this happens not because of any defects found in some particular legal rules but for the sake of replacing the obsolete with the new or the good with the better. Such a train of thought met with difficulties only in the time of the annihilation of legal rules and state institutions, which had been created by and used for Stalin's tyranny.

However, even under those circumstances official propaganda and official juris-prudence tried not to betray the official conception of socialist legality. On the one hand, legal rules subordinated to arbitrariness were declared foreign to socialist legality, which therefore did not lose its genuine nature notwithstanding any mistakes committed. On the other hand, as one leading Soviet scholar in the realm of criminal procedure affirmed during oral discussions late in the 1950s, a summary procedure in political cases or the *Osoboe Soveshchanie* as an agency of extra-judicial repression were, certainly, bad things, but, having been provided for by law, they were not illegal and thus did not go beyond the limits of legality. As will be shown,[33] the idolizing of legal rules in Soviet theory goes hand in hand, if necessary, with a complete disregard for them in Soviet practice. At the same time the executor of laws has no right to discuss their legality. This is one of the most inviolable prerequisites of dictatorial rule and unreserved obedience, and therefore the universally adopted definition of legality in Soviet doctrine reduces it to the strictest observance of the law in force. Meanwhile, law itself admits its assessment by means of legality and this shall not be precluded because Soviet lawyers do not have opportunities to treat their law in a critical way. Law ought to be created for the sake of man, and anything which contradicts human nature as an indissoluble unity of psycho-physical, intellectual, and social aspects, cannot be legal, whether the laws provide so or not. In 1938, when the Soviet government together with the Central Committee of the Soviet Communist Party adopted a secret decree that permitted the torture of people accused of hostile anti-Soviet activity, they acted against the psycho-physical nature of man. In our time, the same features typify Soviet punitive psychiatry, which could not have attained its present scale without secretly adopted governmental regulations. The introduction of secret regulations concerning censorship in the USSR impinged upon the intellectual nature of man, restricting his freedom of self-expression and his opportunity for self-development. In our time, the same features typify Soviet jamming of western broadcasts, which is applied on the basis of orders, but regulated by rules. The prohibition against founding any associations, except those enumerated by Soviet laws, contradicted the social nature of man. In our time, the same features typify Soviet rules concerning punitive deprivation of a telephone, or of other means of social contact, without which modern communication becomes almost impossible or at least extremely difficult.[34]

Thus, the proclaiming of legality together with the demand that the laws must be observed has not always meant real legality. Everything depends on the quality of the laws themselves, on the degree of conformity between their rules and human demands. At the same time, legality as proclaimed by law must be checked against legality as it exists in practice.

Proclaimed Legality in Soviet Practice

Practice in the realm of legality encompasses all aspects of the application of law and should not be reduced to judicial practice alone. For the USSR this is especially important because judicial review of administrative acts is not, in principle, known to the Soviet system. Therefore, in order to form a correct idea of the actual state of

Soviet legality one should pay as much attention to administrative, as to judicial practice. However, owing to the public nature of judicial examination, it is easier to study judicial practice, and since the most severe sanctions of law, criminal punishments, may be applied exclusively by the court,[35] judicial practice serves to some extent as the main barometer of legality in the USSR. In this regard one peculiarity of the so-called guiding explanations, adopted by the Plenum of the USSR Supreme Court and binding to the courts,[36] is noteworthy.

One of its explanations begins with a statement which attracts "the attention of the courts to their duty of ensuring a steadfast and correct application of the laws on responsibility for the issuing of poor quality, non-standard or incomplete products".[37] Why do only these laws need steadfast and correct application? Are other laws not subject to the same requirement? Of course they are! Whatever type of crime is discussed in the explanatory edicts of the Plenum, the formula cited appears *mutatis mutandis* without fail. The courts are obliged to hear cases connected with the stealing of socialist ownership "on the basis of the strict and steadfast observance of the law";[38] they must not forget their duty to "observe strictly the demands of the laws concerning rape without aggravating circumstances";[39] they should distinguish complicity and other forms of involvement in the commission of crimes "in conformity with the law",[40] and so on, and so forth. Then, maybe, such instructions are meaningful in the realm of criminal law, on account of its punitive character, and not in other legal areas, as, for example, civil law, which is not concerned with punishment at all? Even a brief survey of the Plenum's edicts related to civil cases is sufficient to rebut this assumption. "In hearing cases about the right of personal ownership on buildings, the courts should follow strictly the civil legislation of the USSR and union republics."[41] "In hearing cases about the carriage of goods and luggage . . ., the courts should observe articles 72-77 of the Fundamentals of Civil Legislation of the USSR and Union Republics."[42] "In hearing cases connected with discoveries, inventions and rationalization proposals, the courts should follow the Fundamentals of Civil Legislation of the USSR and Union Republics, and the civil codes of union republics."[43] Similar quotations could be produced from any Plenum edict in civil cases. The question arises naturally enough, why it is necessary to be reminded of such self-evident matters. One would think that laws are to be observed without any special mention, simply because they are laws and especially in a country as the USSR, where socialist legality means nothing other than observance of the laws. Meanwhile, the USSR Supreme Court unceasingly repeats its call to obey laws strictly, addressing its plea to all other links of the Soviet judicial system. Does this not indicate that the actual observance of Soviet laws only remotely resembles legality in the Soviet understanding, and that violations of legal rules by judicial agencies are incomparably more significant than one would assume, if one accepted official boasting at its face value?

In providing for the issuance of guiding explanations by the Plenum, the Statute on the Supreme Court of the USSR connects this function with positions taken by courts in individual cases, which indicate an erroneous understanding or wrong application of a certain rule or a certain law.[44] Hence, when the Plenum in its edicts requires lower courts to observe the law or to follow the rule, which applies to the kind of criminal or civil case under consideration, it is implied that the previous practice – known to the USSR Supreme Court on the basis of numerous appeals and its own special analysis – has revealed violations of a certain cluster of legal provisions not in an incidental way, but as a strong tendency or a dangerous regularity. Individual mistakes would not lead to the adoption of an explanatory edict, because they could be corrected by the Plenum by way of abrogation or modification of the erroneous decisions made by any other judicial agency. For example, according to Soviet civil law, the sale and purchase of individual houses needs to be registered by a notary, but if an individual contract does not violate other legal demands and has already been performed by the partners, the court may declare it valid despite non-observance of the requirement of notarial registration. In this way the court of Odessa decided a dispute, having referred to article 47 of the Ukrainian Civil Code. However, the Plenum of the USSR Supreme Court overturned the Odessa decision as violating the rule mentioned, because in order to declare valid a contract with formal defects it would be necessary that the contract had at least been concluded, while in the case discussed the previous owner had received money from the plaintiff, but the latter could not prove that money had been paid to buy a house and that the contract of purchase and sale had taken place at all.[45] Sometimes illegal decisions of lower judicial agencies result not from misunderstanding or misuse of legal rules, but from secret instructions received by judges from high-ranking representatives of the Soviet bureaucracy. Then the Plenum does not respond to the appeals received or simply upholds the decision, using contrived arguments and prohibiting publication of the appropriate materials in the bulletin of the USSR Supreme Court. For example, after the death of a famous doctor and academician in the late 1960s, a dispute about his estate arose between the widow and his daughter from a previous marriage. According to all legal considerations, the daughter should have won the case, but the Soviet leadership thought it better to provide the widow with the necessary resources, and therefore the case was decided in favor of the latter and to the detriment of the former, and no judicial agencies, including the highest ones, recognized her complaints which were well-based in law. When a Soviet professor of civil law expressed his indignation to one of the ruling officials of the Soviet judicial system, responsible for judicial activity in the realm of civil law, he was told that, although the decision of the court contradicted Soviet law, it was nevertheless the only just one under the circumstances, and any other solution would have been irrational in practical terms. Thus, rationality can restrict legality, and observance of law is not binding when its violation seems reasonable. The same attitude can be observed in two other cases heard by the Plenum of the USSR Supreme Court.

Some legal rules in the USSR have been promulgated exclusively for the sake of propaganda, without any serious belief that they could ever be applied in practice. An example is article 71 of the Criminal Code, which states that "war propaganda, in whatever form it is conducted, shall be punished by deprivation of freedom for a term of three to eight years, with or without additional exile for a term of two to five years". The introduction of this rule in Soviet criminal codes by special edicts[46] was to demonstrate the USSR's strong devotion to the cause of peace, when all measures, including criminal punishment, seemed useful, if they could prevent the unleashing of a new war. Moreover, the cause of peace is so dear to the Soviet Union that its criminal law provides more severe punishment for war propaganda than even for anti-Soviet propaganda which – when not aggravated by circumstance of time or by certain personal features of the offender – may be punished by deprivation of freedom for a term not of three to eight years, but of six months to seven years.[47] However, despite the fact that nearly a quarter of century has passed since the introduction of criminal responsibility for war propaganda, not one case has ever been heard by a Soviet court. Meanwhile, during this period events much more serious than simply war propaganda occurred. The invasion of Czechoslovakia was a military campaign, not merely verbal propaganda. As for Afghanistan, the war, initiated late in 1979, shows no signs of an end. Nevertheless, no one speaks about the personal responsibility of those whose decisions have led to these cruel events. Why not? Because there is no war but only friendly help by military forces? Or, maybe, because there are different kinds of wars, just and unjust, as Marxism affirms, and Soviet military suppression of the Afghans is just, while national resistance of the Afghan people is unjust? Or, perhaps, because even more convincing arguments lead to the conclusion that everything is entirely justified by socialist legality? Soviet criminal law provides for the crime of propagandizing war, not unleashing it. Soviet leaders, thank God, do not engage in such propaganda. Nobody does in the USSR. Therefore, the respective rule of criminal law proved to be abortive; it cannot be violated because it is simply not applied. Therefore the Plenum feels no need to issue an explanatory edict on the crime of war propaganda or to remind all other judicial agencies of their duty to strictly observe the law in force in this particular area. Where laws are not applied there is no danger of their violation.

Other legal rules serve as a means of efficacious protection of the most important interests of the Soviet rulers and the most significant ingredients of the Soviet system. Such rules certainly encompass (except for the provision about war propaganda) all other provisions of the chapter of the Criminal Code entitled "Especially dangerous crimes against the state": treason, espionage, terrorist acts, sabotage, wrecking, anti-Soviet agitation and propaganda, organizational activity directed towards the commission of especially dangerous crimes against the state and participation in anti-Soviet organizations, and especially dangerous crimes against the state committed against another working people's state.[48] For various reasons, the enumerated norms do in fact demand an official interpretation. Some of them are ambiguous and lack the precision required for a correct application. For example, nobody can explain with confidence where simple criticism of shortcomings of Soviet reality, as this is encouraged by Soviet law,[49] ends and anti-Soviet agitation and propaganda, prosecuted by Soviet law,[50] begins. Sometimes, distinctions between different crimes, provided for by various articles of the same part of the Criminal Code, are not obvious and can go unnoticed in the absence of special instructions, although an error of classification may lead to a groundless punishment. For example, sabotage and wrecking[51] are similar in many aspects, and their confusion in practice is not impossible, but the former may entail capital punishment, while in the latter case punishment must not exceed deprivation of freedom for a term of fifteen years. Certain types of "especially dangerous crimes against the state" appear outwardly in the same shape as certain other crimes that do not present a "special danger". For example, wrecking[52] and the abuse of official position[53] can be committed by identical actions, and only the subjective attitude of the criminal distinguishes the one from the other. Wrecking requires an intention to subvert the Soviet economy while the abuse of an official position focuses on the objective of satisfying mercenary or other personal interests. How, however, can one reveal this distinction? Should the actual intention be brought to light, or is the character of the actions committed sufficiently by itself for a judicial conclusion? The Soviet court practice in these types of crimes shows utilization of both approaches, and not infrequently actions, which could hardly be considered as even official abuse, have been declared counter-revolutionary wrecking. Intentional or erroneous substitution of one crime by another in the cases considered does not only result in groundless punishment, as when wrecking is confused with sabotage; it also turns ordinary criminals into state criminals. They serve their sentences in prisons or in labor camps with a special regime;[54] amnesty is not applied to them; they cannot hope to be sentenced conditionally[55] or receive an early conditional release from punishment.[56]

Thus, there would seem to be an urgent need for the Plenum of the USSR Supreme Court to issue a guiding explanation concerning judicial practice in cases of "especially dangerous crimes against the state" on account of the frequency of this type of crime and the extremely complicated character of the legislation. However, such an explanation has not appeared up till now, and judicial agencies are neither instructed by the Plenum on how to interpret the appropriate rules, nor are they warned by it about their duty to strictly observe the laws in cases of the greatest importance for the Soviet regime. But there is no reason to be astonished since the solution is quite simple. Political cases, covered by the title "especially dangerous crimes against the state", are heard by the court, but judicial sentences are predetermined by "ruling" bodies. Therefore, the court has no need to understand the corresponding rules since it applies them automatically, and "ruling" bodies should be entirely free in their discretion to rely upon sufficiently obscure regulations without encountering at least formal obstacles in the shape of guiding explanations of the Plenum. As for an appeal to observe the law, it would be too blasphemous under the circumstances to consider it.

Beyond the limits outlined, the preoccupation of the USSR Supreme Court with the strict observance of legal rules by judicial agencies seems quite understandable. When the law does not play a purely propagandistic role or has not become an impediment to the Soviet regime, it must be put into practice for the sake of this very regime. Therefore, appeals to legality, endlessly repeated, have an obvious goal. They serve to strengthen, not to weaken, the existing dictatorship, protecting the latter from legally undesirable and politically dangerous phenomena. It is also clear why judicial practice continues to be replete within violations of laws, despite a great deal of talk about legality. Among the numerous causes of this situation two circumstances attract special attention.

Soviet laws, with the exception of those intended for the general public, are very complicated even to professional understanding, to say nothing of their perception by the man in the street. On the one hand, this is the result of an aspiration to foresee everything in a centralized way and thus to prevent the slightest independence in the realm of the application of law – if such independence is not necessary to allow arbitrariness a free hand. Therefore, in the process of law-making casuistic rules are preferable to abstract ones. For example, the Civil Code includes only one rule concerning the buyer's rights in the event he purchases an item of defective quality.[57] This rule is abstract, and, enumerating the buyer's rights, it refers also to the replacement of the item. However, the 1974 Model Rules for replacement of goods bought at retail trade enterprises[58] consist of 24 articles and establish an order, which demands special training to be correctly applied. It is no wonder that customers do not know these rules and, as a result, can very easily be deceived by sellers. Contracts made in the realm of retail trade seldom become a subject of judicial hearings, but if legal disputes occur, judges, educated in the traditions of the legal system of civil law, have always had difficulties when confronted with casuistic rules, and, owing to this, they cannot avoid making mistakes even despite the greatest care. On the other hand, the complexity of Soviet laws is also due to a system of legal regulations, which, in the case of rights given to citizens, ensures the complete invulnerability of state interests. Therefore general rules are usually accompanied by exceptions; exceptions, in their turn, are subject to sub-exceptions, and, under certain conditions, sub-exceptions annihilate exceptions and restore general rules, etc. For example, according to the general rule, a person who has caused harm is not liable in the absence of fault.[59] An exception to the general rule is that organizations and citizens whose activity is connected with an increased danger for the surrounding persons (transport organizations, industrial enterprises, construction sites, owners of automobiles, etc.) are liable for the harm caused by this activity despite absence of fault.[60] Since, however, the exception cited places the state in an unfavorable position in cases of occupational injuries, a sub-exception appears as well. Victims of occupational injuries must be content with pensions, although the pecuniary loss cannot be entirely compensated in such a way, and only if the harm has been caused through the fault of the state enterprises and other institutions whose activity presents an increased danger will they be liable toward their workers or officials. In other words, the sub-exception annihilates the exception and subordinates the state entities to the general rule. At the same time, the sub-exception is subject to its own exception which provides even more favorable conditions for the state, although not in the way of a return to the general rule, but by means of establishing a special order. The professional disease, pneumoconiosis – widespread among miners – serves as a ground for an increase in pensions according to special rules. Simultaneously with the issuance of these rules, the Soviet legislature decided that victims of pneumoconiosis, who receive increased pensions, may not sue against the state enterprises – although their lost salary remains in part uncompensated – even if the disease has resulted from bad conditions at work or through other fault of the employer.[61] In meeting the need to apply first the general rule and then the exception to it, sometimes the sub-exception and sometimes the exception to the sub-exception, everyone can be confused, and, as judicial practice proves, the judges also are not immune to such a danger.

Not only are Soviet laws often very complicated, they are also frequently impossible to ømplement, a matter which is well-known to those who have to implement them, as well as to the legislator. On the one hand, the Soviet rulers, unable to overcome numerous economic and other predicaments, nevertheless resort to taking legislative measures, which have a calming or encouraging effect – as if legal commands could improve something by themselves, without the necessary economic or other substantive prerequisites. There are dozens of edicts concerning the improvement of the supply of goods in the country, but every day the Soviet population experiences an increasing deficiency of the most essential products, to say nothing of other consumer goods. And, taking into account the deplorable state of agriculture and the insufficient productivity of industry, it cannot be otherwise. The Soviet leadership is astonishingly generous in proclaiming decrees about the improvement of everyday repair services, urban transport, public utilities, etc., but here the real situation is even worse than in the sphere of the supply of goods. And how can one hope that things will really take a favorable turn, if service enterprises do not receive at least a quite modest share of the industrial articles destined for citizens' use. Moreover, matters are made even worse, because production itself has not kept pace with the increase in the size of the population. That part of the governing activity which is concerned with the consideration of citizens' applications and appeals – and which is of great importance to the population despite its non-economic character – has also been exposed to intensive legislative interference in the USSR. "Complaints of working people" – to use the semi-official terminology – have been the subject of general rules issued by the Presidium of the USSR Supreme Soviet in 1968,[62] and also of numerous other regulations, and most of them strive to achieve two things: that complaints shall be considered without delay by officials other than those who are complained against. However, neither of these objectives have been realized. And indeed what grounds are there to assume that the outcome of this affair would be different? In the absence of judicial review of administrative acts, there is no incentive to bring about a decrease of violations of citizens' rights by the illegal conduct of officials and in fact such violations are increasing in number before one's eyes. As a result, the number of complaints is also continuously growing, and the central agencies cannot physically manage to respond to them within a comparatively short period of time. Besides, in order to come to a just and well-grounded solution a thorough investigation of the case at the place where it occurred is required. However, such a task widely exceeds the possibilities of higher-ranking officials, and therefore they usually either refuse complaints received out of hand or impose a final solution upon those against whom citizens have complained. Thus, edicts about "working people's complaints" follow one after another, but the disappointing reality remains unchanged.

The illustrations stated either deal with the normal development of social phenomena instigated by law, as in the case of rules concerning the improvement of the food supply, or, being connected with abnormal events of public life, belong to the sphere of extra-judicial activity, as in the case of rules concerning the consideration of "working people's complaints". On the other hand, the non-enforceability of Soviet laws also affects punitive agencies, including the judicial system. Thus, the eagerness of the Soviet government to protect so-called socialist ownership by fair means or foul can be, if not justified, then at least understood. As the basis of the economic monopoly in the grasp of the dominant stratum, this ownership represents the main source of the unlimited power of the political rulers,[63] and, in protecting "socialist" ownership, the rulers are preoccupied in the last analysis with strengthening their power. However, leaving aside inveterate criminals who would continue their criminal activity under any economic conditions, one should not disregard the unbearable situation prevalent in the country. If the average monthly salary does not exceed the price of a suit,[64] people are doomed either to a miserable existence or to a permanent search for additional income, whether legal or illegal. As a result, what the criminal law regards as the stealing of socialist property (and this notion encompasses all kinds of illegal appropriation, beginning with theft (*krazha*) and ending with abuse of an official position)[65] has attained mass proportions. For many years it has served as the inevitable, although illegal, corrective of a legal, although unjust, economic distribution. Because of this, stealing of socialist property does not provoke – in contrast to stealing of individual property – ethical reproaches beyond the official morality. On the contrary, one part of the population looks upon the failed dodgers with benevolent sympathy, while the other part, which itself has a finger in the pie, looks at them only with a stronger fear for its own fate. The legislature itself has been compelled to mitigate attacks against "plunderers of the property of the whole people", having been discouraged by their overwhelmingly "growing ranks". In order to avoid mass reprisals in the form of cruel punishments, the notion of petty stealing of socialist property has been included in the Criminal Code.[66] This notion also embraces all possible forms of theft, such as appropriation, embezzlement, abuse of official position, etc. However, the punishment, provided for by the same rule, is extremely mild according to Soviet standards and must not exceed six months of deprivation of freedom, or one year of correctional tasks, or a 100 ruble fine. But the most important peculiarity of this legal innovation consists in the provision that criminal prosecution shall take place, if the crime is committed "by a person against whom, taking into account the circumstances of the case and his personality, measures of social or administrative pressure cannot be applied".[67] Hence, comprehensive criminal prosecution of stealing of socialist property has become physically impossible, and it is therefore not the law, but the punitive agencies who shall discretionally decide who deserves to be deprived of freedom, who ought to be punished administratively, and who can get off cheaply with purely "social" rebukes. Unfortunately for the Soviet regime, a similar uncertainty surrounds the question of when, according to the law, stealing of socialist property should be criminally prosecuted without fail. One fact only will suffice to prove our assertion. It would be a waste of time and involve special effort to enumerate all of the Plenum's guiding explanations of legal rules concerning stealing of socialist property, but five of them may be cited on account of their interdependence and for their illustrative effect. On 24 June 1968, the Plenum adopted the edict "On Improving the Activity of the Courts in the Fight Against Stealing of State and Social Property".[68] Less than one year later, on 11 April 1969, the Plenum's edict appeared with the title "On the Progress in Implementing the Edict of the Plenum of the USSR Supreme Court of 24 June 1968".[69] On 11 July 1972, the same Plenum issued the edict "On Judicial Practice in Cases of Stealing of State and Social Property".[70] A little more than a year later, on 8 October 1973, the Plenum promulgated an edict headed "On the Progress in Implementing the Edict of the Plenum of the USSR Supreme Court of 11 July 1972".[71] Meanwhile, all these direct and follow-up edicts appeared to be insufficient, and on 28 November 1975, the Plenum resorted to the edict "On Strengthening the Role of the Courts in the Fight Against Stealing of the Socialist Property, and in Discovering and Removing the Causes and Conditions Engendering These Crimes".[72] The problem, presented so strangely, is completely obvious to those who know the real situation from inside and through practice. The number of people involved in mercenary crimes damaging to the state has attained such a level that the inevitability of punishment as the main ingredient of legality (when it is reduced to inviolability of law) would demand criminal repressions of about the same scope as during the political repressions of Stalin's purges. As a matter of course, the contemporary leaders cannot afford so risky a solution. They prefer to manoeuvre between strengthening and weakening criminal repressions with the transition from one period to another, applying selective prosecution of property crimes, instead of reprisals directed against all offenders. Therefore, the silence of the Plenum suddenly gives way to an abundance of directives with endless contradictions between general and exceptional instructions, followed by abrogation by oral orders in specific cases of that which has been proclaimed as universally binding by written explanations. Under the circumstances the judges feel perplexed, even if they would be accustomed to functioning like robots. If one adds to the inevitable mistakes the judicial abuses, provoked simply by such "favorable" conditions, to say nothing of the numerous other temptations, then one can imagine the genuine state of proclaimed legality in this realm of judicial practice.

The situation is no better with regard to other types of crime engendered by the peculiarities of the Soviet system. For example, criminal law contains a provision about the abuse of authority or of an official position.[73] Such an abuse can be committed not only for mercenary ends but also in order to further other personal interests. However, the interests are assessed as being personal, even where the illegal methods in question were used to satisfy the requirements of the official's enterprise or other state institution. Thus, the temporary borrowing of raw materials from a neighboring enterprise in order to prevent stoppage of one's own enterprise because of a delay in supply, or an exchange of surplus materials of one kind for necessary materials of another kind by two economic associations, constitute the crime of official abuse, as formulated by the criminal law and interpreted by judicial practice, since these operations are legally forbidden. Meanwhile, it will be quite clear that, if Soviet enterprises still continue to function at a tolerable level of productivity in conditions of meticulous regulation of economic activity, this happens to a great extent as a result of non-observance of impracticable rules by economic management. And because exhaustive regulations belong to the universal tendencies of the Soviet system of administration, they meet similar resistance in any area of the administered activity. This is why crimes such as the abuse of an official position are no less common than the stealing of socialist property, and, if all offenders involved were prosecuted, Soviet prisons and labor camps would be overcrowded with convicted officials. Thus, it has also become necessary in this case to apply, first of all, administrative sanctions and to punish violations of criminal law only under extraordinary circumstances. It may be *à propos* in connection with officials' abuses to make some remarks about bribery, which is the most shocking official crime.[74] Of course, no one can affirm that bribery is a specifically Soviet phenomenon. The truth, however, is that it has not attained such enormous proportions anywhere else. Hence, the extent to which bribery has spread over the country, if not its origin, is due to the peculiarities of the Soviet system. Among them the following ought to be especially accentuated: *administrative centralization* (for example, the planned distribution of most products by the USSR planning or supply committees); *overwhelming bureaucratism* (for example, preparation of distribution plans involves so many agencies that the plan for the current year comes into force on 1 January but it actually appears not earlier than in February or in March); *red tape* (for example, the demands for planned supply, elaborated by each enterprise yearly at fixed moments and serving as one of the grounds for planned distribution, occupy an entire volume of required documents); *broad discretion* (for example, each higher agency may decrease demands for supply, produced by enterprises, without any explanation); *procedural nihilism* (for example, in spite of its application for many decades, economic planning in the USSR is not subordinated to a widely-known strict procedure). To overcome all these difficulties and to attain the desired results, even managers of state enterprises not infrequently resort to bribery, finding both appropriate ways and the necessary resources. Then, what can one expect from citizens, trying to realize their rights to pensions or dwellings, attempting to be registered for residence temporarily or permanently, asking for accommodation in kindergartens for their children, etc.? Soviet bureaucratism dominates everywhere, and only its specific features are different if one moves from one kind of governmental activity to another. Owing to this, it will not be the slightest exaggeration to affirm that not one Soviet citizen can manage to avoid bribery completely during his lifetime. As a way of dealing with officialdom, it has become so common in the USSR that most people, after receiving permission to emigrate, consider it impolite not to show their "gratitude" to the inspector of OVIR, with whom they have dealt and who has mocked them with unconcealed pleasure. One cannot deny that the Soviet regime has tried to fight against this social disease, introducing severe penalties for bribery right up to capital punishment.[75] The Plenum of the USSR Supreme Court adopted a special edict on the same occasion,[76] stating that "bribery, being a dangerous crime, calls for a consistent and resolute fight against it".[77] However, the number of such crimes exceeds the real capacity to fight against it on such a scale, and the nature of the Soviet system, which leads to the flourishing of bribery, is so much stronger than legislative innovations, that also in this case the need to manoeuvre between punishing and condoning bribery is as inevitable as in the case of stealing of socialist property.[78]

The two factors described leave little over from the proclaimed legality in Soviet practice, and the picture will become even more unattractive, if one takes into account numerous other factors pushing this practice further in the same direction: the hierarchical position of offenders, considerations of prestige, "social planning" of the desirable decrease of violations of law, and "eyewash" (*ochkovtiratel'stvo*) conditioned by the wish to report favorably about the fulfillment of planning tasks, etc. For example, when in 1982, soon after his coming to power, Andropov ousted Shchelokov, the USSR Minister of Internal Affairs, western media explained this measure as a reflection of the fight against Brezhnev's closest allies. Such a version hardly deserved any credit, because even in his position as the chief of the KGB Andropov could have had no reason to fear Shchelokov's competition and, as the leader of the CPSU after Brezhnev's death, he would not suspect any trouble at all from an official of such an incomparably lower level. In addition, Brezhnev's closest allies, if they really needed to be fought, had stronger representatives than Shchelokov, but they all preserved their positions under the new leader. Those western sources of information which referred to bribery and other abuses of the former minister probably got closer to the truth. Otherwise it would be difficult to explain his all too prompt and resolute ouster. It is also quite natural that the crimes discovered, having led to deprivation of office, were left without criminal punishment. The position of the USSR Minister of Internal Affairs is too high under Soviet conditions to allow, in connection with it, a judicial hearing. However, while in the case mentioned the discussion cannot go beyond different conjectures, in the case of a Soviet writer Sofronov, everything is known with the necessary exactitude. In the mid 1970s his employees literally caught him red-handed criminally appropriating hundreds of thousands of rubles, which belonged to the magazine *Ogonek*, whose editor-in-chief he was. With such irrefutable evidence no one had any doubt that he was finished. But his faithful service to the regime, his unrestricted devotion to the fight against any hint of genuine progress in Soviet literature could not remain without reward. Judicial denunciation of Sofronov's crimes, bearing in mind his high position as an official writer, would also cause harm to Soviet prestige. Therefore, the Party's chief of ideology, Suslov, considered it reasonable to intervene, and the entire case took another course. Sofronov not only avoided criminal responsibility, but preserved his ruling office at the magazine, and the whole story was ascribed to a plot of Zionists who had entrenched themselves in *Ogonek*. As a result, not the criminal but his denouncers were prosecuted. As for eyewash in the fight against violations of laws, it acquires various, sometimes monstrous, forms. In 1967, a professor of law published a book under the title *Sovetskoe zhilishchnoe pravo* (Soviet Housing Law). Several years later the same book appeared under the title *Sovetskoe zhilishchnoe zakonodatel'stvo* (Soviet Housing Legislation). The reasons for these modifications were clear enough to everyone who knew about the Soviet law of copyright, and first of all to the author himself as a professor of civil law, which in the USSR includes the law of copyright. Second editions are paid within the limits of 60% of author's fees for the first edition,[79] but with title modified the second edition could be presented as a new book, which secured certain illegal property advantages to the author. According to the Criminal Code this would simply constitute the crime of stealing of state property. However, the management of the University decided to avoid a scandal which would put the University's reputation in a bad light, and, after the author returned the illegal part of his income, the incident was considered closed. Another case is even more outrageous. One of the victims of Stalin's purges, a famous Soviet actress, managed to survive until the period of post-Stalin rehabilitation. She returned to Moscow and resumed her artistic activity. Once she happened upon her

KGB investigator, and all the tortures applied by him were revived in her memory. His name was known to her, and thus she had no difficulty in finding and denouncing him. Nevertheless, the actress failed in her persistent aspirations for legal revenge: all punitive agencies – including the main pillar of the law, the USSR Procurator General – refused to initiate a criminal case against an outrageous villain, without any explanation. Now this person is a professor of criminal law, and, paradoxical as it may seem, he is primarily engaged in writing books about the arbitrariness of capitalist criminal law and judicial practice. To complete the picture of this peculiar situation one should also know, beyond a number of separate incidents, some of the general methods that have become accepted by punitive agencies: failure to register crimes until it has been decided that it would be expedient to initiate a criminal case; shielding of officials denounced for having applied illegal methods of preliminary investigation and judicial hearing; accusations of anti-Soviet propaganda or at least of circulation of fabrications defaming the Soviet state, if one reveals a certain zeal in denouncing arbitrariness of punitive agencies, etc. And if official legality, proclaimed by law, has been transformed into official arbitrariness, realized in practice – when the law violated may or may not lead to legal sanctions, depending on the unlimited discretion of the ruling bureaucracy – it is no wonder that numerous other opportunities to remain unpunished become practicable, although they sometimes go far beyond what has been secretly permitted or tacitly approved. Important acquaintances, dependable relations, services rendered and numerous other things are capable of replacing a strict law by a friendly tap on the shoulder.

One evening in Leningrad in 1978 a pretty young woman came across a young man who, threatening her with force, pushed her into the elevator of a nearby house, and ordered her to take off all her clothes. When she realized what was happening, she broke the electric lamp to use its glass as a means of self-protection and called for help. The inhabitants of the building came running immediately, detained the criminal and took him to the police. The inquiry started without delay, but was not difficult because it was obviously a case of attempted rape, and neither the investigators doubted it nor did the criminal deny it. However, the father of the criminal was the chairman of the university criminal law department, and, under Soviet conditions, this office entails numerous advantages, including those that stem from professional connections with punitive agencies. As a result, some weeks passed, and the case was terminated by a reference to the mental condition of the accused. It was remarkable, that this condition was explained, not as a mental disease, but as the result of a sudden loss of control at the very moment when the incriminating actions were committed. Such an explanation helped to kill two birds with one stone: the criminal prosecution was terminated because of absence of criminal responsibility and compulsory means of a medical character involving commitment to a special psychiatric hospital were not applicable because the offender's mental condition did not result from a psychiatric disease. Thus, instead of being sent to prison, the rapist returned to his job as a mathematician at one of the military schools. In the USSR only politically unreliable people cannot be trusted with the education of youth. But such strictness does not apply to rapists.

In the winter of 1977 Leningrad became the scene of a more serious incident. Late in the evening a taxi stopped by a building in one of the city's central streets. A young man, leaving the taxi, promised the driver to return with money in a few minutes, but the driver did not trust him and demanded his coat as a guarantee. The drunken passenger, infuriated by this demand, left his coat, ran into his apartment, grabbed a rifle (indeed, despite the legal prohibitions, there was a rifle in an apartment in the very center of Leningrad), returned quickly, killed the driver on the spot, then ran back into his room and locked the door before two policemen, who had appeared at once, could catch him. Then negotiations began between the murderer and his mother, separated by a closed door. The former threatened suicide; the latter pushed him to take this action. The mother's main argument: now your life and my future have been spoiled for ever. The mother's only advice: the best way out for you is to commit suicide. After more than two hours of negotiations, the son followed his mother's advice. The driver and his murderer were buried on the same day. And what about the mother? Was she punished for the illegal possession of a firearm[80] and for incitement to commit suicide?[81] No, the mother was left in peace. However, in this case, which troubled the whole city, she could hardly rely upon her former position as secretary of the university committee of the CPSU or upon her permanent office as chairman of the university department of civil procedure. Another circumstance played a decisive role. She was a people's assessor in the case of Siniavskii and Daniel,[82] and those who had helped the Soviet regime to deal with these foes deserved to be immune against responsibility for the crimes described. But, speaking generally, are not such legal scholars worthy of socialist legality? To answer this question with reference to certain ordinary professors of Soviet law, it would perhaps be useful to have a look at certain leaders of Soviet jurisprudence. One of them contrived at a time when he was head of the Institute of State and Law of the USSR Academy of Sciences, to acquire two country houses (*dachas*), while Soviet law permits possession of only one building by Soviet citizens. Moreover, he paid cash in full for one *dacha* and a half down payment for the other country house. Then a niece of the seller, a legal scholar, visited the buyer and asked for a job at his Institute. The buyer promptly decided to use such a unique opportunity and promised the niece a good position, if she would steal the receipt from her aunt and bring it to him. The niece told everything to her aunt, the widow of a famous Soviet academician, and the aunt alerted everyone so that the criminal could not avoid responsibility. Alas, all her efforts proved to be in vain: the public status of the criminal official was too prestigious to denounce him for the sake of legality. Of course, he lost his office, becoming an ordinary research fellow of the Institute. The CPSU agencies punished him with a strict reprimand, but there was no question of criminal responsibility. The same person, known for his works about Stalin and legality in Stalin's time and about Lenin and legality in the post-Stalin period, simply disappeared temporarily from the pages of Soviet legal literature. But some years passed, and he appeared again, at first by being officially promoted, then by authoring new publications on the topic of socialist legality, and finally as one of the Soviet representatives at the 1982 International Conference on Human Rights in Rio de Janeiro, a position especially appropriate to his professional qualifications. Thus, it cannot be denied that the Soviet regime does not abandon its faithful servants who come to grief, even when they discredit Soviet legality. In its turn, this legality as a practical phenomenon has nothing in common with official definitions and doctrinal interpretations. The solemn proclamation of the strictest observance of legal rules goes hand in hand with gross violations of their demands. This, certainly, could not happen only as a result of actual legality deviating from proclaimed legality. There is every reason to assume that what appears as proclaimed legality in form is legalized arbitrariness in essence.

2. Legalized Arbitrariness

Considering the persistent calls for legality, endlessly repeated by Soviet laws, one would think it impossible to expect direct appeals to arbitrariness from the same laws. Nevertheless, such appeals exist, if not always directly, then at least indirectly expressed in legislative instructions. They are not, of course, as numerous as the calls for legality, and in the process of their formulation wordy disguise is preferred to straightforward frankness. Therefore, the study of legalized arbitrariness in Soviet practice will be more productive from this point of view than the analysis of legal texts, drafted with a similar goal. However, the appropriate laws must also not be ignored, because, if the instructions mentioned are actually ordered by them, this would serve as a formal ground for actual arbitrariness and would become an important clue for discovering the genuine mechanism of its concealed application.

Legalized Arbitrariness in Soviet Law

Two general rules occupy a decisive position in the legalization of arbitrariness in the USSR.

One of them has been established by the Soviet Constitution. In contrast to article 5, which requires the Soviet state and all its agencies to "operate on the basis of socialist legality", article 6, proclaiming the CPSU to be "the guiding and directing force of Soviet society", does not mention socialist legality and is restricted only by the clause that "all party organizations shall operate within the framework of the USSR Constitution". However, the Constitution does not specify concrete legal regulations, and the Party transcends these regulations, since only the Constitution is binding for party organizations. At the same time, as "the guiding force" of Soviet society the CPSU may "direct" the Constitution to any change at any moment. Hence, even the duty to function "within the framework of the USSR Constitution" preserves its binding force only until the Party itself considers it necessary to replace one Constitution by another or to amend the existing Constitution. The CPSU also "directs" the development of current legislation, which formally must correspond to the Constitution. In this regard one of the peculiarities of the Soviet Constitution gains great practical importance. The Constitution carefully avoids enunciating those types of rules which are designed to keep current legislation within the limits of legality, while the general principles, formulated therein, being conveniently abstract, not infrequently allow the CPSU to promulgate new statutory rules without introducing constitutional amendments. If it becomes necessary to issue new regulations, which obviously contradict the Constitution, the methods applied depend on the character of the innovations contemplated. Sometimes, they do not reveal in themselves even the slightest sign of potential illegality, as in the case, when, for example, the functions of union republics are broadened at the expense of the Union. In this case the appropriate new law is usually adopted together with the corresponding constitutional amendment. Sometimes a desired innovation is destined to serve as a prerequisite of arbitrariness, as in the case, when the special courts were established.[83] In this case new regulations are adopted and kept secret, while the Constitution continues intact, as if nothing had happened. In such a way the CPSU supports legalized arbitrariness in the realm of law-making.[84]

The second general rule belongs not to legislation in its normal sense, but to Party regulations, which actually stand higher than the legislation itself. In enumerating the duties of Party members, article 2(i) of the Rules of the CPSU orders them to observe "Party and state discipline". One can assume that state discipline includes observance of laws and thus implicitly refers to legality in the Soviet understanding. There is no need to reject such an assumption or disagree with it. Since, within the limits outlined above,[85] the Soviet regime, in issuing legal rules, is interested in their implementation, one should not be surprised that Party members are also bound by these rules, sometimes even more so than other people. However, it has already been shown how and to what extent Soviet interests may lead to non-observance of the laws and to an extra-legal settlement of problems, or to allegedly legal solutions.[86] In such a situation Party discipline enters into conflict with state discipline. The law demands criminal punishment, but criminal prosecution in certain specific cases contradicts the demands of the system, or, in the opposite case, criminal prosecution in a specific case is necessary to the system, but the opportunity for such prosecution does not legally exist, or the law admits sanctions other than those satisfactory to the rulers. Under all these circumstances, Party discipline prevails over state discipline. This means that, if a judge or other official receives a Party order contradicting the law, he must follow the Party order, by directly distorting the law, or by applying a law that does not directly cover the case considered, or without referring to any law at all – when the case is subject to administrative consideration, which, in contrast to a judicial hearing, does not require an obligatory mention of the legal rule as the grounds for a discretional decision.[87] In such a way the CPSU supports legalized arbitrariness in the realm of law-applying.

Along with general rules, which cover the entire legal system, almost every branch of Soviet legislation has its own norms, forcing their way through legality and thus legalizing arbitrariness.

In civil law this role belongs to article 5 of the Civil Code. It states: "Civil rights shall be protected by law, except for instances when they are exercised contrary to the purpose of such rights in a socialist society in the period of the construction of communism". In other words, the article cited: (1) prohibits the exercise of civil rights contrary to their stated purpose in the USSR and (2) threatens not to protect these same rights, if the prohibition is violated. However, both these ingredients are completely unclear. What the prohibition means has never been officially explained, and everything depends on interpretations suggested by the court in solutions of specific cases. As for refusing protection, this formula is so broad that it encompasses any imaginable sanction, beginning with the rejection of the claims of somebody whose right has been violated, and ending with the deprivation of a right exercised contrary to the prohibition in question. For example, in Komaravo, the most beautiful resort village near Leningrad, there is a group of comfortable country houses, belonging to a building cooperative. One of the houses belonged to a Professor of Physics, who stopped using it after his divorce, and left it in the possession of his former family. In the early 1970s a high-ranking official expressed the wish to become a member of the cooperative, whose management was then ordered by the Leningrad CPSU committee to find a way of expelling a member of the cooperative so that enrollment of the official could take place. In realizing this directive, the cooperative management sued the Professor of Physics on the basis of article 5 of the Civil Code. The arguments of the plaintiff were quite absurd: because the defendant did not use the country house himself and had left it to his former family, this meant that he exercised his civil right contrary to its purpose "in a socialist society in the period of construction of communism"[88] and, as a result, he was no longer entitled to legal protection. The court, having agreed with the arguments stated, interpreted the refusal of protection in this case as involving a loss of membership in the cooperative, and the professor's family was evicted from the house, which was later given to the official in question. This decision was based upon obvious arbitrariness, approved, however, by the law.

In criminal law, analogous results can be obtained by means of article 7 of the Criminal Code. It reads: "A socially dangerous act (an action or an omission) provided for by the Special Part of the present Code . . . shall be deemed a crime." On account of this formula, analogy disappeared from Soviet criminal law. Since a socially dangerous act constitutes a crime only if it is directly provided for by the Special Part of the Criminal Code, one may not – as had been possible before the new codification of Soviet criminal law – consider as crimes other socially dangerous acts, not enumerated by the criminal law but similar to those indicated by it. However, having abolished analogy, article 7 does not affect extensive interpretation, which, consequently continues to be legal in criminal law. On the basis of extensive interpretation, it is quite possible to obtain the same results as could be reached in the past by the now abolished analogy. For example, a crime such as the unlawful use of radio-broadcasting is not directly provided for by Soviet criminal law. Nevertheless, the Plenum of the USSR Supreme Court explained in a 1963 edict, that because "responsibility for hooliganism does not depend on the form of its commission",[89] "intentional acts of radio-broadcasting, connected with a clear disregard toward society and used for mischievous purposes, violating public order in a coarse manner or creating a hindrance to broadcasting and official wireless communication"[90] shall be considered as hooliganism. The Plenum also pointed out that "in the case of using radio-broadcasting equipment for transmissions of other criminal character the actions shall be considered . . . as they would have been considered had they been committed without the use of radio-broadcasting equipment".[91] In other words, if a person may be punished for anti-Soviet propaganda or any other crime directly provided for by the criminal law, then the criminal use of radio transmissions does not represent a separate crime. However, in the absence of such circumstances, it shall be regarded as hooliganism owing to an extensive interpretation of the appropriate rule of criminal law. Is there no analogy in Soviet criminal law? Well, then use extensive interpretation. It all results in the same thing.

In administrative law, legalized arbitrariness is the most blatant. This branch of Soviet legislation, if one disregards certain exceptions, consists almost exclusively of so-called sub-statutory (*podzakonnye*) normative acts: governmental edicts, ministerial instructions, etc. Moreover, most administrative regulations are not only unpublished but even secret. Therefore, citizens who have been ordered administratively to do or not to do something cannot check the legality of the orders received. They may, certainly, complain against such orders, but usually this opportunity is not available beforehand, and, in turning down citizens' complaints, the higher agency also does not refer to the law. The routine formula of denial reads: "There are no grounds for revoking the order complained against." As for the grounds to preserve the same order in force, one would vainly search for them in official answers. For example, during the 1980 Olympic Games numerous "unreliable" inhabitants of Moscow were ordered by the police to leave the capital and remain out of sight for a precisely indicated period. It is clear without saying, that the police could not resort to such orders on their own initiative. The necessary instructions were doubtlessly given by a higher or, maybe, by the highest agency. Are these instructions legal or illegal? Not a single legal rule published in the USSR, answers the question either directly or indirectly. The Soviet Constitution, in proclaiming the inviolability of the person, deals only with the order established for his arrest.[92] But the cases discussed have nothing in common with arrest. Criminal law and administrative law preclude responsibility for acts not provided for directly by the corresponding rules. But the cases discussed do not concern responsibility and thus cannot be assessed in light of the principle mentioned. Banishment as a measure of punishment[93] may be applied only by a judicial sentence. But the measures discussed do not represent punishment, and, as a result, they are beyond the limits of criminal law. Despite, however, the fact that not one of the rules mentioned was violated by police orders, at the same time, not one of the known rules legitimized these commands. No uninitiated person can be certain whether the necessary rule had been established secretly or not. People ordered to leave Moscow had no time to complain before obeying the imperative commands. Hardly any of them complained later on, and even if this happened in individual cases, hardly any answers were received. Legalized arbitrariness does not require explanations toward those who become its victims.

In the law of procedure, criminal or civil, the desired arbitrariness is based upon the rule about the evaluation of evidence. The Code of Criminal Procedure formulates this rule in article 71 with the following words: "A court, procurator, investigator, and persons conducting an inquiry shall evaluate evidence in accordance with their inner conviction, based on a thorough, complete, and objective consideration of all the circumstances of the case in their entirety, being governed by law and by socialist legal consciousness."[94] The formula cited helps to find legal solutions in all cases, when the Soviet regime is interested in the correct application of its laws, and the Plenum of the USSR Supreme Court tried to ensure this result with a 1969 edict "On the Judicial Sentence".[95] However, the same formula becomes considerably more helpful, when for the sake of political purposes it is necessary to adopt an unjust decision. It is true that "inner conviction" is to be based on the "objective considerations" of the circumstances and "governed by law". But, apart from law, "socialist legal consciousness", an obviously subjective factor, also plays a determining role, and "inner conviction" is entirely subjective, whatever kinds of objective circumstances have to be taken into account by the court and other punitive agencies. Therefore, a judicial sentence may contradict the real substance of an individual case, but the only thing that permits any discussion is the fact that the "inner conviction" of the court and the "inner conviction" of the defendant may be quite different. Thus, such a divergence may serve as a very weak ground to frustrate the sentence adopted in accordance with a higher directive – by referring to a more correct evaluation of the evidence by the convicted person or by his supporters. Not one criminal case (hooliganism, rape, stealing, etc.) brought against dissidents – in order to deal with them efficiently without making any political charges – was ever based on convincing evidence, and not one sentence imposed on them on the grounds of "inner conviction" was quashed or even mitigated by way of judicial appeal. In the notorious case of Anatolii Shcharanskii, accused of spying for the USA, something unimaginable happened. Because this case was heard behind closed doors, nobody knew what kind of espionage – bearing in mind the actual position of the accused – could have been engaged in. The Soviet media restricted themselves to vague and uncertain information. Moreover, Jimmy Carter, the President of the USA, publicly assured the Soviet leadership that American intelligence services had no relations with Shcharanskii. This all occurred in the late 1970s, when the politics of détente had attained their zenith, and the two superpowers seemed to be in a good mood toward one another. Nevertheless, nothing was taken into account. Shcharanskii was cruelly punished. Western public opinion, headed by the American President, lost the fight. The "inner conviction" of three judges, directed from above, won the game. Whenever western politicians, scholars, artists and even leaders of some Communist Parties raise the problem of Shcharanskii in their contacts with Soviet rulers, they are informed either that this problem is beyond discussion or that Shcharanskii was convicted by the Soviet court in strict conformity with Soviet law and must serve his sentence, exactly to the day. Thus, when political interests demand it, legality may be replaced by arbitrariness with no more difficulty than when, if necessary, arbitrariness cedes to legality.

Along with these principal branches of Soviet legislation, any other of its separate parts includes one or several rules that can be used for similar goals. For example, one of the most important problems of labor law is the question of payment for labor, especially when such payment is based, not on a system of time-rate, but on piece-rate, which operates depending on production norms. As the Labor Code states in article 83, "establishment of a time- or piece-rate system of payment for labor, as well as the approval of the regulations on the rewarding of manual and office workers shall be effected by the administration of an enterprise or organization by agreement with the trade union committee". Hence, production norms may be established or modified in the same order. However, the trade unions occupy a dual position in the USSR. They represent the interests of workers, and in this capacity the trade unions act as partners of collective labor contracts.[96] However, since the CPSU is "a guiding and directing force" of social organizations,[97] this also relates to the trade unions, and consequently, Party orders about production norms must be unconditionally supported by the trade unions, whether the innovations suggested correspond to the workers' interests or not.

In the realm of land law the rules on withdrawal of land use may damage citizens' interests more than any other rules of this branch of law. Meanwhile, according to article 32 of the Land Code, the right to use a plot of land may be terminated, if the citizen resorts to transactions (sale, gift, leasing, etc.) that directly or circuitously violate the right of state ownership of land,[98] or if he admits systematic violations of the rules for land use.[99] And what is most essential in both cases is that the decision on withdrawal of plots of land belongs not to the jurisdiction of the court but to the agency which has granted the plot.[100] The court has the right to hear property disputes, resulting from the fact of withdrawal of plots of land, but not the right to review the legality of administrative acts concerning withdrawal. One can imagine the scale of permissible arbitrariness allowed by this rule, because – if even criminal cases that have to be heard and solved by a court may be artificially framed, when this is necessary for the sake of political or other important goals – administrative cases, not bound to a strict procedure, and settled bureaucratically, depend in fact exclusively on the discretion of Soviet officials.

Moreover, a branch of Soviet legislation such as family law, very remote from politics on the face of it, is often applied to solve political tasks by using the ambiguous content of some of its rules. For example, article 14 of the Family Code states: "Effectuations of a marriage shall occur upon the expiry of a one-month period after the submission of an application to the state agency of civil status registration by those wishing to be married." But what if, despite the expiration of the period indicated, this agency does not register the marriage? Such events occur not infrequently, when a Soviet citizen tries to contract a marriage with a foreigner which the Soviet authorities consider undesirable or even dangerous. The young people may, certainly, complain, but it is easy to shelve their complaints, since the family law does not include any provision about the procedure to be followed in case the appropriate agency violates the rule cited. Article 33 of the Family Code, concerning the dissolution of marriage by a court, provides that "the marriage shall be dissolved, if it is established by the court that the spouses' further life together, and the preservation of the family, have become impossible". It is clear that a regulation of this nature gives the court a free hand in the adoption of positive or negative decisions. In the post-Stalin era, judicial practice in cases of divorce has become very liberal, and forced preservation of a marriage, despite the demand of one of the spouses for its dissolution, is extremely rare. However, when one of the spouses wishes to emigrate, he or she cannot do so without first divorcing the other spouse if the latter objects to the proposed emigration. If the latter also objects to the divorce, the court usually preserves the marriage in order to make emigration impossible. Such is the generally known practice of the courts, and dishonest people use it to blackmail would-be emigrants, demanding a considerable ransom from them in return for a divorce on the ground of mutual consent.

Most of the rules presented have appeared in Soviet legislation as a result of considerations deliberately directed at ensuring "freedom" from the law in cases when such freedom would seem desirable. At the time of the first Soviet codification, in the early 1920s, Lenin insisted on the need to expand "state interference" into "private legal relationships" in the interests of the working people.[101] Article 1 of the 1922 Civil Code, the prototype of article 5 of the present Civil Code, which allows the denial of the protection of rights in cases when their exercise is contrary to their aims in socialist society, was the logical and practical effect of Lenin's instructions. The distinction between the two articles consists solely in the fact that the former literally repeats Duguit's conception of "social functions", while the latter uses another formula. However, in essence, nothing has changed after the codification of the 1920s was replaced by the codification of the 1960s, in spite of the objections of numerous Soviet lawyers against the continued preservation of this odious rule. The same intentions form the basis for the broad discretion of administrative agencies, provided for by law, which simultaneously precludes judicial review of administrative decisions, because, without special regulations, which have been delayed for an uncertain time, article 58 of the 1977 Constitution – introducing the subordination of administrative acts to judicial control on the basis of citizens' complaints – continues to be a dead letter.

Another group of legal rules, which can in practice be used for the sake of arbitrariness, is not so much the product of deliberate design, as the result of defects in legislative technique and the admission of a great number of "caoutchouc" regulations. An elementary demand of legislative technique assumes that any legal rule shall be backed up by an efficacious sanction in case of its violation. Marxist-Leninist doctrine removes the center of gravity from "formal" to "material" guarantees,[102] and Soviet legislation, based upon this doctrine, is inclined to be astonishingly light-hearted about "formal" guarantees of legal rules, since, according to official propaganda, legal rules are all sufficiently supported by "material" guarantees. Probably, in elaborating article 14 of the Family Code and introducing one month as a term that should expire before registration of marriage could take place, nobody thought it necessary to drop "formal" guarantees, thereby creating unrestricted opportunities for abuse in the future. This happened purely out of habit. However, objectively such a habit helps the adherents of arbitrariness to stand on safe ground. As for "caoutchouc" regulations, Soviet jurisprudence uses this terminology to criticize ambiguous rules of western legislation, for example, reference to *gute Sitten* in West German law or to *ordre public* in French law, which, according to Soviet legal legislature, constitute indisputable proof of the destruction of capitalist legality. Meanwhile, "caoutchouc" regulations are among the most favored methods of legal regulation in the Soviet Union, and article 33 of the Family Code with its formula about sufficient grounds for judicial divorce is nothing but the specific outcome of this law-making approach. What the real effect of such "caoutchouc" rules on the status of legality is from the Marxist-Leninist point of view, has been explained by the Soviets themselves, and in the case discussed there is no need to add anything to their explanation.

Thus, directly or indirectly, by instructions or by hints, through the application of the corresponding – explicit or implicit – indications, Soviet law not only admits arbitrariness but actually legalizes it. Considering this position taken by law itself, one can anticipate what the situation is with regard to the application of law in Soviet practice.

Legalized Arbitrariness in Soviet Practice

In contrast to Soviet law – rarely referred to by western literature as a source of arbitrariness – Soviet practice has been widely discussed from this point of view, not only by western scholars and journalists but also by Soviet dissidents and emigrants.[103] Unfortunately, such a discussion is usually limited to criminal law, without touching upon other branches of Soviet legislation, and even within the limits of criminal law most authors, unconsciously influenced by Soviet propaganda, support the idea that extreme arbitrariness belonged to the Stalin era and has become part of an irrevocable past – albeit that sometimes one can find official disregard of criminal law in our time, in spite of the denunciation of Stalin's tyranny at the XXth and the XXIInd Congresses of the CPSU and by the Soviet media of that period.

Because of the generally known abuses in the area of criminal law, it may be useful in this book to pay attention to other kinds of regulatory activities in the USSR. As for criminal law, the usual accounts do not need additional information so much as essential correction in certain important aspects.

One must never forget that the establishment of extra-legal and extra-judicial terror coincided or almost coincided in time with the founding of the Soviet regime. The notorious *Cheka* (Russian acronym for "Extraordinary Commission") was one of the first innovations after the 1917 October revolution; it was not restricted by substantive and procedural laws, and had the right to apply the death penalty after a short preliminary investigation and a summary hearing of the case without any kind of publicity. Only when the threat of economic collapse compelled the Bolsheviks to proclaim the NEP,[104] with a view to stimulating private initiative, did they understand the need to establish at least restricted legality, because otherwise no one would have been deceived by the call to start private enterprises, to develop private trade, etc. This is why in the early 1920s the Soviets carried out, in great haste, the first codification of their law, including the promulgation of the Criminal Code and the Code of Criminal Procedure. The *Cheka* itself lost its sinister title, and was replaced by the meaningless *GPU* (Russian acronym for "State Political Department"). Meanwhile, at that time, the system of labor camps had already been created, huge numbers of people were continuously sent there by the courts and by administrative agencies, trumped-up criminal cases against former enemies of the Bolsheviks followed one after another, and the leading Bolshevik lawyers of that time, headed by Krylenko, directed judicial hearings of these cases with disregard for the law of criminal procedure. Krylenko himself demanded the abolition of the so-called Special Part of the Criminal Code, which provided for exact measures of punishment for specific crimes, so as to allow the courts unlimited freedom in applying any punishment they considered appropriate. This arbitrariness in the realm of criminal law, veiled in one part and barefaced in another, did not disappear after the proclamation of the NEP.

The purges actually began in the late 1920s with the exile of millions of *kulaks* (rich peasants) and acquired more brutal forms in 1934, after the murder of Kirov, when at first thousands of people were executed or exiled by administrative order with the publishing of lists of their names in Soviet national newspapers. Then a law was promulgated which abolished all procedural guarantees for persons accused of committing political crimes. Thus, in contrast to the established opinion, Stalin's purges were not initiated in the year 1937, but they attained unprecedented levels – when the number of innocent victims of groundless political accusations reached into the millions – and provided for mass repressions with unimaginably monstrous means, when the so-called *troika*[105] (consisting of representatives of the CPSU, the Procuracy and the NKVD, a new acronym for the former GPU), created at local and central levels, determined the fate of the victim in five to ten minutes on the basis of documents produced by the NKVD itself. Sham criminal trials of former Soviet leaders such as Zinoviev, Kamenev, Bukharin, Rykov, etc., were prepared by the NKVD, produced by Stalin and Ezhov, and staged by the Procurator General Vyshinskii and the chairman of the main military collegium of the USSR Supreme Court Ulrikh, also took place. But they were a drop in the ocean in comparison with the extra-judicial reprisals directed against millions. In addition, 1937 was not the final point of Stalin's repressions. Political prosecutions – although in decreasing proportions – continued until the war with Germany broke out in 1941. During the war, any suspicious word could lead to the imposition of the death penalty or to terms in labor camps, and millions of people on the home-front and battle-front shared this horrible fate. In the post-war period hangmen were busy and labor camps were overfilled with 'traitors', not so much real as proclaimed, if one remembers the millions of military prisoners who were directly removed from Nazi death camps to Soviet labor camps. Trumped-up cases were also not a thing of the past. Leaving aside thousands of trials that have not come to the surface, it will be enough to mention well-known events such as the Leningrad case,[106] the case of the Zionists,[107] or the doctors' case.[108] The fact that the last trial was terminated, and the accused were publicly rehabilitated one month after Stalin's death proves that extensive arbitrariness in the realm of criminal law accompanied Stalin's dictatorship from the beginning till the very end.

Khrushchev opened the gates of the labor camps for those innocent victims who had been convicted, and those who had managed to survive were freed, while those executed or deprived of life in other ways were rehabilitated posthumously. This just and brave step was, doubtlessly, Khrushchev's personal achievement. However, there are no grounds for considering it as a restoration of legality, thereby crediting Soviet declarations often repeated in the West. First of all, not all of Stalin's innocent victims were rehabilitated. Many leaders who, like Zinoviev and Kamenev or Bukharin and Rykov, perished in the course of Stalin's fight for personal dictatorship, were left among the criminals, because otherwise the political rise of Khrushchev and other favorites of Stalin would have been compromised, as they attained the heights of power as a result of the vacuum created by the annihilation of Lenin's allies. Then, Stalin's accomplices in legalized crime, who, like Molotov and Kaganovich or Voroshilov and Malenkov, had wallowed in other people's blood, were not charged with criminal offenses after Stalin's death. In such a case Khrushchev himself could have been called to account for his cruel arbitrariness in Moscow and the Ukraine during the time when he ruled these areas as first secretary of their respective CPSU committees. At last, after the denunciation of Stalin's "violations of legality" and when the campaign of rehabilitation had come to an end, Khrushchev proclaimed all over the world that there were no political prisoners in the USSR anymore. Of course, this was an obvious falsehood. Numerous political criminals, unrehabilitated owing to different causes, continued to serve their terms in prison or labor camps. New political cases of adherents to different groups, who demanded either the replacement of the Soviet system or its correction in accordance to undistorted Marxism-Leninism, became the subject of trials under Khrushchev. However, he was unable to apply judicial reprisals as a principal means of the political struggle. Other-wise his declaration about the entire disappearance of political prisoners in the USSR could be denounced very quickly, and accusations against Stalin's arbitrariness could be gradually turned against Khrushchev himself. This is why instead of legal accusations he established a new method to combat dissenters – punitive psychiatry. Of course, the number of victims encompassed by the new method cannot be compared with the number of those executed or imprisoned during Stalin's terror. However, from the point of view of cruelty, Khrushchev's innovation was a match for Stalin's tyranny.

Punitive psychiatry, introduced by Khrushchev, attained its zenith under Brezhnev. Instead of being limited to exceptional cases, the compulsory incarceration of healthy but "unreliable" people in psychiatric hospitals became an ordinary tool in the political struggle. It was also supplemented by such disgraceful means of political suppression as direct banishment from the country, or deprivation of citizenship once departure abroad had been legally permitted, or forced emigration or extra-judicial exile within the Soviet boundaries, or, most insultingly, trumped-up charges of political foes with various crimes that had never been committed, etc. All these types of complicated legal mockery were, naturally, ordered from the very top of the Soviet hierarchy, but their actual implementation was doubtlessly carried out by the KGB. Since Brezhnev's period of political rule coincides almost completely with Andropov's position as the chief of the KGB, there was no reason to assume that the replacement of Brezhnev as the head of the Party and the state by Andropov would mean an end to the suppression that had become so habitual to the latter. On the contrary, judging from his first steps, directed mainly, not at a universal im-provement of the very deplorable situation in the country but at the compulsory establishment of iron discipline, the general tendency of future development could be expected to lead from bad to worse rather than in the opposite direction. A new criminal law about responsibility for "passing information comprising official secrets to foreign organizations"[109] adequately confirmed such a prognosis. Legal develop-ments supported by Chernenko after Andropov's death preserve the same line and strengthen similar trends.

Thus, a short review of the repressions, experienced by the USSR during its entire history, shows that, without perversion of the truth, one can speak, not about the restoration of legality in the present period, but only of the movement first from gross to grosser, and then from grosser to gross violations. Replacement of the ruling persons results in a different scale of arbitrariness. As for arbitrariness itself, it has always remained, and such stability can only be explained in one way: the disregard of legality is due not to the peculiarities of various leaders, but to the very nature of the Soviet system. Khrushchev would swear that Stalin's crimes would never be repeated. Brezhnev would avoid any mention of Stalin's purges. Andropov followed suit with even greater ease, being separated from Khrushchev by the period of Brezhnev's rule. In this regard Chernenko has even more advantages than Andropov. In essence, nothing changed. A law violable *ad libitum* cannot serve as a reliable guarantee of genuine legality, and a system engendering arbitrariness cannot assure necessary guarantees against it. Psychologically, the establishment of Stalinism was easier than its restoration, but politically the restoration of Stalinism seems as feasible as its establishment. So it is with the state of legality in the realm of Soviet criminal law.

At the same time, criminal law does not represent the only legislative branch subject to arbitrariness under the Soviet system. Because punishment of crimes exceeds, in severity, all other governmental sanctions, disregard of the criminal law by law-applying agencies entails more serious consequences. However, when the same agencies neglect civil law or other similar branches of Soviet legislation, the negative impact becomes more extensive than in the case of criminal law, since this neglect touches upon the interests not of only thousands or even millions, but of the entire population and affects human life not incidentally or for a certain period, but daily and hourly.

One can ask, why the Soviet leadership admits arbitrariness beyond the limits of the criminal law, if political oppression is not involved, and the question only concerns the legal regulation of normal human activity. There are a number of reasons for preferring such a system of administration.

1. Demand exceeds supply. In the economic area, the discrepancy between supply and demand has actually always been associated with the Soviet system. Its degree may be changeable; the discrepancy is stable. Therefore, rationing becomes unavoidable. To some extent, it is legalized either permanently or periodically. For example, the Housing Code, in providing for a procedure for granting dwelling premises,[110] establishes permanent rationing in the form of administrative distribution. In contrast to this, the rationing system of goods supplies from 1928 to 1934 and from 1941 to 1947 involved periodical rationing in the form of a contract of sale and purchase, as a civil law institution. However, the first instance was explained by difficulties of socialist construction, and the second instance was justified by war and postwar difficulties. Now, when officially the USSR is a country with a developed socialist society, it is unbecoming to its leader to legally establish a rationing system. Unfortunately, the Soviet economy functions regardless of Soviet prestige, necessitating the introduction of rationing for principal kinds of food in most Soviet cities, without observance of legality, in an extra-legal way. As for the ruling stratum, it does not suffer from illegal rationing, owing to its "closed" shops or other "closed" establishments. However, "special" cinemas and theaters, "personal" planes, trains, and carriages are accessible only to the elite of the ruling stratum. But what is to be done with its other representatives? To settle this problem a special kind of reservation, *bronia*, has been invented. The main peculiarity of *bronia* consists in its constancy. Any theater or cinema, any railroad station or airport always reserves a certain number of tickets in case there is a demand from high-ranking officials. No law regulates this practice, but it has become well-established and inviolable. If a man in the street ordered by telephone a ticket for a plane or a train, and his order was accepted, the ticket would be preserved until the moment indicated by the rules of railroad or air transportation. Then it would have to be sold to any passenger standing in a queue. With *bronia*, the situation is different. It exists without special orders and is preserved without any time restrictions. As a result, a very peculiar picture can be noticed at Soviet railway stations and airports. Many passengers wait for tickets at stations or airports, while trains or planes, which they desire to take, leave or take off with a number of unoccupied places. This practice, causing much uncompensated damage to the state, offers opportunities for enrichment to the appropriate transport workers by admitting passengers for money but without tickets. A similar practice applies to hotels, tourist enterprises, top restaurants, etc.

2. Economic demands exceed the demands of legality. Soviet rulers strive to settle economic problems without violating citizen's rights. However, economic difficulties or economic miscalculations often make this impossible. Then, economic demands are given preference to demands of legality. Thus, in 1928, Stalin introduced the annual state loan, voluntary in appearance and compulsory in essence, as a means of squeezing money from the population. In 1938, when the time came to reimburse the first issue of the loan, an edict about so-called conversion was promulgated, which provided for the exchange of all loan bonds, issued during the period from 1928 to 1937, for new and united bonds of 1938. By this trick, the Soviet government unilaterally postponed the fulfillment of its monetary duties toward numerous Soviet citizens till 1948. In 1947, one year before the expiration of the new term, a monetary reform which applied to money as well as to bonds consisting of a ruble revaluation by a factor of ten, was carried out in the USSR. As a result, the Soviet government achieved two goals at once, in a unilateral way: the scale of its debts was diminished tenfold, and the term of payment was postponed till 1967. Meanwhile, another problem confronted the Soviet leadership. All state loans were issued on conditions of percentages that had to be paid annually in the form of a drawing of prizes. By the mid-1950s, the amount of money necessary for the annual drawings on all loans issued attained the level of the value of a one-year loan. Therefore, it became more profitable to stop paying on the loans issued than to continue the issuance of new loans. Exactly such a decision was adopted by Khrushchev in 1957. As always, unilaterally, he abolished the further issuance of new loans and postponed reimbursement of old loans for twenty years. On the one hand, citizens gained from this decision, because they, at last, were liberated from the compulsory duty to buy state loans "voluntarily". But, on the other hand, citizens lost as a result of the same decision, because postponement of the monetary performance of governmental duties for twenty years was for most people equal to the actual cancellation of these duties. Many state bonds were destroyed by their owners and others were sold on the black market for almost nothing. Only the most circumspect people kept their bonds, to be on the safe side. Brezhnev initiated reimbursement in the 1970s, a little earlier than Khrushchev had expected to do. Considering the level of inflation of Soviet money at that time, it became possible to display such generosity without actually increasing the cost for the government. Not so much the owners of the bonds as their heirs began to receive reimbursement after it had been dragged out for many years. Less prudent people lost everything either completely or almost so, considering the prices which the bonds had fetched on the black market. Purchasers of bonds at black market prices did not win all the way. Some of them were caught red-handed at the moment of purchase or denounced later on; they were tried and convicted of speculation, with the help of a broad interpretation of article 154 of the Criminal Code, which provided punishment for "the buying up and reselling of goods or any other articles for the purpose of making a profit". If bonds bought could be regarded as "other articles", the receipt of reimbursement from the state could still not be considered as "reselling". Apart from this, at the time of reimbursement, people suspected as purchasers of bonds on the black market were obliged to prove the legality of their acquisitions, although bonds, according to the law, are to be payable to bearers without any special proofs. Hence, the history of Soviet state loans alone illustrates, convincingly, how the fact that economic demands prevail over demands of legality led to the appearance of a new kind of crime against the interests of the Soviet system and to governmental violations of legal rules to the detriment of the interests of Soviet citizenry.

3. The demand of the people exceeds governmental demands. This divergence happens more often than one would expect. One example, connected with higher education (education at universities and institutes), will be sufficient to make the point. The number of vacancies at universities and institutes is predetermined annually for the entire country and for each establishment separately by the State Planning Committee together with the Ministry of the Higher Education. No deviation from this plan is permitted, and the plan must be executed fully and without fail. This system has at least two quite significant results. First, because every university and every institute has to be sure of producing the annual number of specialists indicated by the plan, all possible measures are taken to prevent failure, even of one student. Negative marks for exams are to be avoided, any such mark is a signal for alarm, and sooner or later poor students improve their position with the help of a liberal attitude of their professors. If, despite such joint efforts, nothing can be done, and poor students must be expelled, or if some students are lost as a result of other causes, those who study in the evening division are shifted in appropriate numbers to the day division. Second, the ratio between the precise number of vacancies and the number of applications may be as extreme as one to twenty or twenty-five at the top universities and institutes. According to the law, this very complicated problem must be settled on the basis of free and equal competition. It has been shown already to what extent competition is really free and really equal.[111] At the same time, another problem becomes very acute: what is to be done with the children of the ruling elite? The High Diplomatic School or the Academy of Foreign Trade[112] cannot satisfy all demands in this respect. Hence, the ones who are left over are admitted to top universities and institutes in another, easier way than through free and equal competition. For this a special, although unlawful, system has been invented. In the mid-1970s a secret practice, not provided for by law, was introduced, according to which, before the entrance examinations take place, the head of the university or of the institute (the rector) signs lists of applicants who must be admitted in any case. These lists are sent to the deans of the faculties, who secretly give the appropriate orders to examiners, and the applicants included in the lists receive top marks in all exams. Thus, failure becomes completely impossible, and the demands of the ruling stratum are satisfied, despite the divergence between governmental needs and the demands of the people. As with any legalized arbitrariness, this one engenders, or increases, a number of specific crimes. Bribery connected with entrance to the universities or institutes was widespread in the USSR even before the practice mentioned was introduced. In such cities as Moscow, Leningrad or Kiev, where numerous establishments of higher education are concentrated, not one year passes without criminal cases of bribery, although, as a rule, it is not the rectors or their deputies but lower officials who appear in court as the accused. With the introduction of the practice described, bribery has received new stimuli. The rectors themselves, secretly restricted by the number of vacancies to be assigned at their direction, are actually free of any control, since their discretion exists with the leadership's approval, and therefore they may satisfy their own needs together with the rulers' demands. As for the deans of faculties, in instructing examiners about those who must receive the highest marks under any circumstances, they are not only not obliged, but are actually forbidden to produce the rector's lists, and this gives them a free hand to engage in criminal activity as well. Officials and clerks of *ad hoc* commissions which run admission programs to universities or institutes can also receive their "share", since they are in permanent contact with examiners, giving them routine instructions on behalf of the dean or allegedly so. As a result, corruption in the Soviet system of higher education attained such a level that on one occasion, when the chairman of the *ad hoc* commission of Leningrad University arrived in the morning and opened the door of the commission office, he read – together with a crowd of applicants behind him – how somebody had written on the wall of the room: "There are no free vacancies anymore. All vacancies have been sold."

4. The demands of propaganda exceed the demands of legislation. In accordance with its own nature, legislation assumes that its commands will be observed and carried out. Thus, realism is inseparable from legislation. Propaganda, on the other hand, does not require conformity to reality, and the more the latter is distorted, the less truthful the former is. Therefore, when legislation serves such propaganda, its rules are not taken seriously, and their non-execution or direct violation does not present anything extraordinary. Thus, in 1967, the USSR State Plan Committee (*Gosplan*) started elaborating the draft of an edict of the USSR Council of Ministers on the final measures for realizing the 1965 economic reform. A special commission, created for the execution of the governmental errand, included representatives of numerous ministries, several economic and legal scholars, and high officials of *Gosplan*. The first deputy chairman of *Gosplan*, Baichurov, was the chairman of this commission. Before the beginning of the first meeting, the members of the commission were talking to each other. A high-ranking official of *Gosplan* who dealt with problems of food was especially outspoken. With the conviction of a person who knew what he was talking about, he affirmed that there was no hope of improving the goods supply to the population for at least twenty years. When the meeting was opened, Baichurov made some remarks about the rough draft distributed among the members of the commission. His principal remark touched upon the fact that not a single word was devoted to the future increase of the living standard in the USSR, while in fact the draft had to begin with this point. The outspoken official mentioned above objected at once and reminded Bachurin that he knew better than anybody else how unrealistic his suggestion was. Baichurov quietly agreed with the objection of his subordinate, but pointed out at the same time that without the appropriate first article the elaborated governmental edict would be politically vulnerable, and thus would stand no chance of being adopted by the government. After his explanation it was unanimously decided to include the article suggested into the draft. But, if improvement of the living standard is already included in the plan as a fiction, how can one trust the annual statistical data about fulfillment and overfulfillment of Soviet plans? Meanwhile, these data are supposed to be accurate in accordance with the imperative commands of Soviet law. As the Criminal Code states, "padding of state accounts or the presentation of other intentionally distorting accounting data concerning the fulfillment of plans, shall be punished as anti-state actions inflicting harm on the national economy of the USSR by deprivation of freedom for a term not exceeding three years".[113] Sometimes, though extremely rarely, this rule has been applied to low level economic managers. However, even here it does not function as required. Let us look at the building industry. Its enterprises have always lagged behind the plans, and without "padding" and "distorted accounting data" the building workers would never receive increments to wages as bonuses for the fulfillment of plans. To retain the necessary labor force the managers of building enterprises have no other choice but to deliberately violate the strict prohibitions of the criminal law. Local leaders of the CPSU are also interested in reporting to the Central Committee that their provinces or republics have fulfilled the plans, especially the building plan, which determines the further expansion of "socialist production" and thus belongs to the principal sectors of economic planning. Therefore, not infrequently, they compel customers to sign papers as if the work ordered had been finished in time, although in reality the contractors need weeks and months more to perform their planning and contractual duties. The senselessness of criminal punishments in all such cases seems as obvious as in many cases of stealing of "socialist" property or of other similar types of crime. It is also clear that the higher the position of the offender, the less probable is his legal responsibility. Actually, "padding" and "distorting accounting data" has long been a normal system of accounting in the USSR. This is why, when Kosygin was preparing the 1965 economic reform, he could not receive trustworthy data about the genuine state of Soviet industry even from the *TsSU* (Russian acronym for "Central Statistical Department") – the highest governmental agency for economic and other kinds of state accounting. Only with the help of the Novosibirsk division of the USSR Academy of Science, which applied mathematical methods of economic analysis of numerous indirect but more reliable data than those presented by *TsSU*, could more or less realistic findings be ensured. However, despite the defects of the data that are at the disposal of the *TsSU*, they reflect "genuine" reality with fewer distortions than the data published on behalf of the *TsSU* by the Soviet media. This happens because the Politbureau, not the *TsSU*, decides what must be published, and the Politbureau's attitude depends not so much on the demands of legislation as on the demands of propaganda. The most deplorable situation reigns in Soviet agriculture. Thus, the publishing of data relating to it was completely stopped in 1981.[114] There are certain scapegoats, such as the wood and paper industries, which have always been publicly denounced as the sectors of the Soviet economy which do not fulfill their plans. Usually, however, the shortcomings are insignificant: one or two percentages, not more. These exceptions apart, the Soviet economy fulfills and overfulfills state economic plans, if one is to believe official information. If one tries to check this information, by visiting Soviet shops or in contacts with Soviet supply agencies, one will be deeply disappointed. To avoid such disappointment one should never forget that what constitutes criminal report padding and distorted accounting at lower levels, is higher politics at the summit, and, to turn to the ancient Roman formula, *summa iniuria* becomes *summum ius*.

5. The demands of a free hand exceed the demands of a strict law. In the realm of law-making activity the USSR can successfully compete with any country in the world. As for the self-restricting force of established regulations, the situation is essentially different. The Soviet rulers prefer to have a free hand rather than to follow scrupulously their own legal commands. There is one very striking example. In democratic countries additional expenditures by the government are allowed – even where they are absolutely necessary on account of unforeseen circumstances – only after the legislature has approved amendments of or supplements to the budget as already adopted. During the entire history of Soviet legislation, the Soviet legislature has never resorted to such procedures. Does this mean that deviations from the budget are alien to the Soviet system? The facts prove the opposite. At a meeting with Leningrad scholars which was mentioned above,[115] L. Il'ichev, then a secretary of the CPSU Central Committee and a candidate member of the Politbureau, considered it a suitable occasion to say something about the normal activities of this most powerful agency of the country. According to his account, at each of its weekly sittings the Politbureau has to waste a lot of time on procuring financial resources that had unexpectedly become urgently needed. Meanwhile, as any Soviet citizen reading the newspapers can confirm, neither the Politbureau nor the Soviet government have ever addressed the USSR Supreme Soviet with a proposal concerning modifications of the budget. Furthermore, financial arrangements, routinely made by the Politbureau, are kept a secret, and the people know nothing about their amount and destination. What happens to the law of the budget, applies equally to the law of the plan. Those experienced in the Soviet economy know rather well how unstable the planning tasks are and to what extent this fact disorganizes the economic activity of separate enterprises. One can assert without exaggeration that not one enterprise in the USSR manages to work during the whole economic year according to an unamended plan. Either the building plan or the production plan and, in any case, the supply plan, at least in some of its indices, undergo increases, decreases and other modifications, usually not once but several times a year. As a matter of course, these countless changes of planned tasks will inevitably have an effect on the state plan as a single whole; and, what is even more probable, the permanent shifting of the state plan is a major cause of the instability of subordinate planning. Nevertheless, the legislative practice of the USSR Supreme Soviet does not include the promulgation of laws enacted in order to amend the originally confirmed plan. On rare occasions, the population is officially informed that certain indices of the state plan have been changed by the USSR Council of Ministers, owing to certain extraordinary reasons, although in such cases the governmental decisions do not rest upon new legislative regulations. The general rule, however, is that the annual planning laws remain intact, while the real plans are changed again and again in a tightly closed administrative sphere without any needless publicity. Such a practical course is, certainly, *contra legem*, not *propter legem*. But it is impossible to act differently, if one wants to keep a free hand, and for a dictatorial regime, the unrestricted freedom of governing actions has incomparably more value than the uncurtailed observance of the legal order.

6. *The demands of unlimited political power exceed the demands of limiting legal regulations.* One could continue the enumeration of causes that either stimulate or even compel the Soviet regime to establish legalized arbitrariness going far beyond criminal law, and actually affecting the legal system as a whole and in a variety of branches. However, it is hardly necessary, because the numerous individual causes stem, in the final analysis, from a single general ground: unlimited political power precludes genuine legality, which serves outwardly only as a disguising mask and essentially as a practical cover for arbitrariness. The leading stratum of the USSR needs not only the merciless suppression of its political foes and the unreserved obedience of the whole people. A totalitarian system requires the actual support of any command given from the top and resigned subordination by anybody carrying out the same commands at the bottom. These demands, being incompatible with legality, engender arbitrariness not as episodic facts but as a ceaselessly functioning political mechanism, surrounded by the psychological atmosphere of unpunished disregard for established law and the arrogantly insulting treatment of those who possess legal rights but in fact have no hope of their realization.[116] In order to imagine how this happens in practice, let us reproduce the conversations between a potential emigrant and an inspector of the OVIR who has dealt with the applicant's papers. These conversations took place in 1980 and were written verbatim by the applicant.

"Do you have a sister", asks the OVIR's inspector cooly after checking the applicant's documents.

"Yes, I have", answers the applicant apprehensively.

"Is she going to leave for Israel too?"

"No, I do not think so".

"Then let her produce the appropriate written declaration, registered at her place of work or at the office of her apartment building".

"But why? Where did such a demand come from? It is not mentioned in the enumeration of the necessary documents".

"Is today Thursday? You may leave your papers for the present. If you do not bring your sister's declaration on Monday, your papers will be considered as not accepted".

On Monday the sister's declaration was brought, but this did not help.

"What is this? You have been told, but you do not listen", the inspector shows his indignation. 'I am not going to leave for Israel', writes your sister. "What does that mean 'I am not going?' Only not now or never? And why is she 'not going to', owing to what causes?"

"This question sounds very strange. Do you think that, in the absence of special causes, my sister's unwillingness to leave for Israel is inexplicable?"

"Is today Monday? I will wait for the corrected declaration until Thursday".

On Thursday the corrected declaration appears. It reads: "I am never going to leave for Israel because of feelings of Soviet patriotism".

"Well", the inspector sighs with disappointment. "But apart from your sister, you had a husband, didn't you?"

"Yes, I did, but I divorced him thirty years ago".

"Then, produce your former husband's declaration, registered in the appropriate way, that he does not have any financial or other claims against you".

"How can I do this? I have not seen my former husband for several decades. I do not even know, whether he is alive or not".

"Then get a copy of his death certificate".

"But where can I get it and who will give me such a copy?"

"Is today Thursday? As the saying goes, let us live till Monday.[117] What happens later is not my problem".

Monday came. Almost if as in a fairytale, the former husband was found. He proved to be an honest man. Some other former husbands squeeze hundreds and thousands of rubles out of their accidental victims. This one confirmed without hesitation the absence of any demands against his former wife. It seemed that after this the OVIR could not invent anything more, despite all its resourcefulness.

"Well, now that is, probably, all", noticed the inspector with a shade of distress. "You do not have parents, do you?"

"Alas, I do not. But what if I did?"

If she did have parents, opportunities to harass the OVIR's victim would be multiplied a hundred times. But she did not, and the paper stage was completely exhausted. However, only the paper stage. The final decision would require months or years, and what the outcome would be, nobody could predict with certainty.

Disdain for the law is revealed every now and then. If individual conduct contradicts the interests of the system, party directives demand punishment with all the severity of "our (Soviet) law". Thus, Romanov, still in his capacity of first secretary of the Leningrad CPSU committee, once made a military-type raid on one of the many Leningrad foodstores and found plenty of food concealed by the managers of retail trade enterprises. In a time of general deterioration of the food supply, this was considered to be very dangerous, and on Romanov's orders drastic measures were taken against the culprits. On the contrary, if party agencies wish to do something and are warned by lawyers about the illegal character of their projected actions, one can usually see the open indignation of the ruling officials with "your (lawyers') laws". So it was with the attempts of the rulers of Leningrad to withdraw state apartments from owners of country houses[118] or to preserve for Leningrad a privilege abolished by an all-union law.[119] In relationships between economic managers and jurisconsults of enterprises it has long been customary that a manager adopts decisions, paying no attention to the law in force, and expects his jurisconsult to "find" or "create" the reasonable legal grounds. If the jurisconsult objects, by reference to the law, he meets, as a rule, a cry of indignation: "Then why do I need a jurisconsult? In order to observe the law? That I can do without lawyers. You must help me to evade the law. This is why you are necessary for the enterprise." It is true that the jurisconsult has the right to refuse to support illegal orders of his manager,[120] but a broad application of this right leads sooner or later to his dismissal in one way or another. It would, finally, be impardonable to finish our illustrations, without mentioning one of the very impressive thoughts shared with Leningrad judges by the chief of the administrative department of the Leningrad CPSU committee at a closed meeting with them. This thought related directly to the problem of legality and was expressed with exemplary frankness: "Yes, you judges, are independent and subordinate only to law. But you are dependent on me, are you not?" The question was formulated so eloquently and accurately that it did not need either any answer or any addition.

A universal psychology of approved abritrariness, when the latter serves the interests of the system, leads sometimes to monstrous distortions of human relationships, including those kinds of human activity, where one would expect such phenomena least of all. Only this may explain an event that happened at the law faculty of one of the leading universities of the country.

An audience of second to last year students is listening to a lecture on international law. The lecturer is a middle-aged professor with good experience. She deals with the notion of aggression. Numerous features of this notion are explained meticulously and even exhaustively. Everything appears to have been told. Nevertheless, one student raises his hand.

"Well, what is the matter?", the lecturer gets irritated, suddenly losing her composure for some reason.

"I have been thinking over everything you have told us", answers the student, "and it seems that if one follows everything, which has been stated, then not Finland but the USSR must be considered as the aggressor in the 1939-1940 war".

"Stop your hooliganism", the lecturer explodes.

"There is no hooliganism. I simply cannot understand . . ."

"Can't you understand? But do you understand how to deal with political demagogy?"

At that moment the bell announces a break, and the lecturer rushes to a telephone. She calls the KGB officer who guards the University Law Faculty, tells him what has happened and demands him to come immediately and to take the necessary measures.

"What measures", even the KGB officer is astonished. "A student does not understand something in the lecture, he asks for explanations. Shall he be brought to the KGB because of this? It seems a little strange."

"Strange?" the lecturer is indignant. "Well, tomorrow it will not be strange".

That evening, the lecturer forces her son, a student of the same year, to give her a list of students who allegedly have heard anti-Soviet slanders from the culprit. In the morning the list is transferred to the KGB officer. At noon the investigation begins in the building of the Law Faculty. However, something unimaginable happens. At first, the students mentioned on the list do not confirm the son's information. Then, the son himself denies his testimony, blaming it on his mother's relentless pressure. It then becomes urgently necessary to help the lecturer to find an honorable way out of her dishonorable intrigues. Therefore, with the last student on the list, the KGB officer proceeds according to a plan thought out beforehand.

"Where are you going to work after graduating from the University?"

"I would like to work as you do, at the KGB."

"Well, that is not a bad idea. We have interesting work, and our salary is higher than in other places. But how will you succeed, if even now, being afraid of an enemy, you do not work to help us to denounce him?"

"What do you mean I don't? I will do my best."

The last student's calumnies would surely be sufficient, if not to arrest the culprit, then to expel him from the University. This, of course, helped the case. However, it was impossible to correct all blunders made. Everything was crudely done from the very beginning. Therefore, the culprit was compelled to repent publicly and then was left in peace. But what about the lecturer? If a professor of a pre-revolutionary university wrote a report on his student to the tsarist *Okhranka*,[121] nobody would have shaken his hand, and he would have been entirely ostracized and, more probably, been forced to resign. In Soviet society, such a moral sanction simply does not exist. The more terrible the scoundrel the more eagerly one strives to shake his hand either out of fear or in sincere agreement. As a matter of course, no one thought of blaming the lecturer publicly. What for? Yes, she had been a little hasty, maybe she even overdid it a bit. However, her motives were not born of personal malice but by a desire to protect the common cause. Then, why blame her? She selected a form improper for the given case, but in principle she acted correctly and honestly.

In thinking about this case and other similar ones, it would probably be proper to insert a fundamental correction somewhere in this book. It has been pointed out that what Soviet jurisprudence calls the educational function of Soviet law would more correctly be designated as its propagandistic function.[122] The system must pay for legalized arbitrariness, even if it is hidden by proclaimed legality. This falls upon all social institutions, including human education, the moral attitude of people toward the law in force and toward its application. In the USSR, if a newly adopted law worsens the situation, this is perceived as serious from the very beginning. If, on the contrary, the situation must be improved according to a new legal regulation, this engenders scepticism, which may subsequently turn out to be founded or unfounded. As for the application of law, it provokes even more distrust, because nobody can predict beforehand with certainty, whether a case will be solved in accordance with existing rules or not. Outside the limits of public knowledge there are opposing opinions about this practice and its regulation. The ruling stratum approves of it in spite of the absence of any persuasive arguments which might justify its position, apart from an abstract appeal to the interests of the system. The thinking part of the intelligentsia and of other circles criticizes such a negative phenomenon, except in the cases where some of them manage to benefit from the established order. Other people are apathetic in these cases as in all other problems of higher politics, except those who are directly and perceptibly involved. However, as soon as all this becomes a subject of public discussion everything is changed immensely. Apart from dissidents and, in some cases, extraordinarily brave people, any legal rule is generally approved and any operative practice is generally supported. The educational function of Soviet law, if it really exists side by side with the function of propaganda, manifests its capacity to create miracles: while legality has been transformed into an ethical phantom, arbitrariness has become an important moral achievement.

NOTES

1. As E.B. Pashukanis, a famous exponent of Soviet jurisprudence in the late 1920s and early 1930s, said, "revolutionary legality is for us a problem, which is ninety-nine percent political" (E.B. Pashukanis, *Sovetsoe gosudarstvo i revoliutsiia prava,* Moskva 1930, 4).
2. As N.G. Aleksandrov, a famous Soviet legal scholar of the 1950-1960s, said, "the principle of socialist legality means a universal demand to observe the laws" (N.G. Aleksandrov, "Ukreplenie sotsialisticheskogo stroia", *Kommunist* 1957 No.11, 54).
3. *Sovetskoe Gosudarstvo i Pravo* 1979 No.7, 56-74; No.8, 48-77.
4. The 1977 Constitution, art.9.
5. The 1977 Constitution, art.4.
6. *Ibid.*
7. The 1977 Constitution, art.59.
8. The Fundamentals of Civil Procedure, art.2.
9. The Fundamentals of Criminal Procedure, art.2.
10. *Ved. SSSR* 1955 No.9 item 222.
11. *Ved. SSSR* 1980 No.27 item 545.
12. *Ved. SSSR* 1980 No.44 item 910.
13. *SP SSSR* 1976 No.21 item 104.
14. The first volume was published in 1980 by the Presidium of the USSR Supreme Soviet and the USSR Council of Ministers.
15. *Ibid.*, 6.
16. Note 13, art.4.
17. *Ibid.*, art.2.
18. *Ibid.*, art.1.
19. *Ibid.*, art.3. However, the first volume of the RSFSR Collection was published in 1983.
20. *SP SSSR* 1975 No.16 item 98.
21. *Ibid.*, art.5.
22. *Supra*, 6-8.
23. *Supra*, 57.
24. The 1977 Constitution, arts.4, 59.
25. *Supra*, 146-147.
26. *Supra*, 101-103.
27. *Supra*, 101-103.
28. Note 20.
29. *Ibid.*, the Preamble.
30. Note 13.
31. *Ibid.*, the Preamble.
32. *Supra*, 5-6.
33. *Supra*, 193-226.
34. O.S. Ioffe, *Human Rights*, University of Connecticut 1983, 18-19.
35. The Code of Criminal Procedure, art.13.
36. Statute on the Supreme Court of the USSR (*Ved. SSSR* 1957 No.4 item 84, with further amendments), art.9(c).
37. *Sbornik postanovlenii Plenuma Verkhovnogo Suda SSSR*, part 2, Moskva 1978, 204.
38. *Ibid.*, 175.
39. *Ibid.*, 199.
40. *Ibid.*, 246.
41. *Ibid.*, part 1, 130-131.
42. *Ibid.*, 172.
43. *Ibid.*, 227.
44. Note 36.
45. *BVS SSSR* 1982 No.4, 12-13.

46. *Ved. RSFSR* 1962 No.29 item 449.
47. The Criminal Code, art.70.
48. The Criminal Code, arts.64-70, 72-73.
49. The 1977 Constitution, art.49.
50. The Criminal Code, art.70.
51. The Criminal Code, arts.68, 69.
52. The Criminal Code, art.69.
53. The Criminal Code, art.170.
54. The Corrective Labor Code, arts.65, 67-73.
55. The Criminal Code, arts.24(2), 44.
56. The Criminal Code, arts.53, 53(2).
57. The Civil Code, art.246.
58. *Grazhdanskoe zakonodatel'stvo*, (A. Kabalkin, comp.), Moskva 1974, 379-384.
59. The Civil Code, art.444.
60. The Civil Code, art.454.
61. *Ved. SSSR* 1959 No.26 item 146.
62. *Ved. SSSR* 1968 No.17 item 144.
63. *Supra*, Chapter III.
64. *Supra*, 132-133.
65. The Criminal Code, arts.89-97.
66. The Criminal Code, art.96.
67. *Ibid.*
68. Note 37, 164-168.
69. *Ibid.*, 168-171.
70. *Ibid.*, 153-164.
71. *Ibid.*, 172-177.
72. *Ibid.*, 178-184.
73. The Criminal Code, art.170.
74. The Criminal Code, art.173.
75. The Criminal Code, art.173.
76. Note 37, 235-244.
77. *Ibid.*, 236-237.
78. On 14 January 1984, the Soviet agency TASS announced the execution of two high-ranking officials in the realm of foreign trade, sentenced to death because of the systematic taking of bribes on large scale. The future will show whether this is a change in the punitive politics toward official crimes or a measure of deterrence aimed at bribery, which is especially widespread, and at other especially dangerous crimes in this specific sphere of economic activity.
79. *SP RSFSR* 1975 No.9 item 54.
80. The Criminal Code, art.218.
81. The Criminal Code, art.107.
82. *Supra*, 77.
83. They were established in a secret way without promulgation of an appropriate law.
84. One must not forget that, speaking about the CPSU, we mean its agencies at the very top or at another level corresponding to the case in point.
85. *Supra*, 13.
86. *Supra*, 202-206.
87. An exception shall be made only for cases when administrative responsibility is regulated by the Fundamentals of Legislation of the USSR and Union Republics on Administrative Law Violations (*Izvestiia*, 25 October 1980), art.37 of which demands a reference to the rule violated in the decision concerning the administrative sanction.
88. The Civil Code, art.5.
89. Note 37, 323.
90. *Ibid.*

91. *Ibid.*
92. The 1977 Constitution, art.54.
93. The Criminal Code, art.21(3).
94. The Code of Civil Procedure includes a similar rule in art.56.
95. Note 37, 324-334.
96. Art.7 of the Labor Code.
97. The 1977 Constitution, Art.6.
98. The Land Code, art.136.
99. The Land Code, art.139.
100. *Ibid.*
101. V.I. Lenin, *Works*, Vol.44, 308, 401.
102. *Supra*, 56-57.
103. One must do justice to Solzhenitsyn who has made, perhaps, the most valuable contribution to the case of denouncing arbitrariness in the USSR in his work *Gulag Archipelago.*
104. *Supra*, 6.
105. In his blood-thirsty state, Stalin managed to distort even the Russian language. In Russian classical literature, beginning with Gogol, *troika*, a noun derived from "three" (*tri*), has always been a poetical image of a sleigh, harnessed by three horses and gliding along a winter road. In Stalin's political practice, three hangmen, empowered to send people to their execution, became a *troika* as well, and this cruel practice caused its poetical homonym to fall completely into disuse.
106. Late in the 1940s, the leadership of Leningrad was accused of attempting to separate the Leningrad area from the USSR. The highest-ranking leaders were committed to trial and executed in accordance with a judicial sentence. At the same time, thousands of officials of middle and lower rank disappeared in an extrajudicial way.
107. In 1949, the Jewish Anti-Fascist Committee, created on Stalin's orders during the war, was declared a Zionist anti-Soviet organization criminally connected with World Zionism and American imperialism. As a result, the most famous Jewish writers and several Jewish representatives of Soviet culture were executed.
108. In January 1953, the Soviet media announced that a group of doctors would be committed to trial as members of a Zionist organization, which had managed to murder in the past and planned to murder in the future numerous Soviet leaders by means of deliberately wrong medical treatment. In April 1953, the same media announced their rehabilitation. Some weeks later the principal witness for the accusers, Timashuk, perished in an automobile "accident", and some months later the highest investigator of the KGB, Rumin, who had dealt with this case, was sentenced to death and immediately executed. In his 1955 speech in Leningrad, where he came to rehabilitate participants of the Leningrad case, Khrushchev also touched upon the doctors' case. He said that this case was to be used as a pretext for the exile of all Jews from the forty main cities of the country.
109. *Ved. SSSR* 1984 No.3 item 58.
110. The Housing Code, arts.28-49.
111. *Supra*, 145-146.
112. *Ibid.*
113. The Criminal Code, art.152(1).
114. See, however, K. Chernenko's speech, *Izvestiia* 3 March 1984. According to western sources, 1983 was a good year for Soviet agriculture. However, the Soviet statistical agencies abstained from publishing the appropriate data. This can be explained by various causes, including the Soviet policy of future grain purchases from the West. However, the main causes, probably, are the absence of grounds to assume that the achieved success will be repeated, and, as a result, preference must be given to silence over publicity.
115. *Supra*, 125.
116. Especially for these situations, Soviet officials have included in their jargon the expression *kachat prava*, an untranslatable combination of words used in cases when a citizen demands the respect of those rights which are proclaimed by law and rejected in practice.
117. This was the title of a fashionable Soviet movie of that time.

226

118.   *Supra*, 170.
119.   *Supra*, 171.
120.   Art.9(a) of the General Statute on the Legal Section (or Offices), Chief (or Senior) Jurisconsult, and Jurisconsult of a Ministry, Department, Executive Committee of Soviet of People's Deputies, Enterprise, Organization, or Institution. *Biull. Norm. Aktov Ministerstv i Vedomstv SSSR* 1972 No.3, 3-10.
121.   The tsarist security service.
122.   *Supra*, 20.

CONCLUSIONS

As has been discussed, the interdependence between Soviet law and Soviet reality is very complicated. The former distorts the latter in one part, while the latter is adequately reflected by the former in another part. As a result, law itself becomes extremely contradictory, revealing opposite, incompatible, and mutually exclusive principles, rules, and ideas. How can this contradiction be explained? How did it come about and why does it persist? Those who worship Marxist theory would think that similar questions could be addressed to any doctrine but Marxism-Leninism. However, would such an attitude be just and correct? Is not the opposite way of thought more suitable and justified? *Tu l'a voulu*, Karl Marx! Then answer for it.

It is universally known that Marxism rejected all other philosophical doctrines, including those that were recognized as a source of Marxism itself, such as Hegel's philosophy. Marx and Engels perceived that the principal vulnerability of their predecessors was in the aspiration to create a "closed philosophical system",[1] because objective reality develops incessantly while a "closed philosophical system", in order to be closed, must stop at one point or another in its development. According to them, such was the fate of Hegel's theory which, on the one hand, recognized the eternity of any development, but, on the other hand, proclaimed Prussian monarchy the crown of political development.[2]

Let us not initiate a polemic with Marxism on this topic. Moreover, there are serious grounds to believe that, in this regard, Marxism is right. The question, however, must be raised whether Marxism itself does not suffer from the same defect as do other doctrines, or, put differently, has not Marxism itself fallen into the trap set for other conceptions? The Marxist doctrinal system is based upon the assumption that human society is developing on the basis of a struggle between two opposite forces, but that victory always belongs to a third force. The slave-owning society engendered the struggle between slaves and slave-owners, while the fruits of victory fell to feudal lords and landlords. Feudal society was torn by the strife between feudal lords and landlords, on the one hand, and serf peasants, on the other hand, while the capitalists were the real victors of the struggle. Then capitalist society appeared, and it entailed irreconcilable hostility between the capitalist class and the proletariat. Judging from the previous train of thought, one would assume that some third force would here also appropriate victory. But not at all! The proletariat fights against the capitalists, and the proletariat must become the victor in its fight, so that the future development of society will take a turn which has never occurred before. The victorious proletariat will build socialism and communism with the laboring masses;

class antagonism will be replaced by universal harmony; with the entire past now relegated to prehistory, mankind will begin its genuine history; humanity will make a leap from the kingdom of necessity to the kingdom of freedom; in short, the ideal society will be established. Does not this new "crown" resemble, as an ideal, Hegel's Prussian monarchy? Is not such a doctrine a new variant of the "closed philosophical system" with all its defects and vulnerability? Has not Marxism betrayed its own principles, proclaiming that the struggle of contradictions must have as its outcome an all-embracing reconciliation?

The questions enumerated ought not to be ignored by anyone, including those who – not as foes, but as adherents of Marxism – criticize the Soviet system. They think that the obvious defects of this system result not from Marxism, but from its distortion by Soviet leaders and that it will be sufficient to return to authentic Marxism, in order to replace the contemporary repulsive situation by the promised Garden of Eden. In reality, however, the Soviets have not distorted Marxism but rather Marxism has distorted itself: its "crown" has annihilated its doctrine. From the viewpoint of Marxist doctrine, everything in the USSR can be explained, if not indisputably, then at least with appropriate logic and necessary consistency. All the ingredients found by Marxism in the past prove to be typical of the newly created socialism: rulers and subordinates, oppressors and oppressed, exploiters and exploited. Of course, this is a new society, because in the past none of the ingredients mentioned have had the peculiarities inseparable from the Soviet regime. But, despite its novelty, it can be encompassed in the broad framework of the accumulated historical experience. Meanwhile, as soon as one appeals to the Marxist "crown", nothing can be understood, unless one considers propagandistic demagogy as a genuine explanation. Does socialism preclude class antagonisms? Such antagonisms exist in the USSR. Are there no exploiters or exploited under socialism? The USSR relies upon unprecedented exploitation. Has socialism transformed the people from the subjects of political domination into the real bearers of political power? The political power of the Soviet leadership does not have any analogies in the entire history of the human race.

Then, what is to be done? Which part of Marxism shall be preferred – the doctrine or the "crown"? Anti-Marxist critics of the Soviet regime would probably answer: neither. Marxist critics of the same regime prefer one to the other: they would be ready to sacrifice the doctrine for the sake of the "crown". Soviet rulers support both the doctrine and the "crown", with one very important distinction however: the doctrine is used in essence, the "crown" is applied in appearance. This is why everything is so contradictory in Soviet society, and therefore irreconcilable contradictions determine Soviet law, which cannot exist other than as a law of democratic centralism and of centralized democracy, of political freedom and of political domination, of economic emancipation and of economic slavery, of universal equality and of universal hierarchy, of proclaimed legality and of legalized arbitrariness.

NOTES

1. This criticism in a general way, and especially against Hegel, was extensively developed by F. Engels in his book *Ludwig Feyerbach and the Outcome of Classical German Philosophy,* English ed., New York 1941.
2. Precisely this rebuke against Hegel has been sarcastically formulated by Engels. See *ibid.*

INDEX